WHEN DISASTER STRIKES

by the same author

The Anatomy of Bereavement
A handbook for the caring professions

BEVERLEY RAPHAEL

WHEN DISASTER STRIKES

A HANDBOOK FOR THE CARING PROFESSIONS

HUTCHINSON
London Melbourne Sydney Auckland Johannesburg

Hutchinson Education

An imprint of Century Hutchinson Ltd

62–65 Chandos Place, London WC2N 4NW

Century Hutchinson Australia Pty Ltd
PO Box 496, 16–22 Church Street, Hawthorn, Melbourne, Victoria 3122,
Australia

Century Hutchinson New Zealand Ltd
PO Box 40–086, Glenfield, Auckland 10, New Zealand

Century Hutchinson South Africa (Pty) Ltd
PO Box 337, Bergvlei 2012, South Africa

First published in the United States of America by Basic Books, Inc. 1986

This edition first published 1986

Printed and bound in Great Britain by
Butler & Tanner Limited, Frome and London

British Library Cataloguing in Publication Data

Raphael, Beverley
  When disorder strikes: a handbook for
  the caring professions.
  1. Disaster relief   2. Disasters—Social
  aspects
  I. Title
  363.3'48   HV553
ISBN 0 09 165470 X

To Cassie

with love

Contents

PART II

Caring for the Victims

Preface

This book is really written as a tribute to the courage, humanity, altruism, and suffering that are so much a part of the disasters of human experience, whether they be the massive catastrophes affecting communities or smaller personal tragedies. It has arisen from my own work in a number of different disasters, my close liaison with several workers in the field, and my understanding of the studies carried out by many others. The stories of numerous victims have been vividly portrayed by the media and are a further source of this book.

In this volume I have attempted to draw together what is currently known about the nature of psychological response to the various components of disaster, the stresses involved, and some of the many consequences. I have described the experience of many victims of disaster in different communities, the stress faced by workers who come to their aid, and the patterns of care that are needed to cope with the numerous problems that arise. It is my hope that this book will be useful to those who work to prevent or cope with catastrophe; it will help them to understand and contribute to the mantle of care required by individuals, families, and societies that are struck by personal or community disaster.

There are many people to whom I am indebted and whose help I wish to acknowledge. I am especially grateful to Professor Lars Weisæth, Professor of Disaster Psychiatry at the University of Oslo, and his colleagues. Professor Weisæth has generously allowed me to quote from his doctoral dissertation and has shared with me his very extensive experience in the field of disaster psychiatry. Dr. Sandy McFarlane of Flinders University in South Australia has also shared with me his extensive research and clinical experience as well as studies of people affected by the Ash Wednesday bushfires. Dr. Tom Lundin of Uppsala University generously shared his experience with the bereaved and other disaster victims. And I wish to thank Dr. John Clayer, Dr. Paul Valent, Dr. Ellen Berah, Dr. Julie Jones, Dr. Eng Seong Tan, Dr. Bruce Tonge, and many others involved in providing support for disaster victims in Australia, as well as Doctors Green, Titchener, and Shore in the United States.

I am also indebted to all of those who have assisted me in the preparation of this book. I am especially grateful to my secretary and friend Mrs. Wendy Smith, and to Dr. Warwick Middleton, Kath Heggart, Jane Walton, Terry Lewin, and Vicki Price, who all assisted in many ways with references and the preparation of the text. I am grateful also to my colleagues Dr. Jeffrey Cubis, Dr. Ken Nunn, and Dr. Ross Chambers for their special support. And I am especially grateful to the staff of Basic Books for their patience, understanding, and assistance, in particular to Jo Ann Miller and Sheila Friedling for their personal support.

My family have helped me greatly with their love and understanding. I wish to acknowledge particularly my elderly mother who died during the production of this book, but whose wisdom, warmth, and gentleness have been powerful influences in my life; and my daughter, Cassie, now thirteen years old, whose joyousness and love have shone through many difficult times.

PART I

The Experience
of Disaster

CHAPTER 1

The Nature of Disaster

"I dreamt of the end of the world. . . ."

The horror of disaster has been known throughout the ages of mankind. Primitive man struggled to understand the cataclysmic forces that destroyed his tribe and his environment. With the evolution of his capacity to interpret his world, he developed theories and explanations to combat his powerlessness and fears. Such explanations have been incorporated into the myths and legends, the religion and culture, of many peoples and countries. And they are part of the primitive thinking that, even today, so naturally emerges when disaster strikes.

For while it is true that science and technology have given us a much greater understanding of the nature of disaster, disasters can still render us powerless. We see them as "acts of God," reminding us that our fate is often outside our control. And the development of civilization itself has increased the potential for disasters, for instance, when overwhelming natural forces are superimposed on human communities. The complexities of technological development have led to the potential for new disasters, through the failure or collapse of technical systems. Such disasters are often referred to as "man-made," and include the collapse of transportation systems, fires in building systems, and chemical or nuclear pollution. Often, as in earthquakes, natural and man-made processes coalesce.

There are also those disasters that seem to result, to a greater or lesser extent, from the "nature" of humankind itself. The great wars that have devastated the world throughout history, culminating in the genocide of the Holocaust, and the atomic warfare of Hiroshima and Nagasaki, are consequences of this kind. Less obviously, the consequences of man's pollution and destructive use of the environment have led to disasters of death and famine. And then there is the disastrous poverty that affects much of the human condition.

All these circumstances of disaster have their effects on the bodies and minds of men, women, and children. The acute disastrous circumstances of major catastrophes represent much of our struggle to deal with the stresses of existence. As such, they symbolize and condense many factors important to understanding human behavior and alleviating human suffering. The death and devastation of disaster represent the worst of human fears.

There are many costs involved in the various stages of disaster response: the preparatory and preventative, counterdisaster, rescue and recovery operations. Yet most people recognize that one of the greatest human costs is the enormity of the psychological experience—the impact and its residuum—the personal suffering and the "scars on the mind." For those who go through the horrifying threat to life or the loss of loved ones, home and possessions, community, or livelihood, the emotional pain is great. And those who are involved in rescue and recovery operations may themselves confront massive death, threat, and loss, and share it empathically with others, becoming themselves indirect victims of the disaster.

There are also, of course, the personal disasters of human experience, which for the average person in average times may have far greater immediacy and reality. By personal disasters, I mean those events and happenings of day-to-day human life in all cultures and societies that are, for the individuals experiencing them, sources of suffering and distress. These personal experiences may take the form of devastating and acute life events, uncontrollable and unpredictable, imposed on man from without: the death and destruction of loved ones or home, injury, mutilation, assault, disease. Some are the consequence of natural circumstances; but in others, such as automobile accidents and shootings, the person is the victim of human technology and its development. And, here too, the causes are inextricably linked to the human personality and psychology in general, or to the individual's own psychodynamics in particular. Self-destructive and repetitious human conflict, particularly in the sphere of interpersonal relations, is one of the greatest sources of human distress, demoralization, and the sense of personal disaster.

This book reviews the nature of psychological experience in disaster. It draws on my own work and on the many other studies of human response in different kinds of disasters across the world. The emphasis is on themes of stress and response, on how they influence behavior and ultimate adjustment. From such an understanding are developed the implications for the management of disasters. The ways in which people respond to rescue and comfort, and console others, even strangers, reflect an altruism that is hopeful of the human condition in these times of cynicism and despair. This book underscores the importance of this caring in response not only to community disaster, but also, with regard to the many personal disasters of life. There are, as well, special implications for rescue and support workers and all those volunteers and professionals involved in helping. Their experience of disaster is itself a source of both threat and strength, suffering and a sense of worth. The issues of survival evoke basic responses in victims and helpers, as do the threat and actuality of death and loss. How these responses are integrated is reviewed, along with the long-term implications of the psychiatric morbidity that may result. Thus, this book has a dual function. It reviews what is currently known about the psychological and psychiatric elements of disaster and its aftermath; and it provides a framework for the care and understanding of victims—those who were directly exposed or the many others drawn into the maelstrom of the experience.

DEFINITIONS OF DISASTER

According to the *Oxford English Dictionary,* disaster is "anything ruinous or distressing that befalls; a sudden or great misfortune or mishap; a calamity." The word is derived from the Latin *astrum,* or "star," and thus means literally ill-starred, connoting the elements of luck and magic and the powerful disturbances attributed to heavenly bodies.

The term "disaster" is used to denote usually overwhelming events and circumstances that test the adaptational responses of community or individual beyond their capability, and lead, at least temporarily, to massive disruption of function for community or individual. We generally think in terms of sudden and dramatic events, but disasters may also be gradual and prolonged, creeping on almost insignificantly, as in the case of drought and famine.

Disasters are important in the psychosocial sense because of the *stressors* they represent for individual and society. They are, of course, often a threat to survival and the source of extraordinary destruction of person, structures, and social frameworks. Their duration may vary enormously. But there is also, by implication, a process of recovery—a return to some previous or new equilibrium.

Some researchers, such as Harshbarger (1974) and Kai Erikson (1979), define disasters in terms of their effects on communities as well as individuals. Erikson defines the individual trauma as a "blow to the psyche that breaks through one's defenses so suddenly and with such force that one cannot respond effectively." Collective trauma may result in loss of communality and is a "blow to the tissues of social life that damages the bonds attaching people together" (p. 110).

Definitions of disaster are often related to *crisis* concepts. Both are characterized by rapid time sequences, disruption of usual coping responses, perceptions of threat and helplessness, major changes in behavior and a turning to others for help. Obviously there are many overlapping characteristics of relevance to both crisis and disaster, but in the generally accepted sense of these terms, disaster is by implication the more threatening and serious.

Perhaps the simplest definition is that of Cohen and Ahearn (1980): "disasters are extraordinary events that cause great destruction of property and may result in death, physical injury, and human suffering" (p. 5).

The study of individual and community response to disaster and its consequences has led to various attempts to divide disaster reactions into different phases, as well as to various typologies of disaster. Each disaster, of course, is different and has its own particular characteristics. But in attempts to make meaning of such overpowering experiences, it is inevitable that man and society will seek to understand by describing, categorizing, and finding common patterns. In this way not only may response be governed, but some sense of mastery and control restored to counter the sense of powerlessness and helplessness that the very thought of disaster brings.

DIMENSIONS OF DISASTER

TIME PHASES

In an early paper dealing with individual reactions to community disaster, Tyhurst (1950) described three overlapping phases in acute disaster. The period of *impact* begins when the stressors commence and continues until they are no longer operant. In acute disasters, this is usually a brief period but its length may vary quite widely. During the period of *recoil,* the initial stresses are no longer operating, because they have ceased or the individual has escaped, but secondary stresses may have appeared. In the *post-*

traumatic period, Tyhurst suggests that the individual is free from both initial and secondary stresses, but is faced with the losses and effects on his environment and life. This last period, which involves issues of recovery, may be of substantial duration, perhaps the rest of the person's life. Wolfenstein (1957) in her book *Psychological Essay on Disaster* described further phases that take into account the overall span of the disaster experience: threat, impact, and aftermath.

Reviewing the social systems literature in the field, Wettenhall (1975) suggests that Powell's natural history format is a useful one. According to Powell, the stages of disaster time are warning, threat, impact, inventory, rescue, remedy, and recovery. The *warning* phase is one of some apprehension, because there are recognizable conditions that could lead to disaster.

In the *threat* phase, there are specific indications of the approaching disaster force, and communications or observations clearly indicate that danger is imminent. The *impact* stage is the time when the disaster strikes, bringing with it death, injury, and destruction. In the *inventory* stage, which immediately follows, those exposed to the disaster start taking stock of its effects—the destruction and their losses. *Rescue* is the stage when those affected, and often those who have come to their assistance, start to help the wounded and other surviving victims. *Remedy* represents the stage of more specific and formal steps for the relief of those affected. And *recovery* is the prolonged period of return to community and individual adjustment or equilibrium. This version of disaster phases or stages, summarized in figure 1.1, seems now to be the most commonly used. Authors will often make some minor modifications and changes in nomenclature—for example, fusing "warning" and "threat" into a single phase called by either name; omitting a specific "remedy" stage; and using "recoil" for the "inventory" phase.

Such a time phase description provides a useful framework for studying behavioral responses in individuals and communities. Subsequent chapters

FIGURE 1.1
The Time Dimension of Disaster

Pre-Disaster Conditions	Stages of Disaster						
	1	2	3	4	5	6	7
	Warning	Threat	Impact	Inventory	Rescue	Remedy	Recovery

SOURCE: Reprinted from J. W. Powell, "An Introduction to the Natural History of Disaster" (unpublished), in R. L. Wettenhall, *Bushfire Disaster: An Australian Community in Crisis* (Sydney: Angus and Robertson, 1975).

will describe characteristic patterns of experience and reaction associated with these phases. However, another time framework will also be used—one that tends to reflect some of the quality of overall disaster response in terms of activity, arousal, and emotional tone. Cohen and Ahearn (1980) described, on the basis of the literature and their own experience, pre-impact, impact and post-impact phases. The impact phase covers impact, inventory, and rescue, while post-impact deals with recovery. In the impact phase, fear is said to be the dominant emotion, arousal is high, and there are often "heroic" activities.

Post-impact usually begins some weeks later. It may be associated with a honeymoon phase deriving from the altruistic and "therapeutic community" response in the period immediately following the disaster. A disillusionment phase soon follows when disaster is off the front pages, organized support starts to be withdrawn, and the realities of losses, bureaucratic constraints, and the changes wrought by the disaster must now be faced and resolved. Problems arising at this stage in the post-impact phase may be so severe and chronically stressful as to constitute a "second disaster," such as that described by Erikson following the Buffalo Creek flood (Erikson 1976). These phasic components are represented diagramatically in figure 1.2.

FIGURE 1.2

Phases of Response to Disaster

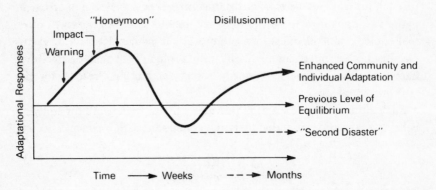

Other factors contributing to the post-disaster utopia are the euphoria at having survived in the face of death and destruction, a denial of loss, the breakdown of social barriers, and the mutual reinforcement of the shared experience. Their combined effect may be to mitigate against post-disaster psychological morbidity. Nevertheless, the reality of loss, death, and destruction, the unalterable facts of changes in community and personal lifestyle, and the prolonged and problematic issues of restitution and recovery must all be faced. Anger and grief, loss of support and breakdown of informal support networks, as well as withdrawal of professional assistance all contribute to the sense of disillusionment. Particularly potent in this context is the attitude of others who may now be likely to make the victims feel that they should have recovered and be "back to normal" and no longer in need of special interest or support.

SPATIAL DIMENSIONS OF DISASTER

For the most part, disasters occur not only in time but also in space. Certain areas are affected almost totally, others more peripherally, others only slightly, and yet others not at all (see figure 1.3). Destruction, disruption, and death thus vary throughout this space frame, as do the capacity for rescue and recovery. This has been represented symbolically by Wallace, and quoted by Wettenhall (1975) as follows.

FIGURE 1.3
The Spatial Dimension of Disaster

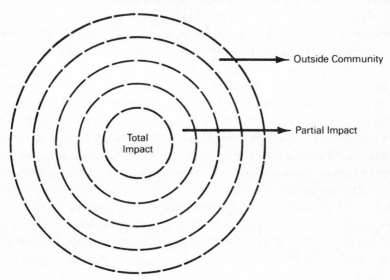

SOURCE: Adapted from A. F. C. Wallace, *Human Behavior in Extreme Situations,* reprinted in R. L. Wettenhall, *Bushfire Disaster: An Australian Community in Crisis* (Sydney: Angus and Robertson, 1975).

There tends to be a phenomenon known as "convergence" in many disasters occurring particularly in Western and relatively affluent societies, though sometimes in other circumstances. Masses of people may be expected to converge on the area or areas where the disaster did most damage and where activities of inventory and rescue may be taking place. Some seek to help or wish to assist, others seek loved ones, and many are simply the curious and investigatory—"the media." Convergence does not just involve people. Usually there is also a rapid convergence of *material goods*— from food and supplies to money, from the essentials for survival to the old and useless items that people seek to donate in large amounts—clothes, furniture, and even the things that might seem to be the "wastes" of their own system. An additional form of "convergence" involves *information,* with messages about the victims and their well-being foremost in this (Fritz and Marks 1954; Wettenhall 1975).

ROLE DIMENSIONS

The typical role dimensions in a disaster are *victim* and *rescuer* or *helper.* Victims are those who have been directly and personally affected by the disaster, by being exposed to its impact or to its effects. It is obvious that someone who has experienced the overwhelming force of the disaster during its period of impact is quite directly affected. Others are directly affected not because they experienced the disaster force itself, but because it has destroyed their loved ones, property, or livelihood. They, too, are victims, although in a somewhat different sense. Rescuers are initially from within the affected population, so they may have dual roles. Subsequently, in most disasters, rescuers also come from totally unaffected areas in surrounding communities. Later there is likely to be a further range of support roles, in helpers who provide medical, welfare, psychological, legal, and other forms of longer-term support. Although these roles in the disaster scenario will be discussed later, a vitally important point should be made here: the roles are not always clear-cut. Short (1979) has shown how stereotypes attached to these roles may lead to a distorted polarization of the victim as weak, vulnerable, and helpless and rescuer or helper as all-powerful, invulnerable, and helpful. Kliman (1976), in discussing a flood disaster, spoke of the caregivers as "the hidden victims" of the disaster, a concept elaborated in later studies (Raphael et al. 1983–84; Taylor and Frazer 1981; Berah et al. 1984).

TYPOLOGIES OF DISASTER

Different classifications and categorizations of disaster have been derived from considerations of their etiology, their qualities, and their course. The simplest is the distinction between "natural" and "man-made" disasters, the former a consequence of the forces of nature and the latter of the forces of man. But this distinction is often artificial for both factors may combine as when a transport accident is caused by extraordinary natural forces. More specific classifications of disaster could be made following this type of model (for example, disease disaster, fire disaster, flood disaster, civilian disaster, and so forth). But the results would be more descriptive than classificatory. We could distinguish between disasters of gradual versus acute onset and duration. Or we could classify disasters by their severity in terms of amount or cost of destruction (for example, numbers homeless, cost to community, lives lost, or numbers injured).

A more complex classification has been attempted by Berren et al. (1982). Theirs is a five-dimensional typology based on the following categories: (1) degree of personal impact; (2) type of disaster; (3) potential for occurrence or recurrence; (4) control over future impact; (5) duration. In this view, disasters may be seen as acts of God or purposeful events; of short or long duration; of high or of low control over the future; of high or low personal impact; and of high or low potential for recurrence. The resulting grid format may be useful in defining certain disasters and providing a rationale for intervention. But thirty-two different possibilities provide a somewhat complex frame in which to place a particular disastrous occurrence.

Many aspects of the typologies discussed apply also to personal disaster. For instance, there may be elements of warning or threat, impact of stressful event, and certainly issues of inventory and recovery. Convergence of offers of support may appear initially, but subsequently the person may feel disillusioned, angry, and alone. Some personal disasters appear to be acts of God, others the consequence of man. Some threaten to recur and seem impossible to control. As with community disasters, those personal disasters that occur with little warning (unpredictable), that cannot be prevented or controlled, and contain highly stressful elements are more likely to lead to prolonged dysfunction and morbidity (Raphael 1981).

DISASTERS AND THEIR LEGENDS

The world has seen many massive disasters. Those before the dawn of recorded history may only be inferred from geological and archaeological evidence. Those since are understood as they are recorded in literature, legend, and memory. By considering different kinds of major disasters of the distant and then the more recent past we can gain a feeling of the ways in which disasters are integrated into human experience.

DISASTERS OF DISEASE

Thomas (1981), in his *Unfinished History of the World,* describes the Black Death, the bubonic plague, which, after a long period of quiescence, swept over Europe in the middle of the fourteenth century, killing over a third of the population. This loss of population was not made up for more than a hundred years. Economies and agriculture declined, for there was no one to work the land. The very fabric of society was destroyed, for those public officials who did survive usually abandoned their duties, fearing anything that would bring them into contact with those who might be affected. The poor and ill were abandoned or cast aside, for to contact them was a very threat to survival. Although this massive episode of the Black Death settled, the plague, as Thomas notes, returned in later centuries. England, for example, had outbreaks in 1603 and in 1666, Spain in 1647 and 1654. (In fact, Thomas categorizes the 1654 episode as probably "the most severe catastrophe of [Spain's] modern history." The plague was taken to the New World, where it nearly destroyed native populations. Further terrible outbreaks occurred in Italy, and Russia, and France. In 1720, for example, approximately 90,000 people died in the area of Marseilles, including nearly all public servants, most surgeons, and all police. Nearly a million died of plague in India in 1895. But then the disease seemed to disappear for reasons that are still not certain.

As with most disasters, the statistics of devastation lack the vividness and emotional impact of individual human experience. In *Decameron,* Boccaccio describes the bubonic plague: "it first betrayed itself by the emergence of certain tumors in the groin or the armpits"; these tumors, or *gavoccioli* as they were called, grew larger and "soon began to propagate and spread . . . in all directions indifferently"; then "black spots or livid" made their appearance, an "infallible token of approaching death" (p. 5). He goes on to describe the terror evoked in others by the "virulence of the pest" and the terrible "energy of the contagion," which led to "divers apprehensions and imagination . . . engendered in the minds of all such as were left alive" (p. 6). Thus, masses fled the advance of death and shunned and abhorred all contact with the sick in a desperate attempt to survive.

Thomas Dekker, an English playwright and poet, wrote of the London plague epidemic of 1603. His work portrays with terrible reality its human impact. Dekker talks of the plague advancing through the land: "Men, women and children dropt downe before him: houses were rifled, streetes ransackt, beautiful maydens throwne on their bedds, and ravisht by sickness." He goes on to talk of "the loud groanes of raving sick men, the struggling panges of soules departing." The grief is overwhelming: "in every house . . . wives crying for husbands, parents for children, children for their mothers." And the scale of death is massive: "A hundred hungry graves stand gaping and every one of them hath swallowed down ten or eleven lifeless carcases," and before the end of the day the bodies in each grave might number three score. The malady was all the more dreadful for there was, for the people of those times, no known way to avoid it; and, as Boccaccio had noted those centuries earlier, "Which maladies seemed to set entirely at naught both the art of the physician and the virtues of physic."

This, of course, was a disaster of disease. Many other endemic and sporadic infectious diseases have caused disastrous mortality through the ages, particularly before the development of an understanding of microorganisms, etiology, modern epidemiological and public health approaches, and more recently antibiotics. But they did not have the awe of terror evoked by the Black Death, and even now by the very word "plague." Even today we are afflicted by viral epidemics such as AIDS. But, although dangerous and frightening, none of these recent epidemics carries the same emotional impact, the same sense of disaster, as is conjured up by the Black Death, the plague.

NATURAL DISASTERS

Volcano eruptions, earthquakes, typhoons, and cyclones probably represent the most overwhelming physical forces in natural disasters. Their effects will obviously be modified by the nature of the human habitations they strike and the sites in which they occur. A prototype of volcanic eruption can be found in the records and remains of Pompeii. The eruption of Vesuvius in A.D. 79 completely destroyed this Roman center. The archaeological rediscovery of the city, with its revelation of citizens preserved at the time of impact by the volcanic ash, gives insight not only into the life of that civilization, but also into the intensity and suddenness of the disaster that overwhelmed it. Other archaeological studies, this time of New World sites, have shed light on the longer-term response to major volcanic eruption. Sheets (1979) has documented the migration of Mayan survivors and their impact on surrounding cultures.

A more recent volcanic eruption, that of Mount Pelée, on Martinique, in 1902, also presents the horrifying picture of a city wiped out in a matter of minutes by the destructive power of a volcano. St. Pierre, a city of 30,000 people, was enveloped in a solid wall of flame as the side of the volcano was ripped out. The captain of a vessel in the harbor at that time described the town as vanishing before his eyes. The destructive effect of the avalanche of white-hot particles mixed with gas and superheated steam traveling at hurricane speed was such that most people died instantly wherever they happened to be, for the temperature was estimated to have been about 1000 ° C. Only two men of the town of 30,000 survived: a shoemaker who survived by some accident, and a prisoner due to be hanged for murder who was protected by the bizarre condemned cell in which he was kept. Rescued after three days, he described his experience: "I smelled nothing but my own body burning . . . soon I heard nothing but my own unanswered cries for help." Much of the human cost of this terrible disaster was incurred because the city administration seemed to have attempted to deny the threat. And once more in November 1985, in a year fraught with catastrophes, a mile-long avalanche of volcanic mud and ashes triggered by eruption of the Nerado del Ruiz volcano engulfed the Colombian town of Armero, killing at least 25,000 of the inhabitants and leaving thousands more injured, orphaned, and homeless. The scene was described as "Dantesque," "a Holocaust of mud," or "like the end of the world."

Despite the overwhelming and violent nature of volcanic eruption, often there is some warning, anticipation, and opportunity to evade the disaster. Yet even when eruption does not lead to complete destruction or loss of life (as with Mount St. Helen's in 1980), it is nevertheless a traumatic and stressful experience for those involved (Adams and Adams 1984).

The insecurity and fear evoked by the shaking and disruption of the very earth itself brings a different element of disaster terror. Earthquakes, when they affect cities or regions of intense human habitation, topple vast buildings, destroy systems of transportation and communication, and sometimes set off great fires, which can add greatly to the ultimate toll of death and destruction.

The San Francisco earthquake of 1906, while by no means the earthquake to cause the greatest loss of life, was one example of earthquake disaster. It is said that the sounds preceding an earthquake can be "as terrifying as the event itself" (*The World's Worst Disasters of the Twentieth Century,* p. 14). There may be a "boom" or sharp snapping sound, or heavy rumbling noises. Shock waves move forward with a pull-and-push motion. "Strike waves" also occur, throwing off impulses at right angles. The terrified person is subjected to both these violent movements as well as their effects on structures such as buildings and vehicles. San Francisco was struck in the early hours of an April morning, just after 5:00 A.M., so that many people woke, dazed from sleep, to the violent shaking, which knocked over furniture or even threw them out of bed. Large buildings shook and wavered and eventually collapsed, leaving behind a mere pile of rubble with no evidence of any survivors. Shocks toppled mansions and shanties alike. Rail lines snapped and "reared up like metal snakes, short-circuiting in blinding sparks as overhead cables fell on them" (p. 15).

In the San Francisco earthquake, the worst damage was caused by fire. Flames from more than fifty different sites coalesced to form a roaring inferno—a "great tide of fire," which was totally out of control. No water was available to fight the fire, both because of deficiencies in fire equipment and because great fissures had fractured all the water mains. These fires brought death as well as further destruction. Many who had been trapped in collapsed buildings, and could perhaps have been rescued, were burned to death. Only after four days did the fires finally burn themselves out. Estimates are that four square miles of the city, with 28,000 buildings, were annihilated and 200,000 people rendered homeless. In this context it is incredible that only 450 lives were lost out of a total population of 340,000. Despite the courage and resilience of the people of this city, the traumatic experience of the earthquake must have been enormous.

Other earthquakes have brought far greater elements of trauma. It is estimated that in the Tokyo earthquake of 1923, which destroyed Yokohama and much of Tokyo, 140,000 people died, and 100,000 were severely injured. The shocks were massive and violent. They created huge chasms which "swallowed" people and vehicles; they brought down buildings; they ripped across the ground in great corrugations. Fires, tidal waves, and the collapse of structures all added to the initial injury and death tolls. Earthquakes in Chile in 1960 caused the deaths of 4,000 people and created tidal waves that had effects as far away as Japan. Peru, which has been subject to earthquakes throughout the centuries, was once again devastated in May 1970. This time, 600 miles of the coast and an enormous area of hinterland were affected. People were killed in seaside villages, and inland hamlets, but especially devastating were the enormous avalanches set off from the mountains in the hinterland, one of which swallowed whole villages in its path. This force was known as the "giant hand," and so it must have seemed to the terrified inhabitants. Total dead were over 50,000—a number no doubt aggravated by the isolation and inaccessibility of many victims. Managua, the capital of Nicaragua, was virtually destroyed just before Christmas of 1972. Between 11,000 and 12,000 people died. Among the many buildings to collapse was the city's general hospital. More than 300,000 people, 75 percent of the city's population, were left homeless. In China in 1976, somewhere between ¾ million and 1½ million people died when earthquakes struck some densely populated regions. Earthquakes caused more than 1,500 deaths in Rumania in 1977 and approximately 2,600 deaths in Southern Italy in 1980. More recently the disastrous earthquake, 8.1 on the Richter scale, that struck Mexico City on September 19, 1985 (along with a milder quake the following day) led to horrifying deaths, mutilating injuries, and prolonged entombments. By the end of November, the death toll had risen to about 20,000, and up to 150,000 had been left homeless. Again, figures of devastation can do little to really portray the human terror and distress that such disasters bring. In the case of earthquakes, these feelings are tied not only to the high mortality and morbidity but also to the ultimate destruction of the sense of security attached to earth and place.

Cyclones, storms, tornadoes, and *hurricanes* bring a different type of threat and devastation. They are also often the harbingers of massive floods. The terrifying forces of wind and rain, which can tear down buildings and throw heavy objects through the air like toys, have been vividly described by survivors. When Hurricane Agnes hit the United States in 1972, the wind and storms destroyed many habitations, and the floods that followed made others at best temporarily uninhabitable. In all, over 72,000 people were dislocated from their neighborhoods and homes. The recovery took a long, long time. The death rate, however, was not particularly high. The hurricane in Honduras in 1974 caused much higher rates of both death (possibly 8,000) and dislocation (more than 400,000 homeless). Poorly built dwellings and inadequate facilities added to the problem. The days that followed were grim: bodies everywhere, putrefaction and decay in the heat, and the dread of epidemics such as cholera.

In Darwin, Australia, Christmas Eve and Christmas morning, 1974, were brutally disrupted by a cyclone. The very time of occurrence made the whole experience unreal. The primitive and overwhelming sounds of the wind, the force of the winds and the rain, and destruction of what had seemed to be solid structures were, indeed, frightening. It was estimated that gusts of wind exceeded 250 km./hour. To quote Stretton (1976, p. 17), "As the full fury of Tracy struck, windows broke, houses were deroofed and finally disintegrated as families were left in the rubble of their own homes in the pitch black, the pelting rain and the shrieking gale. . . . , children were wrenched from the arms of their parents, the possessions of a lifetime were blown away." There was then, "after four hours of this terrifying ordeal, a deadly hush," as Darwin stood in the eye of the cyclone. Then, after a period of eerie calm, the winds returned from the opposite direction with renewed force, bringing further death and devastation, until the final period of calm several hours later. When its impact had passed, people came from their shelters to survey the ruins of their homes and city on Christmas Day. Although only 65 people died and 140 were seriously injured, most of the population of 45,000 had been left homeless. In the days that followed, more than 35,000 were evacuated to southern cities—the nearest of these 4,000 km. from Darwin. Some never returned. Others returned eventually when the city was rebuilt. The ordinary security of their lives had been disrupted by this disaster, and although the city was renewed, for those who experienced the disaster it became, as disasters tend to, a reference point that would never be forgotten.

Tornadoes are a particularly terrifying form of wind and storm disaster, for there may be little warning at all as the funnel-shaped mass of dark rain-laden clouds, swirling with incredible force and energy, moves across the land destroying buildings, nature, and people indiscriminately. Victims describe their homes being shattered around them by terrifying force, cars and people hurtling through the air, children torn away from their parents, and thousands injured and homeless, as in the case of the Wichita Falls, Texas, tornado in 1979.

Fires may occur as natural disasters, as in the great forest and bushfires that have periodically devastated different parts of the world. In regions such as the Australian bush, fires are part of the ecology. Tinder dry conditions, which occur after prolonged drought, dry spells, and burning summer winds can make the occurrence of fire virtually inevitable. This was the circumstance on Ash Wednesday, 1983, in the southern part of Australia when many different fires exploded simultaneously. Some were started by human intervention or indirectly by power wires, but for the most part originated in drought circumstances which combined with searing heat and winds, set off the explosive overgrown foliage after three months without rain. Once started the fires rapidly became uncontrollable, despite the courageous efforts of firefighters and townspeople. There was zero visibility, given the dust, smoke, and flame. Radio transmission did not work in local areas, so it became impossible to communicate about the speed and direction of the fires. Flames were photographed 800 feet high. Fireballs from the burning eucalyptus trees and debris rushed by, with terrifying intensity. People fleeing in cars were overtaken and burned to death. Others were burned in their homes, in some cases while a nearby area was untouched. Stock and other animals were burned to death where they stood. A young couple who had huddled together in a drain, seeking protection from the radiant heat, were later found dead, clasped together, killed by heat and smoke. And when the fires burned out, blackened debris, burned earth and general devastation remained. It was as if the earth were a paper and a flame had been swept across it. In all, 72 people died, over 2,000 homes were destroyed, and more than 300,000 sheep and cattle were lost. And in 1985 disastrous forest fires swept through many parts of Southern California, reflecting similar patterns of destruction and terror.

These "natural" disasters reflect some of the powerful forces that operate when the environment reaches extremes and the very elements that usually nurture man seem to turn against him. In attempts to give meaning to such happenings, primitive man developed legends that interpreted these forces as the acts of deities. This gave people some sense of control, for the deities could perhaps be appeased by sacrifice, or by "proper" behavior, or might even be tricked. Even today, in modern Hawaii, some educated citizens are said to still believe in the volcano goddess Pele. Offerings are made in a ritual way to the lava flow. Belief in Pele is reinforced by the inability of modern science and technology to control the volcano or the lava flow (Lachman and Bonk 1960).

MAN-MADE DISASTERS

At first glance, man-made disasters may seem to belong mainly to recent times. However, the greatest death and destruction, loss and grief, dislocation and relocation are associated with the man-made disasters that have occurred through warfare. The slaying of man by man in either direct combat or through sophisticated weaponry brings cruel mutilating injuries and sudden, untimely, and violent death. Such deaths bring little opportunity for the healing processes of physicians or the healing rituals of grief. And, of course, warfare destroys the homes and habitations, the livelihoods, and even lives of many noncombatants. Much of our understanding of psychological response to disaster has evolved from the need to understand and manage the responses to war. But, mankind's capacity to create psychic trauma through war, to create horrifying forms of warfare, has increased exponentially.

Among the many forms of man-made disasters, the *incineration of great buildings and cities* have had frightening and destructive effects. These are vividly depicted in the records concerning, for instance, the Great Fire of London. Fires in large hotels and the vast structures and crowded conglomerates of the twentieth century have brought their own levels of terror and trauma. Such disasters have been portrayed in the reports of survivors of the Coconut Grove nightclub fire and the Beverly Hills nightclub fire in Kentucky, for example, and captured in startling fiction in movies such as *The Towering Inferno.* Entrapment, choking smoke and fires, heat and flames, an inability to escape, and the collapse of structures all bring threat of death, injury, and destruction.

The *collapse* of man-made structures may occur because of negligent construction or inadequate strength of the structure, or may be triggered by unusual physical forces. Bridges, coal mines, buildings, dams, roadways have all caused such catastrophes. Perhaps the most horrendous incidents have arisen, as at Aberfan and Buffalo Creek, with the collapse of waste and debris left over from other activities. In the Welsh village of Aberfan, a slag heap collapsed with heavy rains and slid as a great avalanche across the town school. Almost half the children of the village were killed.

The Nature of Disaster

The Buffalo Creek dam in West Virginia was "an immense black trough of slag and silt and water, a steaming sink of waste" (Erikson 1979, p. 6) that, with some heavy rain, simply collapsed at 8:00 o'clock one February morning in 1972. Approximately 132 million gallons of black and muddy water roared down the narrow mining valley in the Appalachian Mountains, enveloping and carrying entire communities—homes, cars, buildings, trailers, and human inhabitants. Some of the villagers scattered along the way were able to clamber up the steep valley sides and escape the torrent, but many were not. Many saw family members, friends, and neighbors carried away before their eyes or found their remains in strange postures in the mud during the days that followed. Kai Erikson (1976) portrays the horror of this experience for those who survived. He emphasizes that the disaster was "responsible for a great deal of human suffering," that it left "ugly scars, not only on the landscape, but on the minds of everyone who experienced it" (p. 20). It is interesting that Stretton (1976), in writing of the Darwin cyclone, used almost the same words: "damage to the minds of the survivors can never be calculated" (p. 21). The devastation that followed Buffalo Creek led to the destruction and dislocation of the community, and to loss of communality. Probably this also happened, to some degree, in Darwin. In both these disasters, death, destruction, loss, and grief were compounded by the loss of the familiar environment, which is a part of the individual identity and the fabric of the social system.

Systems of man-made transport are also vulnerable to disaster, although for the most part the risks seem relatively low, given the vast amount of human movement by means of the various modes of transportation. The innumerable wrecks in the history of navigation testify to the vulnerability of ships facing the natural forces of the sea. In most cases there have been high fatality rates. The sinking of the "unsinkable" *Titanic* has become a legendary ocean disaster, although it was not the most costly in terms of loss of life, during both peace and war. Deaths at sea are an accepted fact of life in seafaring nations such as Norway, where each family may lose at least one of its men in this way. There are even particular rituals and myths related to the disposal of wandering souls washed up from the wet graves (Haga 1984). Death by drowning may represent struggle and terror, or quiet fading, but one of the tragedies of shipwrecks involves the fracture of families, as in the saving of women and children from the *Titanic,* who watched helplessly from their lifeboats as the husbands and fathers sank with the giant liner in the sea.

Disasters of *rail systems* bring to mind a variety of images: trains derailing to plunge into chasms or flooded rivers, as occurred in 1981 in the North Indian state of Bihar, when 800 people died; or passengers in the Black Market Naples Express trapped in a mountain tunnel that filled with carbon monoxide fumes; or at Granville, Australia, when a train derailed to crash into a bridge stanchion, bringing down an enormous concrete slab that crushed the train cars beneath, taking 83 lives. And of course, there are, smaller-scale disasters connected with trains, from collisions to suicides on the rails.

Disasters in the *air* have grown with growth in the size of planes. These crashes, sometimes a consequence of human error, sometimes of circumstance, or even physical environment, have usually resulted in the deaths of many, if not all, of those aboard. From the *Hindenburg*—the first of the major air carriers—to the modern jumbo jet, the potential for loss of lives has greatly increased. Physical conditions such as poor visibility or ice, human error, and deliberate human actions have all played a part at different times. For example, the collision between two jumbo jets at Tenerife in 1977 caused 582 deaths; the 1982 crash into the icy Potomac River in Washington caused only 78. But in both cases the deaths were full of horror, lives ending in the exploding flames or in the frozen river. Crashes of large international carriers can bring disaster to many strange fellow travelers, often very far from home, as with the crash of the Air New Zealand sightseeing DC-10 in Antarctica in 1979. Death is usually very mutilating. And those far-distant family members and friends may have little reality when there are no identifiable remains of the loved one.

Disasters of *motor transport* are often especially evocative, given man's love affair with this type of vehicle. The deaths and injuries caused by motor vehicle accidents far surpass most other disasters in Western societies. It has been estimated, for instance, that more Australians died in such accidents over the past twelve years than were killed in the Second World War. School bus crashes have been among the most devastating catastrophes of this type, with their deaths, injury, and the severity of grief for families faced with the loss of child and future. All motor vehicle accidents bring intense personal tragedy to the families involved and are among the greatest sources of personal disaster experience in the community.

New potentials for disaster have arisen with the growth of human *technology*. Many technology-related disasters have been associated with the search for energy. For example, the digging of the earth has traditionally been the cause of death in the collapse of mines and the entrapment of those caught below. And the North Sea oil rig disaster illustrates the terrifying circumstances of a structure giving way to the sea. In the case of nuclear power, its benefits must be balanced against its danger, as shown by the near disaster at the Three Mile Island nuclear plant.

Toxic chemicals and other toxins and wastes have been shown to have the potential for disaster to both humans and environment; even a delayed and slow effect may be especially threatening and malignant. The escape of toxic chemicals from the Union Carbide plant in the Indian city of Bhopal is to date the greatest chemical catastrophe, with over 2,000 dead and many others ill, blind, injured, and dying. The horror of this disaster and the inability of response systems to prevent or manage it highlight the potential for risk in technological advances. Again there are the elements of benefits and costs that must be weighed, but the human cost as vividly documented by the news media must be lessened.

Disasters of the Third World have been marked by great deprivation, famine, and often by a concentration of natural hazards. In Biafra, for example, war and famine came together to produce what has been called "one of the greatest nutritional disasters of modern times" (Brown 1969, p. 315). There was widespread malnutrition among children of all ages, with superimposed anemia, respiratory infection, tuberculosis, malaria, gastro-enteritis, and a variety of other diseases. Stresses on this population included not only hunger and the irritability and nervousness it generates but also the violence and death of warfare, the effects of bombing, the dislocation into refugee shelters, and the disruption of family bonds, and daily life. Indeed, the whole population suffered from extensive catastrophe at every level. More recently, the famine in Ethiopia has brought similar catastrophe to a large population elsewhere in Africa. Bangladesh is yet another "disaster-ridden and disaster-torn nation," overpopulated and underfed, suffering from conflict, political instability, and social upheaval, as well as from typhoons and floods (Feldman and McCarthy 1983). So extensive have been these social and other upheavals that they have significantly affected the institution of the family, leading to a significant increase in the number of families dependent on wage labor and on more than one family member for survival; the character of family relationships is changing as a result. For communities such as these, survival and existence may be a constant battle against catastrophe.

Two disasters of modern times require particular comment, for they have left an impact not only on those who experienced them but, because of their horror and their magnitude, on the course of human history itself. One is the Holocaust, in which the extermination of millions of people, including 6 million Jews, took place systematically, cruelly, and in the most inhumane and terrifying circumstances. The other is the dropping of atomic bombs on Hiroshima and Nagasaki, which resulted in the obliteration of these cities and the horrifying deaths and destruction of much of their populace. The Hibakusha, those who survived, were left with the "imprint of death" forever on them. Lifton's (1967) beautiful and sensitive description of this tragedy conveys so much of the horror that its reality can be felt very clearly—although at another level, of course, its occurrence seems unimaginable.

EFFECT OF THE NATURE OF THE COMMUNITY

The nature of the community that is struck by a disaster may influence much of what happens during the warnings, impact, and aftermath stages. Resources, community structure, and functional patterns are all important. For example, underdeveloped countries may be more severely affected and at the same time have poorer resources to deal with the medical and technical needs that arise.

The ways in which the functional patterns of a community may influence subsequent response are illustrated in a study of the Managua earthquake (Kates et al. 1973). The people of the region had very extended kinship groups and felt primary responsibility to all those within their extended family. This meant that more than 75 percent were looked after by kin afterward. It also meant that bonds to kin and consideration of their needs could take precedence over other important functions, as it did for a number of officials. The lack of a welfare system meant there was no provision for those made unemployed by the disaster. And private property was held to belong to those who took it—looting was within a sanctioned framework.

Many other qualities of communities may be significant. These include patterns of, and access to, communication; the view and trust of authorities who may issue warnings and direction; cultural and ethnic issues; how dependent or independent, rural or urban the community is. The interpretation of disaster by the society may be important, as may the omens and rituals believed to protect against it. The degree to which communities are integrated or disintegrated may also be significant in response and recovery. Similarly, individuals may bring special qualities of personality and coping to the personal or community disasters they meet, and these, too, may influence response and longer-term adjustment. For any disaster, these sorts of background variables need to be assessed and understood.

EPIDEMIOLOGY OF DISASTERS

The epidemiology of disasters deals with their significance from the public health point of view. As Lechat (1979) notes, "epidemiological indices can be of value in planning preventive and relief measures and evaluating their effectiveness." In particular, mortality and morbidity rates can be defined, although difficulties arise in gaining appropriate data if a country has a poor recording system or the disaster itself has had a significant effect on health care units.

Mortality rates are usually accurately recorded, but this may depend on the enormity of the disaster; massive deaths may require mass burials of unidentified bodies. Types and causes of death can provide important information for future disaster management, enabling anticipated casualties to be estimated. In earthquakes the numbers of deaths per 100 houses destroyed may give an indication of the adequacy of building. Injury ratios tend to be higher with earthquakes, and it has been estimated that there are about three casualties to each fatality when earthquakes occur in underdeveloped countries. In most disasters the number of casualties requiring medical attention is usually low relative to the number of deaths: more people either die or survive uninjured. Age-specific mortality rates may be useful in helping to define vulnerable groups. For instance, the very young and very old in some disasters may show higher death rates. Such knowledge may point to causative factors, and in some cases, make it possible to reduce mortality rates in the future. And levels of mortality may be higher than expected for certain types of disaster, for example, flood, indicating that warnings were not given soon enough to allow more people to escape.

Although post-impact death rates are currently poorly understood, it has been estimated that within thirty minutes of impact, more than three-quarters of those who have survived uninjured are or could be involved in the rescue of others. Thus they are likely to be in a fit state to protect themselves and ensure further survival. And, if adequately trained in basic resuscitation and first aid, they are likely to lessen deaths among those injured and awaiting medical care.

Morbidity rates, in terms of physical health needs, are usually relatively low. After floods and many other disasters, they tend to range from 0.2 to 2 percent. The emergency phase of acute need for medical care is usually over within five to eight days of the disaster (Lechat 1979), although in some isolated regions the injured may not receive care until much later. Certain disasters are likely to bring high levels of particular injuries, and medical resources may become severely strained. For instance, after the Ash Wednesday bushfires discussed earlier, the burns units at hospitals in affected areas were considerably strained by the need to care for a significant number of severely burned people, while at the same time maintaining care for the usual number of burn cases that occur in the community. Supplies of eye drops ran out at an early stage because of the vast numbers of people with eyes affected by the smoke, dust, fire, and flying debris. Nevertheless, in most disasters, morbidity rates for the most part return fairly rapidly to those of the normal community. There is an important qualification, however. As will be discussed, stressor effects may have a significant longer-term impact on morbidity, health-care utilization, and even mortality.

Communicable disease and nutrition may be important secondary contributors to morbidity and mortality following disaster, and may require special management. Special variables may also be secondary contributors to morbidity and mortality in man-made disasters, such as the effect of the toxic chemical cloud in the Bhopal disaster.

War, civilian violence, and terrorism all bring high injury rates and are likely to require intensive care at expert levels, as are major vehicle and structure failures. All these disasters bring a special spectrum of morbidity, mortality, and health-care utilization important to understanding and planning for disaster management. Perhaps the saddest commentary in the developing field of disaster epidemiology is that many see it as providing data that will assist with planning for and management of the casualties of an ultimate nuclear war.

WHY DISASTERS ARE OF INTEREST

This review of a few of the world's disasters provides images of disaster so that its possible psychological impact and consequences can be considered. The stressor effects of disaster have been widely recognized by lay observers and by those who have experienced them. Nevertheless, the overwhelming picture is one of human resilience; of suffering that is overcome through courage and fortitude; of altruism, heroism, and human endurance. Catastrophes are survived though they are not forgotten. It is the aim of this book to review and integrate much of what is currently understood about the psychosocial aspects of disasters and their consequences; and to provide a framework for prevention, management, and the nurturing of human compassion and sensitivity in treating the many disasters of life. In this context there have been several rationales presented for studying the psychosocial aspects of disaster phenomena.

1.   Different disasters have evoked descriptions of the behavior and responses of individuals and social groups, and various common themes have emerged.

2.   Disasters may be studied from the behavioral point of view by those who are involved in counterdisaster activities such as prediction, directing disaster management, planning rescue and recovery operations, or developing guidelines for survival and long-term adaptation.

3. Disasters may be of interest as stressors because a single stressor—the one disaster—operates on a large number of people, often at very different levels and with very different concomitants. This peculiarity of disasters makes them particularly helpful in understanding stress and its effects in general, and life event stress in particular (McFarlane 1984).

4. There is a range of psychological or social problems that are associated with or follow disaster. Disasters may be studied to determine which factors in the experience, or preceding it, contribute to these problems and which do not. Knowledge gained could be used to design programs to prevent morbidity, and services might be provided to treat it.

5. Knowledge in the disaster field could be applied to smaller, personal disasters, so that these everyday catastrophes might be better understood and managed.

Of course, these rationales are not the only reason why disasters have been such a source of fascination to social scientists and others. If we consider the reasons for our curiosity and interest, several important themes emerge.

The death, destruction, and mutilation associated with disaster are at one and the same time overwhelmingly horrifying, yet fascinating. People flock to the site of a disaster to see from a safe "distance" what they fear at close hand. The newspapers run stories about "ghouls" at the site of a wreck, or viewing the shattered or burned habitations, but they also fill their presentations with vivid descriptions of death and destruction precisely to increase sales. It is as though people attempt to master what they fear and dread by observing and identifying with it, while at the same time renewing their own sense of life and power by their very survival in the face of death. There is a vicarious sense of mastery over death in this very process.

But, as Wolfenstein (1957) has noted, there is another side to this fascination. Scenes of death and destruction may also allow the vicarious indulgence of fantasies of aggression, again at a safe distance. This may account for some of the excitement generated by disaster, and also for the tension and intense rush of all involved to heal, repair, and make good what has been hurt, injured, or destroyed.

Disasters also reinforce a person's powerlessness and helplessness. Working to deal with disasters—by rescuing from disaster, by helping with recovery, by planning or by involvement in a wide range of counterdisaster activities—restores some sense of control over what is uncontrollable, and thus contributes to the mastery of helplessness.

Yet a further consideration is the excitement and arousal generated by disasters. These feelings are part of a general alertness response in those directly affected, a response that helps them take appropriate action to protect themselves and significant others. This excitement and arousal spreads to those who come to assist. There is, as well, the excitement of surviving—the elation that is natural (although frightening) to feel because one is glad it is not oneself who has died. There is excitement in feeling one can do something (and later frustration if one cannot) to assist in the struggle against powerful forces so that one can avoid feeling helpless. And for victim and helpers there is the intense positive feeling of shared experience and all the emotional strength of active group processes. These factors combine to make people feel that their involvement with disasters, especially in helping roles, is important and worthwhile, perhaps more so than anything they have done in ordinary life.

All these elements may be vicariously mobilized as well, as they are in the viewing of television reports of disaster. In this context, the incredible success of and fascination with disaster movies and stories can be at least partly explained. Here the personal distance grows, yet the opportunity for indulgence in death, mutilation, aggression, excitement, and survival remains. And, of course, this opportunity is indulged by many, for human fantasies and needs in these areas are very great indeed.

THE THREAT AND TRAUMA OF DISASTER

When we look at the potential dangers that a disaster might bring, the potential stressors that operate with its impact, or the potential traumatic variables that arise from it, several relevant themes emerge. These themes have been explored in varying degrees in psychosocial studies of disaster and were, for example, the focus of Norwegian researchers in their studies of the North Sea oil rig disaster (Holen et al. 1983b).

1. *Death and survival.* Inherent in most disasters is the threat of death, or of damage, destruction, and mutilation of the body that might lead to serious injury and even death. There may be actual injury or threat of death to the individual or to those he loves. Or even if this direct threat is escaped, there may be confrontation with the deaths of others or their damaged bodies. Linked to this is the issue of survival, the complex other side of the coin—what it means to have survived when others have died. There may be a range of conflictual threats or stresses regarding who escaped, who died, who could be helped, who could not, who is responsible, who is not.

2. *Loss and grief.* Most disasters bring threat of loss or actual loss and its associated grief. This loss may, of course, be human loss—the death of family or dear friends. But there are also many other kinds

of loss or threats of loss: loss of body functions and/or parts with injury; loss of livelihood; loss of home, with all its symbolic significance as an extension of personal identity; loss of documents and treasured personal possessions; loss of neighborhood, place, and community. Disaster implies loss and threat of loss and thus the anger and despair of grief.

3. *Dislocation and relocation.* Many disasters, especially natural ones but also some made by man, lead to great upheavals, moves, evacuations, or displacements of communities, as well as the separation of family members. These dislocations may result from a natural threat to or destruction of home and place, as may result from earthquakes and floods. Or they may be the man-made consequences of the movement of refugees from war-torn lands. They may be brief, transient, and temporary. Or they may be relatively permanent, sometimes resulting in the destruction of the community as it was known. If the disaster destroys social and neighborhood networks and seriously disrupts social institutions, their restoration after the disaster may be difficult or even impossible. There may be relocation in a new community, or new living arrangements that are positive or, in some instances, disintegrative and negative.

A variety of other threats and traumas arise in the post-disaster period. Some are related to the particular disaster. Others are not even specific to disaster but simply thrown into relief by it. Examples are issues of litigation—who pays for, and who receives, aid or compensation. Bureaucracy and anger combine to make this a potent source of post-disaster distress.

RESILIENCE, RENEWAL, AND REGENERATION AFTER DISASTER

Individuals frequently survive the most horrendous disaster experiences and continue to function as competent and capable human beings, even though the memories of what has happened remain. All who experience disaster are likely to be in some ways touched by it; they can never be exactly the same again. But this does not mean their lives are worse. For even when there may be painful emotional scars, there may also be many new strengths and understandings that have resulted from mastery of the challenge. People frequently find that they are far more courageous than they had thought, although sometimes the opposite occurs. And the encounter with death makes them reevaluate their own lives and what is important for them, so that interpersonal relationships, especially with family, and significant life goals may play a greater and more satisfying role.

There are of course, as will be described below, individuals and communities that never recover and regenerate but are for all real purposes destroyed. Yet Hiroshima, subjected perhaps to one of the greatest disasters to affect a single community, has regenerated and stands as a symbol against any further use of nuclear weapons. Similarly, the Jewish people, both in Israel and in the many countries of the world, have certainly regenerated following the Holocaust, again symbols of human courage and resilience, and the need for such disasters to never occur again.

As Hiroshima and the Holocaust make clear, disasters become a reference point in people's lives. It is of special significance to have known and shared such an experience with someone, however painful, and it is an immediate bond on meeting. Sometimes, if the disaster is too great, the victims may be in some way separated from others by the very extent of the horror they have experienced and others' inability to bear reminders. Thus Lifton suggests that the Hibakusha sense themselves to be rejected and discriminated against—in some way outcasts. He believes that the most important factor is the "death taint," which "outsiders experience as a threat to their own sense of human continuity or symbolic immortality, and feel death anxiety and guilt activated within themselves" (p. 170).

A disaster experience creates not only special roles, but also a special time framework. People may refer to things as having happened before or after a certain catastrophe. Because such an event is so remembered, much may be attributed to it, and subsequent happenings may even be interpreted in terms of it. In looking at retrospective accounts, it is important to keep in mind that disasters exert a powerful influence on perceptions and attributions.

THE HUMAN FACE OF DISASTER

Disasters are frequently described in quantitative and statistical terms: the number of dead and injured, the extent of damage to buildings and other physical resources, the number of homeless, the ultimate economic costs.

Yet for both victims and helpers, it is the suffering disasters bring—the human terror, anguish, and despair—that is most vital. Terror may come with anticipation and threat of disaster. Or, it may come with the impact —with the overwhelming physical forces, with entrapment, helplessness, or nearness of death. The experiences of a disaster and the emotions felt are remembered and relived, and are not readily extinguished in either the vividness of their imagery or the reliving of the emotions. Anguish at death, destruction, and the loss of loved ones, the destruction of home and place may give way to despair when victims realize that, although they have survived and must continue to do so, life can never be the same again. Despair over what has happened, what has been lost, the failed promises of those who offered but were not able to provide help, and even the political and bureaucratic inertia or conflict which inhibit recovery—all these may be part of the suffering of disaster. But, as with personal disasters, it is most poignantly felt and most painfully experienced at the level of the family, the basic human social structure. The separation of mother from child, the loss of a beloved partner, the destruction of family dwelling or livelihood, the dislocation from home and community to an alien place with alien people —this is what is meant by the human face of disaster.

CHAPTER 2

Anticipation of Disaster:
The Warnings and Response

"It couldn't happen here—not here—not this
place—not us;—that sort of thing happens to
other people."

For the most part we do not know what disasters may await us or when
they might occur. It is this lack of ability to know what, or when, that turns
many natural or man-made occurrences into the truly disastrous catastrophes they become. The greater the capacity to predict the nature, extent, and timing of potentially disastrous events, the less likely that their
consequences will be disastrous in human terms.

It is widely accepted by researchers in this field that most people take
little cognizance of the possibility of disaster in their everyday lives. To exist
in a potentially dangerous world, fear must be managed, for if the human
organism were constantly alert to danger, it would be unable to carry out
the functions necessary for existence and cultural development. Yet most
people not only set aside the general possibilities of disaster, but will act,
even in circumstances of risk, as though disaster could not possibly happen
to *them*. What they feel is a sense of "personal invulnerability"—the belief
that one could not oneself be affected by catastrophe. At the simplest level
this is seen in those who build, and rebuild again and again, on the flood
plain, or on the site of a disastrous earthquake. Such behavior also reflects
a general community consensus, a shared avoidance, a joint magical belief
in goodness and protection, as well as, of course, attachment to place. For

some there is the added superstition of defense, the idea that "lightning never strikes the same place twice," that one has suffered or atoned or been so touched by disaster that one is protected for the future. This superstition may lead a person to believe it is unnecessary to protect oneself against disaster, either to take protective precautions in general or even to respond to disaster warnings.

On the other hand, there are communities and people whose lives have been so dogged with catastrophe and deprivation, pain and despair, that their expectancy is one of further disastrous experience. They cannot hope for better, as nothing in their lives seems to support such optimism and hope. Thus, for a different set of reasons, these people too may not respond to the threat of a disaster near at hand. Seeing little purpose or hope of escape, they may passively resign themselves to further catastrophe.

There are other people whose view of the world is not colored by passive acceptance of fate, but rather by a hyperarousal, an alertness, a searching the environment for signs and warnings, for omens that may help them anticipate what they fear and thus protect themselves and those they love against it. To such people, the world is potentially full of disasters; if their dread is great, their lives may be powerfully influenced by the need for avoidance or by excessive attempts to protect loved ones from the possibility of harm.

Any perception of the likelihood of disaster will be influenced by previous experience of disasters, particularly those of the same kind. Thus, the person who has "known" an earthquake is likely to respond in the future to early signs that previously presaged violent movement of the earth's surface. Similarly, those who have known a volcano, tornado, or floods are likely to be sensitive to indications such as smoke, wind, or rising waters. In some instances, if the experience was particularly terrifying, the slightest reminders may trigger a response, perhaps an extreme one, even when there is little real likelihood of serious consequences. But even when this is not the case, persons who have experienced disasters are more likely to understand the importance of a warning and to respond appropriately. Sometimes, of course, the previous experience leads to strong avoidance behavior, such as moving from a flood plain after a severe flood or refusing to travel on trains after a crash. Some of this avoidance behavior may be appropriate (moving from the flood plain); some represents excessive precaution (avoiding all train travel). In all these instances, learning has occurred in response to certain disaster-relevant stimuli; and a range of behaviors, from overreaction to underreaction, may follow.

Response to disaster possibilities or warnings may also show a different type of learning. Thus, when many warnings have been given but no disaster has occurred, it is less likely that there will be an appropriate response to future warnings. False alarms seem to extinguish or lessen the likelihood of responding, as exemplified by the Darwin cyclone in 1974. Many people failed to take notice of the frequently broadcast cyclone warnings because recently there had been other similar warnings, following which the cyclone had veered away.

Scholars such as Wolfenstein (1957), who have attempted to understand the psychodynamics behind response to disaster threat and warning, suggest that individual response may be very much governed by things in *the person's inner world:* both by internalized responses about the possibility of destruction and by value systems acquired from family and cultures. Thus, those people who have had emotionally painful and frightening childhoods filled with hostility may well expect this consequence from any situation of threat and may be overaroused and overresponsive to the threat of disaster, or alternatively, may strongly deny the possibility—attempting to shut it out. A person's response in situations of threat is also influenced by personal, social, and cultural values. For instance, Western and Anglo-Saxon cultural values include the belief that it is somehow childish or shameful to show response in a situation of danger. Wolfenstein suggests that such a belief may be particularly strong for Americans. It is not uncommon for individuals who have responded appropriately to a disaster threat to retrospectively make little of their actions, as though almost ashamed. (This shame may have other sources, however, as we shall see later.) In addition, those who have successfully negotiated a disaster often feel a dread of envy. They fear the envy of those who have been less fortunate and tend to belittle themselves and their deeds as a countermeasure.

Wolfenstein makes another important point that responses to warnings of disaster often involve an element of obedience. Obedience and safety are closely interwoven in childrearing practices. The strictest demands for obedience are essentially in the interests of protecting the child's safety. Not surprisingly, some adults have difficulty with issues of obedience that make them resist being "obedient" to warnings in adult life. Such people are often not appropriately responsive to disaster threats.

RISK ASSESSMENT

One of the psychological processes that takes place in contemplating the possibility of a disaster or a personally disastrous event is the weighing of relative risks. This requires a basic capacity to comprehend, weigh up, and to some degree, quantify the various future possibilities. Not only individuals, but also institutions, from the community level on up, must engage in risk assessment. Thus there are a range of questions to be answered about the nature of the threat: What are the likely human and economic effects, and how severe might these effects be? Might there be any counterbalancing positive effects? How likely is this event to occur? Rare events are far less likely to evoke appropriate appraisal and response than frequent events, even when severity is great. How soon is an event likely to occur? Events that are perceived as likely to be a long way off will be unlikely to evoke an early response, even when long-term action may be necessary to combat them.

Another question related to risk appraisal concerns the consequences that follow recognition of risk. For instance, if there is nothing that can be done, or if people believe there is nothing that can be done, then serious risk appraisal may not even occur. Important in this context, too, are broader system issues. It may not suit an organization or political system to have risks acknowledged. Thus, prior to both the Buffalo Creek and Aberfan disasters it apparently had not suited certain authorities to recognize the potential for disaster. In the Mt. Pelee disaster, authorities apparently may have been unable to acknowledge even imminent threat because of their preoccupation with short-term political goals (*World's Worst Disasters* 1983). If recognition of risk will entail costly countermeasures, then neither governments nor organizations may wish to have the risk made public. In such cases, lobbying or even covering up may result, with the risk or possibility "obliterated" in any public actions.

There are, of course, special groups with an interest in defining risk and drawing it to the attention of authorities and the public. These groups include disaster organizations and hazard-monitoring bodies such as those involved in seismic analysis or other meteorological research.

Other groups may counter warnings or lobby from another point of view, defining risks quite differently. For example, conservationists may argue strongly that natural habitats should be left untouched, although this can mean unbridled growth of forest foliage near human settlements, which increases the hazard of fire. Thus, forest fires in Southern California and bushfires in Australia have occurred in suburban and semirural areas where many inhabitants have uncleared bush and dense dry foliage close to their homes. This had been intended as, and was, a delightful natural environment for living; but as shown by the many homes lost, it was also a potentially risky one.

Even when the risks and likelihood of disaster are defined, they must still be accepted and a plan of action developed. And who will pay for counterdisaster measures, either in personnel or other resources? Many governments do maintain counterdisaster systems, but unless people take some personal measure of risk, unless they are in some way directly involved with risk appraisal, they may not do what is necessary at an individual level to prepare for and respond to disaster. It is only when governments, organizations, and individuals work together in risk appraisal and subsequent circumstances that levels of preparedness are likely to be attained which will enable people to respond appropriately to warning and threat when disaster is near.

THE POSSIBILITIES OF DISASTER

Clearly, many man-made as well as natural disasters cannot be anticipated. Yet geographers, meteorologists, volcanologists, and ecologists are increasingly able to provide highly scientific risk estimates of the possibility or probability of disaster. Thus, likely earthquake zones are well defined, although the precise timing of a quake may not always be predictable. Similarly, active volcanoes are well identified, and in many cases adequate forewarnings of potentially dangerous eruptions are possible. Satellite mapping has enabled enormous advances in the prediction of patterns of dangerous weather, such as storms and cyclones.

As important as the capacity to make predictions, however, is the degree to which such predictive knowledge is accumulated, how it is used, who has access to it and control over its dispersal. It may be of primary interest only to relevant workers, particularly if the disaster seems unlikely to occur. For example, governments and other authorities may have access to relevant information, but for many reasons do not acknowledge or use it. Even if counterdisaster personnel, who are more aware of its importance, obtain the data, their proposals that it be utilized for disaster preparedness may fall on deaf ears if no disaster seems imminent. Here we have one of the key problems in the area of disaster-relevant knowledge and action: unless there is recent experience or close threat of disaster, nobody may be motivated to monitor disaster potential or mobilize preparedness.

This difficulty is even further highlighted in the potential for man-made rather than natural disasters. Private and governmental systems will have important and specific guidelines to ensure the safety of structural and transportation systems and the protection of those utilizing them. They are thus to a large extent "disaster proofed." Obviously, no system is totally disaster-proof, given chance and human frailty. But many systems, particularly in developed countries (international airlines, for example), are highly tuned, well beyond the level of chance. The threat of functional failure may be so unlikely and unpredictable that any disaster preparedness becomes extremely difficult.

The preceding impediments to preparedness are related to high technology. At the other extreme, social systems or cultures may be unwilling to recognize threats for traditional reasons. The possibility of death in cyclones, floods, earthquakes, and the like may be accepted as part of "karma," "God's Will," or "fate." Even though the human suffering involved in disaster turns out to be immense, it may seem only part of a more general deprivation and destruction in some developing countries, and thus mobilize little local response, or even little international aid. Moreover, many developing countries lack the resources and technology to deal with the relatively rare event of disaster in the face of so many ongoing needs.

Thus, for one reason or another, few communities have readily available to the public information on the likelihood and relative risks of natural hazards. People are rarely aware of what might affect them and how, and they are thus poorly prepared to collaborate with authorities in preparing for disaster.

PREPAREDNESS

Information regarding the potential for disaster, if communicated adequately to relevant persons, may lead to general and/or specific responses of preparedness. Such responses, as noted by Mileti et al. (1975), are generally aimed either at vulnerability reduction and possibly thus disaster prevention or at planning for post-impact response. Groups organized to prevent war represent the former, while the International Red Cross is a well-known example of the latter.

On a national level, there are usually government policies, with associated legislation and administrative mechanisms, to pursue both kinds of aims. National disaster organizations or authorities, civil defense and emergency services are examples of groups whose raison d' être is to prepare for disaster and/or to assist the community with its preparations. Operationally, such systems may function with legislative backing and at a variety of resource levels. They may have power only in times of emergency or at other times as well. There are usually provisions for declaring a state of emergency or disaster, so that when disaster occurs, special powers may be given to these counterdisaster bodies. But their powers may be minimal or ineffective at other times. Most workers in the field acknowledge how difficult it is in democratic societies to enact laws that compel individuals to prepare for disasters, as such laws, even though aimed at protection of people, are seen as alien to the values of individual freedom. Thus, even with personal disasters such as motor vehicle accidents, it is difficult to pass legislation making seat belts compulsory or ensuring that those who have drunk don't drive. When such legislation is passed, compliance may be poor and enforcement ineffective, so that little prevention occurs.

Insurance and special financial sanctions can also function to promote preparedness. Thus there may be differential home insurance rates for those building above a flood plain or using materials or design that lessen the likelihood of hurricane damage. But, on the whole, such sanctions and prohibitions have been poorly developed and certainly not uniformly used.

Many psychological and social factors come into preparedness as well, when one examines response at an individual level.

For example, many people do not wish to hear "the bad news" about the possibility of disaster. They may thus be unresponsive to information about something that is personally threatening, particularly if it is difficult or impossible to predict accurately or mitigate. For many people there is a "need" to deny, because to recognize potential disaster would in some way be overwhelming, perhaps because it would evoke feelings of fear, hopelessness, powerlessness, or despair.

A range of psychological responses occur in relation to the threat of nuclear war—a disaster personally known to very few yet potentially totally destructive. Some people simply deny its likelihood or the extent of its destructive consequences (Rogers 1982). Others may displace their concern onto seemingly more particular and manageable threats, such as terrorism. Still others may accept the possibility but find it easiest to believe they can do nothing and adopt an attitude of passive resignation. Some individuals do, however, perceive a threat and act on it in terms of preparedness (Tyler and McGraw 1983). Their responses fall into the two patterns discussed earlier. That is, some work toward decreasing vulnerability by becoming active in the antinuclear movement, whereas others emphasize post-impact mitigation by drawing up survival plans; people who do this have been called survivalists. Tyler and McGraw, in an exploratory study of persons who responded predominantly in one or the other of these ways, suggest that perceived risk and worry are associated more strongly with antinuclear behavior and policy and less to survival behavior. On the other hand, survivalists chose their behaviors because of perception of their likely efficacy. For both groups, behaviors were also related to the degree to which people felt they could influence the likelihood of war, as well as to their sense of moral responsibility in preventing it.

At a personal as well as societal level, a further factor affecting preparedness is that of cost, either financial or otherwise. People may fail to prepare because they perceive the costs involved as too great when balanced against the relative risks. To move to a different area, to clear the forests near houses, to participate in counterdisaster training may all in the absence of disaster, seem to have little relevance or any emotional pull for commitment.

The same applies at a community level, as has recently been demonstrated by Petek and Atkinson (1982) in their book on natural hazard assessment and public policy. They detail the historical shifts in emphasis from "structural" mitigations (for example, dams) to "nonstructural," or behavioral, mitigations. They estimate that in the United States the various rising costs stemming from natural hazards will, by the year 2000, amount to almost 18 billion dollars—that is, as much as, if not more than, the cost of many other major public-sector problems. While conceding that the cost of the most effective mitigations would considerably exceed the probable loss reductions, the authors maintain that implementation of the most economically feasible mitigations could reduce the total hazard costs by 40 percent by the year 2000. At an individual level, a person is probably required to weigh human personal and economic costs to come to a feasible "cost" in emotion, time, and resources that would be equivalent to similar levels of hazard protection or "cost" reduction.

Cultural and system variables may also be influential. Mileti (1983) contrasted U.S. and Japanese organizational response to earthquake predictions. The Japanese organizations tended to view predictions as an "opportunity" to be acted on and were more likely to respond usefully, regardless of the risk. The U.S. organizations, on the other hand, tended to view the prediction as an imposition until convinced they were at risk. They seemed less likely to commit resources to preparation or mitigation activities, unless there were specific reasons to do so. The author notes that six to seven years had lapsed since the data was gathered and suggests there may have been changes with more recent government policies such as earthquake reduction acts and preparedness projects. Nevertheless, it is clear that the influence of underlying sociocultural variables in preparedness needs to be better understood, especially where these appear to interfere with relatively simple and low-cost preparedness measures.

Another factor to be considered is dependency. People often take a dependent stance, believing that "they," the government or authorities, should look after such things as disaster preparation, that this is "what you pay taxes for." "They," of course, are the first to be blamed post-disaster if things have gone wrong, thus "protecting" the individual from responsibility and perhaps associated guilt. Thus, psychologically, hazard recognition, and even a basic general preparedness aiming at prevention, will only come through a range of cognitive and emotional processes. Knowledge about the hazard must exist and be available; there must be communication; motivation to receive it, for those potentially affected; and then intellectual and emotional processing must take place before there are any actions. Sensitivities and vulnerabilities, patterns of individual coping, fears at being powerless or overwhelmed, the realities of the danger, as well as social and cultural variables, will all influence the final common pathway of disaster preparedness behaviors.

When we look specifically at post-impact mitigation, we see a somewhat mixed picture. Response systems are often nonexistent or, at best, lack funding, resources, and trained personnel. However, with greater awareness of disaster risks, international terrorism, and civilian violence, many medical, police, and other emergency service groups have developed disaster plans. Most major cities also have coordinated plans for responding to potential disasters. Some of these—such as the plans for Japan's earthquake-vulnerable cities—are extremely well developed. The resources to support them are available, and both citizens and the local authorities are trained in what to do. In other instances, the sense of personal invulnerability may be carried over into institutions that may be poorly prepared for response if they have never experienced disaster firsthand; certain aspects may be prepared for but not others. For example, most medical disaster plans are well prepared for mass casualties but are often poorly organized to cope with any mental health aspects of the situation (Lundin and Wistedt 1983).

THE DISASTER SUBCULTURE

A disaster subculture may be defined as "a complex interconnecting set of meanings, norms, values, organizational arrangements and technological appurtenances which have emerged in response to repeated disaster threat and impact" (Mileti et al. 1975, p. 18). This subculture is likely to have strong emotional attitudes, for instance, about the best way to respond, how and why lives were lost in a disaster, and what should be done in the future. Like many such systems it is also likely to have its own particular myths, which are powerfully held and reinforced. The disaster subculture is important, for it will influence the way in which communities and individuals perceive and respond to the likelihood of future disasters. Past experience with a particular type of disaster may help people prepare appropriately or it may lead to an inflexible system that is instituted because it had worked previously. Similarly, it may assist with general preparedness for future disasters of a different kind, but not for optimal specific responses. A small rural community may serve as an example of a disaster subculture. Following any flood-threatening rains, for instance, a group of citizens would take responsibility for ensuring that people living close to the river were prepared to move, and they would also act as assistants to emerging disaster workers. During the emergency, they might take on other roles.

Hannigan and Kueneman (1977) show how the subculture is reflected in the social, psychological, and physical adjustments that are used to cope with actual disasters or to prepare for potential disasters. They suggest there are a variety of dimensions: instrumental and expressive, narrow and wide in scope. By means of a case study of a flood disaster subculture in a Canadian town, they demonstrate how the subculture may lead the community actively to anticipate a threat rather than simply to react to it. The changes triggered may be structural (buildings, dams), organizational (voluntary warning and response groups), and internal psychological changes (greater recognition of the threat and consequences of floods). Disaster subcultures are most likely to develop and to be influential when there are "repetitive disaster impacts; a disaster which regularly allows a period of prewarning and the existence of salient consequential damage" (Hannigan and Kueneman 1977, p. 132).

Thus, the disaster subculture can be a powerful force to be reckoned with in understanding individual and community perceptions of hazard and possible preparations to deal with it.

INDIVIDUAL IMAGES AND PERCEPTIONS OF DISASTER

Each person will have his own inner perceptions of disaster in a general sense, as well as specific memories of or fantasies about particular disasters. Dread and fear of disaster in general or of a specific disaster may be deeply ingrained in him, because of a past experience or images acquired from other sources. Special fears may be evoked by images or fantasies related to particular traumatic elements; the death, destruction, survival, injury, mutilation and loss themes being likely to be the most powerful. If a person perceives himself as having successfully dealt with such situations he may feel more confident of his abilities to know what to do. Even if he is fearful, the knowledge that he has survived and negotiated earlier experiences may be valuable to him. If, on the other hand, his image of himself in a previous disaster is one of inadequacy, cowardice, or failure, this may be an extra burden he carries to a new disaster situation.

Training to deal with disasters may also add to inner perceptions and knowledge, so that the individual may be more secure in knowing of likely possibilities, effective preventive and counter actions, sources of help, and most adaptive responses. Lack of knowledge and training adds to anxiety in a disaster situation. Rehearsals and practices, where the potential threats are encountered in role training, are likely to diminish anxiety by allowing a person to confront at least once the possible actions and difficulties that may arise in disaster.

It is not known whether specific inner conflicts or psychopathology lead to a preoccupation with disasters, or to certain patterns of response or preparedness. Wolfenstein (1957) suggests that those people with unresolved conflicts regarding violence, aggression, and destructiveness may be vulnerable to being stressed by disaster threat. But psychiatric patients as a group have not been demonstrated to be particularly or specifically prone. Nevertheless, studies of a threat situation such as the Three Mile Island nuclear power plant leak showed that psychiatric patients were, to some degree, vulnerable to this threat. That is, they reported more distress in relation to the threatened nuclear leak if they perceived it as dangerous and had less adequate support. However, utilization of psychiatric services was not increased compared to a control group of nonthreatened patients (Bromet et al. 1982). Thus, there may be some general impact of disaster anticipation on those who are already demonstrably psychiatrically vulnerable—but it is not marked.

Perhaps those who may be most preoccupied with disaster-type fantasies of an aggressive type would be persons with personality disorder, especially of an antisocial or borderline type; however, there are to date no known studies on the effects that the threat of disaster has on these people. Poor ego boundaries and impulse control may mean that their response to threat appears in actions rather than distress. But we cannot yet identify whether or not such actions are adaptive. The disasters of war would probably be most likely to attract and perhaps lead to disintegration in such personality constellations when under threat.

At a much-deeper and probably unconscious level, images of disaster are likely to be linked with fantasies of destruction and punishment, either inflicted on the self or acted out on others. Apocalypse and horror, blood and violence, the disintegration of body and mind—such fantasies or dreams may represent the darker side of human nature and the disasters that eventuate may seem their ultimate fulfillment. On the other side are the images of heroism and altruism, of healing and repair, that come with the excitement of contemplating disaster and in the wave of convergence offerings afterward. This dichotomy—destruction–healing, cataclysm–peace, good–bad—is balanced out in most personalities and is evidenced in the resilience and integration of so many disaster victims.

WARNINGS AND RESPONSES

When the information regarding a possible disaster becomes specific, a warning will usually be given by the appropriate agencies. Warnings should generally define what is expected and when, as well as suggest appropriate courses of action. One of the most useful models of decision making in response to situations of warning is described by Janis and Mann (1977). Their conflict theory model of basic patterns of emergency decision making is represented in figure 2.1.

Janis and Mann suggest that information, as communicated, leads in various steps to the decisions and outcomes in the diagram. They further state that, if the threatened disaster materializes, vigilance is the optimum effective coping pattern. Defensive avoidance may lead to "evasiveness" (shutting out the need for action), "buck passing" (leaving decisions to others), or "bolstering" (committing oneself to a decision and then rationalizing it as the appropriate one). Hypervigilance is typically an extreme level of arousal that interferes with proper appraisal and decision making. It may be associated with panic, especially where entrapment is likely and there is little time for escape. Janis and Mann suggest that there may be a minimum amount of time necessary for working out an effective plan of response when disaster approaches. They quote Fritz and Marks (1954), who found that death and severe injury were significantly higher in families who were warned less than one minute before a tornado hit than in families who had either longer warnings or no warning at all. The difference may be attributed to this group becoming hypervigilant and taking inappropriate forms of action. However, many factors will determine whether the decision train in figure 2.1 is set into motion. These factors include the nature of the information or warning communicated, its content and source, how it is perceived, as well as what opportunities for verification are available.

FIGURE 2.1
Decision Processes in Response to Warning

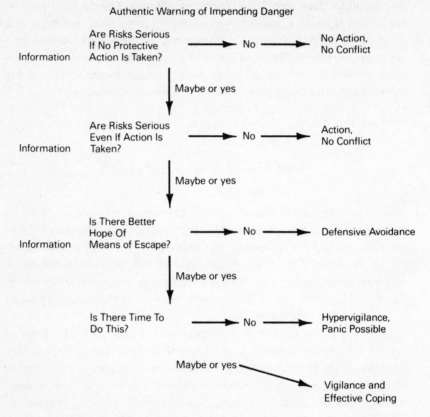

Authentic Warning of Impending Danger

Information — Are Risks Serious If No Protective Action Is Taken? → No → No Action, No Conflict

Maybe or yes

Information — Are Risks Serious Even If Action Is Taken? → No → Action, No Conflict

Maybe or yes

Information — Is There Better Hope Of Means of Escape? → No → Defensive Avoidance

Maybe or yes

Is There Time To Do This? → No → Hypervigilance, Panic Possible

Maybe or yes → Vigilance and Effective Coping

SOURCE: Adapted from I. L. Janis and L. Mann, "Emergency Decision-Making: A Theoretical Analysis of Responses to Disaster Warnings," *Journal of Human Stress* 3 (June 1977): 35–45. Copyright © 1977. Helen Dwight Reid Educational Foundation.

Mileti's group (1975) described the warning and response as system processes, with an evaluation–dissemination subsystem and a response subsystem. *Evaluation* is the detection, collation, and interpretation of information available to estimate threat. The conveyance of the warning message —including the decision to warn, the content of the message, how it is delivered, and to whom—is the dissemination component. The response subsystem is any behavior that is a consequence of the warning received by either individuals, groups, organizations, or communities. Feedback from the response is likely to modify further evaluation and dissemination.

Organizations, rather than individuals, are generally involved in the evaluation–dissemination subsystem. Police departments or emergency organizations are often a key link in the dissemination of warnings, because of their experience and capability for emergency communication. Other groups, however, may be hesitant to become involved in the process and/ or respond. This is particularly so if interorganizational communication has not been good or if the groups do not perceive themselves as having key responsibilities or roles in disaster. Groups such as local government authorities may be hesitant to issue specific warnings unless they feel reasonably certain that damage will eventuate. In part, they may fear that people will panic, although it is actually lack of communication that adds to the likelihood of panic. Groups may also fear humiliation or retribution if their warnings prove wrong and thus hesitate until they are more "sure."

Individuals respond to warnings issued in many different ways, even when the content of the warning is constant. People may hear or perceive the same warning differently, depending on who they are, who they are with, and who and what they see.

Response will be strongly influenced by warning belief. That is, individuals are more likely to respond when their "reflective fear" has lead them to believe that the disaster is likely to occur and the consequences will be negative. Recent disaster experience and closer geographic proximity reinforce the likelihood of an adaptive response. For example, adaptive action is more likely if the person is with his or her primary group (the family) rather than with a peer or work group. Furthermore, since response patterns are also likely to follow everyday behavioral patterns and coping styles, if inaction or denial are characteristic, then they may occur in response to warning. Those with higher education and of younger age are also more likely to respond. Factors influencing response to warning are listed in figure 2.2.

At the organizational level, bureaucratic structures characterized by patterns of highly centralized decision making may delay action prior to impact because they rely on a small group who may not be able to be contacted or to respond quickly unless their normal roles facilitate emergency action. As role conflict between organizational members increases, the ability of an organization to mobilize may diminish. However, as Mileti et al. note, "the greater the continuity between disaster roles and the normal responsibilities of an organization, the less problematic disaster mobilization is likely to be" (p. 53).

Recent investigation of various natural disasters has defined some of the processes of warning and response more specifically. An important example of such research is Perry and Greene's (1982) study of the 1980 eruption of the Mt. St. Helen's volcano. This nonthreatening volcano had not erupted for 123 years and had been a source of jobs, recreation, and pleasure. Thus,

FIGURE 2.2
Factors Influencing Response to Warning

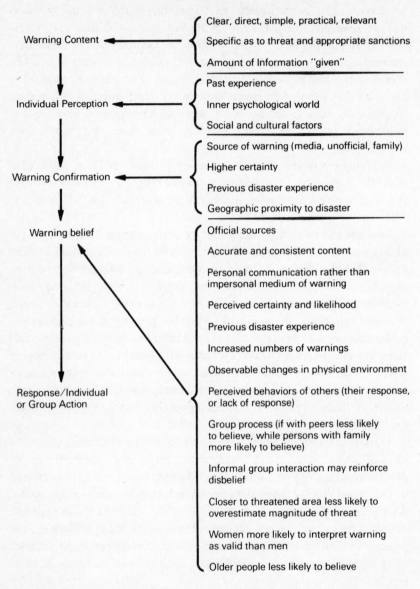

Warning Content
- Clear, direct, simple, practical, relevant
- Specific as to threat and appropriate sanctions
- Amount of Information "given"

Individual Perception
- Past experience
- Inner psychological world
- Social and cultural factors

Warning Confirmation
- Source of warning (media, unofficial, family)
- Higher certainty
- Previous disaster experience
- Geographic proximity to disaster

Warning belief

Response/Individual or Group Action
- Official sources
- Accurate and consistent content
- Personal communication rather than impersonal medium of warning
- Perceived certainty and likelihood
- Previous disaster experience
- Increased numbers of warnings
- Observable changes in physical environment
- Perceived behaviors of others (their response, or lack of response)
- Group process (if with peers less likely to believe, while persons with family more likely to believe)
- Informal group interaction may reinforce disbelief
- Closer to threatened area less likely to overestimate magnitude of threat
- Women more likely to interpret warning as valid than men
- Older people less likely to believe

SOURCE: Adapted from D. S. Mileti, T. E. Drabek, and J. E. Haas, *Human Systems in Extreme Environments: A Sociological Perspective* (Boulder: University of Colorado, Institute of Behavioral Sciences, 1975).

there was low general awareness of it as a hazard prior to activity; but when surveyed following initial steam and ash eruptions, it was found that most people showed an increased willingness to treat the volcano seriously. These authors note how, even in situations such as this, so-called adaptive processes in the society tend to discount risks even when they are defined by scientists. Nevertheless, repeated warnings issued through the media had increased effect especially when reinforced by the first steam eruptions.

The mass media, especially television, tended to be the predominant source of information. Reliance on the media reflected both the lack of any local experience with the volcano and the need for authoritative sources. Furthermore, the longer lead time (April to 18 May 1980) gave people a chance to absorb warnings and seek further information from these sources in a way that would not have been possible with a disaster of more rapid onset. Information was obviously provided intensively: more than 90 percent of the sample in the three areas investigated had received hazard information two or more times a day. Multiple sources and frequency of information meant that more than 80 percent of the population felt moderately certain that they possessed adequate knowledge about all four threats: lava, mud flow, ashfall, and explosive eruptions. However, it is interesting to note that whenever expert information was perceived as in any way vague or uncertain, the situation was, as in other disasters, reinterpreted in a nonthreatening fashion.

Perry and Greene explored the degree to which hazard awareness influenced emergency preparedness. Most people had developed at least some general plan of what they would do should the volcano erupt. In general, the nearer they were to the threat, the more aware they were of the hazards and the more specific was their plan. Greater specificity was also found in a warning system set up in one region by the county sheriff's office. This involved a telephone contact system in which known people linked to the office phoned groups and individuals to offer specific guidance. However, in all areas most people had contact with some official source. Warnings and plans dealt with issues of protection of health, life, and property. Evacuation was also an important issue, although, again, specificity of evacuation plans varied greatly.

This study underscores a point made earlier: preparedness depends largely on the development of warning belief. In this instance those with official warning systems (such as the county sheriff's office) tended to evoke a warning belief system, although it could also be provided by the mass media.

The somewhat prolonged warning in this disaster made possible the development of an emergency subculture. Thus, people could respond to those identified as significant and reliable sources of information within this subculture.

The study also shows how response to warning depends not only on the individual's warning belief, but also on his assessment of personal risk. As we saw, closeness to the volcano was associated with greater awareness and preparedness. The content of warning was also important, for the more specific it was, the more likely people were to take some protective action. Nonspecific messages to communities with low emergency preparedness tended to produce "social milling," with people relatively aimlessly involved, or others continuing their normal routines. At Mount St. Helen's, as in other disasters, the first warnings were greeted with skepticism but warning confirmation led people to respond by taking some protective action.

In the case of a volcano eruption, most authorities consider evacuation to be the most appropriate protective action. Thus, at Mount St. Helen's warnings specified how evacuation could be achieved. Those nearest the volcano evacuated, the most appropriate response for them. People with specific plans had usually planned how to go and where to go. Such plans are adaptive responses to disaster, but of course they are only possible when there is adequate warning time, as well as opportunity for avoidance, escape, or other protective action.

Thus the processes that finally channel into individual response are highly complex and influenced by many factors in the individual and the society (see figure 2.2). The person when warned measures the content of the warning against complex percepts. These generate an affective and cognitive response that leads him to confirm the warning, and subsequently to either believe or disbelieve it. At this point an individual's actions of response may be further influenced by many factors. He may rehearse and plan in his mind beforehand what he will do, a common response in anticipating how to deal with the threats of everyday life. Or his individual, social, and cultural coping styles may influence him to denial, activity, or problem solution.

A person's fear and alertness will rise to deal with the threat, and as Janis and Mann suggest, his vigilance will be heightened—hopefully to adaptive response. In his heightened arousal a number of factors will operate to determine further response as he awaits the likely or inevitable impact.

INDIVIDUAL AND FAMILY RESPONSES

The response patterns discussed here are very much affected when the individual has a family. Ascertaining the whereabouts of other family members, particularly those to whom the individual is closest, and ensuring their safety, becomes a primary motivating force. Families try to be together during a disaster; this can be even more of a priority than confirmation of the warning or taking protective action. Where there is forewarning, families may gather and plan to move, evacuate, or take other protective action as a unit. Where warning sources are uncertain and impact is sudden, family members rely on one another for advice. If evacuation actually occurs, people tend to leave as a family to go to where they can stay with other relatives. There are many implications of this strong attachment behavior throughout the disaster response, from anticipation to rescue and recovery. However, the powerfulness of primary attachments appears first in response to disaster threat and warning, as some quotations from the literature and experience of disaster exemplify:

"When I realized something awful was going to happen the first thing I wondered was where the children were—were they safe—could I get to them, protect them."

"I know that we have planned what we would do if there were a nuclear attack—we would go to one another, my boyfriend and I, at home . . . the need to be together to face whatever it is, is the greatest."

"When I realized the hurricane was going to come and would hit us very soon my first thought was to be with my family—to protect my kids and wife—as long as we were together that was all that mattered to me."

EXCITEMENT

The threat of a disaster, before it comes too close, generates arousal and special activities. Normal roles and responsibilities, such as school and work, are often relinquished. Families are gathered together. Activity is heightened. The specialness of this whole experience may lead to feelings of excitement far beyond most people's everyday experience. This "high" of excitement may make people feel very good, bringing alertness, activity, a sense of importance, and, sometimes, almost a sense of festivity. Children and adolescents are especially likely to respond in this way. If the disaster is not too severe, or if it was not personally threatening, this excitement may continue through impact and after. It may be difficult to relinquish because it is a very special feeling, intense beyond one's ordinary life. However, the excitement may subsequently bring guilt because it was enjoyed when there was so much suffering and destruction. It is a reality that should be recognized and acknowledged in many disasters and situations.

FAILURE TO RESPOND TO WARNING

With disasters such as regular floods there is usually an increased level of expectation, a stronger subculture, and a more responsive community, if for no reason other than the effects of knowledge and practice. But even in such situations, warnings may be misunderstood, misperceived, or simply not responded to. People often have the sense that it can't happen again or to them. They may magically believe that new dams will prevent flooding when they will not (e.g., the Brisbane floods in 1974). They may be skeptical of warnings because of lack of trust in present authorities. Or warnings may take a form that has little real meaning to them. Expected river heights, for example, may seem abstract and unrelated to personal possessions or home.

Some studies of floods and forest fires suggest there may be a differential responsiveness with age to warnings in these situations. The elderly may be more unwilling to move or evacuate, more bound to home and possessions, more resistant to the threat and its implications, even though they have had past experience. Perhaps they cling more to personal invulnerability or are less concerned about death and loss from which they do not feel so distant. People are often very unwilling to make the necessary longer-term adjustments to such threats. They may be unwilling to build above the floodplain, or to take the consequences of land usage, or take the inconvenience. But more particularly people may entertain fantasies about their environment as nurturing and nonviolent, the good earth mother who could not and would not harm them.

Some environmental studies have illustrated the ways in which natural hazards are denied. For example, many people choose to live in heavily wooded suburban sites. Conservation and ecology are popular, and not to have trees near one's house becomes a sin, as does clearing a forest, which may in time and in certain conditions turn into an inferno. This situation is well exemplified by Abraham's (1981) study of bushfire preparedness in the Adelaide hills, which included wooded suburbs on the outskirts of an Australian city that were devastated in the 1983 Ash Wednesday fires. He found that of the 10 precautions listed by the Country Fire Authority, the majority of people had carried out only one of these, even though they stated they had done their best to reduce the fire risk, which they knew to be very high, for that particular season. The majority also believed that the volunteer fire brigade provided adequate firefighting, but only 16 percent had committed this phone number to memory. Although precautions were said to have been part of some general plan of action, few could specify what that plan was. It is little wonder that people did indeed find themselves poorly prepared for fires that would have tested the best prepared systems. Thus, preparation measures for seemingly inevitable disasters, which are nevertheless uncertain in timing and occurrence, may not take place because they caused inconvenience and people are apathetic.

Warnings in such circumstances then inevitably confront the unprepared, and also may bring an additional burden of guilt and regret because people are faced with what they might have done and didn't do. If loss is great—especially if death occurs—then anger, guilt, and blame may be intense.

Another factor influencing lack of preparedness may have to do with insurance. If there is insurance for replacement, people may be psychologically less committed to other precautions and preparations, feeling they have "paid" to be prepared. People may also abrogate personal responsibility if they feel others whose role and function gives them this responsibility (such as voluntary firefighters) should take the precautions. Dependency on others may underlie this attitude, or again it may represent the psychological need to deny disaster as a personal possibility.

These issues are important where warning occurs and threat heightened, particularly within a short period before impact, for people may feel angry, resentful, and let down that they were not "warned" earlier, better prepared, or told what to do. "They," the authorities, are particularly likely to be blamed in such circumstances, since there is a need to shut out the thought of one's own unfulfilled responsibilities. There is also denial of feelings that these very authorities, representing elements of control, were intruders on personal freedom. They were thus resented in the same way as parental dictates were in childhood, even though they derived from the same protective motivation. In this light, one study following a cyclone showed how widespread was the belief that "it just couldn't happen to me." Twenty-eight percent of the respondents said they did not take any precautions when alerted to the cyclone danger. In retrospect the vast majority clearly recognized that warnings had not been taken seriously enough (Scanlon 1978).

THE WARNING AND THE WAITING

Once the warning has been accepted, the person sets in motion a decision train and waits to see what will happen. If his knowledge and experience are appropriate, and the warning has been specific as to the dangers and the protective actions to be taken, he can do little else. People often describe this waiting period vividly:

"I had done everything I could—the waiting was the worst thing."
"We all went into the bathroom, it was the strongest room in the house —like they said to do—it was terrifying with the noise of the wind rising but all we could do was wait and *pray.*"
"I knew we couldn't get away from the fire—we just had to wait and hope it would pass us by."

Clearly, this period is intensely difficult: the warning has been responded to; the threat is real—yet no further activities are fruitful. The reassurance and tension discharge that problem-solving activity provides is lost. There is rising tension and fear. Sometimes the fear may become intense, particularly when onset is uncertain. Individual or group panic may set in. This is especially likely, as has been noted by Quarantelli (1954), when there is still opportunity to escape from the threat, but it is narrowing and will soon close. It is also likely with the pattern of hypervigilance noted by Janis and Mann (1977).

When waiting is prolonged certain things may happen: people may be unable to maintain their degree of arousal and preparation or even their belief in the reality of the coming disaster. Thus the alarm may seem to fade into a "false alarm." With this there is a sense of letdown from the excitement of the earlier arousal. Often there is also anger at those who gave the warning and perhaps a feeling of foolishness or shame for having responded to it—a potentially negative conditioning factor for the next time.

Turner (1983) has investigated some of the effects of prolonged waiting when the disaster does not occur. He conducted interviews with people in Los Angeles County when there were several predictions that a severe earthquake was near. A big area along the San Andreas Fault had lifted, and it was predicted that a great and destructive earthquake would be likely to follow. The population was surveyed on five occasions from February 1977 to December 1978, the period in which there was some ongoing threat of earthquake.

Prior to the survey, Turner had postulated six different, but not necessarily mutually exclusive, themes of waiting:

1. Declining urgency, vigilance, and preparedness, but continued belief in reality of disaster impact
2. Declining urgency and vigilance, but belief that prediction was probably a false alarm
3. Accumulating anxiety and fear, with defensive denial of danger
4. Accumulating personal tension translated into anger and resentment, felt especially toward authorities
5. Familiarization with and sensitization to signs of earthquake hazard and appreciation of its implications
6. Greater preparation for the eventual emergency, as a result of rehearsals and drills in response to early and repeated warnings.

Although there were several significant changes during the period the surveys were carried out, on the whole attitudes were fairly stable. (Perhaps the fact that earthquake predictions were not systematic might have meant less changeable response.) Turner speculated that greater change might have occurred before the survey. People did show increasing uncertainty that an earthquake would occur in the near future. However, it was clear that even after waiting for some time for the earthquake that many had thought would occur within a few months of the warning, the people "showed few of the perverse effects that are often given as reasons for withholding soundly based earthquake forecasts" (Turner 1983, p. 333). Thus, several of the attitudes Turner had postulated were not much in evidence. There was not the disillusionment associated with " 'crying wolf,' or defensive denial associated with accumulating anxiety" (p. 333). Nor was there much anger directed toward scientists and public authorities associated with the prediction. There was some decline in the sense of urgency, but, as Turner notes, this seemed to be associated with "an increased appreciation, selectiveness of attention to earthquake news" which actually seemed to enhance awareness and understanding. It thus appears that such periods of waiting can actually be adaptive. They can enhance understanding of what to do should the disaster occur, thus perhaps helping lessen destructive outcomes.

Obviously, the pattern of response to waiting can vary considerably, depending on personal, social, and cultural factors and the nature of the potential disaster. Further work will be necessary to understand the different types of behavioral response to waiting, and to see how this period can be used in an optimum way.

ANTICIPATION IN PERSONAL DISASTER

Perhaps the personal disaster situation that most closely parallels the anticipation of disaster is the diagnosis of severe or life-threatening illness. Diagnosis may be made early, and there is often a period of uncertainty before
the processes of adaptation begin. Certainly, the initial feeling most people
have is one of unreality. They can't be the victims of such an illness; it is
the sort of thing that happens to "other people." Again, this sense of
personal invulnerability affects assessment of risk. Thus people will engage
in risk-related behavior, such as smoking, and will be slow to take avoidant
actions, such as protection from the carcinogenic effects of sunlight. In some
cases, the only behavior to mitigate impact may be taking out a health
insurance policy. Thus, when the diagnosis is made, most people go through
phases of denial and disbelief. Then angry responses are likely—"Why me?"
or "Why *my* loved one?" And often, there is a feeling of regret mixed with
anger: "Why wasn't I better prepared? Why didn't someone tell me that
something like this could happen?" As the illness worsens and its effects
become directly obvious, the affected person waits its full impact. The
waiting, the failure to respond to warning or to follow therapeutic recommendations, and the shock effects after a person has had little time
to prepare, or has ignored the signs and the disease is far advanced, all
exemplify processes in human response to disaster.

RESPONSE WHEN DISASTER IS IMMINENT

As the impact of the disaster draws near, excitement and arousal give way
to fear—fear for life, fear of injury, and fear of loss. Most people experience
this fear but keep control of it. Cries of terror and panic are rare but do
occur if cultural and personal values accept such release or if threat and
terror of the disaster are very great. In many natural disasters the intensity
of approaching forces override any human sounds, adding to the victim's
sense of his own smallness and powerlessness. Children may become frightened, although previously they had been aroused and excited, as they sense
the change in their parents' responses. As they sense the fear, they will
reverberate with it.

Valent's (1984) description of the Ash Wednesday fires powerfully highlights the experience of this time and up to impact. People told of the noise

of the approaching fires, driven by high-velocity winds "like two jumbo jets taking off next door." The smoke and dust shut out the light, bringing a sense of darkness and night—and uncertainty which way to go if one was fleeing. The fires "rushed in huge fireballs" toward people. For some the fear —as they waited for the fires drawing near—was overwhelming. For others the terror of the flight in hot and burning cars as the fire seemed to rush faster toward them was also a terrifying entry into the impact of the disaster.

OMENS AND THE RETROSPECTIVE INTERPRETATION OF WARNING

Later, in looking back at what happened, people will often alter their perceptions of their response to warning to fit with their present needs. Thus, because of the need to feel in control, people will often suggest that they knew or suspected or saw omens or signs of the disaster. Often, some dream is remembered or interpreted in this way, or the day is said to have been somehow different, or a sense of dread and disquiet is recalled. These rememberings may also be related to the need to explain survival when others have died or to maintain the sense of personal omnipotence. Retrospective interpretation of warnings and lack of preparation may also be justified in this way, to lessen any feelings of personal responsibility. But, for the main part, anticipation is reviewed adaptively—to go over and over something beforehand to mitigate its shock, gain control, and perhaps, magically to stop the horror and trauma from occurring at all.

NO WARNING

Some disasters, such as explosions, air crashes, and even earthquakes, may come with little or no warning at all. In some cases, there is even considerable uncertainty as to what is actually happening. Even under such circumstances, people will usually do their best to protect themselves and those they love, discovering skills and strengths they never knew. But in these disasters without warning, the shock effects are very great and will have implications for recovery.

For the most part disasters are awaited with dread and fear and equated in people's minds with whatever else they have known that is in any way comparable—and often this is war. One victim described his experience of waiting as follows:

"I have never been so scared in all my life—the fire was near—all I could do was wait, in terror, every nerve on edge like a tight string. The only thing like it I've ever known before was the jungle of Vietnam—waiting in fear, death, explosions could come from any direction and get you—and maybe there wasn't anything you could do to stop it."

CHAPTER 3

Impact and Immediate Aftermath

"It was as though we were caught in some terrible nightmare. I felt the jolt of the train on the rails and then—as if it were all in slow motion—the carriage crashed. There was noise —people screaming and then something crashed on top of us. The roof came down. I thought I was gone. I don't know what happened then, but when I came to again I could hardly move. I was trapped and the man beside me was dead. I couldn't see the others but there was blood running down the aisle of the carriage. It was quiet—terribly quiet, and then I heard a moan and people shouting in the distance. I thought at first I was dying and would be crushed too—then a voice near me said 'We'll get you out,' and I knew I was alive and that maybe they could save me."

Whether the disaster comes on with little or no warning or after a period of fearful anticipation, its impact brings to fruition the terrifying physical elements of the particular catastrophe.

SHOCK

When there has been little or no warning a sense of traumatic shock will be the predominant effect. The earliest part of response is taken up with feelings of numbness, unreality, and fear. There is intense arousal as the individual attempts to interpret what is happening to him. For, often, he may not understand the source or even cause of the physical upheaval of his environment. For instance, those experiencing the shock wave of a sudden explosion may think it is an earthquake. The cause and source of a fire may be unknown, and the smoke may be mistakenly perceived as toxic fumes. In a transportation accident, victims may have some period of awareness, even if only brief, but again, the source of the difficulties may not be known and may be subject to many different interpretations. And in such disasters, particularly in plane crashes, there may be few mitigating actions possible, which strengthens the effects of shock, unreality, and fear. For those who do survive, this sense of overwhelming shock and helplessness may become deeply imprinted in a scene that epitomizes the whole experience.

The interpretations of impact in disaster without warning often reflect misconstrual in terms of past experience or fear fantasies. For instance, when tornadoes, hurricanes, and cyclones strike, people who have not heard or taken in the full meaning of the warnings may think that they are under attack, that there is an explosion or bombing. In a recent explosion in Mexico, the mushroom cloud that resulted was misinterpreted by some as nuclear war, come at last.

Not unexpectedly, those who suffered from the first atomic bomb blast at Hiroshima did not know what to believe. The element of shock was enormous, and Janis (1951) quotes a newspaper reporter's comment as typifying the response: "I was just utterly surprised and amazed and awed" (p. 5). In Hiroshima, the timing added to the unreality. For it was shortly after 8:00 A.M., when people were on their way to work, housewives were cooking breakfast, and children were outside. The effect of timing is perhaps most marked when people are aroused from sleep and find it hard to grasp what is happening. This was the case with the Managua earthquake, which struck just after midnight, or the San Francisco earthquake, which began shortly after 5:00 A.M. The *Titanic* hit its iceberg at 11:40 P.M., sinking on Sunday morning. Few people realized what had happened; many had to be aroused from sleep to respond to the sinking.

Thus, the timing of an unexpected impact may make it even more difficult for people to prepare, to interpret, or to respond. In such circumstances the "illusion of centrality"—a person's belief that he or she is the only one affected—is likely to be most prominent. In such emergency conditions, interpretations are inevitably self-focused, with forces initially perceived for their relevance to the self.

Along with sudden and dramatic impact of massive physical forces come dominant sensory perceptions. These trigger some of the most basic and primitive associations. Long after impact, certain sensory perceptions may remain as themes for memory and frightening reminders. The screaming sounds of cyclone or hurricane winds seem to pierce the ears, tear at the senses, and torment the soul. The disquieting rumble of the earth compounds the awesomeness of mechanical force, as the land shifts and cracks in a quake. The loudness of explosions, the roar of fires, the shrieking of the atmosphere—all these are strange and primitive sounds. And especially after impact—when noisy man-made structures have been destroyed, it is the silence itself which is frightening. There is also the quieting of animals and birds, the stillness that has shut out other sound.

Vivid visual experiences are often forever remembered by victims of disaster. Those who lived through the forest fires describe the great fireballs, walls of fire, exploding trees, and towering flames. Survivors of the Buffalo Creek disaster often focus on images of the black mud, debris, and water —"It was like a big black ocean," "I felt as though the water was a thing alive and coming to get us all" (Erikson 1979, p. 9). Those who survived Hiroshima remembered clearly the terrible flash from the first sight of the bomb preceding the shock wave and the subsequent destruction. Even more evocative for some are the smells of disaster—the smell of smoke and dust, of acrid chemicals, of burning human flesh, and, later, of decay and putrefaction.

Mechanical perceptions are usually of the shock wave or force of some power associated with the disaster. This power is often beyond anything the victim could have imagined. It is most frightening of all when it takes away control, flinging humans to the ground or whirling them through the air. The water of floods may do this too, as well as winds and explosive blasts. Like other sensory perceptions during impact, these mechanical perceptions are incredibly strange and intense, and to an even greater extent, they reinforce how infinitely frail and helpless the human organism really is.

When "known" disaster impacts on person and community, there is an anticipatory set of percepts against which it is measured and compared: the last flood, the previous bush and forest fires, the real past disaster or the disaster warned about or fantasied. There is thus greater opportunity for some cognitive comprehension and mastery. The sensory perceptions are essentially the same as in a disaster without warning. But the shock is lessened. Although the individual may be terrified and powerless, at least he knows in general terms the nature of the devil he faces. He can marshal his thoughts and actions to combat it or to anticipate what he will do when it passes. For he is more likely to know both what actions to take and how and when it will pass.

THE EMOTIONAL EXPERIENCE DURING IMPACT

Our understanding of behavior during the period of intense impact comes mainly from two sources: the descriptions of those who have experienced disaster, and systematic studies by sociologists, psychologists, and psychiatrists.

First, there is *heightened arousal,* and the individual is oriented chiefly to the protection of self. Feelings of fear are intense if there is danger and major threat to life. The well-being of the primary group or those for whom the individual is responsible is of primary concern, and, when bonds are intense, as between mother and child, may surpass even the concern for self. Yet survival is the chief goal. The person may feel he is dying, that "this is it," that death and destruction are near, and images of his life may flash before him. Arousal is very high. Attention is heightened. Very few people, however, show maladaptive behaviors in the face of this stressor. Most take actions or control their fears in ways that seem to assist their own survival and that of others. There may be outcry and screaming if terror is great, but this is not common, and may be strongly culturally determined, and varied by factors such as sex role, which allows women this release but not men.

With the increased arousal and alertness, individuals scan the environment for cues as to the level of danger and the nature of the personal threat. There may be many different components of threat, each of which brings its own particular fear—of mutilation by flying debris during storm or explosion, of being swallowed by the very earth in an earthquake, of being buried alive by the crashing of a building. Drowning, burning, choking, crushing, and asphyxiation may all be realistically feared, and with them, the annihilation of the self.

Fear is the dominant and appropriate response when the disaster is severe and survival is threatened. This fear is realistic: anxiety and its physical concomitants are familiar—racing heart and dry mouth, tightness inside, and tenseness of muscle. There is the preparedness for action —for fight or flight—in response to the signal of danger. Fear may be felt for the self, for others, for one's future, for life, for society. Superimposed on this rational fear may be all the irrational fears of conscious and unconscious origin, symbolically linked to death, mutilation, annihilation, destruction, and loss. Even though fear is natural and ultimately adaptive to survival, people are often ashamed of experiencing such an emotion, for in many cultures it is perceived as a sign of inadequacy. When speaking of the disaster, some people will deny this feeling, or make light of it, so it is often difficult to estimate the frequency of its occurrence. No doubt it is more profound and may be more overwhelming in those disasters of enormous physical impact and overwhelming threat to life—the bombing of atomic warfare, the destructive torrent of Buffalo Creek, the inferno of an Australian bushfire.

A *sense of helplessness* is a further emotional concomitant with impact when a person realizes that the forces are such that human action means little, that one is trapped, or cannot escape, and that one's actions may not ensure the survival of oneself or those one loves. As the disaster continues, the person is inevitably confronted with his own ineffectiveness. Fear rises, as do feelings of helplessness, which may lead to further fear. Childhood feelings of powerlessness and inadequacy may be reawakened. And there may be irrational feelings of shame at being so helpless, along with a rising sense of frustration and even anger. But the helplessness predominates; and it is the quality, intensity, and experience of helplessness that is a major factor in the traumatic imprinting of the impact.

> "I felt helpless as we huddled there with the fire around us—there was nothing else we could do—if only there had been something I don't think I would have felt so bad" (fire victim).
> "We felt helpless as the wind tore our home apart and the rain poured in—that was what was so frightening"—(hurricane victim).
> "The edge of the cyclone came back with an unbelievable roar. When our place started to disintegrate it was even worse. There was nothing we could do" (Stretton 1976, p. 19).

The *sense of abandonment* may be another powerful and frightening component of the emotional experience of the disaster. The person or group may feel forsaken by God and man. Wolfenstein (1957) perceives this sense as a major part of the emotional distress of the disaster experience, particularly if the person is isolated and alone. It may also be linked to the experience of helplessness. For some people, earlier experiences of despair and abandonment will be reawakened, adding to the utter alienation and aloneness. Children who are separated from their parents may feel especially that all the trusted good and protective influences have deserted them. But even adults can lose their sense of being safe or invulnerable, or protected, of having others who care for them, and of living in a world that can be trusted.

The *yearning for relief and rescue* is intense. Prayers may be uttered for the first time in years, or people may pray to a God they did not previously acknowledge. Inside there is a longing for it to be finished, gone, and over with, a longing to be safe. Sometimes, especially when the disaster is prolonged, death may be wished for, but, even here, it is an end to fear and suffering that is actually sought. Often, there are also feelings of remorse and regret for what one seems to have lost, and there is a yearning to have a second chance. There may already be a reappraisal of life and values, a process that is often pronounced in the immediate aftermath with the joy and euphoria of survival. There may also be what Kübler-Ross (1969), in a different context, has called "bargaining," where the person, for example, may say to himself, "God, if only you let me off this time, I'll be a better person in future—I'll live life differently. . . . I promise you if only you let me off this time. Let me survive . . . let my loved ones survive . . . let this not be it."

BEHAVIORS DURING IMPACT

During the disaster most people will act appropriately to protect themselves and significant others. Despite the common experience of intense fear and often helplessness, there is usually little panic during the period of threat or impact. Some experiences of impact are vividly portrayed in the following excerpts from an account in the *Reader's Digest* (February 1984) of the Ash Wednesday fires.

An Adelaide radio reporter on direct line to his station yelled through the fire's roar: "The sky is red, then it's white. It's going crazy. The fire jumped thirty, fifty meters high, right over the top of Greenhill Road. . . . We can't see any houses. . . . Greenhill Road is just wiped out. We can hardly breathe. The air is white with heat." The wall of flame shot over his head as he sheltered with others near a farmhouse. He ran toward his own house, reporting as he went: "I'm sitting on the road in front of my own house where I've lived for thirteen years . . . the roof's falling in. It's in flames and there's nothing I can do about it—Goddamn it! It's just beyond belief. My house is gone. It's exploding still and I just can't bear to look at it. And the man across the road thinks his wife may be trapped—and his house is burned to the ground" [pp. 153–54].

In another area a ten-year-old boy ran toward a policeman—his arms out for comfort. His clothes were scorched to his body, his face hardly recognizable. The policeman laid him gently in the back of his car, where he lay crying with intense pain from his burns. The child's body was swollen far beyond its normal size. His father, unknowingly, pulled up beside the police car and fell away shocked as his son called out "it's me Dad, Dad." When the ambulance could not get through, the policeman drove the police car through flames and across melting bitumen to try to get the child to medical care. From the back of the car the boy called out "Oh God, I'm going to die." Their car was trapped by flames and immobilized. Then another came, and the boy and another burned man were transferred to it and taken to the nearest hospital. The child was dead on arrival. His mother, with whom he had been escaping, was found dead beside the road, her thongs burned into the bitumen [pp. 157–58].

Two hundred and fifty people were sheltered in the Macedon Family Hotel, a small hotel in the small Victorian country town of Macedon, as fire raged outside exploding cars and domestic fuel and destroying everything around. Firefighters hosed what they could. These people survived, but the fire with a heat that scientists later estimated had reached 1,000° C had destroyed almost half the town's homes and buildings [pp. 171–72].

Twelve volunteer firefighters died when trapped with their trucks and incinerated by the fires in the Victorian bushland [p. 183].

One fire captain explained the impact of the fires in this way: "Once a major bushfire is raging out of control, there is little that a thousand fire trucks and ten thousand fire fighters can do. Fire becomes a cataclysm creating its own wind and weather, a demon with a mind of its own" [p. 188].

Flight and escape from the threatening forces seem the most logical behaviors. Where possible, this is the first line of action. Usually the person taking it is aware of the dangers and has chosen to flee automatically or as a reasoned choice. It differs from panic in that there is control and a degree of rationality and in that it is still social, recognizing the needs of others as well as the self. Sometimes the person may exhibit power, strength, and speed far beyond his usual levels, to drive his flight and get him to relative safety, or enable him to protect himself or others. At other times, however, there may appear to be a temporary or prolonged paralysis of action that inhibits or delays his response. He will often be motivated to respond in this way when he sees others fleeing and may follow them, sometimes blindly or even inappropriately.

The flight itself may be terrifying, with the threat behind and sometimes on all sides, as in descriptions of flight from the rising flood of the Buffalo Creek dam: ". . . and there it came. Just like a big black cloud. . . . I screamed at my wife. . . . everything above us was coming on down, getting closer and closer and we didn't have much time nohow. . . ." (Erikson 1979, pp. 96–97).

The account by Marit Gilje Jaatun (1983) of a man's attempt to escape during the North Sea oil rig disaster further exemplifies the terrors of flight:

A young man was watching a movie during his off-duty period when the rig suddenly tilted. Understanding at once that something serious had happened he tried to escape through a nearby corridor. Others were running as well. He stumbled over a man he knew, who had been trapped beneath a fallen drum. This man was calling for help, and he tried desperately to free him. But the drum was too heavy to move, and others would not stop to help. As the water came closer, he was forced to leave his work mate. He ran out on the deck and climbed the slippery tilted surface, trying to keep his hold. The rig suddenly tilted further, and a huge container slid toward him. Men he knew were crushed and swept overboard. The rig turned upside down, and he was pulled under the water. He was convinced he was dying. But, finally, after fighting for his life in freezing and tumultuous seas, he reached one of the lifeboats and safety.

Protective postures may also be adopted when flight has ceased or cannot take place. The person may crouch down behind something perceived as strong, or crawl under something, such as a bed. Often a person will assume the primitive protective posture—that of being curled over, head down, knees up, and hands or arms protecting the head and face (perhaps also showing submission to the aggressive forces of nature). Or the person may fling himself flat, holding onto what security the contact of his body with the earth may bring.

Holding onto and protecting others is another frequent behavior during impact. It allows people to experience the reassurance of clinging to another to feel stronger as a twosome, or simply to share the terror. The primitive consolation, security, and comfort in being held closely by another must also come into play. There is also a sense of using one's own body to protect loved ones who are weaker and helpless, especially one's children. This behavior is observed in so many disasters—floods and famine, hurricane and holocaust, accident and apocalypse. Even strangers may cling together when the circumstances are terrifying and the barriers of social distance suddenly disappear.

Family-oriented behaviors, as already noted, can explain much of what happens during impact. There may be fear and arousal and intense concern if family members are absent. Irrationally, people may battle through the forces of impact to try to reach, save, or be with those they love most. When family members are together hierarchical roles of caring may be followed, with the men protecting the women and the women caring for the children.

Such activities may greatly buffer the impact. As Valent (1984) has noted with respect to phases of behavior and response during the bushfires, such rescuing and caring activities complemented the care-evoking, crying, and helpless behaviors of others. There is a sense too that more than anything else family members wish to be together—"If we die, we die together."

Affiliative behaviors, merely wanting to be together with other people, may also generally increase during disaster. Driven by fear as a stimulus, people may seek to be closer to others for the reassurance this humanity brings. Such closeness is comforting in itself. Strumpfer's (1970) study of responses in a severe monsoon rainstorm underscores this relationship between fear and affiliation.

Heroic actions and courage are associated with impact, although perhaps even more with the rescue phase. People may go to undue lengths to assist and save the lives of family, friends, or even total strangers. The high level of arousal, the rapid review of different possibilities for action, and altruistic and humanitarian urges may all lead to this outcome. Altruism and heroism are common themes (Siporin 1976); their frequency speaks positively for basic drives of human concern for others. But, unfortunately, as Rachman (1978) points out, in general the psychological literature tends to neglect courage and focus on fear. Sometimes heroic actions are foolhardy. Sometimes they end disastrously for the person attempting them, although the instincts of self-preservation and the need for the survival of the self usually predominate.

Contrary to popular belief, *panic* is rare. Poorly defined in terms of any scientific criteria, panic is usually taken to mean uncontrolled and inappropriate flight in the face of threat. However, as Weisæth (1983) points out, there is good reason to see panic more broadly. Specifically, Weisæth suggests that panic should be defined to include other disorganized behavior marked by loss of control and not just flight behavior. Thus, it could cover the panic responses of those entrapped who cannot flee and show uncontrolled, dysfunctional behaviors and purposeless hyperactivity. Weisæth's definition is useful: "grossly agitated motoric behaviour which is impulsively driven, with diminished or no cognitive control and which increases the risk of death or injury to the person himself or to others" (p. 165).

It seems likely that panic is limited not only to a very small percentage of persons but also to particular circumstances. Quarantelli (1954), who defined panic as acute fear accompanied by flight or attempted flight, specified some of these circumstances: when there was immediate danger; when escape routes were narrowing, blocked, or about to close; and when the person was highly isolated. Thus, people tended to panic when they lacked communication with others and did not know what to expect or when the disaster might be over and help at hand. Uncertainty, confusion, powerlessness, and helplessness are all likely to increase the possibility of panic. On the other hand, group cohesiveness and the presence of a leader are likely to lessen the possibility. However, panic does not seem to happen very often, even when circumstances are horrendous. Furthermore, when panic does take the form of uncontrolled flight it may not always be nonadaptive, for this very flight, though quite irrational and uncontrolled, may provide escape and safety. Panic is above all nonsocial: it takes cognizance of neither the cues nor needs of others and does not weigh options for the self in terms of others.

Sometimes fire disasters are thought to be associated with panic, as persons attempted to escape smoke-filled areas with limited escape routes. But systematic studies have found it hard to document such an association. For example, in an explosion and factory fire, Weisæth found only three real instances of panic, either in self-reports or descriptions given by others of behavior during the period of impact. These three women met the criteria of extreme anxiety and uncontrolled physical flight. A further eight had shown quite strong disorganized flight behavior, but in this actual disaster, flight, although potentially risky, proved to be adaptive for both groups. Overall, as reported in other disasters, most people were courageous, competent, and in control.

However, when people feel they can no longer combat or endure the impact of a disaster, they may resign themselves to whatever its outcome may be—death, they believe, in most instances. There is a sense of sacrifice, as if one is a sacrifice to the gods or to the forces of the catastrophe. With the feeling that there is nothing one can do may come relief. The survival value of resignation will depend on the nature of the disaster.

The so-called *disaster syndrome* occurs either during the impact or immediately afterward. It is a psychologically determined response that defends the individual against being overwhelmed by traumatic experience. The person appears dazed, stunned, apathetic, and passive. He or she may sit or stand immobile or may wander aimlessly, seemingly unaware of surroundings, the danger, or the presence and needs of others. J. S. Tyhurst (1950) suggested that 20–25 percent of the people in a severe disaster might show this syndrome; Weisæth found such maladaptive behaviors in just over 20 percent of his subjects. Usually, this syndrome is transient, giving way either to hyperactivity or to appropriate activity. Sometimes, though, it may last for several hours, so that rescuers find the victim with a flat and apathetic facial expression wandering aimlessly through the devastation. This person may need care for his own protection in such circumstances. In other instances he may pass into the usual phases of post-disaster euphoria and excitement, marked by altruism and gratitude and strong group identification. From the literature it appears that the likelihood of this syndrome increases with the intensity of the disaster stress and the extent of the devastation (Wallace 1956).

A number of other maladaptive behaviors have been reported in conjunction with some disasters. These behaviors may be classified as panic. They include acute confusional states or even reactive psychoses, dissociative states, fruitless activity, hysterical reactions, and behavior that is out of touch with reality.

Researchers have attempted to delineate the frequencies of various patterns of behavior during impact. For instance, Tyhurst (1950) suggested that responses could be divided into three main groups. A group of 12–25 percent was characterized as "cool and collected," able to formulate appropriate plans of action and carry them through. A group of 50–75 percent showed the "normal" response of being stunned and bewildered, as well as a restricted field of attention, lack of awareness of any subjective feeling or emotion, but behaved reflexively nonetheless. A group of 10–25 percent evidenced obviously inappropriate responses, including panic, paralyzing anxiety, and hysterical behavior.

Quarantelli and Dynes (1973) suggest that most people do not panic. For instance, in the face of a flood threat, 92 percent of families evacuated together in an orderly way. They also contend that only a minority of victims exhibit shock reactions or the disaster syndrome. For instance, in a tornado disaster only 14 percent of the population may have experienced some initial elements of the syndrome.

Lundin (1984b) investigated survivors' reactions following a nightclub fire. He found that 37 percent showed a denying response, 30 percent acute anxiety, and the remainder rational responses to the situation.

Perhaps the most thorough and well-conceptualized review of behavior in a single disaster is that of Weisæth (1983). He examined variables of cognitive control (quality of appraisals of the impact and its consequences); inadequate behaviors (courses of action judged to increase risk); help needed to reach safety (in cases where this reflected some inability of the individual to respond); leadership demonstrated; involvement or cooperative activities; absolute and relative rescue efforts (in relation to available options). These were rated in the 125 survivors of a fire explosion in a paint factory in Norway. Each survivor received a Disaster Behavior Index score. Three groups of behaviors were delineated: optimal, 29.8 percent; adaptive, 49.6 percent; maladaptive, 20.7 percent.

Weisæth also formulated subgroupings and calculated percentages for them (as individuals could fall into more than one subgroup, the percentages total more than 100 percent). He found that 70 percent had some reduction in cognitive control; 24.6 percent displayed some inadequate behavior (usually motor paralysis); 15 percent subsequently needed help to overcome psychological blocks; 33 percent demonstrated leadership activities of a significant degree; 46.9 percent engaged in cooperative activities; 22 percent carried out major rescue efforts; and 22 percent contributed more than could be expected. Overall, these are very positive patterns of behavior in the face of major and traumatic stress. Interestingly, disaster training and experience was the strongest variable to correlate with optimal disaster response and best predicted such adaptive behaviors.

As noted by both Valent and Weisæth, there are also many psychophysiologic reactions during impact. A pounding heart, tense muscles, pains, faints, headaches, and diarrhea are all typical. Victims spoke to Valent (1984) of fear that felt like "a rock inside the chest," of muscle tension that was like being "whipped from head to toe," and of dragging feelings inside. Some of these feelings continued afterward or developed into psychosomatic disorders, but most vanished as the fear and anxiety passed.

THE SIGNIFICANCE OF IMPACT BEHAVIOR AND RESPONSE

The individual's behavior during impact may have great significance for one's subsequent perception of and adaptation to disaster. First and most obviously, adaptive behaviors are likely to ensure survival. This is of primary importance, but it is not the only factor. They must be integrated into a person's experience of the disaster and how it is perceived and interpreted. Individuals may view their behavior positively in terms of pre-existing self-concepts, formed long before the disaster. Or they may feel a sense of inadequacy, shame, and failure. Their response may be a source of conflict —a "responsibility trauma," as the Norwegian disaster workers have called it—and it may be a serious obstacle to adjustment subsequently. A person may feel, for instance, that he or she did not behave courageously enough, or should not have fled, or should have carried out greater protective actions, and there may be a residual sense of shame and guilt. Sometimes the behavior will seem unacceptable because others perceive it as unacceptable. For example, a woman felt her husband's obvious fear during a cyclone, and saw his inability to protect her and the children as signs of his inadequacy as a man. Both the man's self-perceptions and the marriage did not survive this experience.

Special conflicts may arise in this way for those people whose roles involve responsibility for others. This is similar to the situation of leaders in wartime, where the greater threat comes not so much from personal danger, but from the responsibility for lives of others under one's command. More generally, such conflicts, remorse, and regret may be felt by those who could not save their family or friends or who, to escape, had to ignore the pleas of others for help. For example, a man from the Norwegian oil rig suffered somatic and depressive complaints, which improved only when he was able to face and work through his guilt and shame at not being able to save his friend. Such a response may involve the sort of traumatic memory that is later vividly etched in the mind of the survivor, forever being reviewed, and perhaps forever a source of guilt; this is because the survivor may feel that his or her life was purchased at the cost of another's. These reactions on the part of survivors of Hiroshima and Nagasaki have been discussed by Janis (1951) and Lifton (1967).

DURATION OF DISASTER IMPACT

The impact of a disaster may be brief or prolonged. A sudden explosion may be very brief, a flood may last many hours. A person may be trapped in a wrecked vehicle for minutes, hours, or sometimes even days.

Perceptions of duration do not always correspond to the reality. Time may seem brief, or the person may feel that all time is suspended, that he is frozen and caught in the moment of impact. It may seem interminable, as though he is watching all the horror in slow motion, or it may seem to race, like his thoughts. The individual's perceptions of time may stay with him afterward, a vivid part of his memory.

It is often difficult to define when the worst of the impact is past and one's survival is assured. Many disasters bring secondary threats that seem a continuation of the impact—for instance, fires after earthquakes and bombings. The more prolonged this stressor experience, the greater the difficulty and trauma for those affected, as well as the risk to life.

During the disaster, the problem becomes one of how to maintain control: alertness, appraisal of threat, and readiness for appropriate action. Often people can do this, even for prolonged periods, by warding off natural exhaustion and going without sleep. The will to survive seems to give them superhuman strength. At other times there may be periods of shutting off —a conservation of energy, a withdrawal from the intense stimuli—by temporarily erecting a "protective barrier" that seems to cut out some of the threat and pain of what is happening. This may be one factor that helps people to endure periods of incredible hardship and deprivation. Of course, the process also reflects some level of psychic numbing or emotional shutdown.

In some human disaster experiences the duration may be quite prolonged —days, weeks, months, or even years. This occurred in concentration camps or in those areas with long-term drought and famine. Here survival seems guaranteed only if people can emotionally shut out the unrelenting horror of the experience. Feeling may be shut out for many years with prolonged numbing, or it may be locked only just below the surface, as expressed in the outpouring of grief at the death of loved ones seen in recent television coverage of the Ethiopian famine.

COPING FOR SURVIVAL

What are the factors, then, that lead to survival? What are the features of personality and circumstance, and what are the coping behaviors, that bring people through such incredible stress and suffering?

One of the most important factors, it seems, is the powerful *human attachment* people have for each other. Henderson and Bostock (1977) described the coping mechanisms of seven survivors of a shipwreck near southern Australia. These men suffered the ordeal of a shipwreck, followed by drifting on an inflatable life raft in extreme conditions, during which one of the original ten men died. This was followed by a period of several days of heat and then two further deaths until rescue occurred on the thirteenth day. The survivors were interviewed within a few days of their rescue and asked to describe their thoughts and emotional state through this period. Henderson and Bostock conclude that "throughout the ordeal, the most conspicuous behavior was the men's preoccupation with principal attachment figures such as wives, mothers, children and girlfriends" (p. 16). This "attachment ideation," as Henderson and Bostock term it, was reported to be the most helpful component of their experience. As the authors note, this experience is common to many people exposed to serious danger while separated from those they love. Thus, soldiers in wartime or prisoners may feel they can keep going only because of these thoughts and powerful feelings for the loved ones they wish to come back to. A study of coping strategies of concentration camp survivors found that a number of techniques, particularly that of "survival for some purpose," centered around those to whom the person was strongly attached and involved strong attachment behavior (Dimsdale 1974).

The *drive to survive* has been described as prominent among survivors of shipwrecks like the one discussed above. It has also been described as an important force for survival among concentration camp victims (Dimsdale 1974; Eitinger and Askevold 1968). It has kept alive sailors on lone voyages in desperate physical conditions, explorers lost in the desert, and victims of terrorism and humiliating incarceration and torture. More than simply not wanting to die, it is a will to live, an almost aggressive demand for and holding on to life. It may be that the individual is driven by the will to survive for some particular purpose—to see loved ones again, to defeat the forces against him, or even to seek revenge.

Leadership or *group affiliation* can also assist coping for survival. The shipwrecked survivors all commented on the strong influence of their leader, the chief officer. By being decisive and firm but yet compassionate, he had kept up morale and lessened anger and hopelessness. Similarly, in situations as diverse as combat, mine disasters, and concentration camps, the leadership and support of one or more people has often been identified as critical to survival. Mutual aid to one another, the sharing of positive and hopeful feelings, as well as the provision of information, advice, and general support, seemed even in the concentration camp situation to mitigate some of the effects of stress; even there people who could not affiliate with a group were much less likely to survive.

Attempts at mastery may take many forms. Cognitive control, described by Weisæth (1983, 1984), is a search for information or knowledge that will help the person make meaning of, or combat, the experience and its effects. Another coping technique of this sort involves concentrating on the good aspects and shutting out the bad, focusing on the small pleasures, for instance, or on the survival thus far. Review of past coping and survival is another form of attempt at mastery. Intellectualization can be a defensive way of avoiding anxiety and, therefore, may or may not assist coping, because it may lead to avoidance of practical realities that must be faced. Where activities or action are possible for mitigation, self-protection, or the assistance of others, these are likely to enhance the individual's sense of mastery. Where no activity can take place, mental rehearsal of such activity may help, as it did for some concentration camp survivors.

As already mentioned, a temporary *shutting out of feelings,* with a range of *denial strategies,* may help in prolonged stressor situations. (It may not be ultimately adaptive because it may lead to a prolonged psychic numbing afterward.) This shutting out may involve a sense of unreality, of viewing the disaster experience as if it were happening to someone else. Or it may involve a preoccupation with thoughts of an afterlife, the past, or a fantasized future. In concentration camps, complete withdrawal led to a stage of profound apathy, complete indifference to the surroundings, and failure to respond to personal or physical stimuli. While many experienced such withdrawal for brief periods, if it became prolonged the person was unlikely to survive. Another way to shut out feelings is to deliberately suppress distressing thoughts brought on by disaster experience, perhaps even supplanting them with defensive humor. All these strategies can be highly adaptive but can also prove risky for ultimate emotional responsiveness and adjustment if they become fixed. Their cathartic release at a later stage might become an important goal of therapy for those traumatized by the disaster.

Prayer, as noted earlier, is the response of many people, even if never previously religious. It seems to be both a release, a source of appeal, and the vehicle for hope in what may seem a hopeless situation. For example, the shipwrecked men used prayer in this way, quite contrary to their usual way of coping. And the victims of the cyclone, as in other tornadoes and hurricanes, called to their God to save them. Prayers may be linked to man's fantasies that his gods are wreaking their wrath on him, and that he must call on them to desist, to hear his supplication and his acknowledged frailty and to spare him. Or it may be that he calls on the protection of a deity as on a good parent, an omnipotent force.

Hope is mobilized at the level of the individual, the family, and the group. Often, hope is initially high but then gives way to despair and pessimism. At this point, if a good leader mobilizes hope appropriately, the group can maintain the motivating force necessary to take action to survive. Henderson and Bostock (1977) concluded that as a coping behavior, hope has the following characteristics: it means anticipating relief from the distress by one's own actions or the actions of others; it is more powerful when verbalized and shared in the group; and it is used by leaders to sustain morale (even when seemingly unrealistic). Essentially, hope functions to assist survival by controlling mood. In the concentration camps (Dimsdale 1974) it was used both actively to promote the belief that what was happening could not continue, and more passively in stimulating the attitude of "where there is life there is hope."

Behaviors for surviving disasters are also evident in other stressful situations where survival will require endurance. Engel and Schmale (1972) have spoken of *conservation-withdrawal* as a survival mechanism, whereby survival of the organism is supported by processes of disengagement and inactivity vis-à-vis the external environment. This condition gives way to its opposite, action-engagement, when the latter is critically required. Ironside (1979) used this framework to review behavior in a number of extreme situations. He examined, for example, Sir Douglas Mawson's survival alone in Antarctica, Dr. David Lewis's single-handed yacht voyage to the Antarctic, and Millard's survival in his demasted yacht in the Pacific. A number of general themes emerged from his review. There was a preoccupation with food and basic body functions, for to survive the body must be kept strong. Ruthlessness and self-discipline also appeared to be important factors. And like the shipwreck survivors interviewed by Henderson, these men became preoccupied with thoughts and images of those most important to them, their wives and children. When despair or exhaustion were overwhelming, or stimuli were too great for too long, there often followed a period of giving up which seemed to trigger the process of conservation-withdrawal. On awakening from the sleep and withdrawal, the survivors were able to rapidly return to the struggle, often with heightened alertness and new ways of coping. These behaviors are, of course, critical to adjustment during disaster impact. And they take on significance in the immediate and subsequent post-disaster period because of a further component noted by Ironside, the need to give *testimony*. Either during or following the survival process, many people need to write down or tell of their experience—to lay down what they have learned—both for themselves and others.

WHEN AND HOW WILL IT ALL END?

As the disaster impact continues people become preoccupied with when it will end. People feel that they can only hang on so much longer and that "the end" must come soon, either the end of the terrible experience or the end of the self. When probable duration can be calculated from past experience, information available, or obvious environmental cues, there is often a greater sense of control. But even then the impact may seem interminable.

Those who experience hurricanes and cyclones may feel that they will go on forever. Or there are rumors that the storm is returning that confuse its frightened victims. Thus people search the environment for cues to the end, to rescue and relief. Omens are magically interpreted and waves of hope follow even minimal signs. People experience fear about how the end will find them. Will they be alive? Will their loved ones have survived? How great will their losses be? Will they suffer major injuries? What will have become of their homes, neighborhood, community? But the greatest preoccupation is to live through it with those one loves, and at this time all other things seem as nothing by comparison.

It may seem impossible to sustain oneself further, and yet most people seem to gain the new strength they need to do so—even in the most horrific and stressful situations. And eventually the end does come. At first it cannot be believed. The victim does not dare acknowledge it. Then, slowly, relief and joy and euphoria well up. The victim touches himself to make sure it is true and he is whole. With a sense of renewal, he embraces those whom he loves. He has escaped death—survived.

IMMEDIATE AFTERMATH

Once the reality is verified, people attempt to extract themselves from the ruins of their environment. Their sense of relief that they and their loved ones have survived may be overwhelming, shutting out temporarily the enormity of the death and destruction that surrounds. There is the sense "I have beaten death" and a great sense of power.

Then the physical sensations and perceptions start to impinge. People often describe the "terrible silence" of the immediate aftermath. Bird calls and other background sounds may have ceased. Even the roar of the city may be stilled in a great disaster. Then, through this silence may come the cries and moans of others calling for help. The victim starts to see, really see, the extent of human injury and devastation to place. At this point, there may be a fresh wave of shock and fear.

Particularly evocative both during the disaster impact and immediately after are the deaths and mutilating injuries of others. The survivors of Hiroshima described how the burned and swollen flesh made people almost unrecognizable as humans. A sense of repugnance and fear may make it difficult to help those whose appearance is so distorted and distressing. But for the most part altruistic responses are powerful. As noted, most of the initial rescue work is done by those who are themselves victims of the disaster, long before formal assistance arrives. This rescue of others seems almost automatic, a basic human response, perhaps evolved for the survival of the group.

If the person has been separated from close members of his family, one of the strongest responses once the impact has passed is to search for them. The intense anxiety that separation brings is heightened by stress and threat during impact. And these feelings are unrelieved until there is a reunion with loved ones or at least knowledge of their safety—or grief upon knowledge of their loss.

If there is personal injury it may now come to full awareness as the victims take inventory of what has happened to them. Often, the arousal and intense preoccupation with the impact had cut out any awareness of injury, and people are quite surprised to find they are cut or hurt. The pain had simply not been felt. Similarly, those with more serious injuries may have held their pain in check, until now. There is an increasing realization of the extent of the disaster, perhaps previously denied because of the concentration with survival and the illusion of centrality. Property damage and losses may be great, but seem of little significance at this early stage.

Often, however, a sense of shock and numbness, a denial of the emotional impact of loss and death, protects the person at this stage. In this way, what has happened can be faced gradually, bit by bit. For some, the "disaster syndrome" of stunned apathy and nonresponsiveness may continue, or even appear for the first time shutting out the destroyed world with its losses and pain for days. Yet in most cases it passes. The same is true of other disturbed mental states: hysteria, brief reactive psychoses and confusional states, and disorganized and nonresponsive behaviors. But again these generally pass and only rarely become ongoing phenomena of major disorder.

With the growing awareness of needs and of further threats (fires, for example) come various steps for protection. Measures are taken to provide food, medical care, shelter, and clothing. When habitations have been destroyed, people will spontaneously move toward major or safe buildings, such as churches, schools, and hospitals. They will seek one another, forming small groups, of family, friends, or even strangers. These groups are often only temporary but may bring intense involvement. Group identification contributes to the "honeymoon" euphoria and "therapeutic community" effects of this immediate post-disaster period. People also turn to larger, formal groups for assistance. Where such groups did not already or no longer exist, functional groups and leaders often emerge spontaneously.

People have a strong need to be in communication with one another, to know what is happening and to have information. When communication systems are disrupted, feelings of helplessness and uncertainty increase, reinforcing the disaster trauma. Many disasters, both natural and man-made, disrupt communication or render it inefficient. Radio transmission may fail; telephone lines may be down. Communication and information systems may also break down because those responsible are absent or unaware, or injured or dead. Under these circumstances, it becomes difficult to gain or share information needed to deal with the disaster and its aftermath. In the Darwin cyclone, all police, ambulance, radio, emergency, and other communications were destroyed. The repercussions are evident in Scanlon's (1978) analysis:

> "We didn't have any communications. That was our problem. We had no power. The emergency generator wouldn't start. . . . Then the terrible realization came that all forms of communication in Darwin had been destroyed. There was no way of knowing whether the rest of Australia knew that Darwin had been destroyed . . . [and] the anxiety of not being able to let relatives and friends know if you are alive and well—and safe" (p. 8).

Another important element of the post-impact period is the sense of relief and release of tension. Weisæth's (1984) study of survivors of the paint factory fire found this reaction in over two-thirds of the less severely exposed and in somewhat fewer of those more severely stressed. It was seen as abreactive, cathartic, and a sign that the traumatic impact of this disaster was not severely entrenched. Many forms of release *and* letting go are possible. There may be a variety of moods—of quiet, elation, or overt rejoicing in the form of dancing or even laughter, perhaps sexual disinhibition, or even what seems to be absurd or "hysterical" behavior. There may be the beginnings of the talking through process as people share their experiences and perceptions of the terror to gain control and mastery.

The release from stress may also be manifested psychosomatically. For instance, vomiting was reported quite frequently in the North Sea oil rig survivors (Holen, Sund, and Weisæth 1983a) and has been noted following other disasters such as the Granville rail disaster and Cyclone Tracy. Diarrhea is yet another way in which the body symbolically lets go after the tension and stress. Nausea, too, is very frequently described, perhaps symbolizing revulsion.

Other psychophysiological reactions noted include headaches, breathing difficulties, tremors, palpitations, sweating, malaise, dizziness, and exhaustion. Such reactions may be brief or may evolve and merge into an ongoing post-disaster morbidity. The Weisæth (1984) study cited includes what is probably the first systematic investigation of the frequency of psychophysiological reactions in the immediate aftermath period (the first post-disaster week). Such reactions occurred in more than two-thirds of the subjects, often in conjunction with anxiety. In fact, 61 percent experienced tremor of a distressing degree. Palpitations, sweating, and dysphoria also occurred in at least one-third of those most severely exposed, perhaps representing the frequent presence of anxiety. These symptoms and other psychophysiologi- cal reactions tended to be more pronounced and longer lasting in those most severely exposed.

Some reassurance comes with the arrival of outside help. For the victims, the response of local, national, and/or international authorities signifies not only assistance but also recognition of what has been suffered. Communica- tion is reestablished, information begins to flow, and some system of organi- zation to meet individual and community needs is reconstituted.

Yet, despite the release from tension and the increasing sense of security of knowing that help is at hand, fear, anxiety, and arousal may continue or may reappear after a latent period. It is as though people have learned to be alert, that the signal function of anxiety is renewed to protect the person from further danger. Anxiety may be diffuse, general, subjective, or specifi- cally linked to various traumatic components of the disaster experience. The duration of this anxiety is often difficult to pinpoint, as it may merge with the arousal and excitement of the post-impact phase or be disguised in the intense activity that ensues. Perhaps the only systematic study is that of Weisæth (1983), who found that more than 90 percent of the subjects had begun to reexperience anxiety within five hours of rescue. Often, the anxiety came on when "the person went to bed, stopped his activities or in other ways came closer to his internal world" (p. 206). Again, those most in- tensely exposed to the disaster were likely to show the greatest effects. More than 40 percent of such subjects experienced constant severe or extreme anxiety, as opposed to only 13.6 percent of those less exposed and 0.8 percent of the control group. Less severe anxiety tended to be transient and inter- mittent, and some anxiety, even though irrational, is a natural phenomenon in the acute aftermath. Intense arousal and fear do not readily go away.

Perhaps the experience of impact is best exemplified in this account by a disaster victim—a woman who experienced a cyclone at the same time that she went into labor with her first child.

"I felt I must tell someone what it was like. You couldn't know if you weren't there. And people talk about the physical things—but it's the emotions that count. It's what's left in your mind afterwards that really leaves the scars.

"I was frightened when the cyclone warning came—more than most people, because it was Christmas Eve and they were all going to parties and none of them really believed it would happen. But I knew the baby was due any day and I was frightened about that too—it was our first. So I persuaded John to take me to the hospital—he didn't want to—he thought I was making too much fuss and he wanted to go for a Christmas drink with his mates. But anyway he finally took me that evening. They didn't want to keep me at the hospital at first, although I was having a few pains, but by then the wind was really coming up and they could see I might have trouble getting back, so they took me in.

"The night got worse and the cyclone hit—it was screaming with the wind and rain and my pains were coming faster and the waters broke— I was worried about John but there was nothing I could do—I was terrified something might happen to him, but I was scared for me and the baby too. The windows were breaking and the rain was pouring in and the staff were trying to protect us—they were wonderful. When it got worse we got out and sat under our beds—me and another girl—and the women who'd had their babies were trying to save them and there was flying glass everywhere and lots of people were cut and bleeding and the noise was like a horror movie—a space ship screaming or something. I went out of labor and in again and later I had the baby—in the midst of it but I thought I would die—I was sure it was the end of her and me, and that John was out there in it and he was dead too. The noise and the blood and the glass and the rain—it's no way for a child to be born. I never stop thinking about it and all that happened afterwards, and I never will."

IMPACT OF PERSONAL DISASTER

The impact of personal disaster may be either sudden or gradual. The sudden unexpected impact of assault, or motor vehicle accident, or a heart attack fills victims and their families with shock, helplessness, arousal, and fear. Coping behaviors and the chances for survival may be increased by the will to live, strong attachments to others, group support, and guidance from principals such as medical carers. The most common personal disasters with more gradual impact are life-threatening illnesses, which threaten disability, death, and loss: multiple sclerosis, carcinoma, and Alzheimer's and other dementias. Again, helplessness, fear, and dread may be managed, but the pattern of emotional response and the importance of the need for family, prayer, and hope are all similar. And interestingly, recent studies have confirmed the importance of emotional response and its variable expression in outcome. As in larger disasters, there is often a need to shut off feeling and deny for a while, to conserve and withdraw in order to reengage in the battle for self and existence.

CONCLUSION

Many themes will be left with those who have experienced community or personal disaster: triumph over death; loss of innocence regarding death after the horrific deaths of others; devastation and destruction of property and place, community and culture; dislocation; and a new view of the self and of life. These themes, of course, have many variations. Statistics on deaths, injuries, and destruction of home and property help to quantify the impact and will reflect the experience of the individual. But the psychological themes will be significant in many different ways in the days and weeks, and perhaps even the months and years, that follow the catastrophe. Those who have known this impact will never be quite the same again.

CHAPTER 4

Death and Survival

"Every night I would wake suddenly. I was there again in the crash. The confusion. The screams. The silence. The panic. The smell of blood and dust and faeces and fear. I used to dream it all the time. I don't now. But I will *never* forget it."

In the period immediately after the disaster there are spontaneous rescue activities by those who are conscious and able. Some may still be stunned, reflecting the effects of the disaster syndrome. Most are purposive, and work toward the necessities for safety and survival of themselves and others. Once communication is established, or reestablished, with those outside the disaster zone, there is a rapid convergence of assistance and resources, often to an overwhelming degree, which may even interfere with the activities of those already caring for themselves adequately.

This early period has been called "inventory" or "recoil" in the phasic descriptions of disaster. People as individuals "take stock" of what has happened to them: realize they have faced death and survived; acknowledge that they are injured; become shocked by the injuries and deaths of others; seek in anguish for family and others whose whereabouts are unknown. Still there is a level of numbness and shock which may protect against the full emotional impact, particularly of losses, when one is so grateful for survival. Then gradually, perhaps in hours, perhaps in days, the impact of the stress is faced and reactions to it continue or set in. Anxiety may rise, as noted previously, or reappear, particularly linked to traumatic themes. Emotional release may begin; or the numbing and closing off may continue.

But psychological (and physical) energy at this point goes primarily into living, into ensuring continued survival and safety, and in reunion with family or further protection of them. Arousal is likely to continue while there is any possibility of ongoing threat or any continued uncertainty of separation.

The victim's physical state is important, too, as part of his awareness of what the impact of the disaster has done to him. He may be injured, bloody, dirty, burned, bruised, stripped of clothing. This is a further component of the assault he has suffered and the stress he must endure and survive.

Gradually, however, the individual is again in some control of himself and his environment. He knows that help is at hand. His survival is relatively assured, as are food, clothing, or his basic human dignity. He must now begin to integrate what has happened to him.

This confrontation with disaster makes all persons equal in their basic humanity, although each victim must align these experiences with his own unique inner perceptions, past history, and view of self. Traumatic themes of death and destruction are invariably part of this integration process. By no means easily integrated, they may leave their imprint on survivors for a long, long time.

PERSONAL ENCOUNTER WITH DEATH

One way in which the disaster is most disturbing involves the degree to which it threatened one's own life. Perceptions of the threat may vary across a spectrum from an awareness that one could have been at the site (a remote miss) to the belief that one very nearly did die (near-miss). The particular way in which death threatened may have a frightening meaning of its own for individuals who dread certain forms of death in particular (such as crushing, asphyxiation, or drowning). The terror is likely, as studies have shown, to bring a rapid life review of memories flashing before the mind. When it is past there is relief, euphoria, elation.

Then the experience must be integrated. The individual must face the loss of his or her sense of personal invulnerability. Interestingly, this is sometimes replaced by a sense of invincibility. That is, the person feels that although death has threatened, he or she has defeated death and may do so again.

In reviewing how one survived, some people may feel that survival was purchased at the expense of others. Perhaps there were specific instances where others died nearby, or called for help, or one fled to escape and did not stop for those who could not flee themselves. Whatever the circumstances the survivor will ruminate about it in his endeavors to make meaning of his experience and behavior. In any case, the relevant scene or scenes will spring to mind, along with the visual, auditory, and other sensations that symbolize them. Often, the memory seems organized into a condensation of all the most frightening aspects of the event.

When this traumatic stimulus of personal encounter with death has been great, it may be, as suggested by psychodynamic theory, that the ego will be overwhelmed, so that the excitation effect of the stimulus cannot be defended against and traumatic anxiety results (Krystal 1971). Signal anxiety attempts to protect the ego against such traumatic anxiety. Freud (1920) and later Fenichel (1946) suggested that the ego may compulsively reexpose itself in fantasy to the traumatic situation in attempts to gain mastery (the phenomenon of repetition-compulsion) while, at the same time, defending itself against reexperiencing the trauma by avoiding it or shutting it out. Horowitz (1976; Horowitz et al. 1980) has translated these concepts into an understanding of stress response syndromes, with their intrusive memories and reexperiencing, as well as their avoidant, startle, and phobic components. He has developed a questionnaire reflecting some of the post-traumatic phenomena, calling it the Impact of Events Scale. More recently these concepts of the post-traumatic reaction and disorder have been reviewed and consolidated by Brett and Ostroff (1985) and Green et al. (1985).

POST-TRAUMATIC REACTIONS

Psychological phenomena such as the images and avoidance that occur in the days after impact may be considered *post-traumatic reactions*. They are not disorders but quite specific reactions to a traumatic stimulus, and may be, like the wound's response to injury or the grief response to loss, essentially adaptive and healing.

Many of the phenomena involve reliving and reexperiencing what has happened. Vivid flashes of particular scenes may come to mind *intrusively*, forcing their impact when the person would prefer to shut them out. Often, these flashes are accompanied by tremor, palpitations, and even intense anxiety and panic. At night such intrusions may take the form of nightmares of the fire, the crash, the raging torrent, the shaking earth, the collapsing building, and one's own terror at being near death. These traumatic intrusions and dreams may be intense initially, but gradually fade over those early weeks, decreasing in both frequency and effect. Dreams of death encounter and the deaths of others are very common in the early post-disaster period. In analyzing the dreams of Buffalo Creek survivors, Titchener et al. (1976) found that themes of death occurred more than twice as often as themes of guilt and anxiety.

Paralleling the intrusions is the reverse process—the attempts to shut out and repress all memories and reminders of what was so terrifying. Avoidance may occur through mental process or by warding off anything that could trigger a memory—discussions, places or people, pictures, sounds, or other stimuli. Linked to this vulnerability is the response to sounds, sights, and smells that are in any way evocative as perceptual cues. Thus, the sound of wind and rain, the hint of a storm, the rattle of galvanized iron roofs set off anxiety and dread in many people who had experienced a hurricane, cyclone, or other storm disaster. The rattle of train wheels or the screech of brakes may trigger memories and anxiety for survivors of transport disasters. Stimuli may be very personal or almost universal. In either case, they precipitate fear and a reliving of the disaster.

Sometimes the traumatic stimulus of nearness to death will have reawakened old traumatic memories of earlier disasters. Thus, those with wartime experiences of bombing, or being under enemy fire, or of the trenches, may have vivid scenes that they had forgotten, brought to the surface again. One Australian woman, who had not even been directly involved in the Ash Wednesday fires, experienced intrusions of fire and entrapment. She had initially experienced and repressed these intrusive images when, as a small child, she lived through the bombing of Dresden.

Not everyone who is threatened by death in a disaster situation will experience the post-traumatic reactions described. Some people seem protected by past experience or other defenses. Usually for those not so severely exposed, the experience of distressing intrusions settles relatively rapidly, lasting perhaps a few days to a few weeks, depending on the severity of the exposure. The need to avoid also passes, and reminders can be calmly faced —with only a slight memory of fear and pain. For most people the reaction settles within four to six weeks. Disturbance to sleep can be quite distressing, however, and the symptoms worrying, particularly if their natural history is not understood. Furthermore, the anxiety, irritability, and general distress accompanying post-traumatic reaction, and the wish to be finished and free of the experience, may make for difficulties in interpersonal relations, concentration at work, and capacity for pleasure.

POST-TRAUMATIC STRESS DISORDERS

For some people the reactions experienced will become entrenched, or will reappear, as the severe and disruptive *post-traumatic stress disorder*. The criteria for this disorder, which have evolved from Horowitz's studies (Horowitz 1976; Horowitz et al. 1980) of patients with post-traumatic disorders and as listed by the Diagnostic and Statistical Manual (DSM-III) of the American Psychiatric Association (1980), include the following:

1. A recognizable stressor that would evoke symptoms of distress in almost anyone
2. Reexperiencing of the trauma through recurrent and intrusive recollections of the event, recurrent dreams of the event, or a sudden acting or feeling as if the traumatic event were reoccurring
3. Numbing of responsiveness or reduced involvement with the external world, beginning some time after the trauma, as evidenced by at least one of the following: marked decrease in interest in significant activities, feelings of detachment from others, constricted affect
4. At least two of the following symptoms that were not present previously: hyperalertness or exaggerated startle, sleep disturbance, guilt about survival, memory or concentration problems, avoidance of activities that arouse recollections of the event, intensification of symptoms by similar or symbolic events (DSM-III, p. 238).

Just why such intense near-death experience (or other traumatic components of the disaster experience) should lead to disorder for some is not certain. We can, however, draw on some theoretical suggestions and some concrete evidence. In psychodynamic terms, we can say that the shock effects are particularly significant, leaving the ego no time to put up defenses to protect itself. This would be more likely in sudden impact disasters for which the individual is totally unprepared. The severity of the threat to life and self may also make the disaster overwhelming to the ego. And the degree to which the individual feels totally helpless and powerless in the face of the trauma may also contribute. It seems likely that subsequent gaining of mastery may mitigate the effects of this reaction to some degree. And, of course, in terms of this theory, some individuals may be more vulnerable because of early psychological wounding or trauma.

Some concrete evidence comes from Weisæth's valuable work (1984). Paint factory workers who still had, after the first week, a very high level of anxiety, traumatic sleep disturbances, startle reactions, fear phobia of the disaster area, and a degree of social withdrawal were highly likely to be suffering from the disorder seven months later. Several background variables were associated with being at risk for developing the post-traumatic disorder: adaptational problems in childhood and adult life, previous psychiatric impairment, high psychosomatic reactivity, and character pathology. In addition, women were more at risk. Finally, current life stressors and intensity of disaster stress from the time of the catastrophe were two variables. Severity of post-traumatic disorder in the acute (one week) and subacute (seven months) phases, previous psychiatric impairment, and intensity of original exposure were all associated with a greater likelihood of disorder and severe disorder four years later.

Weisæth found that symptoms decreased over time, particularly those symptoms that were not so severe originally, and that improvements were rapid over the first four weeks. Irritability and aggression, which often occurred together, could become persistent, severe, and disruptive, interfering with relationships and function in more chronic cases. Rising irritability has also been associated with the development of disorder in studies of other disasters such as the Beverly Hills nightclub fire (Green et al. 1983).

McFarlane and Frost (1984) examined development of disorders in firemen who combated the Ash Wednesday fires. They found that intensity of exposure alone was not necessarily predictive of stress disorder for this group of men, who were, on the whole, experienced firefighters and who had spent an average of 14.8 hours fighting these major fires. Thirty percent of them had been trapped at some point, more than a quarter had been injured, and 20 percent believed they came close to dying. Intrusive thoughts were often prominent but, again, not necessarily predictive of the development of disorder. The disorder group seemed to be characterized by a general psychiatric vulnerability, as evidenced by a personal and family history of psychiatric problems and a background of introversion and neuroticism (McFarlane 1985a,c). Many of those who did not show signs of the syndrome did, however, need considerable medical care, perhaps suggesting their experience of the stressor had affected them in less specific ways. It seems likely, then, that in very stressful disaster experiences, where there is personal threat to the self, an intense shock effect, and where the person is rendered helpless, reactions of intrusive repetitious images and avoidance are common. Whether these reactions continue, or reach the level of disorder, or lead the person to medical or professional care is another issue. McFarlane's most recent work suggests that the distress engendered by the experience may be the intervening variable in disorder (McFarlane and Blumbergs 1985). The very nature of these post-traumatic reactions are such that people may avoid any acknowledgment of them and often do not wish to talk of them.

ENCOUNTER WITH THE DEATHS AND MUTILATION OF OTHERS

The personal threat to life, the sense that one is dying even when one is not is difficult to integrate. So, too, is massive, shocking, and sudden confrontation with the deaths of others. In every disaster where there are massive deaths, particularly if they involve disfiguring injuries, those who witness them, whether victims themselves or rescuers, are disturbed and distressed.

Thus Janis (1951), discussing the bombing of cities during World War II, comments frequently on the effects of witnessing maimed bodies and extensive casualties. He quotes a German woman's description of the first big raid she experienced: "I saw people killed by falling bricks and heard the screams of others dying in the fire. I dragged my best friend from a burning building and she died in my arms. I saw others who went stark mad. The shock to my nerves and to the soul, one can never erase" (p. 107).

Janis found that for many survivors of Hiroshima and Nagasaki, the strongest emotional reaction was to witnessing the dead and injured. Quotes such as the following one vividly support this finding: "The burns on the faces were horrible. . . . The eyes appeared to be a mass of melted flesh. The lips were all split up and they looked like molten flesh. . . . The wounded were suffering awful pain. It was to me a sickening scene. . . . The death scene was awful. The color of the patient would turn to blue, and when we touched the body, the skin seemed to stick to our hands" (p. 19).

Vivid images of death are associated with many disasters. For example, the rescuers who searched for bodies following the air crash of the DC-10 in Antarctica describe horrific and imprinted scenes (Taylor and Frazer 1981) of "heads with smashed faces, opened skulls empty of brains, bodies without feet, and corpses that were charred" (p. 13). Stretton (1976) commented on the dead of Darwin, "We were all shocked and saddened to see the broken and mutilated bodies of men, women and children" (p. 46).

Images of death were very powerful as part of the traumatic impact of the Buffalo Creek disaster (Erikson 1979):

"I can't forget the horrible expression in her eyes and on her face. She looked as though she was scared to death, not drowned" (p. 120).

"Those bodies were distorted. You couldn't tell who they was. . . . They was all swelled up. Like I say, they was black with muck and mud" (p. 121).

"If you've ever seen anybody die a violent death, it's not like going to a funeral home and seeing people all dressed up and prepared. Instead you see the fear in somebody's open eyes, mouths awry. It's just a horrible thing" (p. 124).

". . . A man will never forget it. If I live to be a hundred years old, I will never forget it" (p. 122).

As Erikson himself commented in conjunction with Buffalo Creek, "Death like this does not retreat into some discrete compartment of the mind. . . . It's all there—an advance look at hell. And the sight does not go away easily" (1979, p. 124). Similarly, in a (Jones 1985) study of those who dealt with the bodies following the Jonestown, Guyana, mass suicide, the author quoted a disaster worker's remark that "seeing the decomposed bodies of the children put an extreme stress on me" (p. 306).

A person's encounter with the deaths of others is distressing and evocative—the sights, sounds, and smells, especially the bodily mutilation, the children. This experience too must be integrated. It may produce the same reactive phenomena as the shocking personal threat of death. Intrusive memories or nightmares, of a body or bodies, of disfigurement or blood, may intrude during the day or disrupt sleep at night. Triggers—smells, reminders of word or place—may bring back all the emotional intensity of the original experience even when it seems shut out and forgotten. These intrusive dreams and memories may alternate with defensive avoidance and repression of the intrusive images and feelings. Again, these reactions may settle in the early weeks after the disaster, or remain as entrenched and painful foci for the development of post-traumatic stress disorder.

Another way in which people may respond to this extreme exposure to death is by what Lifton (1967) has called *"death imprint."* As his term suggests, death imagery is a very prominent component of this response. As in the case of Hiroshima, the degree of exposure, or saturation with death, and the grotesqueness of alterations of body substance add to this imprinting. The survivor has, as Lifton says, experienced "a jarring awareness of the fact of death, as well as of its extent and violence" (p. 481). There may be a sense of pseudo-mastery, of having learned the secret of knowing and defeating death, which is a fragile defense against the fear. The person may seem locked into his death encounter, spellbound by it, and its compelling indelible image may dominate his subsequent life; here it is the intrusive component of the reaction that becomes the prdominant or total one. This imprint may also be associated with grief and impaired mourning. Indeed in his identification with death and the dead, the survivor may reflect "death in life."

While such overwhelming encounters with death do not occur in every disaster they are often pronounced in the disasters of war. Thus, many returned from the trenches of the First World War with deeply etched memories of the deaths and mutilating injuries of their comrades. Man-made disasters frequently bring such trauma, as airplane crashes and the collapse of buildings or other structures (for example, the Hyatt Regency Skywalk; Wilkinson 1983). Where there are fires, primarily or secondarily, the shocking trauma and threat of burns may make such deaths a theme in the memories of survivors. An extreme example of overwhelming immersion in death is the Holocaust, which lives with great intensity in the memories of survivors.

However, when death is massive, a common pattern of response is that of *psychic numbing.* Here it is as though the avoidant, denying, shutting out, repressing component of reaction has become the predominant or only theme. Lifton (1967) suggests that this response may be the survivor's major defense against death anxiety and death guilt. At the time of exposure, it may help him survive by protecting him from overwhelming helplessness, and emotional pain. But it may become nonadaptive, extreme, and chronic; the person is closing out all feeling. Typical of victims of the concentration camps and Hiroshima, this response also appears in many other disasters. Erikson (1976) found it profoundly present in a great many of those who survived Buffalo Creek and felt that it contributed to the destruction of the very fabric of the community.

Again, while it is difficult to define the exact variables that lead to these extreme responses, it seems that helplessness, massive exposure, and shock all contribute. It may be that people can manage to a degree but that once a threshold is reached, survival of the self and the ego requires that feeling be succumbed to and imprinted or shut out and numbed.

Of course, many disasters, perhaps the majority, do not involve such overwhelming encounters with death, either personally or with the deaths of others. The remote miss—or the possibility of death when one is secure and safe—may bring little traumatic stress. Yet the effects of heightened arousal, both during impact and subsequently, may bring excitement, the elation of flirting with death and avoiding the seduction. Some workers have spoken of the carnival-like excitement during and after some disasters which may be explained by this response; here death is at a distance, and met only in fantasy, or in passing by, or through vicarious identification with the lives and exploits of others.

SURVIVAL AND SURVIVORS

What does the experience of surviving the disaster bring with it? Who are the survivors? What are their characteristics? What is the impact? What are the consequences?

Initially there is often elation and even ecstasy that one is alive. There are soon more hesitant, sad, and eventually guilty feelings that crowd in. For it seems wrong to feel joy for one's own life in the face of so much death and loss. If one has lost one's loved ones, all of them or all that matter, there is no elation and there may be only the wish for death.

The guilt of survival comes from many sources, among them the relief at not having died oneself; the sense that one's own life may have been purchased at the cost of another's; guilt for those one did not save; guilt over those who were influenced, perhaps to their deaths, by one's decisions; guilt over being, as one always knew, "undeserving" of having been saved. All the primitive and punitive fantasies are evoked, and the rabid pressures of superego and conscience come into play. There comes a need to hide one's survival, to make little of it, to demean one's losses, so that envy and justice will not point the finger and say: "it should have been you that died."

Lifton (1967) defines the survivor as "one who has come into contact with death in some bodily or psychic fashion and has himself remained alive" (p. 479). He pulls together the elements of survivor experience, some of which have already been discussed here. For Lifton these elements include: death guilt, linked to the issue of survival when others have died and the sense that one's survival was bought at the cost of others' lives—especially pronounced in those who survive their children; psychic numbing, an attempt to cut out the death anxiety and death guilt; feelings of suspicion that others are offering false comfort and fear of contagion from one's death experience; and, finally, formulation—efforts to formulate and make meaning of the experience.

One of the issues that must be faced in the aftermath of survival concerns what one did to survive. Often survival involves competitive aggression, a basic human instinct that has been vital to evolution and to the preservation of the species as well as one's own genetic heritage. In any competition for survival aggressive urges must be mobilized that say "I will live for me, for my life to go on, for my line, for my children, I and mine will live ahead of others, even if the others must die for this." Sometimes the aggressive competition for survival exists only in fantasy. But disasters are a sorting time for genetic advantage and this is reflected in the primacy given to care for one's children and the safety of family. In many different disasters there are stories of people surviving and ensuring the survival of their children by protecting them with their own bodies. In the bombing of Hiroshima, in the cities devastated by wars, in the struggle for existence in famine and drought, the survival of one's offspring and oneself will be fought for first.

This basic urge can rarely be denied. Yet after the disaster the individual must live with it. A person must live with the fact that the food he grasped has kept him alive while another died, that his struggle to the lifeboat pushed others aside, that he knocked others down in fighting his way through the smoke-filled exit. This was the most natural instinct to follow, but may not in retrospect fit with the individual's ideals for himself or the views of his society. The instinct that in primitive times would kill, and in fantasy protect oneself and one's offspring, appears in disasters to have been actually responsible for death.

Further aspects of the aggressive competition for survival require consideration. There may indeed have been killing to survive. Such killing is part of war, but even with justice on his side and the most powerful training and indoctrination, the soldier does not readily forget those he has killed, particularly if they are young or in some ways like him. The first death is especially remembered, even though necessary for the soldier's own survival. To kill in this way, the enemy must be dehumanized and seen as evil. The psychological mechanisms necessary for this process may persist long after safety is insured and war is finished. Veterans, such as those from Vietnam, which seemed to many soldiers such an unjustifiable war, may complain, "I just can't feel for people like I used to." The guilt toward those he killed, even though under the circumstance of battle, may stay with the soldier a long time. Similarly, in situations of escape from terrorist or personal assault, killing may be necessary for personal survival and yet guilt may still be felt. Often, there is also great anger against those who assaulted and forced one to respond violently, revealing the violence and aggression inside oneself that one wished to deny.

There are further rare circumstances where another human's death contributes to one's survival. In extremes of isolation and deprivation individuals or groups have practiced cannibalism to survive. Since cannibalism cuts across deeply entrenched taboos of most societies, the individual will battle to avoid it, yet finally "give up" so that human flesh can be eaten. Survivors may feel that they have been forever altered, that the stigma of the act will be with them for life. Yet they are alive because of it.

Another theme is that of the sacrifice that must be made for survival. Magic, ritual, and taboo may come into play when there is threat of death, in attempts to propitiate the gods to insure one's safety. It may seem afterward that the magic was fulfilled. Or it may be that for prayer or propitiatory fantasy the survivor feels a sense of obligation and future payment. Perhaps an atonement is sought in the suffering of guilt, and for those who suffer loss, this tribute paid in emotional pain may seem far too great a cost. Sometimes those with strong burdens of guilt may be powerfully driven to make reparations in their subsequent behavior, either in material or emotional terms.

Fundamental to many aspects of survival are the necessary resources in terms of the *strength,* bodily *endurance,* and physical and mental *skills.* Often as the individual battles to survive, he seems to be able to mobilize strengths and skills he did not know he had. There may be an inner awareness of these reserves or a sense of some spiritual force providing or guiding them. The strengths to carry out necessary activities may be especially vital, even though the person may be injured, sick, or deprived of food and water. So often survivors from many different disaster situations have been amazed by the strength they have been able to mobilize when needed. When the threat has passed, however, they feel an overwhelming sense of exhaustion as if their reserves have been used up—one has "nothing left" with which to go on. Efforts at rescue and assisting others in the immediate post-disaster phase may add to this. So the survivor survives but, initially at least, may be enormously depleted by the ordeal. Conflicts of survival are exemplified in the following experience.

Andrew was nineteen and a shell of his former self when found by a search party ten days after he and his friends had disappeared while sailing in coastal waters. A violent storm had come up on their second night out and he and the other two young men had struggled to manage the small boat against the powerful wind, rain, and huge waves. This struggle had gone on all night, and all were exhausted when Jim, one of the boys, was washed overboard. He called to Andrew to help him, but Andrew could not reach him as he was swept away by the swift currents. Throughout the evening Andrew had thought that perhaps they would all die, that their parents would never see them again. He had thought of all the things he loved in life and wanted to do and of how unfair it would be if he died. And he had prayed that if anyone "had to go" it would not be him—and then, guiltily, had prayed that they all survive. When Jim was swept away he had been panic-stricken but had felt a brief moment of relief that it wasn't him and of hope that now they might be all right. The boat was so disabled by the storm that he and Allen had great difficulty managing it at all and now had no idea of where they were. A further squall came up, tipping the boat over. The two young men clung desperately to it, trying to stay with it. After exhausting hours Allen let go, calling to Andrew to save himself. Soon he vanished from sight, and Andrew clung desperately; he drifted until finally washed toward a nearby coastline. The search planes found him suffering from exposure, hunger, and thirst 12 days after he had left. His recovery was slow and his mind filled with guilt that he had survived at the cost of others' lives. He felt he could never enjoy life again, for to do so would be to "kill" his friends' memories.

As was noted earlier, a number of factors seem to assist with coping during impact and may correlate with survival: the powerfulness of attachment ideation; the drive to survive and the will to live; the support and identification model offered by good leadership; action and thoughts geared to mastery; the shutting out or closing off of terrifying feelings; and the reliance on hope and prayer. Any or all of these processes may influence the survivor in the immediate aftermath and subsequently. His reunion with those important to him may seem a fulfillment of all that he struggled for and endured. He will be frustrated and distressed if this cannot occur. He may feel an ongoing attachment to the group with whom he experienced the disaster, and this attachment may offer special support for the future. He may internalize what he has learned as a powerful lesson that can make him stronger and more aware. Some endurance groups may attempt to mobilize such processes to heighten personal growth and self-knowledge by exposing people to tough physical and environmental situations. The individual may turn to religion because prayer seemed to save him when nothing else could. And, as noted before, the psychic closing off may be relinquished to allow a return of full emotional experience, or it may continue.

"Survivor syndromes" have been described, particularly in those who survived the concentration camps, and also Hiroshima. Often called the Concentration Camp syndrome, it includes both somatic/organic and psychological effects. The syndrome consists of a recognizable pattern of chronic anxiety, depression, social withdrawal, nightmares, sleep disturbance, somatic complaints, and, often, fatigue, emotional lability, loss of initiative, and general personal, sexual, and social maladaptation. Sleep disturbance would often involve nightmares of camp experiences, with the survivor reliving the terrifying situation and waking screaming, sweating, highly aroused, and anxious. Lifton (1967) found in Hiroshima survivors exhibiting this syndrome, "a pervasive tendency of sluggish despair." They seemed to live a half life, as though "walking corpses" or "living dead" (p. 504). Eitinger and Askevold (1968) found this syndrome in 83 percent of the 227 Norwegian concentration camp survivors they systematically examined; uniformly high percentages have been found in other studies of prisoners of different nationalities, including the surviving Jews. Often the

syndrome appeared after a delay, when things had seemed to be going well in the person's life; its relation to the camp experience was always clear.

The development of survivor syndromes, as opposed to survivor reactions, seems to be principally determined by the degree of stress. Overwhelming disasters such as Hiroshima and the Holocaust, or perhaps confrontation with a great deal of death, as at Buffalo Creek, may lead to this syndrome. The element of man's role in such catastrophes is probably also of significance—inducing further rage, guilt, powerlessness, and identification with what man can do to man.

MASTERY AND COPING

The effects of death encounter and survival have been described. The processes by which individual and group attempt to master these effects may encompass many different elements.

Primary attachments and other important relationships generally play a vital role in the process of adapting to such experience. First, the reunion with those one loves helps undo separation and death anxiety. This reunion seems to deny the impact of death and at the same time offer consolation and comfort to the person who has encountered its trauma. Being with one's loved ones brings back the capacity for good feeling, takes away the sense of abandonment and despair, and at least to some degree shuts out the fear of death. If loved ones have not survived, death will offer a great attraction and may not be denied.

By the reassurance primary relationships offer of one's worth and value, the individual is helped to put aside the guilts of survival, at least temporarily. Family, especially children, represent ongoing life, and death becomes more distant. Beyond this first comfort and reassurance there may be, usually a little later, the wish to share the experience with those closest, to tell them what has happened. This may be possible and cathartic, as long as the need to repress is not too great and the partner or family can bear the emotional intensity of the experience. For it may be very threatening for them, if they have not also been in the disaster, to face the losses that might have occurred and the nearness of death.

The repetitive intrusions may also cause distress that is difficult for family relations, as others may find them hard to understand when the threat is so obviously over and the person safe. Nightmares may disrupt sleep, leading to irritability and further stress on marital or parent-child relationships. Nevertheless, most family members are supportive and understanding and make every effort to help one another come to terms with the experience.

One positive legacy of disaster may be a reexamination of primary family bonds, leading to much greater feeling and personal commitment to them. This outcome has been described in a range of different disasters involving close encounters with death.

Relationships with those who shared the death encounter and survival are always considered of particular significance. Those who have "been through the same thing" seem to feel a special understanding and empathy. Whereas others may not understand or even recognize problems that occur in the post-disaster period, these people are often experiencing similar difficulties. There is enormous recognition and mutual support from association with those who do "know just what it was like." Shared feelings, memories, perceptions, and interpretations of the event are all significant in these bonds. On the whole such relationships are adaptive. For instance, it is this type of interpersonal response that is often the basis of self-help associations formed to support the victims of personal disasters or illness and their loved ones. In the post-impact phase it may lead to some of the spontaneously emergent groups that become important in the drive for the recovery and restitution of the community. Sometimes bonds seem so special and so emotionally important that family members who have not been part of the experience may feel excluded by them, and, as a consequence, there may be stresses on family relationships. Usually, however, their significance gradually lessens as time progresses, the disaster recedes further into the past, and the ritual, frequency, and familiarity of the primary family bonds again take precedence.

Rescuers may develop special relationships and bonds with those whom they saved from death. In one train accident, for example, an ambulance man had for hours held the hand of a young victim who was trapped under a concrete slab. He spoke to her, encouraging her to keep up her hope. When she was finally extracted he visited her in hospital many times. They kept the contact up for some time. Because of their experience, there was a special and intense attachment between them. It was emotionally important to both, although somewhat difficult for others to comprehend. Many people in rescue operations have described similar attachments. There is also the victim's special feeling that he "owes" his life to the person or persons who rescued him. These relationships between rescuer and victim may assist in recovery as well as survival. They offer support, and by symbolizing the goodness, giving, and life in man, they deny some of the evil and death that was encountered.

Death and Survival

Leaders and members of the community at large may also symbolize what might be considered a positive effect of the disaster, working together to overcome the damage and trauma. It is also likely that during the spontaneous phases of the early rescue operation and subsequently in the emergent groups of the community, the victims of death encounter will likely find positive human forces for renewal and life. These provide purpose and support and assist the adaptive processes. The special closeness that comes with friendship and lowered social barriers may reinforce the "therapeutic community" healing effect. Later there may be more formally organized group systems to deal with long-term disaster effects. While the disaster may have disrupted the usual pattern of social interactions and relationships, these new networks may all provide opportunities for the integration of the experience.

It would not, of course, be appropriate to suggest that all patterns of relating facilitate the integration of experience of death encounter and survival, for they do not. The anger generated by symptoms, by the experience of powerlessness, and by the unwanted confrontation with death may interfere with the gratification and roles that these relationships involve. Hostility may be expressed toward the family, or displaced onto them. It is likely that attempts will be made, at both personal and community levels, to find a scapegoat—someone to blame for what has happened; this is a vehicle for anger and also allows the victim to relinquish any burden of personal guilt. Thus there are not infrequently arguments and sometimes breakdown of relationships. Some may simply clear the air and let things get back to normal, but others may reveal long-term vulnerabilities, which finally lead to disintegration in the face of these added stresses.

ACTIONS TO GAIN MASTERY

There are many different ways in which those who have survived an encounter with death attempt to gain mastery of their experience in the post-disaster period. Because one of the most traumatic aspects of encounter with death is usually the experience of helplessness and powerlessness, actions to undo these feelings are especially important.

In the immediate post-disaster phase, *rescue activities* are a way in which these feelings may be partly overcome, particularly when the individual's role is very active, involves leadership, or helps save lives. (Sometimes the individual finds it difficult to relinquish such a role, clinging to it long after its usefulness has ceased.) For men especially, some sort of action seems vital, and those roles which allow the discharge of physical activity may also contribute to a return of power over the environment.

Talking through what has happened, putting it concretely into words and thus outside the self, to be examined and viewed by others, is another method by which mastery is sought. In this way the meaning of the experience may be sought and perhaps grasped and others' responses to it may be judged. The descriptions others give may also assist, as they enable the person to see his feelings, role, and behavior as part of an overall pattern. This talking through may also provide the vehicle for emotional release and abreaction, so that some of the distressed feeling attached to the experience lessens. This is not always the case, however, and sometimes, instead of gaining coping and mastery, the person becomes locked into the role of "performer," telling about the experience again and again, with little emotional release, and sometimes with secondary gain from the attention of others, initially at least. Such people may feel that the death encounter of the disaster has made them into "someone important—someone other people take notice of for the first time" as one man said after the floods he survived.

Giving testimony, either written (as in a book or report) or in some other form (television interviews) is another method by which mastery may be sought. The importance of this testimony to some people (for example, Mawson's diaries) during a prolonged struggle for survival has been discussed by Ironside (1979). However, for many people testimony takes place subsequently as well. Again, it is a concrete attempt to control and make meaning of the experience, to attest to the processes, persons, or actions that made survival possible, and, often, to guide others in the future.

Feelings related to the experience are often the most difficult to integrate. Many of the above processes in interpersonal and behavioral terms may carry strong feelings relevant to the experience, and provide opportunities for their release and relinquishment. This is especially so when the process involve the positive feelings of loving care from family or the cathartic release of talking over the experience with others. The intrusions and repressive processes may operate to allow the feelings to be dealt with bit by bit. Sometimes abreactive release will only come later, with time, with triggers that bring back some crucial aspect, or when the experience seems a safe distance behind and there is some trust it will not return to threaten and overwhelm again.

Tears may be especially important in the release process, and more difficult for men or in cultures where they are not readily sanctioned. The first time a person can cry, not just with relief, but in sorrow, for what he went through, for the deaths of others, and for the near death of self, and for the lost innocence about death, may be the turning point in integrating the disaster into his emotional life. Others' grief and distress may be a trigger for this, as may sanctioned occasions such as funerals.

Communal rituals, ceremonies, celebrations, and public statements may also be vehicles for individual and group release of feeling. Thus special ceremonies, memorials, public performance or reviews, or any acknowledgments by the national or international community of what was suffered may facilitate tears, anger, and grief.

Post-disaster integration of feelings depends largely on the degree to which the individual allows himself to feel. When numbing has been prolonged, there may be a lack of trust in life and emotions. People may be afraid to be involved again because they fear further threat, loss, and pain. Thus, there may be a gradual process of testing out the safety of emotional life, both emotional involvement and expression of feelings, until the world again reveals itself as a place to be trusted. Mostly, however, the release of feeling does not come in a flash or a torrent; such a change is not so dramatic and sudden. Rather, it comes in daily small releases—bit by bit, word by word—and in the gradual fading of memory with time.

Perception of the future as a source of hope is an important aspect of recovery. The need to get on with life and the practical demands of living are part of a process that inevitably draws the individual away from the experience of the disaster. Perhaps from previously internalized good experiences and a basic trust in the world the person can believe that there is hope that he will not experience such trauma again, that life will not be threatening and will be worthwhile. Some changes in attitude may also orient him to the future. He may, stemming from the death encounter and survival, now see his family or his life's goals as emotionally important in a way that he did not before; and he may have a heightened awareness of his own nature, resources, and ability to cope with crises.

DISASTERS OF SHOCK, DEATH, AND SURVIVAL

Although relevant to some degree in all disasters, themes of death and survival become especially significant where there has been severe threat of death to many people and where mutilating and horrific deaths and injuries have occurred. Thus wartime disasters involving bombing or acute frontline contact with highly destructive weapons and technology are likely to bring trauma to survivors. In such situations, the intensity, proximity, and duration of exposure are the major influencing factors in the stress producing decompensation, although some reaction is likely for all those exposed. Wartime disasters of this type are epitomized for all time by the consequences of atomic warfare. Its impact in terms of shock and death, destruction and survival, is so horrifying that the only solution can be to avoid it at all cost. A different sort of immersion in death experience, with pronounced survival syndrome consequences, is that found in the chronic overwhelming stress of the death camps.

Disasters of peace can also involve violence, death, and destruction, as evidenced by studies of factory explosions (Weisæth 1984) and night club fires (Lundin 1984b; Lindemann 1944–45; Lindy et al. 1983). Buffalo Creek, the peacetime disaster most intensively studied in terms of these themes (Erikson 1976; Gleser et al. 1981), has shown the range of responses described here. Earthquake disasters might offer some possible responses of this type, but the studies have not been of such fine caliber. In all these cases, the "man-made" nature of the disasters, as well as their sudden and shocking impact, seems to heighten their traumatic effects.

Traumatic death effects and other imprinting are likely in episodes of terrorism, which tend to show similar reactive processes and syndrome consequences (Fattah 1979). Similar findings emerged from Terr's study of the children kidnapped and held hostage at Chowchilla, although the traumatic stressor effects were somewhat different for the earlier developmental stage (Terr 1983).

When cyclones, storms, and other natural hazards are associated with trauma, the cause is more likely to be personal encounter with death than massive confrontation with the deaths of others, for death rates are usually not high in these catastrophes. Severe fires, because of the terrifying threat and also the disfiguring deaths, seem more likely to bring trauma associated with these themes. For example: McFarlane's (1985a,c) study of firefighters show the impact of these fires in traumatic intrusions, nightmares, and repressive avoidant reactions, some of which developed into disorder.

Survival themes are common following disaster, and some level of survivor guilt may help motivate the intense activities to make good the damage and destruction. But the stronger themes of survival are usually imprinted and entrenched only when there has been competition for life or prolonged and terrible confrontation with death. Buffalo Creek, Hiroshima, and concentration camp victims show strong themes of guilt. But survivor guilt also appears in many other disasters, especially when, as in the North Sea oil rig disaster, there is conflict over escape and the inability to save others.

Where death has been almost total, for instance, following an air crash, the encounter with its mutilating trauma is transferred to rescuers and those who must handle the bodies (Taylor and Frazer 1981). They may then become the ones who are tormented by its legacy of nightmares.

PERSONAL DISASTERS

There are a number of *personal disaster situations* in which these themes of death and survival are also highlighted. Something very like the survivor syndrome may be experienced by those with chronic life-threatening disease who depend on external support systems, such as patients with end-stage renal disease needing constant dialysis. Near death experiences and repeated episodes of trauma or illness that threaten life may lead to personal death encounter reactions, as may episodes of violent assault and rape. But perhaps the personal disaster that best exemplifies all the themes discussed is the motor vehicle accident. Here the victim is likely to have had his own life at risk, to have experienced the sense that "this is it." Family or friends may have died beside him or suffered severe, distorting, and mutilating injuries. The suddenness and shock add to the trauma, and the guilt of survival is pronounced, especially if the individual was driving or in any way saw himself as responsible. In most Western countries the death and traumatization from this cause far exceeds in number and extent that from any natural or man-made disaster. A victim speaks for himself. ·

"I wake up at night in a panic—shaking, sweating, screaming, as I did then. The truck's coming towards me—I'm helpless—there is nothing I can do—it's like some dreadful monster. And then there's the crash and nothing and this dreadful silence. Then there's Emily and John and Mary and blood everywhere and their faces smashed—and they're all dead. . . . And they're all dead . . . And all I want is to be dead too. I'm tortured by my dreams and by the memories of what happened. I can't get them out of my mind. I try everything I can, but the shriek of brakes, the grinding noise of a truck, even the smell of petrol—it all comes back again. I go around in this sort of mute state—I can't concentrate—I can't work. All I can think is that I should have died with them—that it's my punishment. I'm still alive."

CONCLUSION

Personal encounter with death and the horrifying deaths of others in community or personal disasters is likely to produce an intense psychological reaction which may settle and be adapted to. There will always be some feelings about survival when one has faced death and lived—especially if others have died. Many people will be psychologically traumatized by their experience, even with efforts to master it and the supportive care of others. Trauma is especially likely when the stress and death confrontation is sudden, shocking, intense, and massive. Nevertheless, many, although stressed by their experience, will feel a renewed commitment to life and relationships. They will gain an awareness and experience personal growth. They may well view their experience as giving them a valued "second chance in the game of life."

CHAPTER 5

Loss and Grief

"I dreamt of my home and my husband and all
I had known and loved, and they were gone
. . . gone forever."

In the beginning, after the disaster strikes, there is a pervasive sense of relief
at survival, and often an ongoing numbness. There may also be an ongoing
battle to maintain basic functions, for shelter and protection, for food and
warmth. As the sense of shock eases, the feelings of fear and anxiety may
return, or may even have continued from the impact phase. There are the
alerting, signal, and self-protective emotions, aiming to protect against
further assault of disaster forces. Anxiety also may be very high if the safety
of loved ones is not assured, and it may generate frantic searching with great
distress.

Although losses are recognized, with the increasing awareness of other
persons and the environment there may be a continuing numbness, or
shutting off of the emotions of loss. The threat experienced may be in itself
too much to take in, and the further assault of loss cannot yet really
be faced. It may be that psychic energies are still totally committed to
issues of survival—the battling of personal injury, or the provision of life
necessities, or the care of the needy.

In the early post-disaster period, when rescue is completed, there is also
a sense of euphoria: nothing seems as bad as the death that might have
occurred, and to be alive in the face of such devastation is in itself a victory.
The combination of care and the survivors' own "therapeutic community"
of good will may mitigate against the early appearance of emotional response to the losses that have occurred. These losses will, however, eventually take their toll in grief and distress, mourning and morbidity.

99

There are many different losses that may occur as a direct consequence of the disaster, and some secondarily. The most severe grief and pain come with the loss of family members—spouse, children, parents, siblings, lovers. The loss of the home with its treasured mementos and symbols of identity can also have a devastating effect, as can loss of neighborhood and community and loss of work, farm, business, or livelihood. There are also more subtle losses that may require mourning: the loss of self-esteem or identity, the loss of future hopes, and the loss of innocence about death, of the sense of personal invulnerability, or of trust in protective powers. Whatever the losses, the bereavements of disaster are rarely uncomplicated.

LOSS OF LOVED ONES

When a beloved family member dies in the disaster many complex issues must be faced. These deaths are often particularly untimely and under terrible and tragic circumstances. It is always felt that they should not have occurred. A number of different scenarios of disaster-related bereavements reflect these themes.

Those who die in a disaster may die in a far and mysterious place. They may be a long, long way from relatives, friends, and home—on foreign or strange soil. These may be the deaths of air disasters—crashes, hijacks, or international terrorism—or the deaths of war. The person is separated from his intimate group at the time. The bereaved are not themselves personally involved in the catastrophe, although they will suffer its effects. There is often a period of waiting, and uncertainty until the death can be confirmed. During this period, the worst is feared, but there is hope, yearning, and prayer that it will not be the case. Those who are bereaved may gradually and increasingly accept the likelihood of the death if this period of waiting is prolonged. Or they may seek desperately to promote further search and rescue, doing everything they can to put off or deny the moment of confrontation with this reality. They seek every avenue and hope until all are exhausted. When the deaths are confirmed there may be considerable difficulty in making this confirmation into a personal reality. The bereaved may be unable to travel to the site of the wreck or death, for any of a number of reasons. Or he may be unable to see the body because of its total destruction or mutilation, failures of identification, or inaccessibility in the country of death. The remains may not be returned to the bereaved or may be unrecognizable.

Thus in these disaster bereavements there is a legacy of uncertainty and doubt. "Was it really my loved one who died so? Surely it cannot have been. Surely he is alive somewhere, some place, and will come home to me when he can." There is no opportunity in these circumstances to spend time with the dead person—to say the good-byes that one wished to say or to take in images of the reality of death. Often the bereaved are spread out in many different places and so have little opportunity for mutual support and identification. This is what Lindy et al. (1981) have called a centrifugal disaster—its effects are spread widely.

There is, as in most disaster bereavements, a preoccupation with issues of suffering. "Did he suffer?" the bereaved will ask. "How did he die? Was his death quick? Was it long? Was he alone? Did anyone help his pain?" There is a great reassurance if it is known that the death was sudden, that the victim did not suffer greatly, or that he was given succor and pain relief in the process of dying. If final rites are critical to a system of belief, knowing that some provision was made may be another source of reassurance.

The deaths may occur in the person's own country or town but in a disaster in which the bereaved was not himself involved. This situation is most common with man-made disasters, whether wreckage or failure of transport systems, hotel or nightclub fires, or work accidents, or explosions. It is less likely in natural disasters, except by accident of timing or on occasions when impact catches people away from family or home. Here there may also be a period of waiting, uncertainty, and fear—often with greater immediacy, for the disaster is vividly portrayed by the media in every horrific detail and sometimes with sensationalist elaboration. The bereaved may desperately seek information as to the names of those affected, fearing the worst or knowing with certainty that the loved person was at that place, at that time. Supportive family and friends are likely to rally. The bereaved is involved in the disaster through identification with those affected and seems to live every moment of it. He may phone hospitals and police or go to the site or to health care facilities, seeking to deny or confirm the worst fears. There is often intense praying, bargaining, begging with God and the fates for it not to be so.

Finally, the death is confirmed, by police or other authorities, and the bereaved can commence the painful processes of grief and mourning. However, here again it may be difficult for the bereaved to see and say good-bye to the person who has died. Well-meaning others may advise against it, legal processes to do with the disaster may put blocks in the way, medical and other disaster personnel may prohibit it, or the body may simply not be in a state that is humanly recognizable.

This latter situation of bereavement caused by a disaster close to home is exemplified by the rail disaster in Australia. The families of those on the train initially knew only that there had been a very serious accident, involving a particular early morning commuter train. Some heard through friends; some did not hear until late in the day. Television and radio crews were rapidly on the site and there was full television coverage of the huge slab crushing the train and the attempts at rescue. Those who were to be the bereaved in this disaster responded in a number of ways. Some called the sources of information. Some sat with friends waiting to hear. All tried to call the place of work or other destination of those who had traveled on the train to see if they had arrived. But they were not always able to get through, because the crash had brought down lines and convergence of communication made it very difficult to contact parts of the inner city. Some sat expectantly, yet with dread, by the telephone, waiting for a call to say the husband or child had safely arrived. Some rushed to the site of the disaster, trying to find out what they could for themselves but also, of course, adding to the convergence. Some went to local hospitals where they believed the injured would be taken. For many, it was a day of terrible fear and desperate hope, for it was very late in the day when names of the injured and dead started to become available. Because of the massive technical problems created by the giant concrete slab, many of the bodies were not freed for identification until well into the second day.

Identification of the dead in such disaster situations usually occurs through formal mechanisms. Temporary morgues are set up or major mortuary resources in local hospitals or city facilities are used. Formal rescue teams and body handlers—disaster victim identification groups, or teams, as they are called—search for sources of identification on the body and also arrange for it to look as acceptable as possible. The next of kin may then be required to make a formal identification. For cultural reasons this role is usually allocated to a male relative. Both women and children are "protected" from the confrontation with violent death. Because of the pressure of time when there are many deaths, even the bereaved who identify their relatives may not be able to spend any farewell time with them at the morgue. Funeral practice subsequently may or may not make this necessary allowance at a later time. There is, however, a tendency to expect that the deaths of a disaster are more terrible, mutilating, and violent than other deaths, as indeed they may be, and thus to expect that seeing the dead will somehow in itself be inherently damaging. There is very little to indicate that this is the case, however, and much to suggest that *not* being able to see the body may in itself contribute to the difficulties the bereaved experiences afterward (Singh and Raphael 1981). Indeed, in those disasters where this aspect has been investigated, none who have seen the body have regretted doing so (Lindy et al. 1983; Lundin 1984; Singh and Raphael 1981).

Further issues may be relevant to this body identification. Some bodies may be so dismembered that there is difficulty piecing them together in human form, let alone in the form of a particular person. As already mentioned, following the DC-10 air crash in Antarctica, the state of the bodies was such that even experienced body handlers found the experience highly distressing (Taylor and Frazer 1981). Bodies burned during the Ash Wednesday fires were often so charred as to be identifiable only with difficulty by forensic means. And in many circumstances of fire the charred ashes and remains may bear no resemblance to the human who was known and loved. When the remains are so poorly distinguishable the bereaved may be left with even more intense fears, especially with fears of the suffering that must have been inherent in such dreadful deaths.

But at the other extreme, when the person was well and whole and healthy when last seen, and has never been seen again, dead or alive, there is the inevitable issue of uncertainty. In some instances this uncertainty is nurtured by the bereaved. Thus, the bereaved may wonder and fantasize: "Was it really him? Was it really her? Have I buried another—a stranger? Can I give up any bonds to this person I loved?" This element was often prominent in wartime deaths where the soldier died on foreign soil and his grave was never seen or known. One widow spoke of how she felt she had sinned in remarrying until the day she saw her husband's grave in Greece —thirty years after his death. In general, failure to see and say good-bye to the dead person may make it hard to give up the commitment.

Another consequence may be extreme and lingering fantasies of the way the person died. For, because it is known that the death was violent and damaging, the fantasy of the suffering and mutilation is likely to even exceed the reality. This was the case with many of the widows of a major rail disaster, who had not seen their husbands' bodies because others had strongly advised against it. "He must have looked dreadful," said one woman. "I heard the bodies were all bloated. I'm tortured by the thought of how he must have suffered." For children, who often nurture quite violent fantasies and have no real knowledge of death, this consequence is also likely.

The processes of defining the death may also require active legal intervention, for instance, a coroner's inquest. There may be an extended period before cause of the death is substantiated and the body released to the family for burial, which delays the opportunity the bereaved has to "finalize" the death. Both the funeral and the coroner's reports are statements of the reality of the death that must be faced, and they are also occasions to which the bereaved returns in memory when dealing with the event psychologically.

Bereaved people require considerable emotional support to deal with the various aspects we have discussed: the identification (or the lack of opportunity for identification), the farewell, and the bureaucratic processes that may irritate and intervene. This need will be dealt with in further detail in the chapter on the care of disaster victims.

Another pattern of disaster bereavement is that in which the person died in a disaster that affected the bereaved as well. This picture of bereavement will be influenced by a number of factors. Family members may or may not have been together during the disaster. If they were not together, the bereaved is likely to have frantically sought or tried to reach the loved one; a first priority after the impact was probably to continue this search with hope and prayer, foreboding and dread. The body may or may not be found personally by the bereaved. But whatever happened to the deceased, it will be a cause of distress for the bereaved, of soul searching and despair, as all the "if-only's" are gone over again and again.

There may be a shorter or longer period of waiting and uncertainty until the reality of the death is confirmed; it is a period of great stress. The state of the body and the availability of morgue facilities may influence if the bereaved can be with the body and say good-bye. Many stories of disasters tell of the bereaved lying with, holding, or rocking the body of the one they loved.

The bereaved may keen, wail in anguish, or be numbed and nonresponsive. Or he may engage in frantic activity, trying desperately to shut out and undo the enormity of what has happened. Even early in the process of response the bereaved may have waves of anger and remorse, with regret or guilt breaking through. The degree to which grief is experienced in the days and weeks following the disaster will be greatly influenced by the extent of emotional shock and threat that was suffered personally during impact and by the subsequent emotional commitment to issues of survival and basic existence. The individual who is still trying to master his own encounter with death and who is battling, in his mind or even in reality, with issues of life and death may not have any opportunity for the "luxury of grief." Thus many of the bereaved are mistakenly believed to be unaffected by their losses or coping with them well. In fact, they are doing what they are able to do now—committing themselves to the maintenance and renewal of life. It is only later that the full impact of the loss may appear and grief may be released.

If the bereaved was saved by the deceased before his death or in any way involved in a competition for survival with him, or if he believes (rightly or wrongly) that his actions contributed to the death, then it may be even more difficult to resolve this loss. This may appear in survival themes such as numbing, in absent or delayed grief, or in extreme guilt. Because of the violence of most disaster deaths, they are likely to be linked consciously or unconsciously in the bereaved's mind to his own destructive fantasies, and particularly to any violent feelings or thoughts he ever had toward the deceased. In his fantasy his ambivalence seems to have contributed to the death, bringing further guilt and despair to punish him for his survival.

When the bereaved is severely injured during the disaster there may be further problems of survival and blocks to grief. If struggling for his own life, the bereaved may not have an opportunity to see the dead person or to attend the funeral. He may be uncertain as to what happened because of shock and the severity of injuries, and he may not be told of the loss immediately because of his own condition. Those offering him support may find it difficult to discuss the loss, so he struggles on in numbness and ignorance and may never come to terms with the reality of his disaster experience and its consequences.

THE PUBLIC NATURE OF DISASTER DEATHS

In contrast to the "everyday" bereavements an individual faces, disaster bereavements are very public. Everyone knows how, when, and why they happened, at least in general terms. This may mobilize a great deal of public sympathy and support for those so bereaved. Offers of care may converge, even when the family has not been otherwise directly affected by the disaster. Thus, after a rail disaster, no less than fourteen voluntary agencies called to offer support to one bereaved family within a three-day period once the "official" system of care first made contact.

Public sympathy and support often bring public expectations as well. The person is expected to be brave and cope, and his loss is judged as greater or less than that of others in the disaster. In general, people will be expected to behave in prescribed ways and often to show their grief explicitly and when expected. Expectations may be very different from the bereaved's usual or adaptive coping styles, leading to further stress. There is also a certain "identity" of bereavement imposed by this type of disaster death. The person is labeled as one of "the parents of Aberfan" or one of "the families of Buffalo Creek." Another problem of expectation is that of time: there is often a clear message to the bereaved that they should be "over it by now."

REACTIONS TO THE LOSS OF LOVED ONES

The reactive processes of grief are often, as was noted previously, blocked or inhibited in the early stages because the bereaved's emotions are exhausted, shut in, or taken up with the anxiety of death encounter and survival. The *numbness* or *denial* of the immediate response may be prolonged. Yet for many bereaved these issues will be sorted out after the first few weeks and the reaction to the death or deaths will appear.

As I have described elsewhere (Raphael 1983), once the numbness fades the early responses are those of *intense distress at being separated* from the loved person. There is *yearning* and *longing* for him to return, to not be dead, and everywhere the bereaved looks and hopes for reunion. This is most pronounced when the bereaved person goes back to a familiar environment of home or place that was shared with this loved person. When the environment is strange and different—not home, but hospital, caravan, the house of others, or a temporary shelter—the yearning and longing may be accompanied by a sense that perhaps the dead person really is somewhere —somewhere else safe or still in the ruins of the disaster. With the yearning and pain come intense waves of physical distress. This physical distress includes difficulty with breathing, palpitations, weakness, and epigastric discomfort. There appears to be a pain inside, as though something were torn out of one. These sensations are vividly described by Lindemann (1944–45) in his classic paper, "Symptomatology and Management of Acute Grief," where he described the bereavement reactions of survivors of the Coconut Grove nightclub fire. It is interesting that the basis for this influential and classic paper should have been the grief of a disaster population.

Lindemann's work and that of Parkes (1972), Bowlby (1980), and Raphael (1983) all highlight the *anger at the loss*—often termed the "protest"—that is associated with this phase of yearning. The bereaved is angry because he feels deserted by the dead person, even though he knows full well the desertion was not intentional. Present in any bereavement, this anger is especially strong when the death is sudden and untimely and seems so pointless and futile. Why, when it seems so arbitrary in the disaster context, did God or "the hand of fate" choose one's own loved one and not another? Why do the young die, when they have so much promise and life ahead of them? Why was a person cheated of a future together with the loved one? These questions torment the grieving person. The anger felt may be displaced onto others—those who did not warn in time, the authorities, an unspecified "they," the rescuers, the others who survived, or the self. This reaction is likely to be particularly severe and intense when the disaster is man-made, especially if there is any hint or proof that it was the consequence of negligence or insufficient care. Thus the railway or airline, the building or mining contractors, or the government or private agencies connected with the structure or site are likely to be objects of rage for the bereaved—a futile and frustrating rage, because there is rarely any individual to whom it can be expressed.

Anxiety may also be felt in association with this yearning and protest about the loss. The bereaved person may feel panic and helplessness at the thought of life without the person he loved—especially without the comfort of his presence in all that will be required to recover from what has happened.

The bereaved person is very preoccupied with *images* of the dead person, looks for him in familiar places, yearns for his presence, and longs for him to return. If he has been able to see him after death, there will also be images of him dead. When he has not seen him it may seem that he will return. The images bring a longing for the reality of the person's presence, and when he does not come, the pain of his absence may be intense.

The images, like those of the traumatic encounter with death, *intrude into consciousness,* although they may bring a different sort of pain. For the most part, the image is in place of reality, and it is when the dead person does not come to fill in the image that the pain is felt. The images of the death scene itself may intrude in instances where the bereaved has experienced a personal and traumatic encounter with death and helplessness, constituting a post-traumatic stress reaction. The bereaved may try to *avoid* reminders of the person or may attempt to *repress* the feelings of longing, anxiety, and anger, which are so painful. He may also try to repress the traumatic reaction of intrusive memories of the scene of the death, or of his own experience. Thus, reactions to the loss, and to how the person died, may be inextricably interwoven in the post-disaster phase.

Gradually, in the weeks that follow, the bereaved becomes more able to accept the finality of his loved one's death and *mourns* for him. In this psychological process of mourning he is preoccupied with memories of the lost person and their relationship. There is a gradual process of review, an undoing of the psychological bonds, one by one. Memories may be vivid and spontaneous, coming in flashes before the bereaved's eyes like a motion picture. Or, they may be triggered by some place or object, or even by some sound, sight, or smell. Things that have belonged to the dead person may take on a special symbolic link with him, becoming what Volkan (1972) has called linking objects. For instance, a widow wore and treasured her dead husband's watch—all that survived his death in a fire. Another woman who had been involved in a disaster kept for a period of time, unknown to others, part of the body of her beloved friend—the hand—linking her to the person she could not bear to relinquish. With the memories come a continuing range of feelings, including despair, great sadness at what is now irretrievably gone, and anger at the futility of the death.

Guilt is also frequent at this stage, and the more so if the bereaved was in any way involved. The sources of guilt lie not only in survival issues, as discussed earlier, but also in things of special significance in the particular relationship and in the circumstances of the death. Thus, the bereaved may be tortured by thoughts of how much he wished the person dead on some previous occasion or by the lack of love between them or by the bonds of hatred. Sudden and unexpected deaths may leave unresolved some of the ambivalence of everyday life. Thus, a woman whose husband was killed in a commuter train crash was tormented by guilt because that morning she had quarreled with her husband and he had left the house angry and hurt to catch an earlier train—the one that took him to his death. In the normal circumstances of their marriage this disagreement would have been lovingly resolved in the evening; but there was no opportunity for this, and she was left with the "frozen frame" of bitterness.

When the bereaved has shared the disaster experience, *survivor guilt* may be very pronounced. If the dead person died saving the bereaved this guilt may be painfully intense, with the sense that one life was really purchased at the cost of another. Lindy et al. (1983) have described how survivor guilt led to much conflict for those who escaped the Beverly Hills nightclub fire, particularly thoughts that they should not have placed their own survival first, as they did instinctively, and that they should have been able to return to the inferno to save friends and loved ones. Irrational as such thoughts tend to be, they are very frequent in those bereaved in a disaster. The feeling that "if only . . ." is likely to remain.

Just as there are many images and many memories for the bereaved of a disaster, there are likely to be many *dreams*. The bereaved may initially dream of the dead person as vividly alive and find with each awakening a painful renewal of loss and grief. There is a sense of happiness and reunion with such dreams, and all the loving feelings and reassurance return. Sometimes dreams involve the disaster—either fantasies or reality of the dead person's suffering and panic, and especially attempts to escape to safety and be with the bereaved. In certain dreams, scenes of the death are intertwined with the bereaved's experience of it, so that the traumatic reactions and the loss reactions appear together. Sometimes the bereaved will be tortured in dreams by images of the suffering and death. They may be so real that he dreads sleep. It is as though his guilt forces him to experience these fantasies, a guilt that arises from the disaster itself or from previous feelings the bereaved had toward the deceased.

But not all bereavement dreams are like this; others may be full of past happiness and longing memories. As time passes and the loss is gradually adjusted to, the person may appear in the dreams as more distant or sometimes ill or asleep, or his or her face may be seen less clearly.

General stress reactions may appear as part of the bereavement reaction, in complaints of tension, anxiety, and depression (Singh and Raphael 1981). The stressor effects may have a negative effect on immune systems, as observed by Bartrop et al. (1977), and this could explain some of the decline in general health observed following disaster, if other physical factors such as disease and injury are accounted for adequately.

Somatization is also not infrequent with this stressor. In addition to the somatic distress that is part of normal grief (breathing difficulties, palpitations, exhaustion), there may be identificatory symptoms, linked to the way the person died. For instance, some of the bereaved after a transportation disaster suffered from chest pain and "crushing feelings" in the chest, linked unconsciously to their perceptions and internalization of their loved ones' deaths. Thus, somatization may shade into syndromes of morbidity.

These bereavement reactions may often be delayed by a prolonged period of numbness and by the bereaved's involvement in maintaining existence. Where the disaster has been one of natural forces that could not have been changed or prevented, there may be a greater sense of resignation and capacity for resolution. But when there is the hand of man and the possibility of blame, with implications that the disaster *may* have been avoidable, anger is likely to be profound and prolonged. And where losses are multiple, or extreme, then grief may be shut out by ongoing psychic numbing or because it is simply too great to be borne. Perhaps later, and very gradually, in some renewed situation of trust and security, the person's reactions to the loss will appear and the bonds to the dead will be gradually undone.

BEREAVEMENT SYNDROMES

Many of those bereaved in the disaster will react and grieve in the early months or after a period of delay. During the entire first year and at the anniversary of the death, there are likely to be exacerbations of sadness, mourning, and perhaps guilt and anger, as new aspects of the loss are faced for the first time. All the longer-term adjustments to life without the dead person—to a different identity and to different patterns of relationship—are gradually made. Much of this response to loss has been described in greater detail elsewhere (Raphael 1983).

Many aspects of disaster losses make for high-risk bereavements and greatly increase the likelihood that bereavement syndromes will occur as a consequence, rather than reaction and healing. The sudden, unexpected, and often untimely nature of the deaths, plus their violent and mutilating circumstances and the frequent lack of opportunity to see the body and say good-bye, are all contributing factors. The complexities of coroner's inquest, funeral, and legal systems may add to the difficulties. The multiple losses and psychological stresses and crises that occur concurrently are further complicating variables. And the breakdown of social networks that may occur after some catastrophes where there is destruction of community may add further problems, as the supportive and healing care traditionally provided by such networks may be absent. Professional workers may not be available or able to offer the care that is needed to facilitate grief. Medical complications of injuries and the battle for existence may not only delay, but shut out grief, so that time passes and it never appears.

Those who provide support after the disaster may collude with the bereaved to concentrate on material provisions and to deny the emotional realities of loss. This is a very important point as a great deal of energy after the disaster goes into providing for the necessary material deprivations. This may make the bereaved feel that he should not complain about his grief, and both he and those who help him find this easier. Suffering that is shut away and unresolved, however, is likely to lead to problems in the future.

Certain bereavements, that is, the loss of certain relationships, are also more difficult to resolve. For instance, the death of a child is very distressing and terrible for parents. They are always left with the feeling that they should somehow have been able to protect the child and with guilt that they survived in his place. Studies of two major disasters (Singh and Raphael 1981; Lundin 1983) have shown the parents of adult children or late adolescents who die in a disaster to be a group particularly at risk. This is also often the case after the personal disasters of motor vehicle accidents. The death of a spouse may also make for serious problems of resolution, particularly of a wife whom the bereaved felt he should have been able to save and protect. And those who have been intensely and ambivalently loved may not be easily grieved. Sometimes relatively minor losses may cause great grief, because of all they symbolize or because somehow all other losses are condensed into them. Seemingly disproportionate mourning over the death of a favorite pet is a good example. And large losses, the loss of family and intimate friends, or of powerful and important community figures, will always bring extra grief and perhaps the complications of bereavement.

Some of the bereavement syndromes are those of complicated grief, some are psychiatric disorders. *Inhibited grief,* a common syndrome, usually combines psychological numbing, overcontrol, and containment of all feelings related to the death and the disaster. The bereaved does not cry and seems to show little sadness. Reminders seem to have little effect. Often the bereaved is seen as "coping well," because he is "getting on with life" in a very active way. The activity may become exaggerated or compulsive but remains generally appropriate and goal oriented. In this syndrome, the person's nonresponsiveness may be general, involving many or all facets of life, or it may involve only some aspects directly connected to the loss. Inhibited grief is, for the most part, maladaptive and likely to be associated, either immediately or in the future, with impairment and morbidity.

Distorted grief, which involves intense anger, is another common pattern after disasters. Intense anger was first commented on by Lindemann (1944), who noted both the diffusion of hostility through most of the bereaved's relationships and the displacement of anger onto people in any way connected with the death, especially medical personnel and those perceived as responsible for what happened. Lindy et al. (1983) saw anger as an ongoing and often increasing symptom in subjects who suffered impairment after the night club fire as a result of bereavement or death experience. Anger often motivates the search for scapegoats to blame and the litigation that may follow. In the syndrome of distorted grief, it is far more intense and seems the one predominant emotion, defending against sadness, guilt, depression, or despair. The bereaved seems to righteously cling to his anger at all costs, for this in some way locks him into the separation phase and protects him against the finality of the loss. It is as though there is a secret and unconscious belief that anger can punish the "killers" and bring back the dead.

Extreme guilty preoccupation is another pattern of distorted grief that may appear following disaster. There is little sadness and no real mourning for the dead person, but repeated self-recrimination. In thoughts, and often in dreams, the bereaved person tortures himself over his failure to love and protect the person who died, especially if a child or someone otherwise dependent on him. Scenes of the death or the dead person may seem to torment him. This guilty preoccupation may be told to others as the bereaved tries to get them to agree with his self-judgment. No matter how much he suffers he does not seem to atone, and his guilt goes on. It may result in self-destructive behavior, accidents, heavy drinking and the like, or the breakdown of family relationships, as may the unremitting irritability and hostility noted above. The guilt may also merge into a delusional system of depressive illness.

Chronic grief is perhaps the commonest morbid bereavement syndrome seen following disaster. Here there is a picture of intense grief that goes on for months and years after the death—unchanged. The bereaved cries at every reminder, frequently visits the grave, may hold conversations with the dead person, and presents all the hallmarks of unremitting grief. This leaves the bereaved locked into this relationship and eventually impairs all other relationships, as well as the capacity to function in the everyday spheres of life and work.

Depressive illness may evolve from the post-disaster bereavements when the depressive feelings and reactions of the early response deepen and are prolonged. When life does not seem worth continuing, when there are many active fantasies of reunion with the dead person, where depression takes the place of sadness, despair becomes fixed, sleep and appetite impossible, and grief frozen or displaced onto agitated activity, then a depressive illness may have supervened the reactive processes. Depressive illness seems more likely to arise when losses are too great to be borne, or when the person is vulnerable genetically, when the relationship was somehow ambivalent, or when the person had experienced previous losses.

Post-traumatic stress disorders may be superimposed on complicated bereavement syndromes. They may be linked to the circumstance of the death and represent attempts to master it, or they may be linked to the bereaved person's own disaster experience. In either case, shock, helplessness, and death affects are likely to be the stimuli to the development of such reactions and/or disorder.

DISASTERS INVOLVING PERSONAL LOSS

The theme of personal loss will be present in any major disaster where there has been death, but it is especially prominent in those disasters where there are larger numbers of deaths. Airplane, vehicle, and train disasters, ship-wrecks, and explosions and fires may bring such disaster bereavements, but so may flood and famine, terrorism and war. They have been vividly described and studied in the Coconut Grove fire (Lindemann 1944), the Granville rail disaster (Raphael 1979–80; Singh and Raphael 1981), the Boras nightclub fire in Sweden (Lundin 1984b, c), and the Kentucky nightclub fire (Lindy and Greene 1981, 1983). Refugee groups may also experience many bereavements, especially those from war-torn countries, such as Kampuchea and Vietnam recently. For instance, Van der Westhuizen (1980) found that in just one group of these refugees, not one family had survived intact, and that each person had lost as many as thirty members of his or her extended or near family; indeed, some had lost all living relatives. The grief of people in countries torn apart by violent civil and other combat, such as Lebanon, has not been documented in systematic studies but no doubt reflects many of the themes outlined above.

In the personal disaster sphere, deaths in motor vehicle accidents and the violent deaths of murder and assault may also result in complicated and traumatic bereavement processes. But although themes are similar to those in the massive disasters of community, these personal catastrophes attract less public acknowledgment and, often, little empathic and caring response.

LOSS OF HOME

The loss of a home and the personal possessions it contains is likely to bring a special type of trauma to disaster victims. In the first place, this loss may be little acknowledged emotionally, as the person bereaved of a home may be expected to be grateful that he is alive and that his family is intact (if it is) and grateful for the gifts, donations, and compensation that may be showered upon him (in an affluent Western society, at least).

The most devastating loss of a home is when it burns to the ground or is totally destroyed with little opportunity for its inhabitants to rescue any vital, symbolic, or otherwise treasured possessions. Lost in this way may be the whole of the person's past identity in papers, documents, photos, clothes, and books and the whole range of personal items that he used or kept and that in so many ways represent what he is.

Victims always seem to say initially that these "material possessions mean *nothing—nothing* compared to being alive," and, ultimately, this is of course true. But the loss of a home does have a significant impact: even its damage, let alone its destruction, may affect recovery from a disaster (Price 1978; Bolin 1981; Clayer 1984; McFarlane 1984).

The total loss of a home may mean the destruction of important social symbols. Documents attesting to identity and status—for example, passport, birth, and marriage certificates—may be destroyed. This loss may be particularly threatening for those newly arrived in a country and unable to substantiate their rights and status easily in other ways. Photographs of a lifetime of family celebration and sorrow may be forever lost. Thus, people who have lost wedding, baby, and childhood photos may be particularly distressed.

But more than the loss of any one item is the overall effect of the loss of all these possessions, for no matter what compensation is provided, they can never be replaced. The home itself is a private sanctuary and safe environment. Nothing of it may remain after an earthquake, or cyclone; and all that may be left standing after a fire is the chimney, pottery baked hard, and charred rubble. Sorting through these ashes may give little solace in the form of any known or loved objects, as is the experience of many after forest and city fires, when many homes were totally destroyed.

Such is the direct loss effect of the death of a home, but its induced consequences are also very substantial. For instance, there may be the need for new accommodation and the costs of this. Temporary accommodation is almost inevitably with family and friends at first and then in something like a caravan or trailer. There is crowding, shortage of the basic facilities a person was used to having at hand, and inconvenience and unfamiliarity. There may be less than adequate provision for heating and cooling. The post-disaster utopia rapidly fades in such circumstances. Furthermore, the many disasters that lead to the destruction of home lead also to the loss of community, the neighborhood and environment beyond the bounds of home. There may be the stress of dislocation to a strange neighborhood and a new community. It may be a long period before there is a secure, functional, and satisfying home environment again.

The loss of home is potent even where home may seem the poorest type of shelter, a tenement, shanty, or hut. For the home always represents sanctuary, identity, the closeness of family, and the private territory of man in his environment. The home may also be the place of work and business, a farm or cottage industry, for example. In some places the home is the source of food, drinking water, and shelter. Thus, loss of home may also mean the loss of the capacity for an independent economic existence.

The home may be "adequately" or "inadequately" covered by insurance to protect the owner against the financial blow of its loss. Public or government support may provide for or supplement some of the replacement. Yet, even when the home is built again in the same way and in the same place, the inhabitant rapidly realizes that, like all losses, it cannot be replaced. Things are, indeed, "never the same again."

But in many countries, especially those of the Third World, there is little government or other provision to enable rebuilding after disasters, even of shanties and adobe huts. The victims must make their own homes, using whatever very limited resources and support may be available. Traumatized and shocked from their own experiences, perhaps also exposed and hungry, and maybe grieving the death of family members, they must try to seek shelter with extended family until they can in some way reconstitute their place of sanctuary.

It is important to realize that the home symbolizes many important things with respect to the continuity of life and identity, not just for the individual, but for family. Thus when the home is lost this security is lost too.

Reaction to loss of home.   Grief for the lost home has been discussed by workers such as Fried (1982) who have studied relocation of urban communities in nondisaster circumstances. Other workers (for example, McFarlane 1984) have studied the effects of loss of a home, but not the grief process. Loss of a home in disaster is more complex and devastating, however, as not only building structure but also many of the things that constitute a home are lost. Nevertheless, if grief is experienced directly there may be, as in other bereavements, numbness followed by yearning and protest, and then sadness and mourning for what can be no more. Those bereaved of their homes are likely to sort through the ashes and ruins just as the bereaved person sorts through the clothes and possessions of the person who has died—slowly, painfully, remembering and mourning. Even small things found may have important emotional links with the world that is lost. Bereaved people need these opportunities for sorting through. It was sad to note that some people were denied this after the Ash Wednesday fires, for the wreckage of their homes was quickly razed to the ground to enable rebuilding, often while the victims were still in a state of shock and numbness.

There is often a great sense of anger, of "why me" connected with the loss of a home. Not surprisingly, this sense may be quite pronounced if other homes nearby are relatively undamaged. Feelings of envy and guilt may lead to distressing interactions between those who have lost and those who have not. Guilt may also be a problem if people have not taken adequate protective measures as advised or warned, and others may resent them getting compensation under such circumstances. There may be a sense of anger toward the environment or toward those seen as somehow responsible for the destruction. This anger may appear directly or may be displaced onto authorities, insurance companies, and so forth.

When many homes are destroyed together there may be a sense of great loss of place and community as well, leading to further grief and desperate attempts to repair and make whole again. Many people were very eager to plant new trees after the forest fires, to bring back the familiar green of their environment, instead of the stark black.

Frequently, however, grief for the lost home is repressed and denied after a disaster because of the feeling that one should not grieve or complain in the face of one's own survival and others' sufferings. "Others need it more —they are worse off than me—I'm O.K." is a common response from the householders and farmers after many disasters, reflecting both their natural independence and an attempt to ward off sadness that cannot be faced. Others inadvertently encourage such a response, and when compensation is generous, giving and gratitude smother the opportunities for grief.

Fires, bombings, cyclones, tornadoes and hurricanes, avalanches, and severe flooding are all major causes of home loss. The cyclone that hit the city of Darwin, the Buffalo Creek flood, and the devastating Ash Wednesday fires destroyed most of the homes in their respective areas. Studies of all of these have shown that loss of a home has significant emotional impact and affects recovery. Bolin's (1981) work with family recovery after a tornado has shown the importance, too, of financial recovery and the security of home in overall recovery.

Personal disasters caused by fire destruction have been well described by Krim (1976) who studied urban fire disaster families; his findings reveal a number of parallels to the Ash Wednesday disaster (McFarlane 1984; Clayer 1985; Tonge 1984). Characteristic reaction patterns included disorientation and confusion, shock of impact, guilt reactions for real or imagined neglect, anxiety triggered by fire events, separation anxieties, and fears of abandonment. Many victims showed withdrawal, while others showed exaggerated hyperactivity. Some were unable to communicate or were aggressive and hostile to others. Family disorganization was frequent, with isolation and withdrawal of parents from children and regressive behaviors in the children themselves. Grief and mourning were often postponed, sometimes indefinitely. Where there had been the death of a family member or severe burns or injury in the fire, reactions tended to be particularly severe. Fire may have particular symbolic significance as well, in both its "traumatic encounter with death" aspect and its "destruction and loss" aspects. For many describe their fire experience as like "Hell on earth" and see the consequences as God's purification and punishment by flames. Perhaps such associations make the losses even harder to resolve.

LOSS OF COMMUNITY

Erikson (1976) has vividly described what he calls "loss of communality" in his study of the survivors of the Buffalo Creek disaster. He sees this as a collective trauma that is a blow to the fabric of the community, that is, as a loss in "sense of community." Such a loss is likely when the disaster strikes at the very heart and function of the community, as when the black flood of debris and mud destroyed the small mining communities as it tore down the narrow Buffalo Creek Valley. People's villages were destroyed, not only their homes. The trailers and mobile homes that served as temporary accommodations were located in vacant land. There was no renewal of neighborhood or village in the placement of families. People were personally traumatized by their encounter with death, with many showing psychic numbing and survivor syndromes and grieving for lost loved ones as well as home. They could not readily make new networks and had lost their old ones. Thus they had lost their community and communality. A sense of this loss emerged repeatedly in comments by victims:

> "Well, I have lost all my friends. The people I was raised up with and lived with, they're scattered. I don't know where they're at. . . . But down here, there ain't but a few people I know, and you don't feel secure around people you don't know" (Erikson 1979, p. 144).
> "We did lose a community, and I mean it was a good community. Everybody was close, everybody knowed everybody. But now everybody is alone" (p. 148).
> "It has changed from the community of paradise to Death Valley" (p. 147).

No doubt, as in all bereavement reactions, there tends to be a degree of idealization of what existed before the disaster. Yet the description is consistent. The sense of neighborhood and friendliness is gone, sorrow is pervasive. There is a sense of purposelessness and disorientation. Morale is low and there is a loss of community and personal identity. Dreams are filled with sorrow and loss and death, reflecting the death of the spirits of community itself.

The loss of community and communality are likely in disasters that destroy houses, neighborhoods, and the sense of place. This happened clearly with Buffalo Creek. Obviously it is not universal, for other communities suffer similar terror but rejuvenate, and some, like Aberfan and the scene of the Ash Wednesday fires, seem to come through with a stronger and renewed communality. Some communities come closer together to fight the consequences of the disaster and thus even seem stronger as a consequence. A recent example of loss of community through man-made disaster occurred in May 1985 in Philadelphia. More than sixty homes were destroyed by bombing in an attempt by city officials and police to evacuate a disruptive radical group (MOVE) from its home. A fire arose, and part

of a viable neighborhood was burned to the ground with consequent dislocation and loss; it is too early to determine permanent effects on the community. In such kinds of disaster, major dislocation seems to lead to loss of
community spirit. But pre-disaster factors make some contribution to outcome, and the extent of death and disruption of neighborhood networks
may be the critical factors.

GENERAL LOSSES OF WORK, MONEY, AND MATERIAL POSSESSIONS

The disaster may destroy the opportunity for work in a particular place or
at a particular job. For example, the burning down of timber forests in the
Australian fires did away with jobs for sawmill workers in affected areas
(although there was increased demand for construction workers). A factory
may be destroyed or become feared, dangerous, or unworkable, as did the
Union Carbide factory in Bhopal. And the poor circumstances of a community after a disaster may have a general impact on retail business in a town.
Thus, people in disasters may suffer the double trauma of disaster impact
and unemployment. Little is known of their reactions and grief, but there
is usually heightened anger in their response.

A disaster such as flooding may destroy a range of material possessions
or sources of money. Severe and prolonged drought may destroy rural
communities and even affect national income. Such losses should be recognized, but their impact is not well understood. Like the other losses noted
previously they are likely to be denied in terms of their emotional effects,
both because of independent outlook and the fear of grief. Nevertheless,
anger about them, general sadness, irritability, and hopelessness are common feelings.

Looting commonly is rumored to occur in the immediate post-disaster
phase, when people are said to be briefly freed from moral restrictions,
disinhibited, and inclined to take what they want. Often there is a sense that
looting occurs to make up for what has been lost in material terms. It may
be more frequent when cultural or social sanctions accept some notion of
equal rights to property that could be used to justify looting at a time of
trauma. On the whole, sociological research (Quarantelli and Dynes 1973)
suggests looting is rare and more in rumor and in the media than in fact.
It may be the gesture of anger by those who feel chronically angry and

deprived in any community. It may result from envy. It may result from need and poverty.

Compensation may be a source of support, but also a source of envy, resentment, and anger in communities in the post-disaster phase. Initially many people, still feeling numbness or relief, will insist they want no compensation. Then, later, they will see it as their right. Often there is competition, as well as scapegoating, envy, and anger toward those seen as "taking advantage of the system" or unfairly overcompensated. Rumors of false claims are rampant, although such claims are in reality not frequent. These rumors may lead to much community anger, and some individuals and groups (such as ethnic minorities) may be scapegoated. The problem with compensation for personal loss lies in the determination of how much a human life is worth. There is often great bitterness because the death of a child may not be compensable while that of a wage-earning adult is. The bereaved may feel a decision like this says that his dead child, for whom he suffers so greatly, is worth nothing, and that he cannot bear. Nevertheless, despite these factors, most people make reasonable claims and do not in fact see the money as an important goal or as any real compensation for the life that has been lost.

Litigation occurs post-disaster in some instances when compensation perceived as rightful has been denied. It may be sought bitterly under such circumstances, more for what it means in terms of recognition of suffering than for the money itself, though naturally the latter is not unimportant. The substantial litigation and settlement for psychic trauma after Buffalo Creek makes the statement that there is a cost for suffering. No doubt any compensation for Agent Orange or for the dead and injured of Bhopal will symbolize the same—the cost of human loss and suffering.

PSYCHOLOGICAL LOSSES

After some disasters the psychological losses seem the greatest—the loss of belief in oneself, in the safety of the world, and in the trust of others. Sometimes a material loss also has tremendous psychological significance. Examples include the loss of a lifetime of research work in a fire and the similar destruction of a series of paintings of native flowers finally nearing completion in a man's seventy-fifth year. The grief of such losses is subtle and often only revealed in psychotherapy or other in-depth explorations.

POST-DISASTER DISILLUSIONMENT

Often, as the losses are realized and some of their emotional significance faced, there is a growing mood of disillusionment among disaster victims. This is contributed to by many things, but especially the realization and resentment of the losses and of the deprivation they bring. There is likely to be a strong sense of promise unfulfilled. In the euphoria and altruistic convergence of response immediately after impact, the community and government seems to promise all—that losses will and can be replaced, that everything will be as it was before. But only weeks later, as the realization of loss dawns more fully, bureaucrats and politicians may be arguing as to who will pay for what, and it is quite clear that restitution will take a long time, if it ever fully occurs. People strongly feel the letdown, especially in the cold reality of shelter living, with the loss of personal mementoes, the threat to livelihood, and perhaps also personal grief. There can be little wonder that this becomes the phase of disillusionment. It may be resolved or it may turn into chronic distress and dysfunction—the second disaster for the community.

COPING WITH LOSS AND GRIEF

Many different components come into play when individual and community attempt to deal with and resolve the bereavements that have been suffered.

ATTACHMENTS AND RELATIONSHIPS

The support of others is particularly important for the bereaved person. Studies of personal disaster have shown that the support both of those who are close and of the wider social network may assist with the resolution of loss and mitigate against traumatic effects that could lead to morbidity (Raphael 1983). Bereaved people initially need comfort, consolation, and care to assist them with their emotional pain (Raphael 1983). The interactions with others may also be very helpful in allowing the bereaved to share memories and feelings about the lost person and the death, or memories of home and place. This review process has been shown to be a factor in resolution (Maddison and Walker 1967; Raphael 1977a), assisting the bereaved to gradually relinquish what has been lost. Some people will prove more supportive, being genuinely empathic to needs. Others, while meaning to be helpful, may block grief by advising the bereaved not to cry or think or talk of the dead person, or by trying to control anger or sadness. The primary bonds of family will be especially significant to the bereaved person; it may be these attachments that draw the bereaved person through his grief. A mother is thus pulled through her grief by her commitment to her children. Many have said, "I had to keep going, I thought I'd never survive, never make it—but the children needed me and I loved them and so I did keep going." The leadership or guidance of others who have survived the same crisis in the past may also provide coping through relationships, as may sharing the experience and feelings with others bereaved in the same disaster. This is exemplified in descriptions of the mutual support the Aberfan community members provided for one another as well as the emergent groups, community organizations, and self-help associations that have developed for support of those suffering losses in disasters as diverse as mine accidents, earthquakes, tornadoes, fires, floods, and transportation accidents. Sometimes relationships with rescuers, helpers, or consulting professionals may be new attachments that assist the bereaved's coping by both practical and emotional support.

MASTERING THE EXPERIENCE

Helplessness is often a powerful feeling experienced after loss, along with intense deprivation, disruption, and despair. In an attempt to master these feelings and the disaster, those bereaved by losses may seek out action and activity. Committees and organizations for post-disaster reconstitutions, may, as well as any other rebuilding activities, provide constructive channels for this activity. Attempts to master and undo loss may also come through caring roles for others.

Talking through what has happened with the death and loss, plus appropriate emotional release, will be helpful to mastery and integration of the experience (Lindemann 1944; Raphael 1977a; Singh and Raphael 1981; Lindy et al. 1983), as will the formal rituals, funerals, and ceremonies. Public inquiries and the personal seeking of information may assist further by giving meaning and hence some sense of cognitive mastery.

The sorting through of possessions, as well as the sorting through of memories and feelings about what has been lost, is another theme of mastery. As the bereaved learns to live, survive, manage, and have needs met without the dead person, or without home or community, he gains competence and confidence and his sense of mastery becomes more secure. Mastery may be difficult to achieve when all seems lost—loved ones, home and community, and perhaps work and other things as well. It may be felt that there is nothing and no one to go on for and that the trauma is too great to be mastered. This may indeed be the case, and the goals of coping and support are then simply to keep the bereaved alive, surviving, and with enough adaptive function. Some with massive loss seem to go through a period where they merely survive; often, it is only much later that the quality of existence becomes a consideration. Caring for others in need and those deprived may help in such instances, for it seems this brings some mastery as well as some vicarious identification with being cared for.

MANAGING FEELINGS

Workers dealing with the bereaved and traumatized following the Kentucky supper club fire found that helping people to release their emotions in small doses was an important component of psychotherapy with the survivors. This process is important for the bereaved as a stressed group, as it is for those individuals struggling with the intrusive anxieties of death encounter who attempt to control feelings with avoidance, shutting off, and social withdrawal. Both groups need to feel and express grief or distress but without being overwhelmed by emotional pain. In bereavement, there is a need to express feelings—sadness, anger, yearning, or whatever—in a supportive and encouraging environment. There is great release in crying. Feelings may become intense as new aspects of the loss are gradually reviewed and faced. Cathartic release may occur as the bereaved seeks mastery through talking over what has happened and in his review of the lost relationship, particularly when facilitated by supportive interpersonal relationships. Thus, a father said of his daughter's death:

"There are times when I can talk of her and cry and remember how it was. These times are awful but they are real. It's like reliving some of those things we did and part of life again and it hurts like hell because I know it's all gone—I feel so angry and so sad because it's all so hopeless. I feel terrible guilt too—I should have died, not her—I've had my life and it wouldn't have mattered. But God didn't let it happen that way. Then I get to the stage where I can't take anymore—and I've got to keep it all shut out for a while. Whether I like it or not I've got to get on with living and you can't go on if you're feeling like that all the time. So I shut my feelings away until the next time. But it's a help when my wife and I can talk it over together . . . remember when she was little. I'd like to do that more but sometimes it's just too upsetting for us both."

Loss and Grief

HOPE AND THE FUTURE

Again, as with other aspects of trauma and crisis, there is a sense of having to continue with life. The person may have felt that he could not survive such losses, but he has, and the needs of existence and the person's ongoing commitment to life draw him on into the future. Even when the will to live may seem lost, involvement with life is not easily relinquished. And most people have some hope of things getting better—of recovery, of trust in life and love—that again draws them on into the future. The disaster and its losses are left behind, perhaps to be remembered without undue pain, and life is once more lived and enjoyed.

CHAPTER 6

Dislocation and Relocation

> "I felt as though I'd never find a place I could stay in, that we'd be stuck in crowded places like this forever. I thought I'd never find anywhere to call home again."

After survival is assured and rescue completed, losses and damage are faced. The disaster-stricken population begins the long process of recovery. Primary among the problems of this time will be the provision of adequate shelter until home and community are reconstituted. This is the time when administration and bureaucracy may take control, when the population may need to assert itself in order to take an active role in its own rehabilitation, and when the convergence of help, and political pressures, may produce many complications. There is the ongoing stress of adjusting to the disaster experience and losses, but many people may face further frustrations over the months that follow as they struggle to recover.

The disaster may have come as an acute stressor bringing death and loss, but those affected still have their familiar homes and neighborhoods to return to, as well as the support of networks of family and friends. Certain disasters, however, bring dislocation, either brief or prolonged. Individuals may be dislocated from family, from neighborhood, from home, from community—in short, from some or all of the familiar systems of existence that maintain our social framework. Disasters may also bring relocation through evacuation or resettlement into new and strange communities. The stressor effects of such experiences have been described by disaster victims and are increasingly revealed in systematic disaster studies (e.g., Parker 1977; Western and Milne 1979; Bolin 1982; McFarlane 1984) as well as recent reviews (Garrison 1985).

Dislocation and Relocation

What is experienced with dislocation is often a complex mix of many different deprivations, disruptions, and delays, as well as ongoing confrontation with the disaster consequences. Multiple life changes during the prolonged post-disaster period may add to the problems of victims. Often, these chronic, ongoing stresses, even when of lesser magnitude than those of impact, seem unremitting and more difficult to bear. Nevertheless, resilience leads to eventual adaptation for most people and communities, often with a more positive outlook on life. But this may take time. And some never recover.

There are a number of ways in which this stressor experience may arise. Evacuation in response to the disaster threat or its consequences is one. Dislocation of family members from one another may occur through injury, hospitalization, or the splitting of families in rescue and recovery. Destruction of housing, services, neighborhood, and community is another, leading perhaps to evacuation to shelter with family or friends or into temporary shelters. There may be a prolonged relocation to temporary housing and different sites or even to a permanent new home. Or there may be strange dislocations or ruptures of community, as with the Hobart bridge disaster when the breaking of the bridge following the collision of a ship with a bridge pylon led to the splitting of a city and the rise of social stresses for its inhabitants (Whelan et al. 1976). The worst dislocation stress, however, is surely the dislocation caused by war and devastation of homeland. These events bring special and painful stress to refugee populations, who may also have to relocate in strange cultures and societies.

EVACUATION

The bonds to home and place are powerful ones. Many disaster workers have commented on the difficulty in persuading people to leave their homes when disaster threatens, even when leaving is obviously the wisest thing to do. The home seems a place of protection, safety, and sanctuary. It is only when authoritative, specific, and frequent warnings urge evacuation, and when families are able to support each other's decisions, that evacuation in the face of a threat is likely. And even then families may leave with reluctance. Returning after impact, they may find their homes and neighborhood unharmed. There may be some damage, such as mud and debris or broken windows, but essentially, all is intact. In such cases, the dislocation is likely to have been brief and its effects minor. On the other hand, victims may return to rubble and ruins, a destroyed home and neighborhood, a lost environment.

Those who return to find homes substantially damaged or destroyed, or those who had stayed to have their homes destroyed around them, may then face issues of evacuation to another site or place, because local resources and services cannot provide for them, or perhaps because there is ongoing threat. Evacuation implies a move from one's own place—perhaps to somewhere reasonably close, but sometimes to a far distance.

It has been traditional in Western society to evacuate women and children from a place of threat or devastation to "protect" them from the effects of the damage. Evacuation may be purely motivated by this custom. It may also take place because there are primary or secondary disaster threats. The primary threats are those of ongoing disaster damage to shelter and habitat; the secondary are those of the disaster consequences. Thus, when cyclone or tornado assaults a community, it may destroy not only individual habitations but also the sewage, waste, water, and other systems necessary to maintain community life. For these reasons, smaller or larger numbers of people may be shifted by the evacuation process.

Evacuation is often initially to campsites or other temporary shelter; tents are particularly useful portable shelter when numbers of people are large and resources few. This is a form of public shelter, reasonable for the emergency and the early days following disaster, but difficult in terms of physical facilities for any period of time.

However, most people fleeing either on their own or in response to planned evacuation go to the homes and shelters of family members. It has been estimated that more than 75 percent and perhaps as many as 90 percent of people will find shelter with family or close friends (Bolin 1982). Kinship networks will respond readily to the disaster crisis with assistance of this kind.

How long does such an arrangement work out satisfactorily for both host families and victims? In many cases the adjustment can be made for a considerable period of time, but, as Bolin (1982) found in his study of family recovery after tornadoes, after about a month the situation tends to become strained. The crowding, sharing of facilities, inconvenience, lack of privacy, and concerns and worries of the victims are all likely to make for difficulties when the stay is prolonged or, particularly, for an indefinite period. Relationships between the two previously independent family units may become strained, although this is somewhat less likely if younger families move in with parents.

The evacuation of the city of Darwin in northern Australia after the 1974 Christmas cyclone reveals some of the many complexities and associated stresses that may arise in the evacuation process. Twenty-five thousand people were evacuated from that city by air, while many others fled south by car in spontaneous evacuation. Women and children were sent first in the massive airlift; husbands, especially if fit, stayed behind to deal with the disaster's aftermath. There were many reasons for the evacuation, but according to Stretton, the man who ordered and organized it, predominant was the threat of disease and the inability to maintain any services in this devastated city under the tropical heat of summer. The airlift was completed in only five days and was, in practical terms, an enormous accomplishment.

People were highly motivated to leave the city in most cases. The devastation was great. Many people felt a desperation to "get away" from all that had happened, from the reminders of it, and from the risk of its recurrence. The nearest cities to which people could go for shelter were capitals in other states, over 2,500 kilometers or more away. People could take few possessions, and some knew nothing of the cities they were to arrive in—sometimes in the middle of the night. In these cities they were met by Red Cross and other organizations. Some were taken to hospitals, which had in some cases been emptied for them; others went to homes of friends or relatives. Sometimes family members wound up in different cities. For instance, one woman was hospitalized in Sydney, but her children were sent to Brisbane and her husband to Adelaide, both almost a thousand kilometers away.

Sorting out and knowing where victims are and where they are placed or taken in evacuation is one of the most important practical issues. Information about and identification of victims and their whereabouts is critical to the rehabilitative phase of the post-disaster period. Furthermore, it is essential so that families and others may know the fate of intimate relatives. Thus registration is an important part of the evacuation process.

Darwin was a "frontier town," a city to which people often went to be far removed from the very southern cities to which they were then evacuated. Many had "escaped" family circumstances in their move to Darwin and were now thrust back to stay with the very families from which they had needed to free themselves. As one woman said, "My mother and I never got on, and she was no different: telling me what to do as though I were still a child; nagging at the children; making out it was my fault because I'd gone to Darwin. It didn't help that we were all nervy too. The children missed their father and at the slightest sign of wind or rain we'd all be upset and crying. It was one of those things that just couldn't work out."

Those in hostels were not much better off: crowding, isolation, and closeness to strangers all proved difficult. An extreme example is that of a couple whose child had died in the cyclone and who sat frozen in their grief, without any social contact in the hostel situation.

One of the great difficulties came with the separation of families, and there can be little doubt this added to the trauma of the experience. Wives and children were sent south. Husbands stayed behind to work hard in the rebuilding of the city. Rumors had it that other women were in Darwin when the wives and families were not and that the men were "having a good time with women and grog" while their wives struggled on in alien environments. Many marriages did not stand the strain of such separation. Perhaps there were preexisting vulnerabilities, but the stress of what was usually a minimum of six months separation under such circumstances certainly could not have helped.

Some relocated families formed new communities in the cities to which they had been evacuated. These seemed to help lessen the sense of alienation and to assist individuals in working through the traumatic experience and their grief for what had been lost.

Evacuees returned to Darwin in many instances, but some did not. Those who returned often came back to trailer living, mobile homes, or other temporary accommodations, because of delays in rebuilding to insure that structures met a satisfactory code of cyclone safety.

Throughout this period the evacuees faced problems of bureaucracy, the deprivation of basic comforts of home and its resources, the separation from neighborhood, community, and place, and the loss of social networks. Often, they also faced ongoing family problems and psychological trauma. It would hardly be surprising if they found this period stressful.

Several studies identified quite specifically the stressor effects for this population. Parker (1977) in a questionnaire survey of a small group of evacuees noted an early rise (one week after the disaster) in scores on the General Health Questionnaire, which measures psychological distress. He attributed the scores to mortality stressors, that is, to the stresses of having experienced a threat to life. This rise settled, but a later rise at ten weeks seemed related to the evacuation; Parker saw this as being a response to the "relocation" stressor. At this stage many of those who were evacuated had experienced unsatisfactory living arrangements, disrupted families, and unemployment. By fourteen months, scores had settled to a "normal" baseline population level. An interview study by Western and Milne (1979) showed that stress levels were lowest in those who stayed in Darwin, raised in the returned, and highest for nonreturned evacuees. This relationship was retained when impact stressor effects were maintained constant; that is, for the same severity of impact, stress effects were least in the stayers and most in the nonreturned evacuees. Both these studies highlight the stressor effects on mental health of evacuation under such circumstances and call into question its appropriateness. In this context it is interesting to note that although the original groups of evacuees leaving Darwin did so with powerful motivation, in the latter phase people wished to stay and had to be induced to leave with the offer of free return air fares. Perhaps they instinctively knew, as disaster victims often do, that they would have managed best in their own environment.

PLACES OF SHELTER

During the emergency phase, the homes of relatives or even makeshift shelters may prove very satisfactory. But what happens from then on can be in itself stressful and frustrating, taking away the relief of survival and the good feelings of the immediate post-disaster period.

Cultural factors often strongly influence the way in which people can take shelter with other families. People in societies that emphasize individualism and privacy are likely to find any prolonged contact with family members at close quarters somewhat difficult. This may explain Bolin's finding that within a month people perceived this type of shelter as less satisfactory. Other societies, however, have responded quite differently. In Nicaragua, for example, obligations of family are extensive and far-reaching, and privacy is of lesser importance. After the Managua earthquake, people were taken in easily and naturally by their families and lived for extensive periods in this family system (Kates et al. 1973).

The very poor, particularly in extensively devastated developing countries, may be dependent on public shelter. If anomie and demoralization are pronounced, such shelter may be readily accepted and retained, with all the apathy typical of the recovery period in such circumstances. But, in general, people feel a great need for independence. They wish to reestablish their autonomy quickly and return to their homes; they do not want to be dependent on public assistance.

Rebuilding of homes takes time, however, and there is a need for ongoing shelters during that process. Such shelters may be placed far distant. Or they may be on the site of the home, so that the progression of the structure can be supervised. Typically, trailers, campers, or other mobile homes are used. Compared to the original home, these almost invariably have far less space, fewer resources, and no luxuries. Crowding for the family increases friction and is likely to lead to irritability and emotional stress, especially as other difficulties are likely to be present at the same time.

Workers who studied the dislocation of families after several forest fires noted the frequent problems that arose with trailer accommodation. People complained of being crowded in on one another. There was little opportunity for parents to have a private time together to sort out difficulties or offer comfort. Wives suffered from the confinement of such small dwellings for their everyday life. Children had nowhere for privacy or for the release of their energies, so tensions would readily build. Toilet facilities were cramped. The shelter did not protect well in the very cold winter that followed the fires. People were grateful to be on the site of their homes and recognized that the shelter was basically adequate. Yet they could not deny the problems associated with such living conditions, particularly the effects on marriage and family life as well as on psychological adjustment. As one woman explained:

> At first the kids thought it was great fun, like going on a holiday. But it wasn't long before we were all screaming at one another. Jack was depressed because he was out of work after the fires—they burnt down the factory he worked at. I couldn't get out much. We couldn't have the T.V. on while the kids were doing their homework. We never had a chance to really talk things over. Sure, the fire itself was hell, but this was something else—it went on and on. I certainly wouldn't want to live through this again whatever happened, and what's more, if we don't get into our own place soon, I'm pretty certain the family won't make it either.

This trailer living was explored in further depth by Bolin (1982) in his study of tornado aftereffects in Wichita Falls. Approximately 40 percent of those he studied found lack of space and privacy to be a problem, and more than 60 percent had problems with the utilities. There were also major difficulties with the bureaucracies that administered the mobile home shelter program. All these factors contributed significantly to individual and family difficulties.

One special factor observed in this study was the insecurity people felt in such accommodations. The first wind or rain, or any unsteadiness, tended to bring back fears and anxious memories of the disaster and a rebound effect of distress. For many of the victims of the tornadoes it was more than a year before they could move into a place they considered home. Most families had to make at least two moves before being able to go back to a permanent residence, and some three or more. Some of those who were better off could afford to rent somewhere until homes were rebuilt, so that they were protected from repeated dislocations, but on the whole, after such disasters these numbers are small. Overall there was, as with the Darwin cyclone, a great deal of uncertainty in the post-disaster relocations. It is hardly surprising that for the American victims, as for the Australian, there were major emotional and psychological costs. Moving three or more times during the first year following disaster was strongly correlated with reduced leisure time, continued personal upsets over the disaster, and strained family relationships.

A similar pattern of moves and dislocation has been described by Bjorklund (1981) with respect to an avalanche near Göthenburg, Sweden. Victims found stressful the many moves they had to make, sometimes over a three-year period, before they again had permanent accommodations.

The extent to which people return and rebuild on the site of destroyed homes after dislocation and relocation is not known. It seems likely that the majority do return, for attachment to place and home is very powerful, even if it is a place of risk. Communities seem to continue and there is rarely a mass exodus, although sometimes total townships are transported to new sites. This phenomenon is well exemplified by the town of Yungay, Peru. Destroyed by an earthquake, this town rapidly developed again on the site of the temporary camp where victims had fled to avoid the avalanche set off by the quake. It was accepted by the citizens as the new city Yungay North, and despite official attempts to rebuild in another place, the new center grew naturally where the residents had been placed. The social changes that may follow in such circumstances are of considerable interest (Oliver-Smith 1977).

SOURCES OF STRESS IN DISLOCATION

The period of relocation may be extensive, as was noted above, and the place where it occurs, or the new neighborhood, may have many problems. This is shown clearly in the reports of Buffalo Creek (Erikson 1979). Here the residents of the destroyed town were placed in mobile homes if they did not have other accommodations—about half the population of 2,500 people. The mobile homes were situated on vacant lots in the general vicinity of Buffalo Creek. As Erikson says (p. 19), "Most of the survivors found themselves living among relative strangers, a good distance from their original homes . . . they felt alien and alone." In effect, the camps seemed to "stabilize one of the worst forms of disorganization resulting from the disaster" by holding people as if frozen in time in a moment of extreme dislocation. Erikson goes on to vividly describe some of the negative consequences of this in the loss of communality and the ongoing despair and disaster syndrome effects among survivors.

The sources of stress in dislocation are many and include the following:

1. Loss of human dignity and dependence on others
2. Strange, unfamiliar, and often less than satisfactory home shelter
3. Strange neighborhood and place
4. Loss of neighborhood and social networks
5. Disruption of services
6. Uncertainty about permanency of home and place
7. Bureaucratic and administrative problems of the recovery phase
8. Ongoing psychological stresses from the disaster traumas of death encounter, survival, and grief
9. Multiple life changes associated with dislocation and disaster, involving work, leisure, school and life activities
10. Ongoing or new family tensions arising from all of the above.

LOSS OF HUMAN DIGNITY

From the moment he stands in the ruins of his home, dirty, frightened, clothes torn, bleeding, and injured, alone or with others similarly affected, a person feels further assaulted. Whatever his culture or society, there are roles, possessions, and rituals of behavior that contribute to an individual's perception of himself as a human being, to his identity as a man or to her identity as a woman. The more complex the society, the more an individual may depend on these roles, possessions, or rituals for his image of himself. The disaster assaults this self-concept when it takes away or damages these components. In this sense it equalizes people—for naked and without the appurtenances of civilization, all men and women are reduced to a basic condition. Thus disasters are said to be "great equalizers." However, in the stratification of most social systems men and women do not readily accept or feel good about this reduction to basic humanity.

Of course, following rescue, most people rapidly clean and clothe themselves or are provided with these necessities by others. But the lack of one's own clothes and the dependence on others for such basic items reinforces feelings of humility and need. The loss of reading glasses or false teeth may seem trivial but add to the victim's sense of degradation and shame. To have to accept from others the basic requisites of life that as an independent adult one is used to providing for oneself is difficult. It can bring back regressive and childhood feelings, and often considerable frustration and anger. These latter feelings may have to be masked, for the victim is expected to be grateful for all that others have given him. But he may bitterly resent both their generosity and his need for it. Thus a victim of a disaster commented: "Other people's old clothes and other people's cast-offs—even the saucepans. I felt angry and humiliated even though I had to take them, but I have to cover it all up and smile and be grateful. I know they meant well but it really made me feel terrible. They were good to give and we needed—but we did not want to have to depend on other people's things."

Having to *ask* for things one has always been able to provide for oneself is also difficult. This may be further aggravated by waiting in long lines, filling out forms, and by the behaviors of those providing aid. The attitudes of benefactors may add to the sense of helplessness and degradation of victims, even when the opposite is intended.

While this theme is often most intense immediately after the impact and in the early phases of recovery, it may continue throughout the period of dislocation, when one needs to ask for or share basic goods, household items, money, and so forth. It is particularly stressful for those whose sense of pride and self-esteem has been built on a view of themselves as very independent, self-reliant people.

Not only may the need for clothes, material goods, and possessions create this sense of being a lesser person, of losing one's human dignity, but so does the lack of opportunity to carry on the habitual behaviors of daily life and interpersonal relationships. For the daily rituals of meals, interacting with others, work, and social release may be lost throughout the disaster period and, subsequently, with dislocation. People do not feel "the same" when they cannot carry out these functions as they usually did. Thus, the lack of these rituals and roles may disrupt the sense of self and identity and make the person feel in some ways less of a person.

STRANGE ENVIRONMENTS

The change of home environment and place can have many effects. People forget, until confronted with it, how dependent they are on the physical environment of home and its proper functioning. Furthermore, for most people in developed countries the loss of a home in disaster brings dislocation into a lesser environment. Smaller quarters, malfunctioning water or toilet systems, and so forth all add to the frustration and irritability. Problems with the repair and maintenance of the post-disaster shelter add further to stress. It is difficult for victims to make these transitional dwellings into home, especially if the photos, pictures, and curtains were destroyed in the disaster. The trappings of familiarity are lost, and adjustment to the new home surroundings, which are in so many ways an extension of the self, takes time. People are attached to place and home in many subtle ways and may experience ongoing arousal and disquiet in their absence.

Many of those living in temporary accommodations become quite preoccupied with basic utilities. Showers, toilet facilities, cooking facilities, and heating and sleeping conditions are the most frequent causes of complaint, and the more so because of their symbolic meaning. As one woman explained, "It was the toilets and the showers. They were the disaster for me. The toilets would always block, and they would smell, and you could never get them right and no one would take responsibility for it . . . you couldn't get them fixed. I thought we'd all get some dreadful disease . . . and you couldn't wash and get clean either. The water wouldn't come on . . . or if it did it was never hot. I think I'll dream of showers and toilets till the day I die."

Crowding and noise are other sources of difficulty. It may be that walls are thin or the partitions narrow and one cannot help but hear the quarrels and sounds of daily life, both of family members and of others. This adds in a subtle way to the general experience of being stressed.

A further sense of uneasiness may come from the damage to the physical environment: the debris of other dwellings; the blackened or collapsed buildings; the lack of any greenery after fires and the deathly silent rows of black trees. The absence of the subtle background of sounds that one was used to—the familiar bird life or the murmur of traffic—may also contribute to disquiet at the loss of an environment previously taken for granted.

People moved to new and significantly different environments will also feel this strangeness and unease. It takes them a while to familiarize themselves and make this new place feel acceptable and safe. Uncertainty regarding duration of stay and unwillingness to become attached to what one will soon lose add to the feeling of being dislocated and disengaged from the environment.

DIFFERENT NEIGHBORHOODS

Familiarity of place extends to neighborhood: the place next door, the friends across the street, the corner store, the church on the hill. When the disaster has destroyed the neighborhood there is a particular sense loss. Victims may be dislocated from neighborhood as well as home if their temporary dwellings or rebuilding activities takes them to new centers of habitation. Moreover, the basic reliance on neighbors for support may vary with the nature of the society. It is likely to be important in closely integrated communities, or in those like Buffalo Creek before the disaster, where a whole milieu of intercommunity responsibilities, assistance, and mutual concern constituted a strong sense of "communality" (Erikson 1976). The lack of this communality, the inconvenience caused by displacement from it, the strangeness of new neighbors, the difficulty of forming new relationships while under stress, may all complicate the victim's adjustment to a new situation. Sometimes a person will be relocated to a better neighborhood than the one he has known if he was poor, but it is the familiar neighborhood, even its shanties and poverty, that he misses. And the victim's alienation may become more profound, as vividly exemplified by the survivors of Buffalo Creek.

DISRUPTION OF SOCIAL NETWORKS

The social networks, which are held to be important in adversity, are frequently disrupted in the post-disaster period. Distances may be great, communication systems less readily available, and regular patterns of social behavior disrupted. Often, families are too involved in rebuilding and recovery or too demoralized by the disaster experience to be able to put time and energy into social interchange.

Some of the important issues relevant to social networks in times of disaster have been reviewed by Solomon (1984). She notes that disruption of social networks may come through the deaths of members or through the effects of responses to disaster. Such impairment, she contends, is likely to affect psychosocial recovery and increase victim vulnerability to mental and physical health problems.

Social support is likely to be particularly important during times of adversity, and a great deal of research has shown its role in mitigating the effects of stressful life events (Cobb 1976; Raphael 1981; Henderson et al. 1981), as well as some disaster effects (Singh and Raphael 1981). Disruption of the social support available through the family may come when a member is injured in the disaster and hospitalized, or has to move to a new area to obtain work, or some members of a family live with relatives for a period while others do not. Such dislocation may make distances too great for easy contact.

The disaster victim tries first to solve his own problems and then turns to family or significant others for assistance. The type of assistance he needs may be emotional support, tangible practical aid, or the support provided by information and communication. Social network support seems effective in many instances because it is nonprofessional and does not place the victim in a passive role, but is rather an opportunity to exchange services and use aid in a network of services between people. Kin are the first to freely respond to the victim's need but may be less effective when the disaster is widespread, for they themselves may also be affected.

The linkages and availability of nonkin support in the network is also important—friends, co-workers, neighbors, acquaintances and local professionals. It has been suggested that the stronger and greater in number these bonds, the better the victim's recovery, especially when kin are not available. Those who help may offer general support or may be specialists in that their experience, for instance, with prior disasters, gives them special empathy and knowledge. Different people may be best for different types of support or best at different phases of the post-disaster adjustment. The importance of social network support is evident from the following statement of a victim who lacked it:

> One of the hardest things was not being able to talk things over with friends and relatives. Staying in a strange place, being without the car, and being tired all the time because there was so much to do, you just couldn't get to see people. My sister was too far away, my friend had her own troubles and there was nobody near at hand for all those things you normally do for one another: talking it over together, babysitting, sharing the news, sharing resources. We were a family without its contacts . . . and you don't realize how much you depend on them . . . and I guess they depend on you too . . . until they're gone.

As this quote also shows, in some instances opportunities to get together for support are few. However, Bolin's (1982) study showed that visitation rates between victims and their kin and friends did not necessarily decrease significantly. Drabek and Key (1976) also found that support was most frequently provided by relatives and friends. Emotional support is mostly provided by spouse or partner, or otherwise by family and friends, but tangible and informational support may come from other sources.

SERVICES IN THE AFTERMATH

The disruption of or strain on important community services that have been damaged or overloaded by the disaster may create difficulties. Repair, legal, building, power, and maintenance bodies may have long delays before providing services. Goods may be scarce, including food supplies, particularly special foods of religious or dietary significance. Waiting, shortages, and deprivation of what is usually available and taken for granted may induce further feelings of irritability and frustration.

Emergent groups often address such issues by developing appropriate systems or by developing self-help organizations or cooperatives to deal with the deficiencies.

In societies which are already deprived of food, clean water, or other basics such as power for heating, the catastrophe that disrupts provisions

or destroys resources may be the final straw precipitating famine, starvation, disease, and death. As a number of writers have pointed out (for
example, Kates et al. 1973), disasters in underdeveloped countries may bring
only further disintegration for individual and society. Aid may be delayed,
services inefficient, and any opportunity for recovery lost until it is already
too late.

Of particular importance in terms of services are communication systems, providing linkages both within the affected society and to the outside
world. Often, these systems have been impaired by the impact, choked by
the convergence, or left in disrepair. If not remedied, such breakdowns can
add a great deal of further stress and bring on the catastrophe of the "second
disaster." During the early stages, communication systems are needed to be
able to let people and the world know what is happening and what is
required. They are also critical to assessing and monitoring need, until
self-directed activity can take over, or recovery is well established. Moreover, the long-term issues of establishing communication systems between
individuals and organizations may be the biggest problem in the post-
disaster phase. For instance, communication with government bodies to
obtain aid or necessary resources and communication about ongoing or
secondary disaster threats may be very important.

The availability of information services post-disaster depends on the
recognition of their importance and the administrative and other systems
to develop and implement them. If deficient they add further to victims'
uncertainty and stress. Information centers may be developed spontaneously by some of the groups that emerge after the disaster. There may be
a resource or advisory unit where information is accumulated and where
people can go with their questions. Formal post-disaster organizations may
also develop methods for pooling and providing necessary information to
those affected. Newsletters, the use of media, and person-to-person communication may all be utilized to disperse information necessary for the
recovery of the community.

An example of communication and information is given by developments
after one disaster. There was considerable distress because people did not
know which authority could provide for different types of resources and
what steps should be taken to deal with community problems. A single relief
worker for each subarea was provided with all relevant information, which
was updated in regular newsletters and meetings. This worker then had
contact with all the affected people in the area and held local meetings, or
gave information to newspapers, radio, and T.V. through regular sessions,
to pass it on. Similarly, victims developed a feedback system, enhancing
communication in the opposite direction.

UNCERTAINTY

Over the period of dislocation and relocation, there is a great deal of uncertainty for most victims: What will happen? How long will it take? Who should we see to facilitate things? When will it all be back to normal again? Should I have done or be doing things differently? Where should I go? All these and many other questions preoccupy families throughout the recovery period. Being uncertain often seems psychologically equivalent to being insecure and unsafe and is reminiscent of many of the emotions of the disaster experience. As one woman said after her experience in a catastrophic storm, "You just never knew what to expect, where you could stay, when you could go back, what forms to fill in, who would tell you what—or, most of all, when something terrible was going to happen again. It was as though you lived with dread, just because you couldn't be sure of anything anymore."

Information systems are helpful in dealing with this uncertainty and often arise to cope with it.

BUREAUCRACY AND ADMINISTRATION

Ordinary administrative systems are simply not geared to disaster response, unless, as noted by Mileti et al. (1975), their departments usually function with considerable overlap. This is generally not the case. It is true that through the acute post-disaster period, with all the community arousal and altruistic convergence, traditional bureaucratic functions may be temporarily flexible to the needs of the emergency. Then money may be made available, resources requisitioned, orders from other departments heeded, and authority relinquished. At this time, cooperation may be easy and need is not questioned. This situation does not last for long, however. The disaster is off the front pages within weeks, and organizations start to reflect public attitudes: "Isn't it time they were looking after themselves?" "They ought to be over it by now." "Why should *they* get help (money, compensation)?" Soon there are delays of response, traditional roles, territories, and authorities are resumed, and conflict may predominate. Conflict may center on issues of who will pay for the costs of the response to disaster, who will do the work when all departments claim to be overloaded and understaffed, and who will gain the political mileage.

The more rigid and fixed the roles of an institution before the disaster and the less they reflect disaster response objectives, the greater the problems are likely to be. This conflict and rigidity are likely to lead to slow, impaired, or at best reluctant function on the part of bureaucratic and administrative institutions, even though all mean to do their best for the victims. Delays cause irritation, frustration, and sometimes despair for the victims, who get locked into the tangles that result. Clear recovery and rehabilitation systems of administration and function need to be evolved to overcome these problems.

A further issue is the degree to which victims feel able to retain control over their own destinies. Administrations made up of outsiders may seem to interfere, to make decisions that do not reflect victims' goals or needs or what is best for the community. This also leads to distrust and anger. Unless victim representatives are actively involved in the administration of the recovery phase, perhaps directing it, helplessness and apathy are likely to be reinforced and the community and its members may not really recover.

ONGOING STRESS EFFECTS FROM IMPACT

In addition to all the above, many victims are likely to be struggling with ongoing anxiety, psychosomatic effects, general distress, or specific post-traumatic reactions or grief. There may be feelings of exhaustion, difficulty with sleep, fear of going near the disaster site, social withdrawal, inability to concentrate, and preoccupation with the experience.

It is easy to see how these ongoing effects from impact may exacerbate stress from other sources. They may further reduce the sense of human dignity and worth, the capacity to interact with family and social network, the ability to function in work and leisure, and the tolerance for frustration at failures of services and at bureaucratic inefficiencies. Thus a vicious cycle may build. Breaking this cycle may require considerable supportive intervention at a number of levels (see chapter 8), perhaps including specialized counseling or psychiatric care.

> Mrs. B. suffered ongoing nightmares about the floods and was constantly depressed at the sight of her water-stained and damaged home. The children, boys seven and nine, were both "acting up," being aggressive and disobedient, and having considerable difficulty at school. Her husband went off to work each day and returned late in the evening, having "drowned his troubles in drink." Mrs. B. was taking several different tranquilizers and felt constantly angry and depressed as she spent day after day trying to "make it a home again." The ongoing stresses, plus the strain experienced by the family system, were leading to marital breakdown.

LIFE CHANGES AS DISASTER EFFECTS

Many further life changes may occur in the period after the disaster, some perhaps triggered by it. Children may need to change schools or adults their work because of relocation. Increased arguments, legal problems, injury, and illness may all be consequences. Not only are such changes likely to be stressful, but they have secondary effects in impairing physical and mental health. Janney et al. (1977) have shown the greater frequency of life changes and health problems in an affected population following the Peruvian earthquake in 1970, when compared to a control population. These workers also noted a change in perceptions of severity or ranking of life events. Events dealing with shelter and religious experience ranked higher but those dealing with death and illness lower, perhaps reflecting a need to rely on the former and to lessen the severity of the latter. A study of refugees over a two-year period (Masuda and Tazuma 1982) has also noted an increase in life events, with events related to work, finances, spouse, and life style featuring prominently, as would be expected in terms of relocation stressors.

FAMILY TENSIONS

Tension may arise from any of the factors discussed, but a number of specific patterns have appeared where families have been studied in depth (McFarlane 1984; McFarlane et al. 1985; Valent 1984; Bolin 1982). The husband and sometimes the wife may be heavily involved in rebuilding the home or family resources or may have to travel longer periods to get to work. Thus they are away from home longer, emotionally and physically exhausted, and less available to spouse and children. Crowding increases friction, and there are likely to be more arguments among children, children and parents, and spouses. Arguments are also more difficult to resolve, because there is less room for physical activity or escape to privacy. Ongoing distress may deplete emotional responsiveness, either through anxiety or through irritability, which frequently rises during the long aftermath. Psychic numbing may make family members less emotionally involved with and responsive to one another's needs. Fear of being overwhelmed by memories and distress of the disaster may mean family members cannot talk to one another about it; silence and withdrawal may be the result. Resources may be strained, so that little is available for pleasure or the enjoyment of life. There may be little privacy for marital intimacy, and misunderstandings may arise as a consequence, or, as is common, previous difficulties may become exacerbated. Outlets for tension such as drinking may be overused and may bring secondary difficulties. Worries over children are a frequent source of stress for parents. Often, children's behaviors are initially quite restrained and good but problems may start to appear after a lag period and create further stresses for parents. The external support systems of grandparents, neighbors, and friends may be less available. New schools and new work may mean tension of adjustment in crowded quarters. Others may intrude into the family's world—supportive in some instances but disruptive in others, and intrusions may be especially disruptive when there is little separation from the dwellings of strange families, who are perhaps quite different in culture and social background. Disappointments and disillusionments surface as the hope of making things as they were before the disaster is gradually relinquished and the ongoing consequences of loss are faced. Despite these stresses many families do, in fact, respond to the challenge and grow closer and stronger. Certainly some do not, and at particular risk are those where marriage or family structure was marginal before the disaster, which has become the final insurmountable stress.

Alice M. was twenty-five and her husband Tom twenty-four when fire destroyed their home in a small rural community. Their children, a girl of eight and boy of six, had both been having difficulties before this time. Alice had married at seventeen, when pregnant with her daughter, having become involved with Tom to get away from her alcoholic father and depressed mother. Financially and personally they had struggled through the years of their marriage, with Tom leaving on several occasions. He was now unemployed. Janine, their daughter, had been missing school frequently because of stomach problems, and Ken, the boy, had a record of difficult and aggressive behavior in class, stealing, and bed wetting. Both these children's problems worsened after the fire, as did their parents' marital discord. Counseling provided by the outreach team helped a little, so that Janine's emotional problems improved considerably, although Ken's behavior was unchanged. The parents dropped out of counseling after three sessions, and it seems likely their difficulties continued.

TYPES OF DISASTER IN WHICH DISLOCATION AND RELOCATION STRESSORS ARE PROMINENT

Fires, tornadoes, cyclones, hurricanes, massive floods, earthquakes, and volcanic eruptions are all forces that threaten and destroy habitation and can make evacuation and dislocation inevitable. Some man-made disasters may also do this, as with the nuclear leak at Three Mile Island, explosions and fires in urban centers, and terrorist violence such as bombing. War, with bombardment and aerial bombing of civilian populations, is the prime disaster of devastation and dislocation; but psychological studies have concentrated more on the effects of combat and military destruction than on the longer-term adjustments of civilians. Janis (1951) does, however, describe the extra trauma to people from the massive devastation of community with bombing. Many of the same patterns apply. Where they can, people take shelter with relatives or friends, who generally are good to them. Most later seek to return to their own place or home, even when there is nothing there but rubble. It is from the study of refugee populations that an understanding of the gradual making of a new place into home can best be gained. Such studies show the adaptations and problems that are involved and the personal and social costs (Keh-Ming Lin et al. 1982; Eitinger and Schwartz 1981).

The studies that most vividly portray the themes of dislocation and relocation are those of Erikson (1976) of Buffalo Creek, Bolin (1982) of the tornado affecting Wichita Falls (1982), and studies following Cyclone Tracy by Western and others (Western and Doube 1979; Western and Milne 1979). Themes of dislocation and relocation do appear in many other descriptions, however, from Hiroshima to Ash Wednesday, from the civilian violence of Ireland to the floods and hurricanes in the United States.

PERSONAL DISASTERS OF DISLOCATION

Personal disasters that destroy home, neighborhoods, and community are rare, because when damage is so extensive disaster moves from the personal field. But the sense of dislocation and the problems of relocation are reflected in themes of a number of personally stressful life experiences. Forced moves or migrations mean dislocation from a familiar environment and lead to problems of adjusting to a new home and developing new bonds. However, such moves are more frequently able to be anticipated and are sometimes even chosen and not forced. Urban house fires, as noted previously, may have some effects of dislocation and relocation, and likewise also engender intense grief for the lost home. Culture shock may be a reflection of dislocation and relocation at a personal level, and the affected individual may feel all the alertness, disquiet, and disorientation that the disaster victim experiences. The sense of alienation of those who, for one reason or another, find themselves in a strange country with strange customs and a poorly understood language is very similar to that experienced at a community level when all that was familiar has gone. Foreign students may be a group who commonly experience this shock and dislocation stress (Coelho 1982).

The personal disaster that most accurately reflects the dislocation and relocation is the move of an old person from familiar surroundings into a nursing or geriatric home. This brings a strange environment and neighborhood, a loss of social network and support, and numerous assaults on independence and human dignity, sometimes even to the removal of clothes and personal possessions. Services are lost or become unavailable in the bureaucracy and administration, with rules and regulations frequently adding further stress. The losses and grief of the illness, disability, medications, and moves are sources of ongoing and often unresolvable stress. Life changes are multiple, and tensions of family, or what is left of it, are a focus. This relocation personal disaster has been studied as a stressor by Zweig and Csank (1976), who were able to show positive effects for stress prevention and stress reduction programs that helped anticipate and lower the shock effects of relocation. They found that deaths could in some ways be related to the relocation cycle. Anxious anticipation or an alarm reaction was seen as a powerful influence toward mortality effects, and the authors concluded that it was very important to avoid the potential shock and alarm effects of this personal disaster crisis.

Two other personal disasters have themes of dislocation and relocation in a personal sense, and to a much lesser degree in an environmental sense. Unemployment may lead to a sense of dislocation from the familiar rituals and social interactions of work and to a loss of the reassurance that comes from competence and achievement. Prolonged uncertainty, grief for what is lost, loss of self-esteem and dignity, disruption of social networks, multiple life changes, and family tensions may all add to this stressful and traumatic experience. Relocation to the role of nonworker and home, or to a new and perhaps less satisfying level and status of work, may take much adjustment (Raphael 1983).

Divorce represents a crisis of dislocation and relocation in the realm of intimacy and family life. It is often characterized by disorientation, frustration, grief for lost loves and lost ideals, the breakdown of support networks, uncertainty, and altered statuses and roles. These problems may be complicated by ongoing and unresolved distress over what has happened, by many associated life changes such as moving house, and inevitably, by a variety of family tensions. There may be a profound sense of dislocation from life as it has been lived and known in marriage, and a prolonged period before there is any relocation to marital or family roles again.

REFUGEES

Refugee populations are a special group. Their dislocation does not occur from a brief disastrous event, but often from ongoing threat, violence, and persecution. Their homes may be left intact or destroyed; their communities may be in the hands of enemies. They may never have the opportunity to return to their roots or for reunion with (or even good-byes to) their near or extended families. For the most part, they have faced extreme disaster stressors at many levels and on many occasions. They may have confronted death daily, including the violent and mutilating deaths of family and loved ones. Survival may seem to have been bought at an impossible price. Many are left with death imprint, death guilt, and psychic numbing to a profound degree. Their losses may be too many to enumerate and their grief too great to bear. Two groups that vividly represent what has been suffered are the survivors of the Holocaust and, in more recent times, the Vietnamese and many others who had to flee their war-torn homelands.

The victims of the Holocaust (Hocking 1981) suffered not only the stresses of death, loss, grief, and survival, but also dislocation into camps and then, after a bitter struggle, relocation and adjustment to strange and new communities. The survivor syndrome has been described elsewhere. For many the consequences have persisted until the present day.

The experiences of Vietnamese refugees have been more recently studied and documented and throw some of the adaptational processes of refugees into relief. In discussing Vietnamese refugees in the United States, Keh-Ming Lin et al. (1982) point out that the difficulties in adapting to a new sociocultural environment are enormous, especially when there was little opportunity to prepare for such major change. Feelings of homesickness, grief over losses of family members and home, uncertainties about the future, and many sources of frustration all lead to ongoing stress. Refugees showed a significantly raised score on the Cornell Medical Index, even into the second year after their arrival; and psychosomatic symptoms and general feelings of nervousness and sadness were frequent and persistent. More than 50 percent of the refugees could be classed as having emotional difficulties in the first two years. When symptomatology was initially high, it tended to remain so. However, the early stressful effects seemed related to basic tasks of adaptation, which affected refugees indiscriminately. In the second year, age and marital status seemed to contribute to vulnerability, with divorced or widowed women who were heads of households often being overwhelmed and highly vulnerable. This is not a small group, as it may constitute between 10 and 15 percent of all refugees. Older and younger males and reproductive-age females were also, to some degree, vulnerable: the males perhaps because of language, work, and status adjustments, and the women perhaps because of stress related to multiple roles and changed status as women. This study and others have highlighted the importance of status discrepancy, an element of human dignity, in contributing to the difficulties of refugees and migrants. Manual work and the need to accept public assistance also seemed to reinforce negative feelings.

The authors concluded from their own work and that of others that a two-to-three-year period of adaptation may be faced before the relocation is satisfactorily made. The multiple life changes they demonstrated for this group (Masuda et al. 1982) must have compounded the problem, for these extended over the period of the study and included finances, marital relations, and life style—all facets of relocation.

Bureaucratic problems are a further difficulty for many refugees, especially if the host country may have taken them unwillingly or has few, poorly defined policies to deal with them. Policies should, but often do not, pay special attention to the need to keep families intact and to allow adequate time for adjustment. Children are likely to be particularly vulnerable and to have special needs that may not be recognized.

The need to adjust to a new language and culture requires special recognition for all migrants and refugees. Thus status discrepancies, the altered roles of women, and isolation from the main society or from the refugee's own ethnic group may all contribute to dislocation (Nann 1982).

Recent studies in Australia (Krupinski 1984; Tsang 1984) have highlighted the intense and ongoing nature of refugee problems, for the Vietnamese at least. High levels of stress, frequent relocations after arrival, difficulties with employment, and separation from family members who have been left behind all contribute. But above and beyond this, most of these refugees experienced a painful period of dislocation in refugee camps before departure, a terrifying escape, and a desperate struggle for survival as boat people on the open seas. In the process of becoming refugees, they suffered life experiences that are too frequent and dreadful to enumerate—rape, murder, and violent assault—often losing most or all of their families and sometimes witnessing these deaths before their eyes. Children arrived alone, and many others came hoping for families to follow. For many, psychic numbing is the only mechanism of survival.

The extent of the refugee problem is enormous; refugees are the greatest disaster population currently to be dealt with. A United Nations report includes estimates that 45,000,000 persons were denied residency in their homelands from 1945 to 1967 and that at present there are probably at least 15,000,000 refugees in the world.

COPING WITH DISLOCATION AND RELOCATION

Coping with dislocation and relocation may require techniques and adaptations that can be used over a considerable period. Oliver-Smith (1977) has described some of these processes at a community level when he speaks of the "rehabilitation system" that operates in a community, as exemplified by his study of Yungay after the Peruvian earthquake. He discusses the role of individual aid, which he saw as significant, in that it was at least in part responsible for the resumption of many traditional patterns of behavior in the population that had been affected by the disaster. People were evaluated for individual aid in terms of urban or rural origins, and the aid they received depended on whether they were directly involved in the disaster or indirectly affected by its consequences. When the givers of aid tried to provide it on an equal basis to all, conflict and friction arose and helped to divide and reinforce the highly stratified society that had existed before. Yet, ultimately, more of the upper classes became involved in the community, and it seemed likely that there would be a more integrated and cooperative society. Community aid also assisted in coping because communities that were already in the process of forming and dividing off were accelerated by the disaster process. Furthermore, part of this aid came through a program whereby food was given as payment for work. Many of the peasantry learned not to provide their labor free to the towns, but instead to exchange it for provisions; thus a new and more positive sociocultural ethos, that of paid labor, developed. And in terms of system-oriented reconstruction, the temporary site where people had camped became—at their insistence and not where the authorities suggested—the new relocated city. And thus it was that the place for the new city was "based on a very real appreciation of the structural pillars of their social order, as well as deeply felt emotional ties to the site of their destroyed homes and deceased families" (p. 13). In Yungay, then, coping resulted in the adaptive development of the new community, with preservation of many socially important facets of the old society and many emotionally important aspects of place. It was a newer group of people who would ultimately, though not immediately, provide the community with a broader base and with the new, adaptive custom of paid labor.

Coping with dislocation and relocation often occurs at community or systems levels. Coping is facilitated by strong social bonds, which are enhanced by the experience of having faced the disaster stress together. Emergent groups and leaders seem especially important in this context. By offering leadership and direction, they help avoid disintegration, schism, and scapegoating, as well as anomie and alienation in the community. In terms of mastery, goal orientation and active striving to master the trauma experienced by the community are helpful. At practical and political levels, the development of information and organizational systems involves active participation in the planning and management of relocation and reconstruction, with at least some degree of community control over these processes. Rebuilding of community structures or the development of new groups and structures seems valuable, as illustrated by the mobilization of community resources and development in the town of Aberfan. Mastery may also be gained by the development of subcommunities, which retain contact with the parent center. Thus evacuees of one destroyed Australian city established a self-help group in the city where they were moved. They held meetings to reform social networks, viewed videotapes of friends left behind, and sent back similar communication. This coping proved adaptive; it meant both lessened stress in relocation and an easier return "home."

The emotional tone of the community may vary from bitter disillusionment to inappropriate trust, hope, and even euphoria. The most adaptive coping probably allows some opportunity for community release of feeling and discussion of the experience and of future plans. The feeling release may come through public meeting, protest and petition, memorial ceremony, or celebration. One cathartic release in a small town during the long recovery after a catastrophic fire was a community theater in which many citizens participated and in which the fire dragon was ritually destroyed. Country dances, weddings, and births may be opportunities for celebration of rebirth and regeneration, as noted by Valent (1984). The reviews, reports, testimonies, and writings of the disaster may further facilitate this release of feeling as they do for individuals.

At individual and family levels, interpersonal relationships continue to be critical but, often, also particularly vulnerable. Rebuilding social networks, or making new ones, and maintaining bonds with family from whom one is separated are likely to enhance coping. Models of others who have made or are making similar transitions are likely to be particularly helpful. This was noted by Coelho (1982) as one of the coping styles used by foreign students. Mastery again involves information and active involvement, as well as opportunities to talk through stresses and modify them as far as possible. There is a need to look at options, plan toward goals, and to be able to retain autonomy in terms of one's own recovery, rehabilitation, and the management of places of relocation. Emotional release and control may involve the use of opportunities for catharsis and the development of controls to manage the circumstances where the discharge of frustrations is counterproductive. The use of friends and professionals to help with the working through of ongoing disaster stressors is a positive coping mechanism, as are discussions and sharing of feelings with others facing similar frustrations. Also, having a future orientation with hope helps draw people through this period, even when it is prolonged. Garrison (1985), after reviewing mental health implications of disaster relocation in the United States, suggests that critical variables in determining mental health outcomes with relocation include perceptions of housing quality, a sense of belonging and being at home, financial considerations, access to social support, other sources of life stress, and degree of perceived control in the situation; class and ethnicity may also influence vulnerability.

Dislocation is distressing, painful, and often full of anger. It may be prolonged, and those affected by the disaster may be relocated in many strange shelters and dwellings before they find the place that feels like home. They may feel stripped of human dignity and independence in the process of their recovery. Or they may be strengthened by the challenges they have mastered. Their lives and communities may show a rapid rebirth or a sad and gradual process of recovery. Yet, eventually, most people come "home" again—either to their old home or to a new habitation that the bonds of attachment have slowly made into "my place" again.

CHAPTER 7

The Young, the Old, and the Family

"Will the wind come back again, Mommy? Will it? Will it?"

CHILDREN IN DISASTER

The experiences of children, particularly younger children, are usually inextricably interwoven with those of their parents and families, unless, at the time of the disaster, they have been separated. The fear and threat are experienced both directly and indirectly through identification with and response to parental reactions. In the immediate post-disaster period there is often a tendency to "protect" children by sending them away from the scene of destruction, but this may add a further trauma of separation rather than alleviate distress. Children's attempts to make meaning of their experience and integrate it will take a variety of forms: dreams, games, storytelling, play enactment, or repression. The experience may leave them with specific or general vulnerability.

Until recently, studies of children's responses to disaster have been fairly limited. However, Terr's sensitive, in-depth studies of the victims of the Chowchilla bus kidnapping, McFarlane's epidemiological studies of behavior after the bushfires, and Burke et al.'s studies (1982) of behavior after severe storms have all added considerably to our knowledge. Further work deals with children affected by war, violence, and bombardment. And there have been a large number of descriptive and case studies commenting on responses in disaster situations ranging from tornado to flood, earthquake to evacuation.

THE CHILD'S ENCOUNTERS WITH DANGER AND DEATH

A central theme that emerges from exploration of children's responses to disaster situations is that, in a way that is not generally appreciated, they, too, experience fear of death and destruction. To some extent, this experience of fear may often be age-dependent, in that it is related to the child's ability to comprehend the nature of death. Even so, it is clear that quite young children can become distressed and traumatized. Particularly influential in the young child's experience are the presence or absence of his parents and the terror of overwhelming physical forces that seem to render the "all powerful" adult parents frightened and powerless. Some examples may help to clarify the nature of children's experience.

When the cyclone hit Darwin, children were, for the most part, with their parents. Parents, when they realized the severity of the threat, pushed their children into bathrooms or under tables or even into heavy cupboards, in an attempt to protect them from the violent physical forces. Most of the homes in which parents and children sheltered were torn apart by the force of the winds, which howled and whistled with great intensity. Parents often had to protect their children by throwing their bodies across them. Then there was awareness, when the cyclone had passed, of the total destruction of the city. The poignancy of the children's experience was reinforced by the timing: many saw Christmas trees and toys spread afar by the forces of the storm. A time of anticipated happiness and good feeling, gifts and food, had been turned into a time of devastation and loss—particularly for children, the loss of one of the familiar rituals that would normally reinforce their sense of security. The extreme physical forces of this disaster, far beyond anything known to most children, were influential in children's subsequent response to the experience, in their fearfulness of wind and rain, and in their games of "cyclone."

Similarly, Australian forest fires brought the terror of violent and extreme physical forces that were totally beyond most children's comprehension, and until that time, perhaps also their fantasy. The fires occurred at mid-afternoon, when many children were traveling home from school in buses. Visibility and knowledge of the fires' course were so poor that several buses were trapped near the path of fires. Children had to lie down while flames surrounded the vehicles and passed. In a rural area, bus drivers were uncertain as to whether to leave the children at their usual roadside stops, where parents would expect them, or to take them on to some other unknown place. Some children were left at such stops—fortunately, safely. In another area children lay on the floor of a school building, which parents hosed and kept wet as the flames surrounded them. Valent (1984) reports a six-year-old boy who experienced a terrifying drive through the fire, his own terror reinforced by his father's screams of helplessness and anger. And, indeed, several children died in these fires. Others lost playmates, friends, and family members in this "hell" of heat and smoke and flame. They knew that death was possible and that they might have died.

Vivid descriptions of children's experiences in and responses to the Buffalo Creek disaster are given by Newman (1976). When she assessed them two years after the disaster, even children who had been as young as twenty-six months revealed evidence of the traumatic experience. One, Peter, was unable to take a bath without screaming, wet his bed frequently, and screamed in his sleep. His preoccupation with the disaster related to the experience of his father getting the family out of the house just in time, to then see it being swept away, and to seeing other children floating by with someone screaming for help, with his father being unable to rescue them. Other children showed similar themes of fear and fearfulness linked to their specific traumatic experience with the flood of black water that swept past, leaving death and destruction behind. Many children saw the deaths of others, including infants and children. Some found the dead remains of other children in the days that followed.

The Chowchilla bus kidnapping was a very different type of disaster, brought on not by overpowering natural forces but rather by human malevolence. Here, too, there were trauma effects linked to the potential for death and destruction. Terr describes these children's experience and the longer-term consequences in a series of important papers (Terr 1979, 1981a, 1981b, 1983a, 1983b, 1983c). In this disaster, twenty-six schoolchildren, of ages five to fourteen, some of them siblings, were kidnapped and held for twenty-seven hours before escaping. The kidnapping began when their bus was blocked and taken over by three men wearing stocking masks, one of whom had a gun. The children were then transferred to two vans, the older children to one and the younger to another. This meant that in many cases siblings were separated. The van's windows had been painted over. Thus the children were driven around in total darkness, and without food, drink, or toileting, for a period that lasted eleven hours. Early the next morning, they were transferred into a hole, which turned out to be a buried truck trailer. There they remained for sixteen more hours, before finally managing to dig out and escape. They were taken for debriefing before reunion with their parents, which meant a total separation of approximately forty-three hours. As Terr notes, even though no one died or was seriously injured, the children were all subjected to the experience of helplessness and to the danger of a prolonged life-threatening situation, whose outcome was unknown and was to be feared.

Children have also faced disasters of war, riots, and violence. Frazer (1973) discusses the impact that constant threat and danger have on children in Belfast. He notes earlier work that showed how children in bombed cities were often more distressed when they had been evacuated and separated from home than when they stayed to face the threat and danger during bombing. He relates this to the fact that even children who faced bombing may not have seen injuries, blood, or death and rarely saw the enemy. They rarely experienced the naked aggression of battle, as those near the military front may have done. In riots such as Watts and Belfast, in contrast, children may have had prolonged experience of death encounters in scenes of violence, injury, and killing. Similarly, refugee children may also have had many such traumatic experiences.

There are many other disasters that have brought children to a realization of death and destruction. In his description of Hiroshima survivors, Lifton (1967) aptly referred to a loss of the "innocence of death." This loss of innocence may be all the more so for children who have such experiences.

PATTERNS OF DISASTER RESPONSE

What happens to children exposed to such traumatic experiences? What is their pattern of disaster response?

In the warning or pre-impact phase, children are generally with their parents or other adults such as teachers. Unless they have had previous disaster experience, which might bring an automatic response of fear, they tend to share the arousal of others and a sense of excitement. The suspension of routine activities such as school may make the occasion seem special. The dangers may not be apparent, especially for younger children, who cannot conceptualize such abstractions. But, as parents become fearful, the children will seek to be close to them and will fear separation. They sense and respond to the protectiveness of adults. Valent (1984) notes that, in certain instances, children can see dangers even more clearly than adults. This observation is supported by Terr's (1979) finding that children may not use denial to the degree that adults seem to in the face of such trauma.

When the disaster strikes, there is both the fear of the threat and the need to be cared for and protected, to survive. As Valent sensitively depicts, adults show intense feelings of love and altruism and wish to save and protect children. It is not always easy for parents and others to meet children's needs. The terrifying physical forces, extreme danger, and entrapment may bring a return of primitive childhood emotions, and adults may have their own needs to regress and be cared for. There have in fact been disaster circumstances where parents have regressed and children taken over the more adult roles. Nevertheless, most children are very frightened during the disaster impact, for they respond directly and appropriately to the physical forces and to the threat they appraise.

The only really systematic description of children's responses to impact is Terr's discussion of the Chowchilla episode. These children clearly realized that their lives were threatened, only occasionally and briefly responding with denial. They later remembered most aspects of their own experiences and responses, as well as those of their peers. They cried but apparently did not show "paralysis of action," numbing, or other responses of the disaster syndrome (Terr 1979, p. 563). They did experience considerable fear—fear due to separation from parents and siblings, fear of death, and fear of further shocks and surprises. It is likely that similar feelings and responses are experienced by most children during disasters and that they represent, as Terr suggests, the ego's response to the traumatic experience. The Chowchilla children showed evidence of the effect of fear on their psychological functioning by misperceptions and even hallucinations during their imprisonment. For instance, some children misperceived the presence of an additional kidnapper. Younger children and some older children as well may respond to their fear by clinging, crying, and displaying all the emotional concomitants appropriate to situations of threat and danger. Nevertheless, as far as published reports indicate, most children seem to respond sensibly and directly to the disaster impact, particularly when supported and protected by parents or other trusted and caring adults.

After the impact of such traumatic situations, children attempt to master and integrate what has happened to them, as do adults. Experience, research, and clinical reports tend to show the same common themes appearing for most children. Like adults, their reactions will start to appear in the post-impact period. Their further experience during that period will be colored by parental responses and ongoing losses and stressors. Most families share the enormous sense of relief at personal survival and at the intact status of the family group. When members are absent, there is an intense preoccupation with insuring that they, too, have survived and are safe; arousal and active searching will continue until this has been established. Perhaps the most vivid examples of this drive to reestablish the primary group intact are in John Hersey's description of the parents and children of Hiroshima seeking one another through a field of death and utter destruction, often with horrific burns and injuries.

On the other hand, in many disasters where death and destruction are not overwhelming, children seem to share in the post-disaster euphoria of adults. Again, there is excitement or even elation, with the high arousal, good feeling, and intense and supportive interpersonal interactions that occur at this time. Children's elation, laughter, and games may be threatening to adults, who feel guilt about their own joy at survival and who may attempt to repress what they see as wrong in themselves in order to stop it from appearing in their children.

Children may share in the breakdown of traditional barriers, rituals, and discipline ("hamburgers for breakfast!") and in the excitement of rescuing and helping others. For them, as for adults, it may be hours or, more frequently, days before the letdown of the post-disaster period occurs. Then there is a growing awareness of what has gone. Parental disquiet, distress, grief, and despair impinge on the child. Disruption of family ritual now bring irritation and insecurity. There is a longing for things as they were before. At this point, even the rituals of school, discipline, or tasks may bring reassurance, whereas previously they had been resented. The child, like the adult, must get on with life, integrating his disaster experience and living within the framework of its consequences.

REACTIONS TO ENCOUNTERS WITH DEATH
AND DANGER

Children's reactions reflect many of the features and patterns found in adults but are often more direct and less disguised. Their reactions may also reflect the general stress response syndrome described by Horowitz (1976).

Many children who have directly experienced the disaster go through a period, which may be extended, of fears associated with what has happened to them. Any physical reminders may trigger such fears. After storms, cyclones, and tornadoes, there are fears of high winds, rain, lightning, and noise like thunder or wind. Even the rattle of a window may suffice to trigger *startle* or *specific fear responses.* These have been described after the Darwin cyclone (Milne 1977), the Omaha tornado (McIntire and Sadeghi 1977), a tornado in Mississippi (Silber et al. 1957), and severe winter storms (Burke et al. 1982). After fires, triggers are likely to be smoke, flames, or sirens (McFarlane 1983). After floods, water or rain are triggers to fear, as noted by Newman (1976) in her descriptions of the children of Buffalo Creek, where some children were even afraid of their bathwater. Children surviving Aberfan (Lacey 1972) showed fears of heavy rain, bad weather, wind, and snow—all conditions that had been associated with the slide. After earthquakes, fears were triggered by movements, rattling, rumbling, or other specifically related circumstances (Blaufarb and Levine 1972; McIntire and Sadeghi 1977). In addition to these specific fears there is a more general fearful response, which seems to represent heightened *separation anxiety*. Children regress, cling to parents, are fearful and distressed if parents are absent, even if only in another room, and wish to sleep with them again at night. Specific triggers may also induce this general fearfulness.

Sometimes these fears will be well hidden when there are no obviously threatening circumstances, so that adults do not realize that the disaster trauma is still operant and powerful. Children seen eight months after the Ash Wednesday fires were believed by their teachers to have no ongoing fears or effects from the disaster. Yet McFarlane observed their reactions to a fire siren when it went off while he was in their classroom. All the children showed an immediate and intense response ranging from crying to general distress. Burke et al. (1982) and Bloch et al. (1956) also observed fear reactions in children considered by adults to be over their fears.

Also characteristic of traumatized children were *disturbances of sleep* and *nightmares,* particularly in the weeks following the disaster. Children often dream directly of what has happened and may wake up frightened and screaming or shaking with reexperienced terror. Like the fears, these nightmares usually fade with time and with the love and reassurance of parents, but for some children they may not. They have been described after the fire disasters, after cyclones and earthquakes, and in most disasters in which children have been systematically studied.

In commenting on this phenomenon in the Chowchilla children, Terr (1979, p. 587) distinguishes several different types of dreams, based on the degree to which the kidnapping experience was disguised or directly represented in the dream. She described these as "exact repeat playback" dreams, "modified playback dreams," and more fully "disguised dreams." All these children had dreams relating to the kidnapping after the event. Terror and exact dreams tended to appear in the early period; disguised and repetitive dreams tended to appear later. Terror dreams were often not remembered by the children but reported by parents. These traumatic dreams seemed, as with adults, a repeating of the events and did not bring relief from the distressing internalization of the experience. Relief may occur only when the child gains understanding that allows for emotional release, as Terr suggests.

The dreams of children in such circumstances may also reflect their encounter with death. As Terr notes, it is unusual for children to dream of their own deaths. Their experience of being "buried" in the hold or believing death likely might be responsible for such dreams. The Buffalo Creek children also showed sleep disturbances, including terrifying nightmares of the experience and, in some cases, even somnambulism.

Thus many children experience a period of sleep disturbance after the disaster, both because of traumatic dreams and because fearfulness may make them afraid of darkness, sleep, and, particularly, separation from parents. Many sleep with night-lights when they had previously not done so or regressively seek the comfort and security of their parents' bed, showing separation fears that are also revived.

Play is another important aspect of the child's response and of his attempts to integrate what has happened. After a hurricane, children played many hurricane games involving chiefly themes of wind, destruction, rescue, and hiding for safety. Often, their parents found these difficult to tolerate, as they triggered a reawakening of the parents' own traumatic experiences. A range of games appeared after a fire. Again these were often reinforcing the child's powerlessness against fire, yet seemed to represent attempts at mastery. Fire engines, firemen, and police games symbolized the child's need to identify with the strong forces that checked the fires. Lacey (1972) noted that the games played by children who survived the Aberfan disaster in some instances involved "burying." Often, however, their play seemed inhibited by the loneliness of having lost so many friends, and the children retreated to the security of their family circle.

Play may also involve *drawing.* Newman (1976) and Tonge (1984), looking at the Buffalo Creek and bushfire children, describe the impact of disaster and its representations through this medium. The drawings of the Buffalo Creek children tended to traumatic regression, wish fulfillment, dehumanization of human figures, interference with body image concepts, condensation of the traumatic scene, denial, and bizarre expressions of unconscious imagery. Many creative expressions also emerged, however, alongside indications of hopefulness that were mostly absent from the responses of adults. Tonge's bushfire children drew pictures expressing anger and fear of loss of control and depicting the "fire-ghosts" who separated them from parents. Terr (1981a) describes the drawings of the traumatized children she saw as being "unelaborated and simple in their stark representations of the traumatic experience" (p. 759) and sees them as showing the same characteristics as post-traumatic play.

Again, it is only through Terr's careful exploration of Chowchilla (California) children that we have a detailed description and explanation of the different facets of children's play in disaster (Terr 1979, 1981a). She notes how almost half the children played games specifically related to the kidnapping, monotonously and regularly, without relief, and for the most part, without realization of the connection with their experience. Retelling was also seen by Terr as a version of *traumatic play,* with many repetitions and elaborations, which still did not alleviate anxiety and distress. Terr concludes that fourteen of twenty-three kidnapped children (ages five to fourteen) played or retold their experience. She goes on to make the important distinction between ordinary play, which helps all children master everyday stressful experiences, and traumatic play. In ordinary play, the child plays a few times, perhaps taking over the powerful role and caring for the hurt one, and is able to master the experience. But when the experience has been too overwhelming, rendering the child especially helpless, the play does not allow the same successful retrospective mastery. It is compulsively repeated, but each repetition brings fresh anxiety because it still doesn't produce a happy ending that would have prevented the bad experience. Such traumatic play does not stop spontaneously; someone else must usually help the child, with support, to master the trauma or to stop. Reenactments were further behaviors in which children repeated dramatically, and almost directly, segments of the experience, but not in the sense of play or the enjoyment of play. These reenactments seemed to represent further pathological aspects of the traumatized children's responses. As Terr's study is the only systematic exploration of children's play post-disaster, it is important that further research explore the significance of such patterns in other disasters. For it is obvious from work such as McFarlane's (1983b) that some children continued fire-related play for as long as ten months after the fire, although its specific form and significance were unknown. In further systematic evaluations that examined fire-affected children eight and twenty-six months after exposure to the disaster, McFarlane et al. (1985) found that, according to parents' reports, over one-third of the children showed (eight months) and continued to show (twenty-six months) significant post-traumatic phenomena. These phenomena included dreams, games, upset over reminders, and talk. The phenomena were very reflective of ongoing parent problems, especially the mother's preoccupation with and disturbance by her own intrusive thoughts of the disaster.

There are other elements of reaction to the threat of danger that children have experienced that should be considered. Some are similar to those found in adults. For instance, children tended to interpret occurrences that took place before Chowchilla as omens or warnings (Terr 1983a). These retrospective interpretations, together with other alterations of time sense, have been found in a variety of traumatized individuals and seem to represent an attempt to gain control and mastery. If omens can be found, the mind seems to say, future traumas and disasters may be predicted and prevented. Similar experiences are reported by many bereaved individuals following traumatic and unexpected deaths, and here, too, they seem to represent attempts at mastery and protection of the self and ego from future trauma.

Psychosomatic or psychophysiological reactions in the post-disaster period, which have been commonly described in adults, also seem frequent in children. They have been described in children following the Ash Wednesday fires by McFarlane (1983), who found an increased incidence of headaches and stomachaches, as well as of absences from school. It is interesting to note the frequency of gastrointestinal disturbances, as in adults' reactions.

POST-TRAUMATIC SYNDROMES

These have been clearly described in Terr's studies, which have shown that every one of the twenty-six children who had been kidnapped exhibited significant post-traumatic effects four years later (Terr 1983a). Effects included residual traumatic anxiety and fears; cognitive restrictions such as thought suppression, denial, and repression; memory preoccupation with associated psychological concomitants; misperceptions such as hallucinations; disruptions of time sense; and the repetitive phenomena characteristic of post-traumatic syndromes, manifested in dreams, play, and reenactment. Terr found that although there were many similar features when the children were assessed one year and four years after the event, some symptoms seemed to become more pronounced with time. These included feelings of shame, suppression of thought, splitting off of feeling from some memories, misperceptions, death dreams, a sense of a foreshortened future, and repetitive play and reenactment. These symptoms were of sufficient severity to constitute a post-traumatic syndrome for every child and to have significant effects on development. Terr noted differences from the syndrome in adults: psychic numbing or amnesia and intrusive flashbacks were not observed in the children, while the limited view of the future was particularly striking.

Post-traumatic syndromes in children were also assessed after Buffalo Creek (Newman 1976), and one-third of the children of Aberfan (Lacey 1972) received care at child guidance clinics, probably for ongoing disorder. Burke et al. (1982) found increases in aggressive conduct, antisocial conduct, and anxiety among boys five months after severe storms. McFarlane (1983), while observing few effects in a survey taken two months after the disaster, found effects appearing after a delay in the survey taken after eight months. He also noted that at least 43 percent of children continued to talk spontaneously about the fires and that at least 35 percent were still upset by reminders. These effects continued at 26 months (McFarlane et al. 1985) and were more significantly frequent in children with disorder. Tonge (1984) found syndromes of emotional disorder and conduct disorder, the former with many components of post-traumatic syndromes.

Variables associated with the development of syndromes include previous vulnerability or family disorder (Tonge 1984; Burke et al. 1982; Terr 1983a,

1983b, 1983c; Bloch et al. 1956) and stress effects in parents continuing in the post-disaster period (McFarlane 1983, 1985b; Tonge 1984; Bloch et al. 1956; Newman 1976). Some studies emphasized the vulnerability of younger children, others that of older children, especially the senior child in the family, who is often also the most vulnerable to bereavement-induced disorder (Raphael 1983).

Survivor themes and syndromes do not seem to have been systematically studied in children. The loss of childhood, the impairment of development, or the shutting out of the capacity to feel may be consequences, leaving children inhibited, afraid, and withdrawn.

Thus, children are affected by such traumatic impacts. Initially, the effects take the form of reactive phenomena, but they may continue and lead to troublesome illness and disorder if the child is personally vulnerable, and may continue even after a significant latent period (McFarlane et al. 1985). Not only may illness appear but absence from school, educational impairment, and entrenched symptoms may have an adverse effect on development (McFarlane et al. 1985). Or, the stresses may interact with ongoing, or preexisting, difficulties in the parents, who may either deny the child's disorder or, because of their own ongoing disturbances (McFarlane 1985b; McFarlane et al. 1985), may be unable to provide the care and reassurances the child needs in order to integrate the experience adaptively.

CHILDREN'S LOSSES IN DISASTER

While there have not been systematic studies of children's bereavements in disaster, there are a number of observations and findings that are relevant.

As with adults, much will depend on the ongoing situation after impact and whether there is shock, threat, or struggle for survival. Once safety and security are guaranteed, children begin to perceive their losses and react to them. Their perceptions will be strongly influenced by the degree to which such losses disrupt their lives and by their capacity for an awareness of the future. However, even very young children react with grief to the absence and death of family members and to the loss of people or objects that are emotionally meaningful to them.

In the younger years of infancy and childhood, it is difficult for children to realize the permanency of the loss. They may ask again and again for the lost person, even though they have been told that he is dead and gone and cannot come back. Their interpretations of what has happened are likely to be very concrete, as is their understanding of where the dead person has gone. The nature of the disaster deaths—their suddenness, shock, and trauma and the fact that the child may have had little opportunity to see the body or participate in the rituals of farewell—may add to the difficulty in comprehending and resolving what has happened.

The immediate reactions and confusion of children are well exemplified by a five-year-old boy's reaction to his father's death in a rail disaster:

In the morning his father leaves home as usual to catch the train to work. It is a "normal" family morning with a few disagreements but a basically loving atmosphere. His father is running late and so does not kiss him good-bye as usual. After his father leaves, the family morning ritual of breakfast and play is resumed. He plays with his favorite toys, especially the train set that he and his dad have enjoyed together since Christmas a few weeks before.

Suddenly, his mother is in a state of intense distress, telephoning many people, crying, listening to the radio, watching something on T.V. His uncle arrives, and the neighbors come in. His mother leaves him to go to police and hospital, seeking information, desperate for reassurance about her husband. She cannot contact his work, for the disaster has brought down telephone lines and other communications are jammed. She comes back, still upset and crying. He sees the television coverage of the train disaster, which, although dramatically and frighteningly portrayed, is to him just the play and make-believe of television—something you switch off so that it goes away. He becomes frightened, though, on seeing his mother upset, and he starts to cry, to demand, and to cling to her. She holds him and sobs. Then others take him away, and she seems oblivious to his presence, caught up in her fear and her tears. His happy, loving mother is gone.

This continues throughout the day—the relatives, the tears, no proper meals; he is ignored. Everyone is upset. Then one of his uncles returns, much, much later, and tells his mother something. She collapses in further anguish and grief. He is put to bed. In the morning his grandparents are there, and someone tells him his father is gone—not coming back. Much later, someone tells him he is dead and has gone to be with God. Everyone is upset. He wants his father, who always seemed so strong and able to make things right. But, when he asks for him, everyone becomes even more upset and angry. He is minded by strangers while there is something called a "funeral." Later someone tells him his daddy was killed in the train crash and will not be coming back again. He knows little of death and finds it all incomprehensible. All he knows is that his beloved father has gone—in some way to do with trains—trains that he and his father had played with so happily. His mother cries and is distraught. She cuddles him sometimes and tries to comfort him often. His whole world is in a state of upheaval: insecurity, fear, misery, and distress.

The situation of disaster bereavements where the child was not involved in the impact is likely to be very similar to that of other sudden, unexpected deaths, like those in motor vehicle accidents. As the disaster may indiscriminately affect the young and the old, these deaths are often untimely, for example, affecting parents of young children. The violence of the deaths may add to the frightening fantasies the child has about death, especially when he has no opportunity to test reality in any other way. The public nature of disaster deaths may also give a special sort of identity—"the boy whose father died in . . . ," for instance. When there has been a man-made disaster, litigation may be significant and prolonged. Issues of blame or scapegoating may mean, especially to the younger child, that someone "killed" his father, brother, or other family member.

Especially important in the child's understanding of and response to any personal loss will be its effects on his parents and, to a lesser degree, any other family members. He is likely to be powerfully affected by the degree to which their grief disrupts the security of family life. He may identify with his parents' reactions. He is likely to take up their interpretations of what has happened, perhaps reinforcing them with his own guilty, aggressive fantasies. But, particularly at the egocentric state of development, there is a danger that he will see what has happened as a consequence of his own unlovableness, aggression, or as a rejection of him. Thus, reassurances of ongoing love and care are vital.

Losses of home and possessions are also likely to have effects. Because they are so much more evident and can be understood and experienced in concrete terms, the child's grief reaction to them may be more direct and obvious. He may grieve easily and overtly for pets who died in the disaster, or beloved lost toys, while his grief for his mother is shut away and unrealized. The disruption of daily patterns of love and care will again be most likely to affect him directly.

REACTIONS TO LOSS

Children's grief varies with age, developmental stage, and the degree to which it has sanctions for release. As noted by Burke at al. (1982) and McFarlane (1985a), parents often deny children's responses to the impact and threat, and the same has been demonstrated with bereavement (Raphael 1983, chapter 3). It is commonly believed that children are unaffected, because they do not show the same patterns as adults and their behavioral and emotional responses during bereavement may go unrecognized. This may be because parents are too overwhelmed by their own grief or, alternatively, too afraid to tune into the children's distress, which makes them feel helpless and reawakens painful separation experiences from their own childhood.

Babies and certainly infants as young as three months will react to the loss of their primary caregiver, usually by general distress and crying. The infant from six to eighteen months is very sensitive to separation from his mother and to her distress or grief. If she is grieving or he has prolonged separation from her, he may show considerable disturbance and vulnerability to subsequent losses.

Given appropriate circumstances, children as young as eighteen months to two years show sadness and longing for the lost person if there has been a strong emotional attachment. The two- to five-year-old child will not only ask for and cry for the lost person, but may also show anger and denial about the death. Yearning and protest, sadness and despair may appear. At this younger stage, the child shows an inability to conceptualize the finality of death. He may interpret the absence as rejection of him or sometimes as the fulfillment of his own angry feelings toward the dead person. He is concrete and wants to know where the dead person is. Although some children of this age understand the physical nature of death, many do not. Thus the child may believe, unless helped to understand otherwise, that the dead person is really alive somewhere else, somewhere from which he could return but does not.

The five- to eight-year-old has a greater understanding of the finality of death and its physical reality, but may also have more guilt, for his ambivalence to those he loves may be more pronounced, as may his capacity to blame himself or see things as a consequence of his wishes. Children in the latter part of this age span may be frightened because they become aware that they, too, could die. Nevertheless, children in this age can grieve and mourn, although they may defend against emotional release and use denial.

The older years of childhood bring responses nearer to those of the adult. The child of ten to twelve years has a greater awareness of the future and the differences he will experience because of the death. On the whole, responses often show denial, pretense, or the wish to believe the death has not occurred, yet also appropriate grief, sadness, and mourning for the lost person when there is opportunity for these to be expressed. The children's reactions to the loss will, however, always be complicated by their reactions to the grief and distress of parents and by the disruption of family life (see Raphael 1983).

Adolescents' reactions to bereavement are even more like those of adults but colored by the adolescent's developmental crisis and by peer and social expectations. The adolescent struggles to behave in an adult, "controlled" fashion, yet feels the fears and insecurity. Such emotions are to his thinking "childish." Others may criticize him if he does respond with grief or, again, if he doesn't. He is often expected to take up adult roles in support of a bereaved parent and may thus have to set his own grief aside. His peers are afraid of what has happened to him and find it difficult to offer any support about the death. He may act out the tensions of his grief and need in reckless behaviors or by attempts to console himself rather than dealing with the emotions directly. And he will be fearful of and reactive to the disruption of family life.

In short, children may react to the losses of disaster with typical patterns of grief and mourning. But often they do not, because their insecurity and the responses of others to them may lead to inhibition of the emotional release and to a blocking of the psychological processes of mourning.

Behavioral responses that may appear unrelated to grief are often the more frequent pattern. Thus children, especially boys, are likely to show an increase in aggressive behaviors. Regression is also frequent. Separation responses are pronounced, with exaggerated clinging, dependency, or demandingness. With withdrawal, another frequent pattern, the child seems "good" and "quiet," and his sadness and depression may not be realized. Sleep is often disturbed. Insecurity may appear as preoccupation with food and eating or a loss of appetite. The child fears being alone. Irritability is common. Stomachaches and headaches may reflect psychosomatic reactions.

BEREAVEMENT SYNDROMES

It is very likely that bereavement syndromes will appear in children who lose a primary and important person in a disaster, particularly a parent. As Bowlby (1980) has pointed out, much childhood bereavement may take on pathological forms, because of the child's immaturity, because of the difficulty others have in recognizing and responding to his needs, and perhaps also because of the possible impact of the deprivation and trauma on his development. This is especially true with respect to deaths in a disaster, which are so often sudden and unexpected, and have been shown to make the child's reaction more complicated and pathological (Raphael 1983). The fact that parental grief is more likely to be pathological also places the child at greater risk. The trauma is further compounded if the child personally experienced the impact or if he was involved in the circumstances of the death.

Studies of children after war bereavements indicate an increased likelihood of pathological bereavement syndromes (Elizur and Kaffman 1982); this is also the case for many children facing the personal disasters of bereavement (Raphael, Field, and Kvelde 1980). Elizur and Kaffman (1982) followed up twenty-five Israeli children whose fathers had died in the Yom

Kippur War in 1973. Assessments were made six months, eighteen months, and three-and-one-half years after the disaster. These workers defined the syndrome of pathological bereavement by the number and severity of symptomatic reactions, which were expressed in manifest behavior change after the father's death. Children were seen as having pathological bereavements when they had exceptional difficulties that disrupted their daily function in the family, at school, or with peers and when parent, teacher, and investigator were likely to agree on the child's need for professional help. Children who managed, despite stress, to adjust were said to have a normal bereavement.

These workers found the percentage of pathological bereavement to be high at six months and eighteen months and to have lessened only slightly by forty-two months. There was an average of nine handicapping problems per child, with problems tending to peak in the second year after the father's death. Nearly 70 percent of the children showed signs of severe emotional disturbance in at least one of the assessment phases, and about 40 percent showed criteria of pathological bereavement during all phases of the study. The reactions were subdivided into mourning reactions (crying, denial of the death as a fact, remembering responses, sadness, and yearning), which tended to decrease during the second year, and behavioral problems (representing a fight-flight style of coping with the pain and frustration), which persisted at a high level for the entire period. The behavioral problems tended to be of two main types—overanxious-dependent and unsocial-aggressive—but both modes were found in many children. These responses are represented as follows in figure 7.1:

FIGURE 7.1

Children's Response to War Bereavement

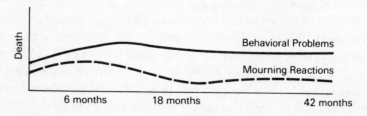

SOURCE: Based on data from E. Elizur and M. Kaffman, "Children's Bereavement Reactions Following the Death of a Father: 2," *Journal of the American Academy of Child Psychiatry* 21:474–80.

On the whole, those children with high levels of emotional impairment in the early months tended to develop the most serious and prolonged pathological bereavement.

This picture is very similar to that found in our own studies (Raphael

1983; Raphael et al. 1979b), where there were high symptom levels and distress for the majority of children following bereavement of parents, especially with unexpected and violent deaths. Similar findings appear from Bowlby's work (1980) on children separated from parents in war. The symptom pattern may vary from child to child or may distill out into specific disorders such as anxiety states and depression, as well as conduct disorders. The role of bereavement in disaster-related disorder has also been substantiated by McFarlane's (1985b) study where loss of someone in the family, one parent coming close to injury, or property loss added to the risk of pathology at follow-up. Bloch et al. (1956) also noted the contribution of bereavement to problems children developed after a tornado. For instance, eleven of the twelve children who had immediate family members killed or injured suffered emotional disorder.

Thus the bereavement experienced by children in disaster has in itself, and through its effects on those the child loves, a very significant impact.

THE CHILD'S EXPERIENCE OF DISLOCATION AND RELOCATION

The loss of home, a strange environment, the breakdown of family ritual, separation from parents, from familiar neighborhood and environment, and from school and friends, the loss of toys and treasures, and crowded and strange accommodations are all likely to be stressful for children in the post-disaster period. If these experiences are prolonged by evacuation and temporary shelter, especially if there are repeated disruptions and moves that affect school and family life, the impact on the child is likely to be substantial. An intervening variable of often critical significance is the way in which parents respond and how much they are able to reassure the child and deal with his emotional responses.

In the early post-disaster period, the child is likely to be "compliant" and "good," and the effects of the disaster and its changes do not appear to be significant. But the family tensions associated with dislocation soon take their effect, as do the child's own day-to-day experience and response to disaster traumas. As noted from work with children in other settings, repeated disruptions and parental disharmony are likely to be significant in contributing to the development of problems.

Reactions to dislocation and relocation are likely to be manifested in the child's behavior and are often not recognized for what they are. Irritability and aggressive syndromes, isolation and withdrawal, and particularly acting out are likely to appear. Somatizing reactions may also be present, as well as the common forms of emotional and conduct disorder. Separation fears, clinging, and demanding behavior may lead to negative responses from stressed parents, further complicating the child's feelings.

Disorder associated with dislocation and relocation stressors appears to follow the pattern of conduct and/or emotional disorder, as indicated by Bloch et al. (1956), McFarlane et al. (1985), and Tonge (1984). Tonge in particular emphasizes the role of ongoing but worsened parental dishармony in contributing to conduct disorder. He also notes the difficulties with therapy for such children. Bloch et al. (1956) emphasize the role of parental decompensation which was dissociative and demanding, and seemed to interfere with the child's capacity to integrate the reality of the disaster by failing to provide the necessary support and reassurance. Similarly, McFarlane (1985) has also found that ongoing disaster-related problems in the parents contribute to the child's disorder.

PERSONAL DISASTERS IN CHILDHOOD

It is the childhood experience of assault or *abuse* that probably most closely resembles the child's response to the death encounter and danger of disaster impact. A great many workers have researched child abuse and its impact on children's behavior and development (e.g., Oates 1984). Here, too, the child becomes fearful, anxious, and responsive to trigger reminders of the assaults. They may have the added terror of repetition, and the child may become preoccupied with avoidance. Green (1983) sees such response as a post-traumatic disorder in these children.

A range of other situations may produce similar response to death and danger. Children's involvement in motor vehicle accidents and other reactions to witnessing murder of a parent have been described in this context, including both post-traumatic reactions and bereavement responses.

Bereavements such as the death of a parent or sibling, especially when unexpected (for example, through accident or massive heart attack), seem likely to produce considerable personal disaster responses (Furman 1974; Raphael et al. 1980; Raphael 1983).

Dislocation and relocation are reflected in events such as repeated moves or the placing of a child in foster care or even in a boarding school or institution. Such frequent dislocations have been shown to create emotional problems for children, as have the disturbances of family harmony that are often associated.

CHILDREN'S COPING WITH DISASTER

Attachments and relationships with family, teachers, and friends will be very important in helping the child's coping in the post-disaster period. The reassurance of love and care in family life appear primary; when this is disrupted by separation, especially in the early days after the disaster, problems are more likely to result (e.g., McFarlane 1983). This was also noted with war stress effects (e.g., Bowlby 1952): children developed symptoms of anxiety and behavioral disturbance when evacuated to peaceful areas, and these symptoms improved only when the child was reunited with his family in the war-torn city. Children seem to especially need to be with family members and need demonstrations of their love and physical closeness. They also need parents to accept their regressive behaviors, especially in the early stages, and to comfort them without making demands. Later they may need the reassurance of discipline from parents and a return to the normal expectations of family life. However, the need for reassurance in the form of physical closeness and factual information about what is happening cannot be overemphasized. This has been found with children following the Ash Wednesday fires and the Darwin cyclone; it is described by Bloch's (1956) group, as well as by Fraser (1973) in his study of responses to Belfast riots. When significant relationships have been lost, whether because of death, injury and hospitalization, or dislocation, the child's needs for care from his other important attachment figures will be particularly great. If parents are so distraught from their own grief or psychological traumatization or from the burdens of the relocation and recovery, then they may require support so as to be able to meet the child's needs. The family as a unit may strengthen through the disaster experience and so be better able to meet the needs of members for emotional support; but, if it does not, it may require assistance or the children may need to seek their reassurance and closeness from other relationships. Teachers are very important to school-age children in this context, and the world of school with its regulation and discipline may be reassuring. Teachers may also offer empathic emotional support to individual children with whom they have a relationship. As with parents, however, this may not be possible if the teacher is too overwhelmed by his own experience or by fears of the child's emotional distress.

Efforts toward mastery come in a number of different ways. Older children and even many younger ones attempt to ask questions about their experience and sort out what has happened. As with adults, information is of vital importance to them from the period of anticipation on. Younger children often fear they have somehow caused the disaster. For example, one child thought he had "turned on the tornado," another that his playing with a candle had made the "world burn." Or they may simply not know what is happening; thus the child experiencing an earthquake thought "the world was sliding into the sea." Providing factual explanations and allowing the child to discuss his fears and theories helps his mastery of the situation.

Talking through will not be the main mechanism of young children who have difficulty verbalizing their feelings and experience: they will, through play, work out some of their experience. If not just repetitive traumatic reenactment, play gives the child the opportunity to do things better and to lose some of the fear and helplessness. Drawing or painting the experience is valuable in this context too (see figure 7.2). For adolescents, writing it out as an essay, or as some sort of testimonial or review, may be similarly helpful. Within groups, play, discussion, and even formal playacting can help toward mastery. It is also useful for children if they can help others (while still being able to lean on parents) and carry out age-appropriate practical tasks toward recovery.

Children may need to be able to review and question the event and to understand the deaths and losses that have occurred. Thus, they may gain mastery from attending the funeral of a family member who has died or from being able to share in discussion of the death with family, rather than being falsely protected from realities they must ultimately integrate. Important in parents' interactions with children toward such mastery are consistency and lack of confusion (Silber et al. 1957). As Frazer (1973) notes, children may need quite a bit of encouragement to talk about their fears and experience, and this may be helped by asking them about the reactions of other children, such as brothers and sisters as well. It may be very helpful if, while recognizing and responding to the child's distress, parents or others

FIGURE 7.2
A Child's Drawing of Bushfires

SOURCE: Drawing courtesy of Dr. H. Julie Jones, Royal Children's Hospital, Melbourne, Australia
Reprinted by permission.

168

can convey the optimistic expectation that the child is competent to handle the stress (Yates 1983).

Emotional response and release may be particularly difficult for the child to achieve. He needs to be able to share and let out his fears, longing, and sadness, as well as anger, in manageable amounts so that he does not feel overwhelmed by them. This may happen through interactions with parents or through play and drawings, but it may not. The younger child, with less capacity to monitor and control his feelings, may be particularly vulnerable to being overwhelmed by them and may even be traumatized in subtle ways that leave him at risk for the future. The pain of bereavement may be particularly frightening for the child if a parent dies. Children are likely to be intermittent in the release of such feelings, and as Elizur and Kaffman (1982) note, many use various defensive measures to lessen the acute pain and assimilate the loss gradually. Younger children may do this by denying the finality of the death, older children by withdrawal and ignoring the subject. In any case, the child copes by gradually sharing his fears and distress in some relationship or interpersonal environment that gives him the emotional support to do so.

As with adults, feeling hope about the future is often a part of coping, although children probably need to have internalized at least some good experiences to experience this feeling. Newman (1976) noted that such hope was more prominent in the children of Buffalo Creek than in their distressed and disturbed parents. However, to sustain it the child probably needs to see some stability in his environment and to sense that the rest of his family feels that good times and feelings will return.

Children's coping may be at risk if they are vulnerable from previous traumas and from preexisting parenting problems. The stress of the disaster may affect the child-parent dyad in different ways. Its intensity is very likely to significantly affect the child's coping, for if it is extremely severe, the child's experience is likely to have been bad and his parents are likely to be suffering from ongoing effects, which may make them unable to meet his needs. Then, ongoing disturbance or family disharmony may be the intervening factor leading to the child's failure to cope. As already mentioned, some suggest that younger children are more vulnerable (e.g., Milne 1977; McFarlane 1983), while others suggest that older children are (e.g., Bloch et al. 1956; Frazer 1973). It seems most likely that different children are affected in different ways and that, if the parents are very disturbed, the younger child, in particular, may have few other resources to help him. Boys and girls seem equally affected in most studies. Those who have had to take parental roles because parents cannot cope may have difficulties. But ultimately it seems that the severity of the stress, and particularly its impact on the family, will be the main variables that affect children's coping with disaster. And for the most part, children, like adults, show considerable resilience in their recovery from such trauma.

FAMILIES IN DISASTER

Families have particular significance in disaster. The stress of the threat or impact will intensify the bonds between members and often the family will respond as one unit—a system. This system has flexible boundaries, open to interaction with other systems in the recovery process, either systems of extended kin or organizations that provide necessary aid and resources. Family interactions and responses have been studied in a number of disasters (Drabek et al. 1975; Drabek and Key 1976; Drabek and Boggs 1968; Erickson et al. 1976; Bolin 1976, 1982; Trost and Hultaker 1983).

At the time of *threat,* families attempt to come together and confront the disaster as a unit with mutual protection and planned courses of action. Decisions are made within the family about appropriate responses, one of which may be the response of evacuation—a decision rapidly reinforced and carried out by members when together. The family unit often evacuates to kin outside the disaster area or may go to other family members within the impact area to weather out the disaster together. The function of the family as a unit may be helpful to the overall disaster responses if its actions are appropriate, but may create difficulties if they are not, for instance, if the family refuses to evacuate from an approaching flood. The family is likely to evacuate or leave in the family vehicle and to try to get as near as possible to other family members and neighbors at the place of evacuation, reconstituting a familiar social system. There is likely to be distress if members are separated and intense behavior directed toward bringing them together, even at the personal risk to life.

During *impact* the family behaves as a unit primarily directed toward its own survival. Help during any prolonged impact such as a blizzard (e.g., Perry et al. 1983) is directed first toward family members. In a brief impact disaster, family activity is likely to be directed toward staying together and avoiding injury and death.

In the *immediate post-disaster phase,* families as units will be primarily concerned with the rescue and safety of members, but will then help friends and even strangers. Desperate searching for trapped or absent members is likely, and it may be virtually impossible to keep members away from the disaster site if they fear someone is still trapped or injured there, or if they are dead. Protection of the youngest and most vulnerable members seems foremost.

For the *longer-term aspects of recovery,* family units tend to turn to one another and extended kin for shelter and support, aid, and other resources. Formal organizations such as the Red Cross, the Salvation Army, and religious groups may provide what relatives cannot. Some studies suggest that families of lower socioeconomic status may rely more on these bodies. The family response may be heavily influenced by social and cultural variables, such as resignation to fate or perception of control of the world as being external to the self. Some family structures may be more vulnerable, such as those with single (especially female) parents.

Factors influencing the recovery of families in the fullest sense have been studied extensively by Bolin (1982). Examining response to a tornado disaster, Bolin concluded that a number of factors influenced recovery. Bereavements of family or close friends were likely to be associated with a lower level of recovery. Relocation, with frequent moves, was associated with reduced leisure, continued personal upsets over the disaster, and strained family relationships. Emotional effects for the victim families tended to be persistent. Thirty-five percent of the families had not gotten over upsets due to the storm eighteen months after the disaster. But despite the many strains, especially among those who had experienced major losses, the vast majority of family ties were strengthened. Contrary to expectations, the elderly seemed, for the most part, less severely affected. Storm-related anxiety, sleep disturbance, and bad dreams tended to persist for those who had had intense exposure to the tornado, particularly if friends, neighbors, or family were injured or killed, or if there had been little warning and greater shock effect. The common response, as in many other disasters, was along the following lines:

"It is a once in a lifetime experience and makes you place more importance on human relationships and less on material possessions."

"We feel closer as a family" (Bolin 1982, p. 131).

This is, of course, quite different from findings after the Buffalo Creek disaster (Titchener et al. 1976), where families perceived major impairment in their functioning. Similarly, a victim of the Ash Wednesday fires commented, "Our family just isn't the same anymore. We can't seem to talk to one another, everybody's shut off in their own world. Things will never be the same again."

In Bolin's study, family recovery seemed to be affected by bereavement, material losses, and extended stresses. Larger families were more vulnerable to stress aspects of the experience, but the older and better educated seemed less vulnerable. Support networks helped mitigate these stresses. Higher income also seemed to make things easier for affected families, as has been noted in other studies and as is hardly surprising, for such families usually have many more resources to call upon in the face of crisis.

Bolin classifies recovery into four types: emotional recovery, economic recovery, housing recovery, and quality of life recovery. Using his tornado data, he attempted a path analysis to discover the contributors to recovery. He found a number of interactive variables to be important in a general model, as shown in figure 7.3.

Bolin concluded that economic recovery had the largest causal effect on emotional recovery. But this finding may have been particularly relevant to a disaster such as the one he studied, where life loss and injury were not substantial, where death encounter and bereavement were not great, and where housing, shelter, and daily life issues predominated. Bolin's diagram may, in fact, represent more the path of family recovery from relocation stressors than from the range of disaster traumas.

The effects of disaster on families are many, and the intricacies of family dynamics may be thrown into relief by the stress produced by the impact and aftermath and the need for different coping patterns. It may be that some family members are allowed certain roles during and after the disaster and others are not. Such patterns often have a function. For example, the person allowed to be afraid during impact may carry the fear for the family.

FIGURE 7.3
Family Recovery

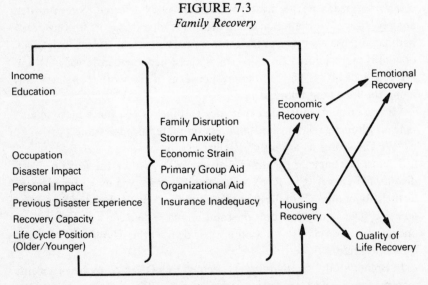

SOURCE: Loosely adapted from R. C. Bolin, *Long-term Family Recovery from Disaster,* Monograph No. 36 (Boulder: University of Colorado, Institute of Behavioral Science, 1982).

The person who becomes anxious, cautious, and preparatory in response to warning may, by doing so, allow the rest of the family their feelings of invulnerability. The member who is shocked and distressed after the impact may be the one who is allocated the role of receiving care, thus allowing the rest of the family to maintain its sense of strength and coping. Conflict of roles may create difficulties, as, for instance, in cases when the person who is supposed to be brave is afraid, and the one who is supposed to be sick is well. Similarly, children who take over adult roles during and after the disaster may be vulnerable. It is also difficult for others, especially those fulfilling adult roles, to have needs for regression and care met.

The impact of the distress of some members on the functioning of others may have considerable implications for family dynamics and stability. The distress of parents is likely to be a source of upset for children (McFarlane et al. 1985), as is the disturbance of children for parents (Milne 1977; Bolin 1982). Parents are likely to be overprotective, and children testing. Between husbands and wives, marital harmony and intimacy may be threatened, because of a need to avoid the topic of the disaster, or because of psychic numbing and other reactions or disturbances that have resulted. Self-medication, alcohol, and acting out are likely to be further detrimental to family functioning. Stresses of dislocation and relocation, especially the disruption of normal family life and the impairment of networks (Bolin 1982; Erikson 1976), are likely to further mitigate against the recovery of individual members and the family as a unit.

And it is the children who in so many ways will reflect and respond to stresses in the family system following disaster. Their recovery may symbolize the recovery of their family, or their problems may reflect dysfunction that still exists.

THE ELDERLY IN DISASTER

Those who have studied disaster have looked at the responses of different sectors and groups in the community and have often theorized that some groups might be more vulnerable than others. Women with young children, children, adolescents, and the elderly have all been considered in this context in different studies.

The elderly are often seen as being particularly vulnerable. It has been suggested that they are more attached to place and slower to move from it in response to warning or that they may find recovery more difficult, especially if they have lost the home and possessions of a lifetime. As noted earlier, Bolin's studies suggested that they were, in fact, less vulnerable, with older victims tending to show better recovery in many instances after the tornado than younger victims. This pattern is substantiated by the work of Bell et al. (1978), who found that older tornado victims were less anxiety-ridden than younger victims, resolved their anxiety earlier, had fewer associated physical and emotional stress reactions, had less disruption of family and social network interaction, and reported improved relations with relatives and friends. They found the aged placed fewer demands on service agencies, as did Poulshock and Cohen (1975) in a study of aged flood victims who had suffered major dislocation.

All of these findings are contrary to the expectations held about the aged, who, because of their general ill health, lack of mobility, and lower incomes, are seen as more at risk. And, in fact, Bolin and Klenow (1982–83) show that many studies do highlight difficulties among the aged. They may be less likely to perceive a situation as hazardous and to heed warnings and evacuate. Thus, they may be more vulnerable to death, injury, and loss. A number of studies suggest that they are overrepresented among the dead, so that those who do survive may be the stronger. They may be in need of aid and rehabilitation after a disaster, because there is much to indicate that they suffer greater losses and show slower economic recovery, yet may be relatively neglected because they are slow to demand or complain. Emotional problems have been described for this group in some studies, but others have not found such problems. It seems in any case the elderly are hesitant to identify their problems and less likely to seek help and use services available to them.

Bolin and Klenow themselves found that the elderly in their study did not suffer more losses but did perceive themselves as more severely affected. More of the elderly suffered injury and death, however, and this may have added to their sense of deprivation. As with other studies, it was found that the older people did underutilize aid from most significant sources, including their primary groups. Although the elderly showed a lower incidence of emotional and family problems than did the younger victims, their rate of emotional recovery was much the same: both groups reported significant levels of lasting emotional effects from the disastrous storm. And, as a group, the older people showed slower economic recovery, perhaps because of their greater economic vulnerability, as well as their underutilization of aid.

In conclusion, then, the old may be slow to accept the realities of disaster threat and may be injured or killed as a consequence. As survivors, they may suffer many dislocations and considerable economic difficulty. But they seem to "make the best" of the situation and they do not complain. Their emotional hurt may go deep, but they tend to suffer it quietly, often failing to use resources that might be available to help with their economic and emotional needs. This tendency is evident in the comments of one older woman: "It was terrible, awful, and we lost everything we had. I'll never get over it in some ways. But it was worse for the young ones—it was such a shock—they're just starting in life and everything. Bill and me—we've had our lives and we've gone through bad times before—we'll make it. And we don't want to be no trouble to anyone. Not our kids or anyone else. We'll manage."

PART II

Caring for the Victims

CHAPTER 8

The Problems of Mental Health and Adjustment

"These figures represent the immediate casualties: damage to the minds of the survivors can never be calculated" (Stretton, *The Furious Days: The Relief of Darwin*).

The experience of disaster, whether of a major disaster affecting the whole community or a personal disaster affecting only the individual and his family, inevitably tests coping ability and brings forth varied behavioral responses. There may be distress associated with the experience itself and with the process of adjustment to its consequences. This distress may be so great as to lead to dysfunction, impairment, disturbance, disorder, or disease. Or, it may be brief and reactive, settling in the early days or weeks after the experience. And for some people, the challenge of disaster, even though distressing, seems to lead to a new and positive process of life adaptation.

There is a need for further systematic study of disasters in order to understand the levels and patterns of disorder that may follow and the factors that correlate with such morbidity. In this way, we will be able to both understand increased vulnerability and protect against morbidity.

A number of valuable review papers have attempted to address the issue of post-disaster morbidity, starting with that of Kinston and Rosser (1974), Perry and Lindell (1978), and, more recently, Chamberlin (1980). Many studies are bedeviled by their lack of appropriate methodology, their descriptive and retrospective nature, and a failure to use control populations and careful criteria of morbidity. A further difficulty arises from the frequent failure to define the outcome criteria, and whether or not distress or disease is being studied. Nevertheless, in very recent years, there have been some important studies, from which a number of consistent patterns appear.

A recently established International Study Group for Disaster Psychiatry has addressed many of the methodological problems in the field and has attempted to develop a core methodology for future research (Raphael, Weisæth, and Lundin 1984). Collaboration between such bodies, the Center for Mental Health Studies of Emergencies of the National Institutes of Mental Health (NIMH) and the World Health Organization (WHO), should contribute to the development of a data base for disaster-related psychosocial morbidity. A further issue that has complicated studies in this field is the lack of and need for ethical constraints when investigating distressed populations (Singh 1984). Moreover, the use of "hard" data from social indices, hospital admissions, and records is often problematic, because the disruption of disasters may lead to considerable community breakdown. Such statistics may have meaning only when there is little disruption of services, as in Adams and Adams' study (1984) of the Mount St. Helen's ashfall or Bennet's (1978) study of the Bristol floods.

In dealing with disaster-related morbidity, it is necessary to consider a multitude of aspects. These include the reactive responses to the disaster stressors: early patterns of distress and disturbance; established patterns and levels of morbidity in health and social terms; common symptom patterns; psychiatric syndromes associated with disaster, including the "disaster syndrome"; post-traumatic stress disorder, bereavement pathologies, psychic numbing, and other survivor syndromes; responses of those with preexisting psychiatric morbidity; psychosomatic disorder, physical ailments, and mortality arising from disaster stress; and protective factors that may lessen the likelihood of pathological outcome. Special aspects also need to be considered, such as reactive responses of children, of the injured, and social indices of morbidity for the community.

REACTIVE RESPONSES TO DISASTER STRESSORS

It is clear from all those who have observed or been involved in disasters that many behaviors that are "different" from normal appear in response to the disaster and in the period immediately after. There are many emotional reactions, and most people experience at least some. The "disaster syndrome" of stunned, dazed, and apparently disengaged behavior has been described as a response to impact and immediate aftermath. It is said to occur in perhaps 25 percent of those affected by disaster. Wallace (1956) has suggested that this syndrome is most likely when there has been utter devastation of the victim's environment. The reaction usually settles within hours or, at most, days, although in rare cases it is prolonged and becomes a psychic numbing or other severe disorder.

Anxiety or anxiety-related reactions are extremely common. They may continue from the high arousal that comes with impact or, more often, emerge after a latent period of a few hours or days. These reactions have been most thoroughly studied by Weisæth (1983, 1984), in victims of the Norwegian paint factory fire. Weisæth found that of those who were exposed to the disaster, more than 90 percent experienced an anxiety reaction within five hours of rescue. He called this a "traumatic anxiety syndrome," "a normal stress reaction to danger trauma" (p. 417), which included repeated attacks of anxiety, anxiety-induced sleep disturbances, startle reactions, and fears of approaching or staying at the site of the disaster. Those most severely exposed (his "A" group) experienced these reactions to a clinical, symptomatic degree. Weisæth felt that other symptoms at this time were secondary, either actually induced by the anxiety or, as in the case of social withdrawal, aimed at protecting the individual against being overwhelmed by the anxiety. Irritability, depression, guilt, and shame were also secondary and much less frequent at this stage.

Weisæth found that 43 percent of those most directly exposed had symptoms and impairment equivalent to post-traumatic stress disorder at one week after the explosion. Of those who were not directly exposed only 25 percent had such traumatic anxiety symptoms. Of the control group (workers who had not been at the factory but who had seen the explosion) only 10 percent had such symptoms. Certain anxiety symptoms tended to improve in the first week, especially sleep disturbance, fear of the area, and anxiety itself. Nevertheless, others, such as social withdrawal and irritability, increased, and mean anxiety measures were also generally raised. Only a few delayed reactions of disorder appeared, however. Although more than 20 percent showed impairment of their work function during the early weeks, early return to work and social cooperation were seen as helping them to cope. It is interesting to note that many people who saw the explosion and suffered the trauma of not knowing what had happened to their family members also suffered from anxiety symptoms, especially those related to the people who were in greatest danger. Spouses showed anxiety responses and their children regressive symptoms.

A number of workers have used Goldberg's (1978) General Health Questionnaire (GHQ) to examine reactions in terms of a measure of general psychological dysfunction, with cutoff points denoting the likelihood of being a psychiatric case. Parker (1977) showed 58 percent of Darwin evacuees to be stressed to "caseness level" during the week following their evacuation after the cyclone. Seventy percent of women in his sample were so affected. This decreased to 41 percent at ten weeks post-disaster. With victims of Cyclone Osca in Fiji, Fairley (1984) showed a GHQ decrement from 45 percent of the population at eight weeks to 19 percent at twelve weeks. Patrick and Patrick (1981) estimated a diminution in anxiety and distress from 70 percent of the cyclone-affected population they studied in Sri Lanka to 46 percent at the end of four weeks. Other studies have examined the decrement of reaction over longer periods of time. The percentage reacting over the first week seems to vary from 70 percent or more to 20 percent, in large part correlating with the severity of the experience. Levels may remain high in the early weeks, at least for general reactions. Then, by ten weeks, there is usually a significant drop, with a gradual ongoing decrease over the first year (see figure 8.1).

This picture is not dissimilar to that seen using the General Health Questionnaire following personal disasters such as bereavement (Vachon et al. 1982) and involvement in motor vehicle accidents, or other stressful life events (Singh et al. 1985).

Other reactive patterns of behavior, which have been described but not systematically studied, are disinhibited and antisocial behaviors. Usually evident only in the immediate post-disaster period, these may include looting, stealing, aggression, promiscuity, sexual acting out, and heavy drinking. Most give way rapidly to increased social controls and stricter moral standards, as if to purify, and to prevent further "punishment" from the disaster.

Psychophysiological reactions are also not infrequent in the immediate post-disaster phase, especially vomiting, churning feelings in the stomach, diarrhea, and physiological concomitants of anxiety such as palpitations. These, too, are usually transient, as both Fairley (1984) and Parker (1977) have documented.

Mr. A., twenty-seven, was married with two children. He was in the first carriage of a train that crashed. Although trapped and slightly injured, he was eventually able to free himself and walk away. He recalls being terrified by the shock of impact and being able to coolly and automatically appraise his situation and struggle out through the wreckage. He was shocked to see blood pouring down his arm, which was

FIGURE 8.1
Disturbance Over Time

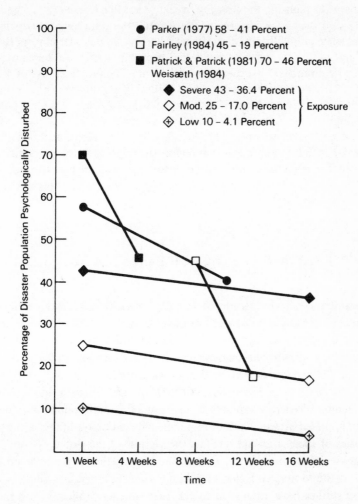

● Parker (1977) 58 – 41 Percent
□ Fairley (1984) 45 – 19 Percent
■ Patrick & Patrick (1981) 70 – 46 Percent
Weisæth (1984)
◆ Severe 43 – 36.4 Percent ⎫
◇ Mod. 25 – 17.0 Percent ⎬ Exposure
⊕ Low 10 – 4.1 Percent ⎭

Percentage of Disaster Population Psychologically Disturbed

Time
1 Week   4 Weeks   8 Weeks   12 Weeks   16 Weeks

superficially lacerated, for he had felt no pain and did not realize he was injured. Once he sat down, he felt overwhelmed by feelings of panic— his heart raced, he was sweating, and his hands shook. He vomited. Waves of panic came over him in the days that followed. He could not return to work and felt terrified of ever traveling on the train again. Intrusive memories of the train, the feelings of panic and helplessness, and the shock would overwhelm him. He felt he wanted to avoid anything that would remind him of what happened and anyone who might ask him about it, yet he had an urge to talk of his experience again and again. His sleep was disturbed by nightmares in which he relived the shock and entrapment and from which he would awake, screaming as he had been unable to do at the time. Gradually the dreams and panic lessened. The levels were high for the first few weeks, but after friends drove him to work and then took him to regularly catch the train again, his painful experience gradually receded. His wife had been able to let him share his feelings with her, and his friends had been supportive and encouraging when he discussed his experience with them. The practical task of work and his own attempts at coping by ventilating his thoughts and feelings helped his recovery. Most of his symptoms had settled by three months, although if the train stopped suddenly or he heard a loud crash, they would be briefly renewed. He felt the whole experience had somehow strengthened him and made him realize the importance of his family life and that overall the positives were what had brought him through it.

PATTERNS AND LEVELS OF DISASTER MORBIDITY

Post-traumatic stress disorder has only recently been systematically defined, on the basis of Horowitz's work (1976) and operational criteria such as DSM-III. Many of the symptoms found after disaster were classified as traumatic neurosis in earlier descriptive studies that attempted to assess morbidity following disaster. Epidemiological studies of post-disaster psychiatric morbidity are chiefly those of the Bristol and Brisbane floods, Three Mile Island, Weisæth's valuable assessment of a total population after a factory fire, McFarlane's studies of people affected by bushfires, a number of studies of specific groups such as the victims of the Buffalo Creek and Kentucky nightclub disasters, and, more recently, the longer-term studies following the Mount St. Helen's ashfall (Tatum, Vollmer, and Shore 1985).

Most studies have attempted to compare disaster problems with those existing beforehand if there is background information about pre-disaster levels of problems, or with control populations who have similar background factors but have been not exposed to the disaster or have been exposed only to a minor degree. Such studies have, for the most part, addressed general levels of morbidity and complaint, and some have included data on health-care utilization. The general levels of morbidity that can be derived from studies that have attempted to quantify morbidity in the first, second, and subsequent years post-disaster are summarized in figure 8.2.

As can be seen, morbidity levels tend to cluster around 30–40 percent

FIGURE 8.2

Levels of Impairment in First and Second Years Following Disaster

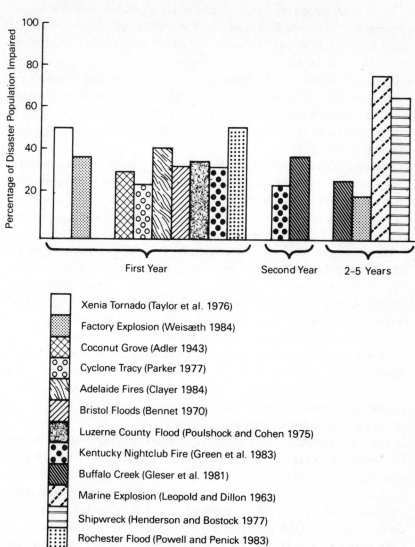

(with systematic measures) at one year, with about 20% (a small sample) near normal population levels and others nearer 50% of the populations sampled. At two years, levels are generally less but with a persistent level of morbidity that seems to have become chronic for some individuals and some disasters. Disasters that are man-made and with high shock and destruction, such as Buffalo Creek, show persisting levels of over 30 percent severe impairment, and some, such as one marine explosion, as much as 71 percent.

These levels are, on the whole, general levels of psychological distress and impairment. More specific evaluations of morbidity patterns have examined mortality, psychosomatic illness, mental health problems, physical symptomatology, consultation-based health-care utilization, hospital admissions and alcohol and drug usage. Some of these findings for major community and personal disasters are summarized in table 8.1 and comparison is made with the personal disaster of bereavement. Mental health problems, as defined by a range of different measures, are shown as increased in all these systematic studies.

What constituted the bulk of this increase in mental health problems? Descriptive studies have shown that a range of symptoms are commonly reported, as have some of the systematic investigations. The commonly reported symptoms from those studies in which there has been systematic evaluation are listed in table 8.2.

The diagnostic categories these symptoms represent are clear in only a few instances. For instance, Weisæth (1984) described a prevalence of posttraumatic stress disorder of 36.4 percent in his most severely affected group after seven months, with 17 percent in the other disaster group and 4.1 percent in the control group. There was only one other case of any other disorder in his population, and it was unrelated to the disaster.

Bromet et al. (1982a) showed that within two months or so of Three Mile Island mothers of young children were at greater risk for developing episodes of anxiety and depression, especially if they perceived the incident as a source of danger. A number developed new cases of these disorders, as evaluated by diagnostic interview (SADS).

After the cyclone in Fiji, Fairley (1973) also examined those considered by General Health Questionnaire scoring and general interview assessment to be psychiatric cases. He found that of the thirteen cases detected in the group of seventy-five, six showed post-traumatic stress disorder, three major depression, one bipolar affective disorder, and three mixed anxiety and depression, all by DSM-III criteria.

As indicated in table 8.2, depressive reactions and symptoms are frequent. Popovic and Petrovick (1964) note that depression appeared after the Skopje earthquake, as did some transient physical problems, confusional states, and psychosomatic reactions.

The survivors of the shipwreck studied by Henderson and Bostock (1977) showed, in five cases out of seven, severe ongoing impairment, much of it with a depressive quality, as have the survivors of two night club fires in Sweden and the United States (Lundin 1984b; Green et al. 1983). Studies

TABLE 8.1
Significant Health Morbidity in Disaster-Affected Populations (as Shown in Controlled Studies)

Community Disaster	Mortality	Psycho-somatic	Mental Health problems	Physical symptoms	Health-care utilization	Hospital admission	Alcohol/drug use
Mount St. Helen's ashfall	↑18.6%	↑100+%	↑236%	↑200%	↑21%	↓7.2%	↑20%
Adelaide fires	↑	↑45%	↑300%				↑104%
Bristol floods	—		↑	↑	↑	↑	
Brisbane floods			↑	↑	↑		
Three Mile Island			↑(Mothers)				
Factory explosion			↑Post-traumatic Stress Syndrome				
Earthquake, Greece	↑Heart		↑			↑	
Flood, New York				↑Leukemia, ↑Miscarriage			
Cyclone, Darwin			↑				
Cyclone, Fiji			↑	↑			
Cyclone, Sri Lanka			↑	↑			
Hurricane Agnes flood	↑		↑	↑	↑	↑	↑
Personal disaster bereavement	↑	↑	↑		↑	↑	↑

NOTE: Mount St. Helen's (Adams and Adams 1984) — Flood, New York (Janerich et al. 1981)
Adelaide fires (Clayer 1984) — Cyclone, Darwin (Parker 1977)
Bristol floods (Bennet 1970) — Cyclone, Fiji (Fairley 1984)
Brisbane floods (Abrahams et al. 1976) — Cyclone, Sri Lanka (Patrick and Patrick 1981)
Three Mile Island (Houts et al. 1984) — Hurricane Agnes floods (Logue et al. 1979; Zusman 1976)
Factory explosion (Weisæth 1984) — Bereavement (Raphael 1983)
Earthquake, Greece (Trichopoulos et al. 1983)

TABLE 8.2

Commonly Reported Symptoms in Disaster Studies

Community Disaster	Anxiety	Fears	Nervousness	Sleep	Nightmares	Fatigue	Gastro-intestinal Symptoms	Headaches	Withdrawal	Irritability, Anger	Work Function Impaired	Depression	Physical Illness	Sedative Use	Alcohol Use
Bristol floods	X			X			X	X		X		X			
Brisbane floods			X				X	X		X		X	X	X	X
Hurricane Agnes floods	X					X								X	X
Rochester floods	X		X	X	X			X				X	X		
Buffalo Creek	X		X	X	X					X		X		X	X
Cyclone, Sri Lanka	X	X							X			X			X
Cyclone, Fiji	X	X	X				X	X	X				X		
Cyclone, Darwin	X												X		
Three Mile Island	X											X			
Factory explosion	X	X		X	X				X	X		X			
Adelaide fires	X	X	X	X	X			X		X	X	X	X	X	
Skywalk, Kansas	X	X	X	X						X		X			
Night club fire, Sweden	X			X	X					X		X			
Personal disaster bereavement	X		X	X		X	X	X	X	X	X	X	X	X	X

NOTE: Bristol floods (Bennet 1970) — Cyclone, Darwin (Parker 1977)
Brisbane floods (Abrahams et al. 1976) — Three Mile Island (Bromet et al. 1982)
Hurricane Agnes floods (Logue et al. 1979) — Factory explosion (Weiseth 1984)
Rochester floods (Powell and Penick 1983) — Adelaide fire (Clayer 1984; McFarlane 1985a)
Buffalo Creek (Gleser et al. 1981) — Skywalk, Kansas (Wilkinson 1983)
Cyclone, Sri Lanka (Patrick and Patrick 1981) — Night club, Sweden (Lundin 1984b)
Cyclone, Fiji (Fairley 1984) — Bereavement (Raphael 1983)

after the Brisbane floods showed considerable evidence of depressive symptomatology as well. Special disaster syndromes, such as those following Buffalo Creek, Hiroshima, and the Holocaust, all evidenced high levels of depressive symptoms. Depression to suicidal level was noted following the Sri Lanka cyclone. Transient situational disturbances of mixed anxiety and depression are probably not uncommon. They are exemplified in the case described by Grant et al. (1975) following the Darwin cyclone and in Boman's (1974) description of cases after the Granville rail disaster.

However, more prolonged reactions of anxiety, whether specific post-traumatic stress disorder or other anxiety conditions, seem to follow the disaster reaction. These may lead to high levels of residual disability, for example, 71 percent of the marine disaster survivors studied by Leopold and Dillon (1963). The anxiety spectrum includes phobias, post-traumatic reactions, panic and general anxiety state, and mixed anxiety depression; their specific patterns and levels have not been systematically studied in many disasters, although Weisæth, Parker, Fairley, and the Patricks all found significant levels of general anxiety responses.

More specific symptom clusters have been described for specific disasters, for instance, the "Buffalo Creek Syndrome" (Gleser et al. 1981) of depression, somatic concerns, belligerence, agitation, social isolation, and changes in routine and leisure. Sleep disturbance was also prominent, as was the survivors' preoccupation with water and death. Survivor guilt and shame, a sense of meaninglessness and helplessness, unresolved grief, and anger are all described as prominent (Titchener et al. 1976). Other survivor syndromes described include the conflict, guilt, and shame over not having saved others, as was felt following the North Sea oil rig disaster, and the more potent and entrenched problems of many of the concentration camp survivors. Psychic numbing, or the cutting off of feeling, has been one such effect that has been found to a greater or lesser extent in many disaster studies.

The pathology found may be clearly related to the disaster, either by its symptomatology, as with post-traumatic stress disorder, or by time relationship. A study that attempted to refine the differences between severe psychiatric illnesses precipitated by a disaster and those occurring coincidentally involved victims of a Rumanian earthquake. Predescu and Niga-Udangiu (1979) studied those victims they considered earthquake disordered (i.e., who had been psychiatrically healthy before) and those for whom the earthquake seemed to complicate or worsen preexisting disorder. They were able to show that both groups of patients had similar patterns of disorder. However, those whose disorders were believed to have been caused by the earthquake had significantly greater levels of bereavement, property and home loss, and involvement with the earthquake generally, and had lower levels of disorder in their families, that is, less predisposition. The authors also noted that there was a lower general utilization of psychiatric hospitals in the early days, perhaps due to the priority of somatic emergencies. The patients whose disorder had been precipitated by the earthquake tended to have a better prognosis. However, these authors do not comment on levels of disorder, either incidence or prevalence.

The following case history reflects some of the morbidity that can be found in this general sense.

Mrs. K. was forty-one. She and her daughter were caught in forest fires, and their home was damaged but not totally destroyed. She was shocked by her experience but not injured. She was anxious initially and involved herself in organizing the repair of her home. Her anxiety symptoms seemed to settle after two or three weeks. All seemed well until about ten weeks afterward when she became increasingly tearful, lost interest in food, and had trouble sleeping and upsetting dreams of the fire. She felt constantly irritable and angry, especially with her husband, who had been away from home at the time of the fires and did not seem to realize what she had suffered. She suffered from churning feelings in her stomach, nausea, and repeated headaches. When her local doctor suggested that her condition might have some relationship to the disaster, she insisted that she was "over all that," that others had been "much worse and lost everything." As her symptomatology worsened, she was finally persuaded to see a psychiatrist and diagnosed as suffering from a major depressive disorder. During therapy it became obvious that the losses she had suffered had reawakened feelings from earlier deprivation, as well as guilt that she had not taken further precautions. The lack of support and her own coping style of denying and repressing her anger had added to her disturbance. She responded well to therapy in this, her only depressive episode.

RELATIONSHIP TO MORBIDITY OF PARTICULAR DISASTER STRESSORS

When the different stressor components of the disaster experience are examined alongside the disaster pathology, their contribution to the development of this pathology, in terms of severity and levels, may be seen. In some instances, it is even possible to define the very specific effects of particular stressors. Table 8.3 gives the general contribution of such stressors in studies where they have been evaluated.

It is critical to note that in the majority of these studies the *severity of the stressor* (for example, threat or loss) *has been strongly correlated with the severity of the pathology or reaction engendered,* although other vulnerability factors are also important.

Much of the material presented here has been described in discussions of the specific stressors, the reactions to them, and the syndromes that develop. This will not be repeated; rather, the reader is referred to death, shock, destruction, and survival stressors and effects in chapter 4; loss and grief stressor effects in chapter 5; and dislocation and relocation stressor effects in chapter 6. The main clear-cut syndromes that appear following disaster in these contexts are the post-traumatic stress syndrome, the survivor syndrome, and the disaster bereavement syndrome.

The *post-traumatic stress disorder* has been most carefully studied in its epidemiology and natural course by Weisæth (1984) and by McFarlane and Frost (1984) and McFarlane (1985a, 1985b, 1985c). As noted earlier, the former found the disorder in 36.4 percent of the severely affected group after seven months and in 18 percent at four years. Early response was predictive of disorder at seven months, especially high levels of traumatic anxiety and sleep disturbances, startle reaction, fears of the area of the disaster, and social withdrawal. Weisæth showed that if the illness was severe at seven months it was likely to become chronic. Risk of illness was increased for those with adaptational problems in childhood and adult life, past psychiatric impairment, high psychosomatic reactivity, character pathology, current life stressors, and greater intensity of disaster stress.

On the other hand, McFarlane noted that exposure levels (but not necessarily danger and threat), life events, and stressfulness of the experience contributed to morbidity, which seemed to have a threshold level before it became disabling. Both he and Weisæth noted the degree to which post-traumatic symptoms could be present without leading to the patient seeking help or defining himself as ill. Weisæth believes the social withdrawal contributes most to impairment dysfunction, while McFarlane emphasizes the patient's response to the question of the degree to which symptoms interfere with his life. Intensity of acute and subacute reactions was the strongest predictor of chronic morbidity in Weisæth's group, and there was some effect of previous psychiatric illness contributing to vulnerability to chronic disorder. Both these workers found little evidence of psychic numbing, although repressive mechanisms were certainly used.

A further interesting finding in Weisæth's study was that irritability and anger/aggression increased over the four-year follow-up—the only symptom to do so. He noted the possible problems it could lead to, including

TABLE 8.3

Disaster Stressors Correlating with Disturbance

Disaster Study	Time of assessment	Stressors of Disaster/Outcome							
		Death threat	Injury to self	Bereavement	Property loss	Dislocation	Work loss	Severe injury to relative	Major exposure to disaster
NATURAL DISASTER									
Cyclone Tracy, Darwin (Parker 1977)	1 week	+							
	10 weeks	+				+			
(Western and Milne 1979)	9 months		+			+	+		
Cyclone Oscar, Fiji (Fairley 1984)	10 weeks	+			+	+			
Tornado, Wichita Falls (Bolin 1982)	1 year and 23 months	+		+	+	+			
Flood, Wilkes Barre (Logue et al. 1979, male subjects)	5 years				+	+	+		
Flood, Bristol (Bennet 1970)	1 year					+			
Flood, Brisbane (Abrahams et al. 1976)	1 year		+		+	+			
Bushfires (McFarlane 1985a)	4 months		+		+		+		
(Clayer 1984)	1 year				+			+	+

TABLE 8.3 *(Continued)*

Disaster Study	Time of assessment	Death threat	Injury to self	Bereave-ment	Property loss	Dislocation	Work loss	Severe injury to relative	Major exposure to disaster
MAN-MADE DISASTERS									
Buffalo Creek									
(Gleser et al. 1981)	2 years	+		+					
Nightclub Fire									
(Green et al. 1983)	1 year	+	+	+					
(Lundin 1984)			+	+					
Factory Explosion									
(Weiseth 1983)	7 months	+							
	4 years	+							
Rail Crash									
(Singh and Raphael 1981)	1 year			+					

NOTE: Disaster Stressor—Factors shown in systematic studies to be significantly related to high-stress/morbid effects as measured by general health questionnaire, symptom check list, or interview. (Variables not scored may not have been relevant to the particular disaster, or may not have been investigated, or may not have been found significant for group investigated.)

impairment of interpersonal relationships. Similar increases had also been noted in the Three Mile Island mothers who were pregnant and in victims of the Beverly Hills nightclub fire. As is evident from table 8.2, irritability is a common problem post-disaster and is perhaps especially so with "man-made" catastrophes, where someone may be a focus of blame.

Bereavement disorders have been described by Lindemann (1944–45), Singh and Raphael (1981), Lindy and Green (1981), Lindy et al. (1983), Green et al. (1983), Lundin (1984a, 1984b), and Elizur and Kaffman (1982). Forty-five percent of the bereaved followed up in our study did badly; their pathology included general health deterioration and chronic grief and depression. Concrete manifestations included a continual preoccupation with the dead person, frequent visits to the grave, repeated tears, and grief to the extent of total preoccupation and impairment of social capacities. High levels of anxiety may also be present in these chronically grief-stricken people.

Most of the above workers note the high levels of impairment following the deaths of children, especially late adolescent or young adult children. This is similar to recent findings of parents' bereavement following the deaths of children in motor vehicle accidents (Shanfield and Swain 1984). The bereaved made comments such as "My life is devastated" or "I am finished—I have nothing else to live for." On the whole, women appeared to show more severe pathology psychiatrically, although in some instances the men developed severe physical impairment. These bereavement disorders, when chronic, are notoriously resistant to treatment. Factors such as the opportunity to see the body, social network support to help with grief and mourning, and facilitative bereavement counseling may all lessen the likelihood of such severe pathology (Raphael 1983). Weisæth suggests there may be some similar preventive effect with post-traumatic disorders in adults, although Terr (1983a, 1983b, 1983c) noted the failure of counseling to prevent traumatic stress disorder among the kidnapped children. It is interesting to note that both these disorders have also been feigned, as has been noted with Vietnam veterans for post-traumatic stress disorder (Sparr and Pankratz 1983) and with general, nondisaster populations for bereavement (Snowdon et al. 1978; Phillips et al. 1983).

Some case histories exemplify these long-term disorders:

John S., thirty-nine, was involved in a transport disaster, suffering a back injury that was relatively mild. He had problems with dreams and nightmares, tiredness and fatigue. His irritability and startle reactions were intense and increasing. Each time he considered returning to work his symptoms seemed to increase. He remembered vividly the hour he spent while others tried to rescue him and his horror that the car would explode. He resented the government for not fulfilling its commitment to "make things right for all those affected" and spent his time in isolation. He lost his interest in sexual relations and would drink heavily in the evenings. Two years after the disaster, his problems were the same and he was seeking compensation or an invalid pension.

Mrs. E., aged fifty, could not believe that her son Alan, the "light of her life," could have been killed in an air disaster. She did not see his body and felt it was all some terrible nightmare. She kept her son's room untouched and grew increasingly angry at her husband's attempts to reinvolve her in life. She would spend many hours in her son's room, which she kept as a "memorial to the most wonderful young man who ever lived." Enlarged photos of her son filled the house. In the evenings she would hold long conversations with him. Her whole family was in despair because she rejected all offers of help. Her picture of unresolved grief, with tears, anger, and despair, continued unabated for four years.

SOCIAL PATHOLOGY POST-DISASTER

There have not been many studies that have addressed the issue of social pathology following disaster. The study of Mount St. Helen's ashfall showed increased episodes of family violence, increased legal convictions, and some increase in violence and aggression compared to pre-disaster levels. Follow-up studies a year after the Ash Wednesday fires showed an increase in family and marital problems and problems with children (Clayer 1984), and similar findings appeared following the Darwin cyclone (Milne 1977). Increased family tensions associated with the disaster experience, its effects, and the added stress of dislocation have already been noted. Powell and Penick (1983) described similar effects after the Rochester floods.

Increased alcohol problems and drug consumption have been described following the Ash Wednesday fires, the Mount St. Helen's ashfall, and the Brisbane floods. Buffalo Creek led to social pathology of this kind, as did the Sri Lanka cyclone. It is probable that such disorder has developed with some other disasters but has not been systematically evaluated.

Acting out of disaster-induced tensions and self-destructive reactions linked to unresolved guilt or anger may cause delinquency, promiscuity, and other social problems. Guilt may occur, with depression and self-destructive behaviors. It is more likely after near-miss situations and situations in which there are conflicts. Wilkinson (1983) noted it in survivors of the Hyatt Regency Skywalks collapse, but it was also prominent after Buffalo Creek and in survivors of the concentration camps and wartime bombardments.

Social withdrawal, particularly in association with numbing, may be the most frequent form of morbidity in interpersonal relationships. It may be primarily a consequence of the disaster or precipitated by it in those who are already introverted or tend to cope with stress by such defenses. Social withdrawal is rarely noted or complained of and is difficult to assess in surveys, and so its level may be underestimated.

Rather than social pathology or community breakdown, there may be enhanced social and community functioning, as suggested by Williams and Parkes' study (1975) showing the increased birth rate in Aberfan five years after the disaster. Improvements in both community and individual social functioning may be substantial when people reevaluate their lives positively in terms of their commitment to others, as they often do after a disaster.

IMPAIRMENT OF PHYSICAL HEALTH

Increased mortality, related to stressful effects and not directly to disaster injury, has been described after disaster in the Mount St. Helen's ashfall, the Athens earthquake, and the Brisbane floods. And increased psychosomatic disorders have also been reported (Clayer 1984; Adams and Adams 1984), as well as the suggestion of increased leukemia and spontaneous abortion (Janerich et al. 1981). Supposing these increases are real and not physical effects of the disaster, which most workers seem to have excluded as causative, then stressor mechanisms are likely to have operated, as indeed they do post-bereavement (Bartrop et al. 1977). Obviously, further data is necessary in this field. This may be similar to long-term effects of extreme stress, as reviewed by Hocking (1965). It is necessary to bear in mind, however, possible physical effects of the disaster, change in services, service utilization or health awareness, and different health or personal habits.

VULNERABILITY AND PROTECTIVE FACTORS

The factors that make for vulnerability to disaster in terms of the risk of subsequently developing problems have been explored in a number of studies; and it would be most apt to conclude that there are, as yet, no answers.

Problems of Mental Health and Adjustment

Some studies point to *age* as a factor, in some cases showing the greater vulnerability of the young, in others of the old. Women have been shown to be at slightly greater risk in some studies (Abrahams et. al. 1976; Bennet 1970; Weisæth 1984), at least in terms of psychological morbidity. But in most studies there are no obvious sex differences, with men and women being equally affected. *Education* has been shown to have some positive effects, with the more highly educated having less morbidity, but the effect of this variable is not a great one. *Socioeconomic status* may contribute, as those of lower status are often less able to bear the assaults and consequences, especially economic, of the disaster. And there is much evidence that people with poor socioeconomic resources in underdeveloped countries may be greatly at risk from disaster and its consequences. In such circumstances the individual may be more likely to succumb to death or the other destructive disaster stressors than someone who is protected by better warning systems, stronger buildings, and effective medical follow-up. The protective effect of social class on survival generally has been well demonstrated by Hall (1985) in his analysis of survival following the sinking of the *Titanic,* where many factors combined to assist the upper classes. *Family status* has been suggested to have some influence. For example, bigger families are seen as slightly more at risk, and first-born or elder children may carry a disproportionate vulnerability. *Marital status* has been shown clearly by Clayer (1984) to correlate with disaster morbidity, in that "married previously divorced" are particularly at risk, as, to a lesser degree, are "married previously widowed," although this variable has not been so defined by other studies. *Occupational* status has not been shown to directly correlate, except inasmuch as higher and professional status may afford some degree of protection, although loss of work status post-disaster, as in the case of refugees, may add stress. *Employment* seems to contribute, for the unemployed seem at greater risk of impairment. *Religion* may influence the person's way of coping: it has been suggested to correlate with how people protect themselves, with those who are more fundamentalist tending to leave things to fate and thus suffering more damage, injury, and stress. This observation has not been substantiated, however. Different *cultural and ethnic* background factors may be influential as well, and there is a great need for studies to investigate this. Fairley's (1984) study of Fiji included both Indians and Fijians but found no major cultural variables that influenced outcome. It has been suggested that different ethnic groups may be more at risk of being scapegoated and this could increase vulnerability; but again, there are as yet no systematic studies.

Some background experiential and family factors are of interest. *Past disaster experience* has been suggested by many workers to lower vulnerability (Weisæth 1984), and studies where this has been investigated offer some support. It has been suggested that even wartime experience may help, perhaps through a process of "stress inoculation," which makes the individual more confident, less aroused, and gives him greater mastery. *Past psychiatric history* has been suggested to increase vulnerability in a number of studies. It may do so to some degree but has not emerged as a powerful variable, and patients have often improved in the face of disaster or managed well overall. *Family history* of psychiatric disorder has been investigated in the Romanian earthquake study, where positive family history was found to be less likely among those whose disorder was caused by the disaster, but others see it as contributing to vulnerability.

Disaster stressors seem to be a critical variable in risk, as has been discussed earlier. The more intense the disaster experience, the greater the confrontation with death, mutilation, destruction, loss, and dislocation, the greater the likely effects on psychological functioning and mental health. Whether specific disasters lead to greater risk of mental problems is not really clear, but certainly high levels have been found in association with many of the "man-made" disasters that are extremely destructive, such as Buffalo Creek. Being injured in a disaster seems to add to the stress, but there have not been any adequate systematic studies to evaluate this effect. Losing home and property has been shown to be more significant than expected in a number of disasters, including fires, floods, and tornadoes. Perhaps this is because of all that property symbolizes as well as the reality of deprivation. Similarly, long-term follow-up of Mount St. Helen's (Tatum, Vollmer, and Shore 1985) showed that death of a family member or friend, or major property loss, added to risk status; and Green, Grace, and Gleser's (1985) long-term follow-up of the Beverly Hills nightclub fire showed also that death encounter and loss were powerful contributors to outcome. Intensity, duration, and quality of disaster stressors, the shock effects, and the degree of helplessness may all be significant in adding to risk.

Mitigating and protective variables may also intervene. These may include personal coping styles reflecting aspects of personality. Those who engage their environment and undertake active mastery through activity to deal with the disaster and its effects, or who talk through their experiences, seem likely to do better. Social support has been shown to have a powerful influence in lessening the risk of post-disaster morbidity (Solomon 1984; Green et al. 1985), and when absent or inadequate, in increasing vulnerability. The heightened interpersonal closeness of the post-disaster period—the therapeutic community of social interactions—has been said to be one of the factors that prevents high levels of post-disaster pathology. But Abrahams et al. (1976) showed that those who perceived the help they were given as inadequate were more likely to suffer morbidity after the Brisbane floods, as has been found with the bereaved (Singh and Raphael 1981). Social support decreased the effects of the Three Mile Island incident as a stressor for workers and for psychiatric patients (Bromet et al. 1982a, 1982b). Clayer (1984) has shown how much people rely on help from their informal social networks, even with medical problems and certainly with those of the disaster, and how this support may influence outcome. Most workers argue that the disruption of social networks in the post-disaster period has a negative impact. This same influence has been noted in personal disasters such as bereavements and accidents (Raphael 1977; Bordow and Porritt 1979). It seems likely that the most important members of the social network are family and immediate relatives, with friends also of significance. Relatives seem to take on a special importance in disaster and provide emotional, informational, and tangible support that may mitigate against stressor effects.

Specific aid provided not just by family and friends but also by government and other sources plays a role in the recovery of the disaster victim. Bolin's study (1982) shows how significant the influence of economic recovery may be, for emotional recovery may come only when economic recovery is assured. The resources to provide shelter, lessen the number of dislocations, and assist the victim to return to previous or improved standards of living will be helpful to mental health, particularly by lessening some of the stressor effects of dislocation.

Specific counseling and intervention to help with coping and the working through of the stressful experience has been demonstrated to have some mitigating effects (Singh and Raphael 1981), as suggested by many workers in the field (e.g., Cohen and Ahearn 1980; Parad et al. 1976; Lindy et al. 1983; Lundin 1984b; Weisæth 1983). The most appropriate forms of counseling intervention for particular individuals, specific groups, and specific disaster stressor situations need to be more carefully refined, in view of Terr's and others' findings that some substantial morbidity may persist or appear despite intensive work with victims.

The resilience of human beings is perhaps the strongest protective factor of all.

DISASTER AND COMPENSATION

In natural disasters, compensation issues revolve primarily around insurance or government and private grants to assist victims. There are often problems in determining who should be compensated and to what levels. Judgments of those giving the compensation and those receiving it may differ considerably: there is usually some division of opinion about need and loss as bases for quantification of amounts of money, goods, or services provided. Thus, the issue of compensation may in itself become a source of conflict, interpersonal difficulties, bitterness, and stress, which can add to disaster-related morbidity.

The problem becomes even more complicated when compensation is sought against persons or organizations for deaths, injuries, psychiatric impairment, or property loss associated with catastrophes where human negligence was involved. The litigation that arises may influence the outcome of the disaster experience, and perhaps even the views psychiatrists take of any disorder that develops (Simon and Zusman 1983). It is suggested by many that the delay of waiting for compensation, or the need to "maintain" disorder for compensation, may prolong and exacerbate morbidity. "Nervous shock," or psychologically induced morbidity over and above normal stress reactions and grief trauma, has in recent years been an increasing factor in litigation claims, particularly since the settlement of $13,000,000 to the Buffalo Creek litigants. Yet there is much to suggest that here, as with personal disasters like work accidents that involve compensation, gaining compensation does not reduce the morbidity. This is clear in Weisæth's prospective study, where all victims were guaranteed work and whatever they needed to recover, so that issues of material compensation did not apply at all. The levels of morbidity that developed and became chronic were still substantial.

Obviously, issues of litigation and compensation may create difficulties in the post-disaster period and, in some but certainly not in all cases, may have effects on disaster-related morbidity. The danger lies in assuming that ongoing morbidity will somehow be "fixed" by compensation, when it is very clear that other factors, such as the changed social role of the victim or the nature of the stress, may be far more significant in determining the course of post-disaster pathology.

MORBIDITY IN CHILDREN AND ADOLESCENTS

As noted earlier, the reactions of children to disaster stress will reflect their own experience and their response to parental reactions to the disaster and its consequences. In table 8.4, the systematic studies that have examined the

TABLE 8.4

Studies of Problems and Stressors in Children

Disaster Study	Time of Assessment	Level of stress	Relevant Variables					
			Threat	Bereave-ment	Dislo-cation	Parent effect	Dysfunction of family	Age
Fires								
(McFarlane et al. 1985)	2 months	↑ 2.7%	X	X	X	X	X	(young)
	8 months	↑ ↑		X		X	X	(young)
Cyclone								
(Milne 1977)	7–10 months		X		X	X		(young)
Flood								
(Ollendick and Hoffman 1983)	8 months	↑ 43%				X	X	(6–12)
Storms								
(Burke et al. 1982)	5 months	↑				X		(young)
Tornado								
(Bloch et al. 1956)	> 1 week	↑	X	X		X		(6–12)
Kidnapping								
(Terr 1983)	5–13 months	↑	X					(5–14)

morbidity of children are summarized in terms of relevant variables, including levels of stress, impact of disaster threat on stress levels, effects of disaster on parents, dysfunction of family, and age.

The problems of children are perhaps best exemplified in several brief case vignettes.

Simon was four and had spent the time of the hurricane hiding in his mother's arms in the bathroom of their house. Any wind disturbed him, and when it rained heavily he would refuse to move from his mother's side. Nightmares about wind woke him frequently. He played hurricane games, where he acted as the wind, running through the house and knocking over furniture. He was treated in some brief play sessions, and his mother was given guidance for managing his behavior.

Alison was eight when her father was killed in a train crash. She became withdrawn and quiet, and her work at school declined. She had trouble sleeping at night. She would cling to her uncles when they visited her mother, and was angry and rejecting when her mother attempted to console her. At times she was fearful. Her behavior improved after therapy. She and her mother dealt with their longing for her father and were enabled to talk of him and what had happened.

Ten-year-old Phillip had been exceptionally good in the early days after the fire, as he was shocked by the horror of it, although, before their farm had burned, he thought it very exciting. His parents' total preoccupation with rebuilding left him and his younger brother and sister very much to themselves in the cramped quarters of the trailer, although he had many tasks to do to help the family. He was reported by his school for aggressive and defiant behavior, a falloff in his schoolwork, and suspected stealing. When counseling sessions with the family helped all to communicate and function together again, recognizing needs and feelings, his problems disappeared.

As the various workers have noted, fears and separation anxiety are common initially after children have been exposed to the threat of disaster impact. Other symptoms include sleep and dream disturbances, aggressive behavior and fighting, conduct disorders, and play or talk about the disaster. There often follows a period of exceptionally "good" behavior, although close observation may reveal increased separation responses and clinging. The younger child is more likely to directly reflect parental responses, and may also show clinging, crying, and regression with intense separation anxiety. Older children may show conduct or emotional disorders, with the latter, as Tonge (1984) has noted, generally being more reactive to the disaster. Aggressive behaviors are not uncommon.

Adolescents may show delinquent behaviors or withdrawal. There has been little systematic study of their conditions and pathology, however, except for Crawshaw's (1963) observations on how adolescents have reactions that fall between those of children and adults and may be simultaneously excited by and fearful of the disaster.

The long-term effects for children and adolescents are uncertain, as are effects on development. Personal disasters such as abuse are known to have long-term consequences, and substantial pathology is found following parental divorce and after bereavement. Some longer-term studies following up children in the post-disaster period found that disorder at two years was greater than at two or eight months after the disaster (Higgins and Schinckel 1985). Children in this study (following fires) showed more morbidity when there was family dysfunction, overprotection, or post-traumatic stress symptoms for the parent—and up to 30 percent were affected, indicating the problems were not minor. The patterns of behavioral and pathological response found after personal disaster and general community disaster are very similar. In both cases, effects may be mitigated by ongoing supportive relationships and especially by parents providing children with information and answers, as well as with opportunities to share feelings about what has happened. The state of family function, parental adaptation, integration and emotional support, will be critical to facilitating adaptation to the traumatic experience and associated life changes (Raphael 1983).

DIFFERENT TYPES OF DISASTERS

Systematic cross-disaster comparisons of psychiatric morbidity have yet to be made. It is clear from many of the studies quoted above, however, that the effect may not be great in disasters with little life or property loss and little threat of death. The predictability of disaster, by contributing to psychological preparedness, may lessen shock effects. Thus, the morbidity found with regular flooding may be substantially less than that associated with a highly traumatic and unexpected man-made disaster such as Buffalo Creek, or with the uncertainty and terror of civilian violence. Earthquakes may be very stressful as natural disasters, with the shock, death, mutilation, and destruction, as well as the secondary impact of the severe fires that frequently follow (Arvidson 1969). Yet their death rates may be substantially less in developed countries, where buildings are often earthquake-proof, than in developing countries, where overpopulated cities may be filled with crowded shanties and slums and, consequently, where psychological effects may be much greater. This observation has not yet been established in research studies, but comparative reports from different areas—including the recent earthquakes in Mexico City (September 1985)—lend support to this idea.

Although systematic comparisons of disaster effects are lacking, a look at some very different disasters may prove helpful.

"POISONING"—CHEMICAL AND TOXIC WASTE DISASTERS

The recent disaster in the Indian city of Bhopal highlights the risk of acute emergency from a toxic chemical, and this is only one of the innumerable possibilities of such a disaster in modern industrial communities. The thousands of deaths involved and the immediate impact on health for tens of thousands of people are likely to lead to many psychological traumatic effects and pathological bereavements. The fear of the environment, the loss of work, and the dread of longer-term consequences for the health of present and future generations are likely to produce chronic stresses for most of the population. Litigation sought may or may not help people's sense of rage and impotence about what has happened to them and their families. Psychological morbidity may be substantial.

With the more chronic experience of exposure to chemicals such as Agent Orange, it is often difficult to separate out the physical and psychological contributions to any ultimate morbidity. It may be that the fearful circumstances of, or belief about, exposure may in themselves be psychologically stressful, particularly when its physical implications are perceived as threatening.

Exposure to toxic or radioactive materials may bring immediate threat of choking or poisoning, followed by longer-term distress and concern, as well as fear of genetic damage. Such exposure may occur suddenly and unexpectedly, as the result of explosions, collisions of vessels or vehicles containing such materials, or accidents during manufacture; or it may come gradually and insidiously, through leaks or slow release, possibly without the knowledge of victims.

Ridington (1982) provides a fascinating case study of a Canadian Indian community's response to the threat of a hydrogen sulphide leak from a nearby oil well. These people, tribal hunters and gatherers, with their highly tuned natural intelligence, believed the slight chemical leaks to be threatening and poisonous. They made many efforts to persuade the authorities to do something about the threat. These efforts had little effect, however, as the authorities interpreted the situation differently, that is, from the point of view of the needs of a highly industrialized society. When the gas later escaped in a major leak, the band chief heard the sound and saw the cloud moving toward the village. He was able to alert the villagers, so that all escaped without serious injury. Had the leak occurred at night or in winter, loss of life would have been inevitable. The authorities closed the well temporarily, and legal actions followed. The Indian people of Blueberry maintained that the risk and threat were substantial and asked for assistance to move their village away. The industrial authorities defined the situation as nonthreatening, claiming that the risk was negligible and that in an industrial society risk was one of the costs for the benefits derived. The latter argument was in fact not relevant to this Indian group. The issue was still unresolved at the time of report. Given that stressful effects such as headache and general lack of well-being appeared even before the major leak, it seems likely that such a situation of ongoing threat and conflict would engender many further difficulties psychologically. This episode exemplifies the difficulties inherent in many chemical and toxic disasters, which may be very differently defined by the victims and the authorities or industry. For the Indians, "The poison gas came down like a fog" to destroy and threaten their community and way of life.

The effects of chemical leaks and explosions may be substantial, as they are likely to occur in communities with large populations, for example, at docks in cities or storage centers in industrial suburbs. McLeod (1977) reported on effects following the leak of "Morphos" (organophosphates) from a ship at Parnell in New Zealand. There was wide news coverage of the emergency, which emphasized the highly toxic nature of the chemical. Many people presented symptoms of dizziness, headaches, weakness, sweating, nausea, confusion, and anxiety. McLeod concluded that among the hundreds treated for such complaints, there were *no* instances of organophosphate poisoning and that the condition treated was most likely anxiety. That is, the morbidity may have been that of "mass panic" in response to the threat and the intensive publicity that surrounded it. This report highlights the problems of defining organic and psychological effects in such chemically threatening situations, and the fear that they induce; see also study of the toxic oil disaster (Lopez-Ibor et al. 1985).

Most thoroughly studied has been the Three Mile Island disaster. In this case there was a prolonged period of threat from the potential "toxicity" of the nuclear power plant, but no lives were lost or property damaged. Nevertheless, mothers of young children and pregnant women showed both acute and chronic impairment of their mental health. Clinical anxiety and depression as well as milder psychiatric symptomatology contributed, and risk was increased for those who were closest to the plant, vulnerable in terms of a past psychiatric history, and having inadequate social support

(Bromet and Dunn 1981). Workers at the plant felt their health had been endangered, and consequently experienced greater uncertainty, conflict, and lessened job satisfaction (Kasl et al. 1981). This and other potential nuclear power disasters constitute a powerful source of threat, a "toxic" dread as it were.

"FEAR OF FLYING"—AIR DISASTERS

Crashes are not common, but when they occur, they usually produce many deaths and few casualties. They most frequently affect groups that have widely scattered origins, so there is little "therapeutic community" response to support survivors and the bereaved. Needs for mental health support may be substantial (Duffy 1978). The sites of crashes are often a further element of the disaster, for they may occur in isolated or desolate places, making it difficult to reach any survivors and creating further stress for those waiting for news of the disaster.

Issues of blame and negligence may lead to bitter feelings among all those affected. Air crew, especially the pilot, may be greatly affected by what happens, and feelings of guilt are likely to be profound for such survivors. The victims' previous experience with personal crises and their life situation at the time may complicate recovery. Emotional reactions described include psychic numbing, disbelief and bewilderment, guilt, fear, phobias, irritability and mood swings, anger, and depression. Repetitive intrusion of memories and dreams may lead to intense emotional reexperiencing of what happened. Psychophysiological reactions are frequent. Nonadaptive behaviors may appear, including alcohol abuse, withdrawal, self-neglect, displacement of anger or exaggerated activities to avoid memories (Barbeau 1980; Perlberg 1979). The bereavements may be very traumatic and complicated, especially if there is no opportunity for seeing the body or availability of emotional support for working through. Anger is likely to be intense, for the bereaved always feels "it should never have happened."

These feelings and reactions are exemplified by Mrs. S., age fifty-four, whose son, daughter-in-law, and two grandchildren were killed in an international airline disaster. Having heard of the crash, she was full of dread but was unable to confirm whether they had been on the plane or not. It was a week before their deaths were confirmed. She could not see their bodies or go to the site of the crash. She dreamed constantly of it and of them. She was despairing and filled with anger that they had been cheated of life by the accident, when all had seemed to be going so well for them. She felt that she was "old" and had had her life and that somehow she should have died in their place. Psychotherapy over a number of months helped her resolve some of these issues, but she still had a profound sense of loss and of the meaninglessness of life.

Other air disasters involve a plane crashing into a town or city. These may range from personal disasters, when few are affected, to major disasters, hurting many. The shock is great, of course, for such disasters come without warning. Injuries and mutilation may be severe. Both those on the aircraft and those in the community are affected. A description of response to such a disaster is provided by Baren (1976). In this particular disaster, a plane crashed into an ice-cream parlor, killing ten adults and twelve children and injuring fourteen others. A crisis intervention program was provided for those injured and bereaved. There was an initial period of numbness and shock, but anxiety about the disaster appeared within a few days, with many experiencing nightmares. There were feelings of guilt and anger about the deaths and complicated bereavement reactions.

It was noted by Baren (1976), and identified by Taylor and Frazer (1981), Butcher (1980), Barbeau (1980) that air disasters may bring special stresses to the helpers as well, through both the encounter with mutilating injury and death and the stresses shared with those they help (also Davidson 1979; O'Brien 1979). Airport staff and rescue personnel may also be stressed, because of intense pressures from distressed relatives, feelings of responsibility, and the often prolonged periods of uncertainty.

Another type of disaster related to air travel is that of aircraft hijack. The psychological experiences of passengers under such circumstances are highly distressing, because of the fear of death or crash, the separation from family and friends with no opportunities for communication, and the victimization that is likely. The victims are powerless and in a state of constant threat, and they recognize that even a rescue attempt may lead to their losing their lives. They are often with strangers and deprived of physical comforts. It is likely that subsequent psychological morbidity will be substantial and that the hostage syndrome, in which hijacked victims may identify with their captors, may commonly be found (Ochberg 1978). Systematic studies of the morbidity in such groups have yet to appear.

Disasters related to aircraft and air travel are relatively rare. But when they do occur their effects are likely to be very psychologically traumatic because of high levels of disaster stressor for victims, bereaved, and disaster workers—death encounter, mutilating deaths and injuries, and bereavements that will be difficult to resolve. These same themes are important in small aircraft crashes. The numbers are less but the disaster experience just as great.

Elvira was waiting for her husband, a competent pilot, to return from a business trip in his small plane. Her brother and father had also gone with him. The night became stormy, and she waited in terror on hearing that he had not arrived at the expected time. The plane was found in isolated Australian bush four days later after intensive search. The bodies were unidentifiable. She stayed numb, her grief totally blocked. "She carried on bravely," as her friends put it, until a severe physical illness on the second anniversary of the deaths brought an opportunity for delayed grieving and help through psychotherapy.

BRIDGES—"THE CUTOFF"

The collapse of a bridge, like an aircraft crash, may hold a group of strangers in its grip. As vividly described in Thornton Wilder's *The Bridge of San Luis Rey,* such a disaster may have implications not only for those injured or bereaved but for all those who are joined by it. And the destruction of a bridge may alter not only individual lives but the very fabric of a community, as demonstrated by the collapse of the Tasman Bridge in Hobart, Australia.

On a Sunday evening in January 1975, about two weeks after the Darwin cyclone, the Tasman Bridge, which spanned the wide Derwent River to join the two halves of Hobart, broke when an interstate freighter collided with the pylons, leading to the collapse of 127 meters of decking. This crashed down on the ship, sending her rapidly to the bottom. Several cars ran over the edge of the broken span; others stopped precariously, their occupants just escaping. Seven seamen and five motorists died, while many others survived after undergoing terrifying experiences that threatened their lives. Many of these showed "delayed shock" effects of the disaster. The captain of the ship was found guilty of careless navigation and was said to suffer delayed shock so that he was invalided out of the merchant navy.

A sociological study of the effects of this bridge collapse on the city of Hobart was carried out by Whelan et al. (1976), who examined a variety of social and psychological indicators as well as criminological indices in the six months following the disaster. The study showed that psychological adjustments were complicated, with some specific effects. The loss of the bridge disrupted travel to work and recreation, contact with relatives, and many services. Frustration and anger rose, and lethargy and hopelessness about the situation appeared in many cases. Increased use of tranquilizers was reported. Isolation, stress, and fatigue were found to interfere with satisfactory adjustment. There were increased claims for financial support by deserted wives and single mothers; in fact, such claims doubled. This may have resulted from the friction and fatigue, as well as from a lack of casual work, previously used as a financial support by vulnerable families. Phobic disorders were not uncommon. Some lonely neurotics who had previously found solace in the city became more isolated and impaired. Alcohol consumption rose, and there were increased crimes in some areas, especially against persons and perhaps associated with alcohol. Disputes among neighbors increased. It seemed that families kept their troubles to themselves but displaced or projected their discontent onto others. The disruption of many services, including medical, transportation, and police services, may have added to the stresses of the population, but it also created some difficulty in the interpretation of these results. Nevertheless, the authors conclude that there is adequate justification for seeing some of these problems, at least, as the end product of the fracture of the city. And, in most instances, the period of adjustment took many months.

"BURIED ALIVE"

Mine disasters continue to occur even with careful safety measures. They are part of the culture and expectation in many mining communities, where rituals of superstition—vividly and sadly portrayed in novels such as *How Green Was My Valley*—may become part of family life, as people defend against the possibility of such loss. Often, the men who are trapped in a mine collapse die below, and the disaster then wreaks its effects on their bereaved families. Grief of widows and children in such circumstances is profound. They may have prolonged waiting at the pit-top and may or may not see their dead husbands brought to the surface. Their anger at coal authorities is intense, especially if there is any suggestion of negligence or inadequate safety measures. They are usually well supported by the community, which shares their loss. Although their bereavements may be bitter, there is little else known about their outcomes, except perhaps their legacy of loneliness.

The men who survive the disaster are likely to have severe psychological consequences in the form of post-traumatic stress disorder, with phobic reactions to their underground experiences in many instances. Ploeger (1977) found that ten years after a disaster, nine of the ten miners he followed up showed an irritable-explosive change in personality and post-traumatic stress symptoms of nightmares, fears, and phobias. Beach and Lucas (1960) also reported on coping techniques and problems in adaptation to the stress of a mine disaster.

Earthquake disasters may also involve the trauma of being "buried alive." As detailed in a number of reports, the shocked, frightened, and sometimes injured victims may call for help and wait, perhaps futilely, for rescue. One story is of a woman who, with her mother, struggled to keep them both alive, only to be rescued after three days when her mother quietly died. Specific pathology found with entrapment is not defined, but the grief and post-traumatic effects are likely to be significant. The relatively high levels of psychiatric morbidity in some earthquake studies may reflect this. It was found, for instance, that after the very disastrous Managua earthquake, admissions for neurosis rose 209 percent in the first three months and 46 percent in the first post-disaster year (Ahearn 1981). Post-traumatic symptoms have also been commonly described. Fear of enclosure and entrapment, breathing difficulties, and feelings of panic are commonly described following both these types of disaster, perhaps symbolizing at a very primitive and basic level feelings and fears of entombment and death. More recently, in the Mexico City earthquakes of September 1985 there have been experiences of prolonged entrapment whose effects are not yet known.

"HELL ON EARTH"—DISASTERS OF FIRE

The terrifying experiences of fire have been vividly portrayed in a variety of disaster studies. For example, McFarlane (1984) and Valent (1984) have depicted the experience of adults and children in the Ash Wednesday bushfires. Morbidity patterns for that disaster have been shown to be substantial in Clayer's (1984) follow-up of 1,515 victims twelve months later. At least 40 percent of the affected population reported levels of impairment equivalent to psychiatric cases. These people reported a 300 percent increase in mental illness, as well as a 200 percent increase in psychosomatic disorders.

The morbidity for victims and bereaved has been substantial following a series of fires in night clubs—a man-made fire disaster scenario. The reports of Lindemann (1944–45), Abe (1976), Green et al. (1983), and Lundin (1984a,c) all depict the horror and trauma involved, as well as the serious psychopathological consequences. Canter (1980) has reviewed many of the relevant issues concerning the effects of fires on behavior.

Other disasters may bring death or threat of death by fire. Earthquakes, shipwrecks and air crashes, as well as explosions and bombings may all be complicated by fires. The particular contribution of fire to the traumatic experience of victims in such cases is not fully understood but is probably difficult to disentangle from other stressors.

Several themes appear in response to fire disaster. Feelings of terror are profound, and panic, which occurs only rarely, is most often described with such catastrophes. Thus, victims have been described struggling over one another to flee smoke-filled hotels and night clubs, or fleeing forest fires in panic. The choking effects of smoke, the heat, and the poor visibility may add to the fear. These perceptions are all triggers to subsequent traumatic anxiety. Bereavements are complicated, especially if the individuals were themselves involved in the fire or if the bodies were barely identifiable. Burns injuries are problematic for the patient and his family. They require intensive care and a long period of readjustment, often with significant psychological complications.

For many, particularly those of Judeo-Christian origin, fires seem to symbolize the fires of "hell." Thus, many victims make remarks like "It was hell on earth," or "It was like the 'Devil's Inferno,' " or "I thought I was in hell." There are strong associations of punishment, atonement, and purification of evil. It is little wonder, then, that guilt appears as a frequent symptom, further complicating the traumatic neurosis for survivors. This may become manifest in strange ways. For example, a clergyman delivering a sermon at a large memorial ceremony for the victims of the Ash Wednesday fires preached from the Book of Job on the "burnt offerings" to God —a logical choice of imagery to him, yet for many of the audience a painful reminder of inner fantasies.

"DEATH BY DROWNING"—SHIPWRECKS AND DEATHS AT SEA

The literature on shipwreck shows high levels of post-disaster psychiatric morbidity (for example, Leopold and Dillon 1963; Henderson and Bostock 1977). These disasters are likely to bring traumatic neuroses, reflecting the helplessness and fear of the experience. More recently, a large and controlled study of traumatic aftereffects was carried out with men and officers of the U.S.S. *Belknap,* which had collided with another ship (Hoiberg and McCaughey 1984). In the three years following the disaster, significantly more of the men from the collision ship, as compared to the control ship, were hospitalized or left the service because of neurosis. These rates were highest among the uninjured men who were evacuated, perhaps indicating that they may have lacked the opportunity and support to work through the experience. The symptoms commonly reflected post-traumatic disorder and effects. Those bereaved by marine disasters have not been studied, but their grief is likely to be complicated by the loss of the dead person's body and the uncertainty that may be a consequence. Guilt is likely to be reinforced in those who have survived when others have died, especially if life is lost when the survivors were given first priority.

Death in water and drowning is part of the threat of flooding when this is sudden, severe, or overwhelming. Buffalo Creek exemplified this experience, but natural disaster floods may equally be frightening. Bodies found may be in a disturbing state of disintegration. Those who die in such disasters may struggle desperately to reach safety and their deaths may be full of panic and fear. These aspects, too, are likely to fill the fantasies of survivors, perhaps reinforcing the traumatic experience.

Tsunami perhaps represent the ultimate in the overwhelming force of water and drowning—the tidal waves of fantasy. One study of behavior (Lachman et al. 1960) showed that few responded to warning when this "unbelievable" disaster occurred in Hawaii in 1960. Little is known of effects on survivors.

"ROTTEN WEATHER": TORNADOES, CYCLONES, HURRICANES, BLIZZARDS

Frightening winds, noise, physical forces with great destructive power, rain and floods bring disasters characterized by some death and loss but especially by dislocation from community. Morbidity patterns are significant, sometimes associated not so much with the frightening experience as with its consequences. In some community studies, 40–50 percent may still be emotionally affected many months afterward; children seem particularly vulnerable. Blizzards, freezes, and icy storms bring threat to survival for those caught in them, but to date there are few descriptions of the psychological morbidity found in association. One description of the John F. Kennedy Airport snow-in (Hammerschlag and Astrachan 1971) showed lack of group interaction and support, irrational fears, a dependence on technology to magically solve the problem, and a sense of abandonment. The sequelae are unknown. More recently, Dombrowsky (1983) discussed the importance of family solidarity and Perry et al. (1983) the role of giving and receiving aid in dealing with such disasters. None of these workers have reported on the longer-term psychological effects. Most people seem to deal with the stress of disastrous weather, even though the experience may have been fearful. The outcomes seem most likely to be related directly to the level of stressor experience, with numbers of deaths and death encounter relating to short-term effects and dislocation from community relating to longer-term chronic morbidity.

"GOD'S WILL"

The Guyana mass suicide represents the most obvious disaster related to following a religious or other leader to death and destruction. Obviously many psychological factors contribute to the involvement in such movements. Psychological consequences for the survivors are unknown, but the bereavements are likely to be difficult. There is also likely to be both anger and resentment at the leader and over the self-choice of death. At Guyana, positive identification of the bodies of the 911 who died was not achieved in nearly two-thirds of the cases. The tragedy had many complex medicolegal aspects (Curran 1979). Thus consequences of morbidity for those who recover and handle the remains of such seemingly purposeless mass deaths may also be substantial (Jones 1985).

"MASS MURDER"

Another type of disaster, as yet poorly studied apart from the genocide of the concentration camps, is that of multiple and senseless killing of others. The atrocities of warfare or civilian murders may be examples, while assassination and individual murder carry the same implications at a personal disaster level. Studies of children surviving family murders have shown the enormous psychological trauma they suffer. The concentration camp survivors reflect some of the stresses engendered by mass murder, including post-traumatic disorder that is prolonged and that may even extend to the next generation or the broader community.

"A PRESENT-DAY PLAGUE"

The AIDS epidemic has brought two components of psychological trauma and will no doubt lead to many psychopathological consequences that have yet to be defined. First, the epidemic has aroused fears associated with sexuality, especially about homosexuality and contact with homosexuals. Scapegoating and a return of prejudice against homosexuals are already in evidence. The fear of contamination and rumors about the disease's contagion may make people hesitant to accept homosexuals (or those identified as at risk) in many walks of life and business. The disease's further association with drug use leads to fantasies about it as a retribution for the deviant. And its power to contaminate blood given or used in medical systems will bring fears to the health field as well. The "mysterious" contamination is very frightening and has some of the threat that the plague held in the past, but greatly attenuated by present-day dependence on the miracles of technological medicine. The disease is having a significant impact on behavior and generating considerable anxiety and depression in those who fear it.

The second component of psychological trauma relates specifically to those who contract the disease, which is in most cases fatal. Psychological responses to such terminal disease, acquired as it may be through homosexual behavior, abuse of injected drugs, or in the course of medical care, are likely to be strongly influenced by feelings of anger and guilt, as well as difficulty in family and interpersonal reactions. Deuchar (1984) has described some of the stresses and psychological consequences faced by AIDS victims, and potential victims, in New York. He notes how the furor created by publicity about the condition has led to "AIDS panic" in some risk groups who seek "AIDS testing" at the first sign of any skin lesion or infection. This panic has led to changes in sexual behavior and a lessening of the use of "impersonal sex" as an outlet. The public outcry has led to a return of rejecting attitudes toward homosexuals, who may be shunned. Grave psychological upheaval faces those who contract the disease, and such patients display a range of psychiatric symptoms. There is often self-imposed isolation, as well as rejection by family, lovers, friends, and society. Many patients experience a sense of guilt and punishment, and commonly following diagnosis, feelings of regret, shock, derealization, and depersonalization, as well as sleep disorders. These feelings may give way to great anger and hostility toward sexual partners, families, the community, or doctors. Financial worries may complicate the condition, because of the costs of illness and problems with work. Depression is also common. All these reactions are, of course, superimposed on whatever psychiatric problems and disorders may have existed beforehand. The sad consequences for many victims of this modern plague are anger, guilt, rejection and isolation, and a lonely death of despair.

"STARVATION"

Starvation can be a component of many different disasters—drought, famine, concentration camp or other imprisonment, wartime sieges such as that of Leningrad, or other disasters that bring isolation. The lack of vital supplies of food is the ultimate threat to life but is not necessarily acute; however, its psychopathological sequelae may be complicated by organic brain damage. Those who survive it may become apathetic, depressed, and preoccupied with issues of food and personal security, or narcissistically preoccupied with their bodies. Neuropsychiatric complications may also appear.

Thus, there are many different disasters whose impact on health is variable, sometimes leading to extensive psychosocial morbidity. The meaning of these different disasters is often influenced by the symbolic significance of their physical effects. There is much to support the view, proposed by Luchterhand (1971), that when disasters are "man-made," their effects in inducing pathology may be more severe. And throughout the various types of disasters run the common themes of disaster stressors—shock, death, helplessness, loss, and dislocation—and for many the common equation: the greater the stress, the greater the likelihood of morbidity.

CIVILIAN VIOLENCE AS DISASTER

Many parts of the world suffer from the acute and chronic threats of civilian violence. Highly destructive homemade or technically sophisticated weapons are used alike in the streets of Belfast, Beirut, and many other cities throughout the world. Riots are also commonplace in many major cities of both the developing and developed world, bringing sudden shock and threat followed by death and destruction. Loss and grief can become frequent experiences for families in areas plagued by urban violence. They occur against a background of antipathy and hatred, and often provide further fuel for vendettas and escalation of violence. There may also be large-scale destruction of homes and property and even dislocation to shelters, camps, or the homes of others. Unlike a natural or other man-made disaster, however, these disasters do not simply occur and go away. Most continue, bringing the need to adjust to ongoing personal threat of death and loss while maintaining everyday existence.

The impact of such ongoing violence and atmosphere of danger has been studied by a number of workers. Lyons (1972) proposed that there might be an inverse relationship between aggression and depression and tested this proposal by examining the effects of the riot situation in Belfast on the incidence of depressive illness. In essence, he hypothesized that the externalization of aggression with civilian violence might lead to a decrease in depressive illness. His findings supported the hypothesis. There was a significant decrease in depressive illness for both sexes and all age groups. The decrease was more pronounced in males, who were more involved in the aggression and violence, and in those social classes in which people were also more likely to be involved. The decrease was more significant in the riot areas. The suicide rate fell by 50 percent. There was a notable increase in other indices of aggression and violent crimes including homicide. By contrast the rural areas, away from the riots, showed a sharp increase in male depression.

In a later review of the psychological aspects of civilian violence, Lyons (1979) showed other reactions to be common in this community stressed by riots and bombing, common features of modern terrorism. Post-traumatic stress reactions were frequent, even in the children of Belfast. Adults showed, like other disaster victims, affective disturbances such as fear, anxiety, irritability, and depression. Somatic symptoms, such as abdominal discomfort, chest sensations, headache, sweating, and trembling—all associated with the feelings of anxiety—were frequent. There was a significant increase in the number of prescriptions given for tranquilizers and sedatives. Lyons also commented on the fact that, as in wartime generally and in other disasters, there was no increase in psychiatric admission rates.

The children and teenagers of Belfast also reacted to the riots and violence. They did not, on the whole, show many anxiety or emotional disturbances, unless reflecting these from their parents. They did show excitement and often identification with and acting out of violence and conduct disorders. Most older children (teenagers especially) belonged to paramilitary gangs, and group antisocial behavior was common. Lyons concluded that these children had become conditioned to violence, that it had become an intrusive part of their lives.

The bombed of Belfast—those who had suffered in explosions—usually had psychological symptoms of affective disturbance, or phobias. Sometimes they developed agoraphobia, which might well be seen as an appropriate defensive adaptation, protecting them against exposure to further explosions. Children who had experienced this were also likely to show separation anxiety. Depression appeared in 22 percent of cases. Irritability was not only common, but was often serious enough to disrupt marital relationships. As noted with other victims, anxiety, sleep disturbances, and trigger reactions to sounds such as gunfire were common: 65 percent of these people had a post-traumatic anxiety state.

Lyons concluded that although the bombing and violence of civilian upheaval in some ways resembled civilian experience of bombing in wartime, there was an important difference: in wars, the community was united against an outside aggressor; with terrorism, the violence might come from anywhere and the community was divided.

Tan and Simons (1973) studied the effects of riots in the very different context of Malaysia. Psychiatric admissions reflected common disorders even when related to the riots. However, sleep disturbance, appetite disturbance, and depression were common symptoms. As in many disaster situations, people were disturbed by fears of danger, by the threat of loss of relatives and of home or other property, and by the sight of mutilated bodies. Although their morbidity was that commonly presented by psychiatric patients, some presented brief reactive psychoses and neurotic disorder. The vulnerable tended to have suffered threat and to be less well integrated into the multiracial society. For the most part they responded well to crisis management. Frazer (1973) has studied the effects of such similar violence on children, as noted previously, and supports the notion of major effects on development and behavior, especially when parents are significantly affected.

Civilian violence, which is increasing throughout the world, may be clearly predictable, if not for the timing of its episodes, in cities such as Belfast, or in the civil wars of Lebanon. The psychiatric effects of civil war in Lebanon have been considered by Nasr et al. (1983). These workers found that while most of the population weathered the war remarkably well, perhaps because of the strength of the family system and the internal cohesion of the different groups, there was an increase in psychiatric referrals with the hostilities. Post-traumatic and depressive symptoms were common, and drug addiction and alcoholism both increased.

But bombings and terrorist violence also occur sporadically and spontaneously in many other situations in both developed and developing countries. Such anticipated episodes bring an extra impact of shock and terror. The emotional and mental health problems that arise as a consequence may be substantial. A study of psychological sequelae among those who were involved in but not injured by hotel bombings in Birmingham, England, in 1974, showed significant effects on mental health and functioning (Sims et al. 1979). Social functioning was considered worse in those who had directly suffered, and work capacity was often impaired. Neurotic, phobic, and post-traumatic symptoms were frequent.

Another form of civilian violence involves terrorism and the taking of hostages. There is, in these situations, the threat to one's own life and perhaps to the lives of loved ones. And there is often a prolonged and strange relationship with captors, who may submit victims to many threats, deprivations, and humiliations; in some instances, strong attachments may develop between captive and captor. Torture is sometimes a factor, as may be senseless violence and death. Those, such as Ochberg, who have studied hostage situations have commented on the lasting impact and morbidity that results.

There are a number of personal disasters that also follow such patterns of civilian violence. The danger and threat of assault, mugging, rape, and robbery are frequent in some cities. The victims of such violence also show marked psychological reactions afterward: fearfulness, anxiety, startle response, anger, gastrointestinal upset and headache, as well as depressive responses and guilt. Post-traumatic disorder may develop and may be prolonged. The victims of violence may need ongoing support to deal with and work through their trauma. Paranoia, a lack of trust in others, fear of being alone, and depression are commonly reported in those who have suffered such personal disasters, and as noted by Nadelson et al. (1982) in a follow-up of victims of rape, problems may persist for years.

WAR AS DISASTER

There can be little doubt that war is a disaster on a large scale. The psychologically traumatic effects of combat on soldiers have been systematically studied in several recent wars and in both world wars. Romo and Schneider (1982) have reported on war and disaster, with implications for future war. They note the correlations found between psychiatric casualties and the numbers wounded in action. There is a strong correlation between combat-induced psychiatric disorder (a traumatic stress disorder) and severity of stress. The longer time in action and the more comrades killed or severely injured, the higher the rate of psychiatric decompensation. The soldier is confronted by personal encounter with death, the massive and mutilating deaths of others, and loss and grief. In addition, he is dislocated from home and familiar environment, protected only by the social support and cohesion offered by the men of his fighting unit and his leaders.

The Vietnam veteran has been considered one of the major disaster victims of war in recent years (Boman 1984). This group has shown psychological morbidity as a reaction to the stresses of a special type of jungle warfare, which included use of defoliants. The lack of public support for the war and the political conflict surrounding it added to the stresses experienced in combat. Recent studies have shown considerable levels of stress disorders. Thus, Frye and Stockton (1982) found 43 percent of veterans in a group they surveyed to be suffering from moderate to severe symptoms of post-traumatic stress disorder ten years after combat. This level was surprising considering that the men of the sample were extremely well educated, financially secure, professionally successful, and, in many cases, had been commissioned officers in Vietnam.

A number of factors seemed to contribute to the development of the disorder. The lack of helpfulness of the veteran's family (wife or parents) following his return home was one of the most critical factors. In general, these men were unable to talk to their families about their war experiences on their return home, because of the strong antiwar sentiment or the family's inability to listen due to fear, anxiety, reluctance, or general avoidance. The men's difficulty in resolving these issues was compounded by the immediacy of their discharge; many arrived home within forty-eight hours and thus had no transitional period in which to adjust and arrive at a sense of justification and personal meaning. The lack of a transitional period also meant that comrades or military personnel were not available to help the veteran work through his crisis. A high level of combat also contributed to the development of disorder. The mechanisms the soldier used to survive in the face of this catastrophic stress were denial, numbing, and repression: these seemed to facilitate his survival but place him more at risk for disorder. The extreme unpredictability and uncertainty of the jungle warfare also added a particular stress, making events seem outside the soldiers' control.

This picture of disorder, with intrusive thoughts, sleep disturbance, startle reactions, emotional constriction, detachment from others, guilt feelings, and depression, is well representative of the psychological morbidity of warfare for the combatant. Further complications such as drug abuse or serious violence were also noted during the war. And despite later improvement, there is still the suggestion that many veterans have ongoing problems with alcohol dependence, violence, and poor impulse control (Boman 1984).

Boman (1982) reviews evidence that many veterans also continue to suffer from depression, personality change involving psychic numbing and constriction in some cases and preoccupation with violence in others, and some ongoing survivor symptom effects—guilt, withdrawal, and despair. The picture of war-related impairment in this group is sobering; and some professionals suggest it is more severe than for soldiers in other wars (Keane and Fairbank 1983). However, the picture seems to be typical for those who have faced extreme combat stress in war. The stresses of other kinds of warfare such as air combat have also been clearly demonstrated to produce problems of psychopathology that must contribute to a high level of morbidity.

Studies of some of the "smaller" current wars, such as those in the Middle East, have demonstrated similar effects, since the stresses of death, mutilation, and loss are all intrinsic to battle. However, an extra contributing factor has appeared in studies of the United Nations peace-keeping forces. Weisæth and Sund (1982) show that soldiers in such forces might be affected even when combat is not intense, because they cannot retaliate. The fact that these soldiers too were at risk for typical post-traumatic stress disorder indicates the strong effect of helplessness in contributing to traumatic consequences.

War as disaster also has effects on the civilian population that is assaulted or conquered. The impact of bombing on civilian populations has been carefully studied and reviewed by Janis (1951). He showed that effects of air raids were proportional to the level of death and destruction, particularly to the personal experience of seeing others mutilated and dead, of being knocked down or nearly killed by the blast, or of having one's home destroyed. These "near miss" experiences contributed strongly to the development of severe fear reactions, as well as higher levels of psychiatric casualty due to anxiety and depression. Those who experience "remote miss," on the other hand, may show diminished levels of fear and greater capacity to withstand the emotional stress of later air raids, provided they do not then suffer a "near miss." Thus, Janis showed it was possible to predict that the incidence of severe emotional reactions from: (1) the number of nonfatal casualties; (2) the number of survivors in public shelters or homes damaged during the attack; (3) the number of families in which a fatality occurs; (4) the number of homeless people; and (5) the number of visible casualties, that is, of dead and mutilated seen by survivors. Thus, the disaster stressors of death and destruction, loss and grief, and dislocation are clearly operative in producing morbidity, and the level is again directly proportional to the intensity. Other experiences of war such as separation of family members, especially children, wartime bereavements, and general fear of invasion, bombardment, capture, and occupation may all add stressful effects.

Concentration camp and imprisonment experiences are another of war-related stress inducing psychiatric morbidity and problems. This has been best described by the work on the concentration camp syndrome referred to previously. Human reactions to such extreme environmental stress have been summarized by Hocking (1965). He acknowledges that physical effects from starvation, illness, and injury may complicate the picture but asserts that a psychological syndrome with a prolonged and chronic course was very frequent in those who survived extreme stress such as the concentration camps. These people showed anxiety, difficulties in concentrating, fatigue, apathy, illogical feelings of guilt, and sleep disturbance, often with terrifying nightmares of their experiences. This was found not only among Jewish survivors, but also in 78 percent of Danish resistance fighters who had spent a relatively short time in camp and 63 percent of the police force who had been interned in Denmark. Even years later, more than 40 percent of these groups still suffered considerable neurotic impairment. As in so many other situations of extreme stress, it was not preexisting personality factors that contributed the greatest effect to subsequent development of disorder but rather the duration and severity of stress during imprisonment. Eitinger's work has contributed greatly to an understanding of these stressor patterns (Eitinger and Askevold 1968).

Refugees, as noted previously, may be other victims of the disaster of war.

The principal stress they face in their refugee status may be dislocation, but a great many of them have also experienced danger and personal encounter with death, as well as the loss of family members, home, and possessions. The numbers of refugees are very substantial, and recent studies (Lin et al. 1982) suggest that there may be significant levels of morbidity for more than 50 percent of these people. Sadness, depression, grief, and somatic complaints are common; post-traumatic disorders may also appear for many. The longer-term morbidity patterns are not clear, and adjustment to the new culture may take a long time for those who are given a new home country. Little is known of the psychological morbidity of those who are not given a new home, for their struggle is to survive. In sum, the psychosocial morbidity of war is substantial, and is directly related to the stress of the experience. The following case study highlights some of these issues.

Frank W. was thirty when he presented for psychiatric care. He had been having "terrible nightmares," in which he was again in the jungles of Vietnam, "terrified," among the "mutilated and dead bodies" of his friends. His wife complained that he had lost all interest in her and was constantly irritable with the children. His work as a clerk was unsatisfying to him, and he seemed able to relate to others only when drunk. At such times, he would get violent and was easily drawn into fights. He had even frightened his sons with his ferociousness when playing war games with them. In therapy he remembered how much he had feared going to war, how much he had resented his conscription, his horror at the first death he saw, and his guilt at the first man he killed. On several occasions others were killed beside him; he survived in the midst of their dead bodies. His adjustment prior to Vietnam had been good, although he had been a shy young man, perhaps as a defense against being like his father, who was alcoholic and sometimes violent. His own capacity for violence in the threat of battle and his own desperate fears as he struggled to survive had overwhelmed him. He had felt guilt at killing but was driven by terror if he did not kill during battle. He developed a secret fantasy to justify his actions—that for each person he killed, he saved the life of one of his comrades. He could not talk to his wife about these feelings or any of his experiences, as she thought he should "put it all behind him" and the topic obviously upset her greatly. In therapy he was able to deal with his fears, particularly those of becoming like his father. His post-traumatic stress disorder improved considerably, although he was still sometimes troubled by bouts of depression and occasional bad dreams.

There can be little doubt that war is disaster and that it, too, may scar the minds of its survivors.

CHAPTER 9

Victims and Helpers

"I wanted to help so much. There seemed to be
so little I could do. I didn't know it would affect
me so much. I'd seen death before and I
thought I was hardened to it. . . . But I wasn't.
. . . All those dead people . . . the blood . . . the
children . . . the waste of it all. . . . I'll remember
it as long as I live."

When a great disaster strikes a community it will reverberate through it:
all will feel to some degree the death, fear, loss, and devastation that the
assault comprises. Many members of the community are victims and many
are helpers. These roles and experiences may be changed and interwoven
so that the distinction between victim and helper has little meaning. This
chapter looks at these roles: their special characteristics and the relationship
between them. And it explores the nature of the helper's experience as
victim of disaster.

VICTIMS

The word *victim* means "a person or thing injured or destroyed as a result
of an event or circumstance" *(Oxford English Dictionary)*. Thus there are
implications of injury and destruction for the person, or of being damaged.

Also inherent in the concept of victim is passivity, the sense that something is done *to* the person, something over which he has no control; so feelings of helplessness may also be evoked by the label and the experience.

It is clear that those who come to assist victims may themselves in turn be stressed by traumatic exposure to death, destruction, loss, and dislocation as they work in rescue, recovery, and restitution roles. Helpers may share the victims' experience of seeing mutilated and dead people, devastated homes and communities, because they are there. They may also, when working supportively with victims, empathically share, through identification, the painful emotional burdens the disaster has brought. Often the stressful experience or victimization of the helpers may not be recognized: they become the "hidden victims" of the disaster (Kliman 1976).

Some of the attempts to define the different degrees and types of victimization are useful in increasing awareness about those who may be affected by disaster as a traumatic experience. One such attempt is Dudasik's (1980b) description of four different types of victims in association with the Peruvian earthquake of 1970.

- *Event victims:* "those persons who were subjected to deprivation, suffering and hardship attributable both to [the disaster] itself and to its physical, psychological and sociocultural repercussions" (p. 331).
- *Contact victims:* Those who were affected, either directly or indirectly, by consequences of the disaster. This category would include those affected by disrupted services, contaminated or broken water supplies, or loss of food and other necessities. It is intended to describe those who must exist in or deal with the destroyed and devastated community.
- *Peripheral victims:* Those who had strong ties to the affected area and suffered as a consequence. This would include individuals with family or friends in the area.
- *Entry victims:* Those who converged on the stricken area during the period of crisis, for example, volunteers, people searching for relatives, or members of professional disaster aid groups. These may add to the victimization levels of any disaster, and their needs must also be recognized.

Dudasik described clearly how some of the volunteers who came to help following the earthquake had to suffer the lack of accommodation, shortage of food supplies, ongoing tremors, poor sanitation, threat of illness and injury, as well as the devastation, the stench of decaying human flesh in the rubble, and the "ever-present misery of the victims." These were all superimposed on a basic experience of "culture shock" in many cases. Thus, it is not at all surprising that many foreign helpers, as well as quite a number of the locals, themselves became affected by the disaster syndrome. It is reported that some became lethargic and apathetic, feeling helpless and inadequate. They often stayed in the compounds where they were based, drinking, sleeping, even playing cards or going through mechanical activities—anything that would help them "avoid tasks which immersed them in a sea of misery" (p. 336). Some reacted in the opposite way, flinging themselves into every task they could find and pushing themselves to exhaustion. These reactions have also been experienced by helpers in other situations (e.g., Berah et al. 1984).

Another way in which to classify the victims of disaster has been proposed by Taylor and Frazer (1981) as follows:

- *Primary victims:* Those in the front line who have experienced maximum exposure to the catastrophic event.
- *Secondary victims:* Grieving relatives and friends of the primary victims.
- *Third-level victims:* Rescue and recovery personnel who might "need help to maintain their functional efficiency during any operation and to cope with traumatic psychological effects afterwards" (p. 5).
- *Fourth-level victims:* The community involved in the disaster, including those who converge, who altruistically offer help, who share the grief and loss, or who are in some way responsible.
- *Fifth-level victims:* People whose emotional equilibrium is such that, even though not directly involved in the disaster, they may be precipitated into states of distress or disturbance.
- *Sixth-level victims:* Those who, but for chance, would have been primary victims themselves, who persuaded others to the course that made them victims, or who are in some way indirectly or vicariously involved.

The classification is somewhat complex, and perhaps the different aspects may be best represented by a diagram as in figure 9.1.

This classification does not allow for the different effects among helpers, who should probably be subcategorized in terms of whether they experienced the disaster effects directly or only indirectly. As will be discussed later, there are often some quite different experiences and effects for these two groups as well as a number of common themes.

In some ways the disaster that strikes a community is like a stone that is dropped into a pond. Ripples of its effects will spread through the community, reaching and affecting different elements at different times. Some of the waves set off will stir up their own currents in those already vulnerable.

FIGURE 9.1
The Various Disaster Victims

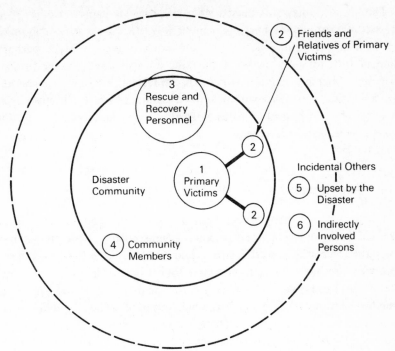

SOURCE: Adapted from A. J. W. Taylor and A. G. Frazer, *Psychological Sequelae of Operation Overdue Following the DC-10 Aircrash in Antarctica* (Wellington, New Zealand: Victoria University of Wellington Publications in Psychology, No. 27, 1981).

Some will create their own havoc, because their force is great and not spent, because they are close to the center of the intrusive effect. And as in the pond, it will take time for the effects to fade out. Ultimately, things may or may not be changed in the pond, depending on the size of the rock, the size of the pond, and the forces involved.

VICTIM DYNAMICS

Being a victim in a disaster means being exposed to many of the disaster stressors outlined in previous chapters. The specific dynamics will depend on the particular disaster, the person who is a victim, and the role expectations for that particular victim situation.

THE VICTIM AS A PERSON

The "victim" may be a person who, in earlier life experience, has been stressed or emotionally hurt in a similar way. This early stress may have left him or her vulnerable or, if it was not too overwhelming, perhaps "inoculated" to some degree against the adverse effects of the present experience. Being a victim may have special relevance for anyone who has had a "victim" experience within family dynamics or who has been a victim of other abuse, physical or psychological, during childhood. It may, for some people, lead to reverberations of masochistic feelings or of feelings of punishment.

THE ROLE OF VICTIM

This role carries many expectations, for one of the traditional myths of disaster, both community and personal, claims polarized and stereotyped roles: the "helper" is powerful, strong, and resourceful, the "victim" powerless, weak, resourceless, and ineffective (Short 1979). The victim may feel that he has to be weak and inadequate, that he must accept any help given whether he wants it or not, such as a handout of other peoples' old clothes or orders as to how to behave. There is usually a role expectancy of gratitude: victims are expected to be pleased and thankful for what they are given and not to complain. This expectancy creates great difficulties for victims, who often find it hard to express their distress, grief, and anger because people have given them aid and feel they should now be "all right." There are some similarities between victim role and patient role; both imply submission in a system of relationships and interactions with helpers and healers, as well as an abrogation of the rights to independence and complaint in return for care.

Mr. J. was fifty-six, an astute and competent tradesman. He had been injured in the cyclone, but only mildly, and was transferred to another city. There he was hospitalized for both assessment and accommodation purposes. He could not readily accept his loss of independence, having to wear hospital pajamas, for instance, and to obey the nurses, when he had previously given the directions for others to obey. He was too proud to let people know he could not read without his glasses, which were lost in the disaster. He had neither identification nor checkbook in the early stages. Each time he tried to express his distress about the terror of his experience and about the humiliation of being so dependent on others, the senior nurse told him how "lucky" he was—he hadn't been badly hurt —and how grateful he should be—everyone had done so much for him.

Victims and Helpers

THE CIRCUMSTANCES OF VICTIMIZATION

As important as expectations regarding the victim's role are the circumstances under which the person becomes a victim. A provoking editorial in *Disasters* (1980, 4:127–28), entitled "How to Succeed as a Disaster Victim," informs readers that they would do best to be a victim in a rich and affluent country, in a disaster brought on by an "act of God," rather than, for example, by chemical contamination or radiation. Things are far more difficult for those who are victims in poor countries. International interest and aid may be capricious, depending on publicity, the nature of the disaster, and other current world events. Short-onset disasters, such as floods, hurricanes, and earthquakes, are more likely to bring notice and help than the slow starvation of famine or drought. Political issues may mean that some victims' needs or roles are accepted and others' are ignored. And the aid provided may be more in line with stereotyped perceptions of the victim's state (clothes and toys) than with the real necessities (food and fuel). Success as a refugee will hinge on factors such as countries of origin and intake and how refugee status arose. But, in any event, being a disaster victim in a poor country is certainly bad news.

Becoming a victim because of "fate" has certain implications—of being chosen, picked out, punished, or spared by the gods. Becoming a victim because of the actions of others, as in war, civilian violence, and terrorism, also brings particular psychological implications—of being the target of specific or pointless human hatred.

Victimization by terrorism, especially in the hostage situation, is a special example. Stressors include the threat of death, separation from family and others, and control by captors. The victim tries to cope in many ways, as Ochberg (1978) and others have described. He is likely to remain alert and aroused, to attempt to gain the reassurance of familiar roles, or to rehearse what he should do. He tries to contain his anxiety, for he can see that its release may not help his survival. He tries to maintain his self-esteem while preserving relations with his captors for he senses that this may be the key to his survival. The victim may need to see the captor as a good person and to develop a sympathy for him, in order to maintain hope that he will be allowed to live. And when the victim becomes a real and human person to the terrorist, someone like him, with a personal life, family, and children, it is less likely that he will be killed. This is shown by Ochberg's (1978) discussion of Mr. Vadus, a hostage on a train in Holland. Vadus's attempts to send a message to his wife and his descriptions of his problems in family life made him real to the terrorists, who could no longer execute him, as they had intended. They later executed someone else, who was not "a person" to them. No doubt survivor guilt creates difficulties for the survivors of such incidents too.

A special relationship of this type, between victim and captor, can become positive and intense. This phenomenon is the so-called Stockholm syndrome, named after a situation in which a hostage in a Stockholm bank vault had sexual relations with her captor and lasting affection for him afterward. The victim "loves" his captor, perhaps even to the point of sexual intimacy, and at least with affection and positive feelings. This situation is more likely where the experience is intense, where the duration is more than three or four days, and where the hostage depends on the captor for survival and, at least to some extent, is suspicious of the authorities and psychologically distant from them. Ochberg (1980) gives several examples of the syndrome, including that of a senior Italian magistrate who, after being held captive by young Red Brigade terrorists, came to regard them as his own children. Afterward the victim may retain this special feeling. He or she may also maintain a paranoid suspiciousness of authorities and a lack of trust in interpersonal relationships, except perhaps with family.

A related type of victimization is that of torture. Here the victim may also attempt to cope by maintaining self-esteem and a sense of superiority to his persecutors, even if only in fantasies that deny the reality of the degradation and pain inflicted (Weisæth 1984, personal communication). The same stresses of confrontation with death and powerlessness are extant, and the same psychological sequelae may result.

Victims of crime may experience similar traumatic effects and be left with post-traumatic stress problems, as well as with paranoid suspiciousness and fear. They, too, have the need to deal with emotions aroused by the fact that the violence was committed by a person and to make meaning of this in terms of other people and relationships. For instance, in studying the reactions of those who were victims in crimes such as bank holdups, Weisæth (personal communication) found that at first the assailant may be remembered without a face or with a black hole in the place of a face.

Longer-term consequences of such victimization by other human beings include a chronic paranoia, a lack of trust in others, and sometimes post-traumatic stress disorders, anxiety, and depression. Some of the more positive consequences of such victimization may include a renewed commitment to family relationships and a sense of rebirth. Some victims have gained support and helped others by helping train those who would negotiate in future terrorist situations. Concern for such special issues of victimization in both community and personal disasters has lead to quite a few movements to deal with the needs of victims, for instance, to self-help support groups as well as care and legislative systems to provide counseling and compensation afterward.

Sometimes victims develop a special identity based on the circumstances of their victimization. Thus, the survivors of the Holocaust may feel they are forever so labeled and known. Publicity may lead to intense and sometimes distressing interest in the victims, their views, and their outcomes. There may be such public expectancies and interest that the victims' own individual reactions and needs may be submerged. In some instances, the publicity may maintain the victimization, rather than allowing the victims to be perceived in other roles or from other points of view. The identity of "victim" may come to exclude all others.

A special group of victims are those who have in some way been responsible for the disaster, such as train motormen or airplane pilots who, through chance or negligence, have caused a crash and survived, or, even if they did not cause it, may have been seen by themselves or others as somehow responsible for the deaths that occurred. These people usually suffer enormous emotional distress from public response and their own powerful feelings of guilt, and they are usually given little support. There may be prolonged periods of waiting before blame is established or the person exonerated. Yet even if exonerated, most of these people never recover, remaining "broken men."

A final comment on victimization involves the cultural context. In some societies there may be an element of nobility and greatness in suffering; those who are victims may in some way seem elevated in status. At an individual level this may make the victim feel important and significant for the first time in his life. Yet, in other societies or circumstances, there may be images of degradation and inferiority, perhaps even intimations that it was in some way the victim's own fault. In such cases, self-esteem may be negatively affected, adding further to the stress and to the likelihood of psychological consequences.

HELPERS

A helper is, again according to the *Oxford English Dictionary,* "one who aids or assists . . . or succors in some distress or misfortune." But there are many differences among the helpers who come to the disaster. Each brings his own special wish to assist, his own drive to succor, his own personality and past life experience, and most importantly, his own perceptions of what is needed and what he will do. A helper may also be a victim, giving aid to family, neighbors, and others more severely affected than himself. Or he may be a professional helper in one of many different roles, from rescuer to counselor, coming from outside to help the affected community.

THE HELPER AS A PERSON

Each individual will bring to the disaster his own internalized experience and fantasies that bear on what "disaster" and "helping" mean. Past encounters with death, destruction, grief, or dislocation may have left him psychologically vulnerable. For instance, he may have been bereaved of a parent in childhood. Or, he may have been involved in an overwhelming accident or subject to the loss of home or to the insecurity of not having a fixed home. Sometimes, but by no means always, such past experience may lead to stronger coping. Certainly those with previous experience of helping in a disaster may feel better equipped to face the various threats entailed and may be far less likely to be stressed by the experience unless, of course, it is overwhelming. Taylor and Frazer (1981), in their study of those who had been involved in body recovery in the Mount Erebus Antarctic plane crash, found that even some who had had extensive past experience with body recovery were stressed by their work with such great numbers of frozen and destroyed corpses.

Certain personality patterns and inner conflicts may lead the individual to respond to the disaster situation. Those who have conflicts concerning their own violent and aggressive fantasies, which the disaster now seems to have fulfilled in horrifying reality, may feel drawn to the disaster site. It is as though they may unconsciously feel they have somehow caused the catastrophe and have a need to help and heal. Sometimes the helper is drawn by natural curiosity about death and destruction and what these may mean personally. Another facet of the motivation to help may be the response to survivor guilt. The helper feels glad that he has not been the one directly killed or affected, then feels guilty and so must help in order to atone. He may feel the natural need to master the inner dread aroused by catastrophe through action, reparation, and control. None of these motivations is of necessity pathological, and all are likely to occur to some degree in most people. In some instances they may be exaggerated, and the helper may be overdriven in a particular way, perhaps through intrinsic needs to undo, for instance. This may add to his need to be involved to an excessive degree, and also to anxiety or resentment if he is frustrated in doing so. For a small number of helpers, underlying motivations may lead to distress, disturbance, or breakdown during the helping process; but for the most part they are dealt with defensively through activity and, when the disaster period is over, recede from the person's mind.

Another motivating force for the helper is often the wish to be involved in the excitement and special nature of the disaster: something quite different from the boredom and regularity of day-to-day activities. Such helping may bring far more than is bargained for, so that instead of arousal, there is a sense of being shocked and overwhelmed by the extent of the tragedy and the suffering of others. Nevertheless, in many helping disaster situations there is a sense of special involvement and excitement, a "high" which makes everyday tasks pale in comparison.

Above and beyond these natural and very human motivations is the motivation of altruism. A cynical view denies the importance of altruism as a factor in human behavior. Yet most people who have been in any way involved in a disaster will agree that it is a frequent and powerful force in the helping provided to others. It may be that the cataclysmic threat of disaster brings this drive to the surface for the survival of the group and thus of the species, which is so dependent on the functioning of the group. The importance of altruism has been commented on by Siporin (1976), who sees it as a phenomenon of crisis situations. He calls the therapeutic community effect after a disaster the "altruistic community" and says: "People give of themselves, even sacrificially, in a tremendous self-help effort, characterized by much chaotic collective behavior, by inefficient but effective mutual aid" (p. 217). Individuals show love, caring, and responsibility toward others who are in need or distress, over and above the needs of self. Altruism is more likely to be associated with personality traits of self-esteem, maturity, self-control, and empathic tendencies. Careful exploration of the various descriptions of disaster and disaster behavior shows that, even in situations like Hiroshima, people extended altruistic care and concern to others.

THE HELPING ROLE AND ROLES

Being a helper of one sort or another carries certain sorts of role expectations. As noted above, the helper is expected to know, to do, to be in control, to be powerful and resourceful, and to fix what has happened.

Helpers come to their roles along a number of different pathways. The circumstances of a disaster may be such that a victim finds himself helping others who have been more severely affected than he has. Or the helper may be someone who responds spontaneously from outside the impact area, as one of the many who converge. Or he may be a trained disaster worker, trained either for direct counterdisaster roles, such as impact management, rescue, or recovery, or for indirect roles, such as supporting victims in their efforts to deal with the consequences of the disaster. Such helpers may be either volunteer or professional. And what they do may be very similar to their day-to-day tasks or so different from them that a dramatic switch is required. Several other variables may be important in role performance. Sometimes there will be clearly defined goals and procedures. On other occasions the expectancies are very poorly defined: the helper may not know what he is expected to do, why, or how. His role in relation to his organization may be dictated by the defined systems of authority and responsibility he is used to. Or he may be uncertain about his place and function in special disaster systems of authority or in emergent groups.

The uncertainty of role expectation may in itself produce stress for the disaster worker or helper, who may fear that his work will be inadequate, that the wrong things will be done, or even that victims will die because of his actions or inaction. Thus, clearly defined roles involving practical tasks and activities, such as those of police and ambulance workers, are less likely to be associated with strain than vaguely defined roles, such as those of social workers and other support personnel (Raphael et al. 1983–84). Our studies found that uncertainties about goals and expected function could result in greater levels of depression among such support helpers. One important factor in lessening uncertainty and increasing effectiveness of functioning is disaster training. Helpers who have been trained in their roles and have practiced performing them are far more likely to perform without undue stress or with lower levels of stress. Past experience in disasters or other emergencies may also mitigate against negative responses, giving the helper a greater sense of command.

Once the person enters the helper role during or following a disaster, there is likely to be a high level of arousal and involvement. Attention is closely focused on the emergency tasks, and people feel that they are functioning most effectively. The mind races: thoughts, plans, and actions follow one another in rapid succession. This "high" is most rewarding and helps solve problems and frustrations. The helper will often become overactive and overinvolved, believing that he is the only one who can manage the situation or help victims. He may work nonstop, far beyond the optimal time of duty, and refuse to leave or relinquish responsibility. This behavior, called the counterdisaster syndrome, has been described in many helpers in many different disasters. It may reach an extreme degree and become inefficient, disruptive, or even counterproductive.

The helper or worker feels intensely good in helping others, in "undoing" the damage and trauma through altruism and reparation. This work may also involve him intimately and closely with others who share the special experience, creating a closeness he is unwilling to relinquish. Many disaster workers or helpers find their experience at this time more important and fulfilling "than anything in everyday life, and much more worthwhile," and so wish to hold on to it. The publicity and public nature of such roles often leads the helper to identify himself with his role in the disaster and make it a reference point in his life. It may also have brought the gratification of certain privileges or relief from responsibilities. For all these reasons, the helper may seek to continue his disaster role in whatever way he can.

CIRCUMSTANCES OF PARTICULAR DISASTERS

Particular disasters may have implications for helpers as a group or for individual helpers. If there is massive death and destruction or if children are affected, there is likely to be a strong helper response. An ongoing situation such as the AIDS epidemic may evoke a much weaker response, both because of its chronicity and because of fears of contamination. The helper who comes to offer assistance (and who is not himself a direct victim) has some image of the disaster circumstances and often also some fantasy of what he can offer in response. These images and fantasies are important to understand, as they may powerfully motivate the helper, or lead to anger if they are frustrated. When understood, they may more easily be channeled into appropriate helping modes. Furthermore, the helper's reparative needs are such that when he cannot make good the disaster effects, he may feel stressed or overwhelmed and may become a victim himself if his responses are not dealt with.

VICTIM-HELPER RELATIONSHIPS

As noted earlier, there may be special relationships between the victim and helper. Intense bonds may develop because of the needs of the victim and the mutuality of the roles. However, because of role expectations, some relationships of this kind will work only as long as the helper feels needed and in control. In the beginning, when the victim is still stunned, shocked, hurt, dependent, or needy, the helper will feel a positive glow from what he can do for and has given to the victim. Later, as the victim needs him less and can once again function independently, the helper may feel threatened, rejected, or inadequate—or simply grateful that his role obligations are finished. Problems of gratitude and ingratitude often arise where there are different expectations.

Another aspect of the victim-helper relationship is empathy and identification. The crisis of the disaster is likely to bring victim and helper closer together emotionally. The helper often feels that "that could have been me, or my family." Furthermore, the victims may in some ways be more like himself in social class and background than those he works with at other times. All this means that he is usually much more emotionally open to the suffering of these people. This may bring many good feelings of common humanity or it may be very threatening.

As already mentioned, some helpers continue relationships with victims well beyond the period of necessity. Thus, they may be reluctant to hand "cases" over to the appropriate local health, welfare, or other workers. They may even be reluctant to refer victims to others such as psychiatrists when there is clearly a need for more in-depth assessment (McFarlane 1984). Sometimes the specialness of this relationship may interfere with other relationships, even personal and family ones. This problem is made more likely by the fact that there is less professional definition of roles at a time of heightened need and demand. Furthermore, and appropriately, the disaster situation calls for the natural response of one human being caring for another.

STRESSES FOR THE DISASTER HELPER

In recent years there has been an increasing awareness that a disaster may bring stressful effects for those involved in a variety of counterdisaster and support roles, even if they themselves are not directly affected by the disaster. Contributing to this awareness is a developing body of theory and study of "burnout" in those working in high-stress roles, for example, in emergency, intensive care, and terminal care units in hospitals. The stressors faced by helpers may be severe and may lead, as they do for other victims, to reactive processes in the immediate post-disaster stage or to significant and longer-lasting effects on mental health.

The stressors are similar to those experienced by other victims but with additional aspects related to role functioning. There are now a number of studies that address these issues: studies of rescue and support personnel involved in the Granville rail disaster in 1977 (Raphael et al. 1980; Raphael et al. 1983–84); studies of those involved in body handling and victim identification following the DC-10 air crash in Antarctica in 1979 (Taylor and Frazer 1980, 1981, 1982); studies of those involved in the helping after the Kentucky nightclub fires (Lindy et al. 1983; Titchener and Lindy 1980); studies of firefighters (McFarlane 1984; Cook et al. 1984; Innes and Clarke

1984), health workers, and relief workers following the Ash Wednesday bushfires (Berah et al. 1984).

Our own studies of ninety-five workers after the rail disaster showed that they perceived the following aspects as the most stressful of the experience: feelings of helplessness, magnitude of the disaster in terms of the numbers of dead and injured, the unexpectedness, the sight and smell of dead bodies, the anguish of relatives, the suffering of the injured, and the need to work under extreme pressure. Similar findings regarding stressors emerge from other works cited.

ENCOUNTER WITH DEATH

For helpers who are directly involved with the dead of the disaster, the multiplicity of the deaths, their sudden and unexpected nature, the shocking injuries they may involve, and the deaths of the young, especially children, may all reflect the special traumatic effect of confrontation with human mortality. Following the Granville disaster, policemen and rescue and mortuary workers commented on the stressful nature of this experience, even though their daily work brought them into frequent contact with death. Even doctors and nurses were horrified by the magnitude and nature of the deaths; as one doctor spoke of his experience:

I'm used to death . . . but it's usually quiet death in the home . . . or clinical death in the hospital. It's cleaned up by the nurses beforehand if it's an accident. There was nothing in my experience that equipped me for this. The bodies were so mashed; there was blood and guts everywhere . . . and so many were dead and some of them were so injured . . . and it was such a terrible way to die. It seemed so unfair that they were caught and trapped like that by the hand of fate. I could see them all . . . just like me or anyone else . . . going off to work in the morning . . . the same old way for an ordinary day, and then this . . . and life was cut off forever —gone—finished. It just made me realize . . . well . . . how it can all end —and then there's nothing. I felt so helpless too, as though there should have been more I could do and there wasn't. I was inadequate to deal with all that death somehow; it shocked me in a way I wouldn't have thought possible. I dreamt about it for weeks afterwards; I'd wake up in a panic trying to resuscitate someone in my dream . . . not having the equipment . . . calling someone to get it for me, and no one coming. I felt bad and guilty, and sometimes the memories of it would flash before my mind. I kept going over and over what had happened to see if I could have done more . . . although I really knew in my heart I had done all I could. I drank heavily for a while too, and I was angry with everyone: my wife and kids, the patients. That's settled now but it's had an effect on me that I'll never forget.

I, too, experienced this sense of massive confrontation with death, in my role of organizing and carrying out support services for bereaved relatives at the city mortuary following the disaster. Still clearly imprinted on my mind are the rows and rows of sad, gray human bodies. This same feeling was described by those helping the bereaved families following the Kentucky nightclub fire, where Titchener and Lindy (1980) comment on "the fear in the presence of so much death—made grotesque by the grey faces in neat rows" (p. 9). They call this "traumatic overload," and others have called it "death overload" (Pine 1974b).

Our work (Raphael et al. 1983–84) showed that at least 70 percent of the Granville workers studied experienced some degree of strain, as assessed by a questionnaire administered about a month after the disaster. Although the representativeness of the sample is unknown, there is much to suggest that it is likely to have covered a considerable proportion of those directly involved. The sample included rescue and organization workers (police officers, rescue workers, firefighters), medical personnel (doctors and nurses), and support personnel (social workers and Salvation Army workers). There appeared to be no significant differences between these three groups in the general experience of being stressed by the disaster. The encounter with death contributed substantially to stress response, leading to nightmares, anxious feelings, sleep difficulties, and to a degree, depressed feelings, although these last tended to be more commonly associated with uncertainty of role functioning.

In this disaster, some of those dealing with the dead at the site were themselves in danger of dying from the slab that was crushing the train. These people were significantly more likely to have positive feelings about life subsequently, as though their personal encounter with death had lead them to reevaluate their own lives and goals.

Similarly, Taylor and Frazer (1981) review the experience of the body handlers after the Mount Erebus disaster. The sight of smashed and mutilated bodies was a grisly one, and the men tended to defend against their feelings by redefining the bodies as frozen carcasses. When these dismembered remains were taken in clear plastic bags to the ice strip before transfer back to New Zealand for identification, the heat melted some of the contents. The sharp bits of bone sometimes punctured the bags, and they burst, with body juices and flesh splashing over the workers. Then, in the city mortuary in Auckland, Disaster Victim Identification teams had to work with "unmarked . . . to charred, carbonized torso fragments with the majority of flesh singed, arms and legs badly gashed (usually), ankles broken, and feet either dangling or missing, the stumps badly lacerated, with varying degrees of skull damage. . . . Several plastic bags were opened to reveal an unrecognizable mass of humanity, thick with aviation fuel and hydraulic oil" (Taylor and Frazer 1981, p. 17).

The study of 180 workers who had dealt with the bodies at various stages after the Mount Erebus crash showed that one of the most prominent stressors faced by this group was the encounter with massive death and mutilation. As measured by the Hopkins symptom checklist, only 18.5 percent were free of symptoms initially and 53.5 percent showed symptoms of moderate severity. Moreover, the initial assessment revealed that 80.5 percent experienced changes in sleep, 76 percent changes in appetite, 48.9 percent dazed feelings, 40 percent changes in interaction, and 33 percent changes in social activities. Some people still continued to experience these effects at the time of the one-month assessment, although by follow-up at twenty months 80 percent considered they had resolved their problems quite satisfactorily. The changes in symptoms over time are represented in figure 9.2.

In terms of constellations of symptoms and ongoing disorder, the symptom patterns for the Mount Erebus workers was very much that of post-traumatic stress reactions, with reports of "intrusive unpleasant thoughts," "bad dreams," "sleep disturbance," "wanting to be alone," and "tension." It seems likely only a small proportion continued these reactions to the level of disorder at twenty months, although the numbers are not fully clear from Taylor and Frazer's reports. The symptoms found in our study (Raphael et al. 1983–84) and reported descriptively by Titchener and Lindy (1980) are similar in type.

THE ANGUISH AND SUFFERING OF OTHERS

Whether involved in rescue and recovery operations or in longer-term support services, most helpers are likely to have contact with the directly affected victims, sharing their suffering firsthand or hearing from them of their experience. The human, empathic response, together with the heightened arousal, engagement, and the often intense relationships, means that the helper will become acutely aware of grief, pain, and distress. This distress may be awakened in the helper on top of his own grief and anguish about what has happened. Sometimes, the helper can cope with this awareness only by withdrawing, retreating into important practical tasks, or denying the emotional suffering of the victims. Feelings of inadequacy and helplessness may be readily aroused, because what the victims really want

FIGURE 9.2
Changes in Stress Effects Reported by Workers

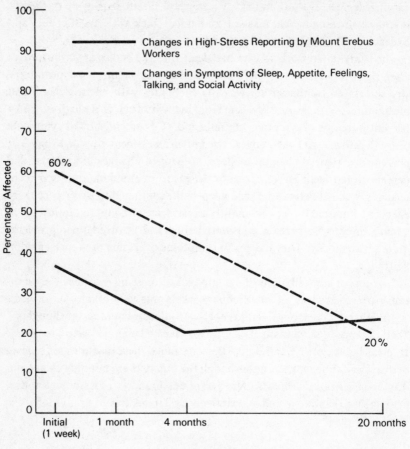

Source: Based on data from A. J. W. Taylor and A. G. Frazer, "The Stress of Post-Disaster Body Handling and Victim Identification Work," *Journal of Human Stress* (December 1982):4–12.

is for things to be as they were before and here there is nothing the helper can do. Police and social workers after the Granville rail disaster and support staff helping grieving relatives following the Mount Erebus disaster all commented on experiencing such feelings. Titchener and Lindy (1980) note a variety of defensive responses used by psychiatrists and mental health workers to stop themselves from being overwhelmed by their identification and empathy with bereaved relatives. These included a sense of protest about the extent and reality of the deaths, feelings of helplessness and fatigue, denial and disbelief, anger and rage, and a sense of giving in to the traumatic overload of death and loss.

More recently, commenting on a team of helpers in the Ash Wednesday disaster, Berah et al. (1984) noted how "intense and intimate engagements with distressed victims often *taxed empathy, emotional resources and therapeutic skill*" (p. 358). The "vivid emotions" and graphic descriptions of the victims made their experience come alive for helpers who had not been there, as did the blackened and devastated countryside. The helpers may have traumatic experiences of their own brought to the surface or may suffer traumatic intrusions and dreams related to the experience, their own variety of post-traumatic stress reaction. Two-thirds of this team of nineteen mental health workers whose job was to provide counseling and support reported suffering from fatigue, and one-third reported disturbed sleep patterns and increased muscle tension. Feelings of shock and bewilderment, dependency, confusion and uncertainty, depression and sadness, and helplessness were common. After three or four visits to the affected area and its people, the emotional and physical reactions of stress did diminish somewhat. It is important to note that about half the team became ill during their disaster work, and nearly one-half had accidents or changed their smoking, drinking, and eating habits. Post-traumatic dreams were present for about a third of the group. It cannot be concluded that the anguish of others was the sole cause of the stress reactions experienced, for role conflicts also appeared for this group as they visited and worked in the devastated area. Nevertheless, their principal role was to share the suffering of others, and there can be no doubt from their own reports that this was indeed a substantial stressor for them, even though they were very skilled and experienced in this work.

Role functions in a disaster may be less clear for those whose principal function is to offer emotional support. These workers are likely to feel greater uncertainty and helplessness, and in our studies this seemed likely to be more associated with feelings of depression afterward; perhaps the overwhelming loss and grief contributed to this depression as well. The workers are often involved in outreach programs, seeing people in their own homes or shelters and seeing people who could be themselves—not the traditional welfare or mentally ill clients, who normally define themselves as dependent on the helper. Thus, there is less role protection and role training for workers in this field.

Empathy with grief, suffering, and loss is indeed painful (Raphael 1981, 1983), as my own experience as a disaster worker has revealed,

I remember clearly lying awake the third night after the disaster and feeling inside me the overwhelming load of grief that was ahead for those people and families we had met at the morgue. I knew I could not personally counsel them all. I knew there were very few resources for counseling in the outer areas of the larger city where most of them lived.

I knew their grief was complex and terrible, and that they could be helped, yet we would not be able to do it all. I felt a terrible sadness and a sense of loss, as well as a great personal burden.

This empathic response to the victims' loss and grief, plus any uncertainties of role and training, leave the helpers emotionally vulnerable; earlier losses, or fear and dread of loss, may be awakened in the helper. The actual effects of such vulnerability and the stresses involved in terms of reaction or disorder over longer term remain to be defined.

ROLE STRESSES

Several different kinds of role stresses appear. For those with practical disaster tasks, the feeling of not being able to accomplish these adequately is stressful. Difficulties of communication, inadequate resources or equipment, staff problems, lack of access, or bureaucratic problems may all be immediate sources of stress and frustration. A senior police officer commented after the rail disaster: "We couldn't get in there with acetylene torches—there were gas cylinders and we were afraid of fire. We couldn't break up the slab—it took us quite a while to see how we would free them. Those were the terrible frustrations. The people involved were terrific—they did everything anyone could do and more, but we couldn't get the victims out. Not in the beginning."

Exhaustion is another kind of role stress. Many workers become overinvolved and may, because of this or through necessity, be unwilling to relinquish their posts until exhaustion supervenes. Strict requirements for relief may help prevent exhaustion, but it nevertheless is a very frequent source of stress.

Another source of stress is the helplessness felt when the overwhelming nature of the disaster or a lack of training or resources makes fulfillment of role responsibilities difficult or impossible. This may also be added to by personal factors in the helper. For example, expectations of the self and others to be all-powerful may reinforce helpers' feelings of inadequacy.

Relationships with authority systems and with other relief organizations involved in the disaster may become a source of strain. If the helper is uncertain of lines of authority or his role in terms of other bodies helping in the disaster (and there may be many with the convergence that occurs), he may find himself or his group involved in conflict. Berah et al. (1984) comment on this in their study, as do Heffron (1977), Zurcher (1968), and Leivesley (1977). Problems may even reach the point where there is conflict between groups over who "owns" or has the right to treat victims—a sad state of affairs for helpers, organizations, and victims alike.

Family interactions may be a source of stress if the family feels excluded or deprived by the worker's involvement. Differential responses in family members have clearly been seen as stressful. The helper may be torn by his responsibilities to family and to victims. He may be unable to share his distress, for example, his preoccupation with intrusive memories of what he has experienced, or his spouse may be unable to tolerate his needs to talk it through (McFarlane and Frost 1984), so that distress and disharmony result. Conflict between regular work and disaster roles is also not infrequent. The helper's colleagues may feel excluded and angry because they did not share in the limelight of the disaster aftermath but had to "keep things going back at the shop." The special relationships the helper forms with victims and with those who worked in the disaster with him may lead to a sense of exclusion for colleagues and family alike.

Injuries may also be a problem, as may loss if the worker was personally affected by the disaster. All in all his role is a complex one, and it is not surprising that he will be affected by it. The effects may be negative or positive, taking the form of symptoms and impaired role performance or reevaluation and reinvestment in life.

Reactions to role stressors seem to include depression, but this is more likely for support workers (Raphael et al. 1983–84). Drinking problems, marital difficulties, accident proneness, and illness have all been described but not systematically studied.

HOW DO HELPERS COPE?

Like all those affected by disaster stressors, helpers, as indirect victims, use a variety of techniques in attempting to deal with the experience. Among the most important of these is the use of supportive relationships.

The support of family and close friends is one of the main factors that will enable the helper to successfully negotiate the stresses the disaster brings. They are a secure and loving base to which he returns. They offer consolation, succor, security, and ongoing life. They help him heal.

Other supportive relationships are also very important. Close bonds with other workers who shared the experience and professional support systems are both likely to be of great value. Perhaps the most effective way in which supportive relationships may be used to help is through the process of psychological debriefing after the disaster; here the leaders of the working team may informally or formally provide an opportunity to review the disaster experience, so that those involved may talk through their feelings, fears, frustrations, and successes. This seems to help by providing the catharsis of emotional release, by allowing individuals to test their perceptions of the experience against those of others, and by enabling them to actively review the experience and thus gain mastery. This process is sometimes undertaken in informal social situations and may include family members, who are also given an opportunity for open discussion about what has happened. This same process may be conducted more formally by involving an outside expert to review the disaster and gain perspective on it. The evidence points to the usefulness of this supportive group interaction, plus the processes of review and catharsis, in preventing negative psychological sequelae of the disaster. The mechanism of using this process preventively will be discussed in the next chapter.

Gaining mastery of the stressful experience comes in many ways. The review process helps the person to see that his job was well done and that there was little he could have done differently under the circumstances. Praise from his leader is likely to reinforce his sense of mastery. If he has been somehow inadequate in his functioning, he may have considerable psychological adjustment to make, especially if living with a burden of guilt over any serious adverse consequences of his actions or decisions. Training and education help in the sense of mastery, in that the person feels he has learned from this experience and is better prepared to deal with the next. Reports, reviews, and testimonies all help in this way, as does involvement in future disaster planning and counterdisaster activities.

Dealing with the feelings involved may initially be through distancing or shutting off, so that functions can still be carried out. Thus, the workers who must identify the bodies may find it necessary to temporarily dehumanize the remains to carry on their task although later they experience distress and grief. Such a temporary emotional shutting out has been described in many disaster helpers (e.g., Titchener and Lindy 1980; Raphael 1981). As with victims, it is adaptive as long as it does not lead to psychic numbing or ongoing denial of emotions. Given the importance of gradual release of feelings in supportive personal situations, family closeness and psychological debriefing may be critical to adjustment and the helper may be "at risk" if these are lacking. The experience of helpers, from initial motivation to response to outcome, is summarized in figure 9.3.

FIGURE 9.3
Helpers as Hidden Victims

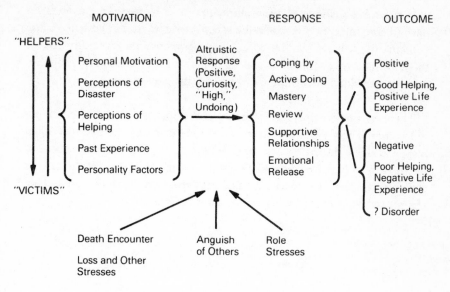

PERSONAL DISASTER VICTIMS AND HELPERS

The close identification helpers experience with those affected by a wide variety of personal disasters has been noted by many workers in this field. The need to maintain the delicate balance between empathic concern and compassion while avoiding overinvolvement has also been highlighted (Raphael 1981). The stressful effects for workers stem from the encounter with death, from sharing the anguish of the victims and their families, and from role stresses. A number of recent studies (Vachon et al. 1978; Livingston and Livingston 1984) have shown how high levels of stress may become. For instance, Vachon's group found that staff on a newly opened palliative care unit were only slightly less stressed than a group of newly widowed women; physicians also experience stress and "burnout." Younger and less experienced personnel may be more vulnerable, and training and anticipatory group work may be needed to help lessen negative effects. Here, of course, the confrontation with death is much less and is anticipated, but it is continuous, whereas the helper at a disaster generally leaves the scene and goes back to his ordinary work. Both groups need supportive interpersonal frameworks that can facilitate their adaptation to the inevitable stressors of the work. Debriefing and support groups are likely to lessen morbidity, just as good training and education will provide the helper with more resources to deal with these community and personal disaster responsibilities. But in both types of situations, victims and helpers readily merge, boundaries are blurred, and impact on personal life is considerable. And in both cases, the outcome for helpers may be considerable psychosocial morbidity. But if there is not an overinvolvement or exhaustion of personal resources, positive reevaluations of life and relationships may result.

There are many helpers and workers at the time of disaster. Their efforts reflect all the best of human values, on a complex background of individual response. They do their work well, for the most part, and are critical to recovery. Yet there may be much personal strain. Awareness of their needs and their disaster experience may prevent them from becoming the hidden victims, who suffer long after the disaster has passed.

244

CHAPTER 10

Psychosocial Care

"I had to talk about it, over and over again.
. . . I couldn't get it out of my mind in the
beginning. It helped that others would listen,
and accept my feelings. Then it started to
fade."

The shocked, stunned disaster victim requires care at many levels: he needs the caring acknowledgment that he has been affected; he needs comfort and consolation from others—family, friends, and all those who come to help him; he needs care for his injuries and maybe assistance to bury his dead; he may need shelter, food, and clothing in the short run, and aid and compensation over the long run. At a community level, similar needs— social and material—must be met if recovery is to occur. Care can be provided in indirect ways; through actions or statements or responses that indicate others are concerned, or more directly in terms of concrete provisions of support to the victims. This chapter discusses different levels of care, their utility and effects, and patterns of care ranging from diffuse to specific.

RECOGNITION OF SUFFERING AND STRENGTH

The first and most general level of psychosocial care for disaster-affected people and communities lies in the recognition, by statement or actions, that they have suffered from the disaster. This recognition may come from the authorities, the government, or the surrounding community. It may be evidenced by the declaration of a state of emergency, by the use of emergency resources, or by political action directed toward stating the special case of the victims. At times of such disaster emergency, political leaders may visit the disaster site or make statements that the government will come to the aid of those affected. These statements symbolize the general community's recognition of suffering.

The media response also provides recognition of what has happened, and its "human interest" stories are likely to underscore the suffering and need of the affected community. This media interest again indicates to victims that their plight is being taken seriously—it is on the front page or headline news. However, it may not be followed through by the ongoing response that many will require, just as the promises of some leaders cannot always be fulfilled by total reparation for what has been lost. But these initial reactions are helpful, even if forgotten promises later lead to disappointment and resentment.

The effects of inappropriate recognition of suffering is well exemplified by a city where the state government is said to have failed to declare a "state of emergency" in the wake of major floods, although it had done so a few weeks earlier when demonstrations had occurred during a football game. People felt angry that their need had not been appropriately acknowledged. In another instance, several small towns showed anger and resentment because they had not been mentioned by the media during the forest fires even though they had been as severely affected as others who got "all the publicity." People felt they were not recognized as disaster victims. A similar phenomenon occurs in personal disaster situations. In a casualty/accident study, many patients who had experienced the shock of accidents but only mild injury felt that they had been dismissed by the casualty surgeon, who had not recognized their distress.

In some cases, just the statement "I know you've been hurt and upset" is sufficient care to enable victims to regather their resources and start on the pathway to recovery. A further aspect of the recognition of suffering may be the recognition of the victim's spiritual needs—thus, for instance, by the chaplains who comfort at the site of the disaster.

Another important issue of disaster care and management is that victims and communities need recognition not only of their suffering but also of their strengths; these strengths may be mobilized in recovery. The recognition of strength and capacity to cope is in itself important in undoing the helplessness that is likely to have been so overwhelming during the impact. Such strengths may need to be acknowledged at an individual level by conveying to victims a respect for their capacities while offering support or care, and by indicating that help will probably be needed only for a short while until the victims' own strengths again take control. At a community level, recognition of strengths means engaging the community from the beginning in the assessment of damages and the process of reparation. Strengths will vary for different individuals and different communities, but they are always there. Any post-disaster plans must acknowledge them. Otherwise, victims and affected communities may be forced into further passivity and dependency or into feelings of inadequacy, which will complicate recovery.

An adequate plan for post-disaster management—an overall mantle of care—will do all of the following:

1. Offer every possible comforting human response and physical necessity to those affected in their period of shock and subsequent realization.
2. Recognize and support the strengths of those affected as they gradually become able to take control of their own lives and destinies again.
3. Facilitate the supportive understanding of victims and those who will be in contact with them, about the natural responses, reactions, and recovery following a major disaster.
4. Ensure that necessary specialized care is provided to those whose coping is threatened, who are decompensating, or who are at risk.
5. Provide for the integration of psychosocial care with the provision of other forms of aid.
6. Recognize and provide for the many different "victims" of the disaster.
7. Plan and monitor the smooth and gradual transition of care of the victims, their representatives and their community caregivers as appropriate during the post-disaster period.

The levels of psychosocial care in disaster may be symbolized by the model of an "umbrella of care" diagrammed in figure 10.1 and analyzed below.

PSYCHOSOCIAL CONSULTANCY

A vital part of the umbrella of care is consultant work with organizations and groups involved in disaster response. Educational and consultative

FIGURE 10.1
The Umbrella of Care

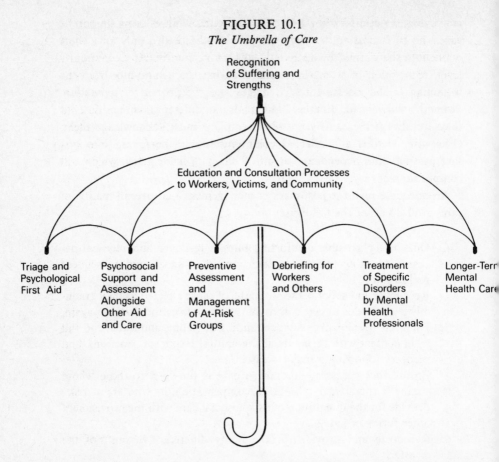

models are very valuable in helping the many who are involved in disaster —from those in counterdisaster planning and management to the victims themselves—understand and respond to the different biological, psychological, and social processes that may occur. Such consultancy may not, however, automatically be recognized as valuable and important by those involved in disaster management and response, unless previous experience has indicated a need or sanctions have been negotiated.

As initially described by Caplan (1964) and discussed more specifically in the disaster context by Cohen and Ahearn (1980), negotiation of sanctions may mean that the mental health professional who wants to develop post-disaster services and offer consultancy advice must be seen as trustworthy and as offering something of practical value in the emergency and chaos of the post-disaster convergence. Practical workers such as rescue personnel and police, or those in charge of the disaster response organization, may view mental health services as unnecessary, a luxury, or even a nuisance.

They may see such services as getting in the way of the "real work" and offering poorly defined or incomprehensible services.

Sanctions will need to be negotiated at federal, state, and local levels with the authorities likely to be responsible, and then specifically with counter-disaster and community leaders. It needs to be clear what is offered, to whom, how, and why, who will pay costs, and who will be accountable. Both at the initiation of consultancy and throughout the process, boundaries and relationships with other professional and volunteer groups may need to be negotiated. These groups may not have a clear idea of what can be provided within the framework of mental health or psychosocial care or, if they do, may see it as intruding on their own domains.

PRE-DISASTER

Liaison with community bodies involved with disaster awareness, disaster prevention, and counterdisaster management, needs to be established. The consultant may, through conferences or presentations to these groups, develop awareness of the psychological variables that influence behavior at the different disaster stages. Topics would include the nature of adaptive and nonadaptive responses during impact, the importance of information in lessening anxiety during and after the disaster, the advisability of keeping primary groups intact whenever possible, the need for victims to have a role in their own recovery, the importance for the bereaved of seeing the bodies of those they have lost, and so forth. Training in the principles of emotional first aid for a wide range of disaster workers is also important alongside the basics of physical resuscitation, in view of the evidence that people often respond best to support offered at the same time as other services (Singh and Raphael 1981; Valent 1984; Cohen and Ahearn 1980). Consultation should also aim to increase awareness in mental health professionals of the range of psychological morbidity that may appear in the immediate post-disaster period and the necessities of triage (the allocation of treatment to victims according to priorities that will maximize survival) if there are indications of risk or developing problems. If disaster workers are aware of or have previously used psychiatric consultancy to discuss cases and increase their understanding of mental health problems, they are more likely to be able to utilize this knowledge in the disaster context. It is also important, if there is any opportunity pre-disaster, to acquaint workers with some of their own possible patterns of response and with the management of stress by techniques like psychological debriefing. Many organizations will be resistant to the psychological component of disaster management and counterdisaster activity unless they have had recent experience of human behavior during a catastrophe and perhaps also some awareness of recent developments in this field. Thus, many hospitals have little in the way of a mental health component in their disaster plans, and it is only in recent years that psychiatric consultants have had any involvement in community organizations with disaster briefs.

An example of pre-disaster consultancy can be provided from work in an Australian state prior to the bushfires. Because of previous disaster experience in two emergencies (cyclone and rail disaster), there was a heightened awareness of possible difficulties and needs.

Workers had been made aware of the emotional needs of victims. At the time of disaster they were provided with handouts and further education on emotional first aid. There was recognition of the need for a single resource person for the longer-term contact with victims, instead of multiple, converging, and chaotic caregivers. Government subsidy was provided to hire these workers, and they were trained in mental health aspects and offered opportunities for regular case review. Recognition of the stress of the helpers led to special group debriefing and review to assist with stress management. Workers in different areas met to review their experience. Public awareness of disaster stress and post-traumatic stress reactions was encouraged by arranged media presentations. Finally, public acknowledgment of the mental health needs was made by hiring an outside expert to work with workers, organizations, authorities, and the public during the emergency periods and to assist with plans for the later aftermath.

Another state developed a somewhat different model, involving a direct outreach to local communities and the provision of both grass roots consultative services and direct mental health interventions in affected areas.

Both these programs were only possible because of pre-disaster work, which had led to an acceptance of the importance of victims' mental suffering, and of worker stress. However, much implementation and detail only followed the disaster impact, with the further negotiation of sanctions at various levels of the community. As a consequence of this disaster work in the mental health field, psychiatrists and other senior mental health professionals now have an established role in counterdisaster planning and activities in both states, and at a high level.

Thus, sanctions for the mental health component are developed on the basis of trust and respect for the contribution that this expertise has provided in disaster and everyday problems. These sanctions may require maintenance, for with change of personnel the gains may be lost.

As has been noted by several studies, the closer roles during the disaster are to roles held in the pre-disaster period, the more readily transfer of knowledge and skill can take place. Thus, police or emergency workers may respond to consultancy about disaster that is offered by mental health workers with whom they collaborate in other emergency situations. Often such prior collaboration is in personal disasters, for instance, in bereavement crisis work following accidents or sudden infant death syndrome or in crisis intervention work following rape or other assault.

DURING DISASTER IMPACT

Consultancy at this stage is often geared to advice about behaviors and about methods of lessening stress (preventing separations, lessening shock, and maintaining contact with and information flow to victims) and to developing plans for needs that will arise in the aftermath (crisis intervention, aid, outreach services, community groups). The consultant's work may also be geared to directly helping the disaster workers and authorities and to offering support for their emotional needs. For instance, the consultant may help workers define duties for optimal effectiveness or may help them talk through decisions to lessen guilt conflicts.

Immediately following the rail disaster, consultants were involved in acquainting authorities and public with the likely mental health consequences and needs and how best to handle them. Their work included setting up a team of mental health support workers with expertise in the field of bereavement to assist the relatives of those who were killed. When relatives came to identify bodies, workers offered them emotional support and made initial contact for longer-term follow-up in the weeks ahead. During this period media presentations informed the general public of the best ways to support those who had been directly affected. Other presentations were made to hospitals, about support for the injured, and to the authorities, about the needs of the bereaved. Some early educational tasks were undertaken with workers in the communities who were likely to have contact with victims (see Raphael 1979–80). This work helped sensitize the community to needs and prepared many for the contact they were having or would have with those more directly affected. Some preliminary planning was also carried out regarding the needs of workers in the disaster aftermath. Similar programs have been set up in other disaster situations, for example, those described by workers at the Traumatic Stress Study Center at the University of Cincinnati after the Beverly Hills supper club fire (Titchener and Lindy 1980; Lindy and Green 1981).

IN THE AFTERMATH PERIOD

Here consultancy can provide a number of major inputs to disaster management that will assist with recovery and contribute, hopefully, to the lessening of psychiatric morbidity in association with the stress. It will be important to assess the likely mental health needs following the particular disaster and plan services accordingly. Thus, consultancy extending from the impact and acute aftermath will be able to suggest services related to high death levels in terms of care of the bereaved. These services may need to incorporate aspects related to body identification, funeral, and coronial aspects, support to families, as well as encouragement and facilitation of grief work. If there have been many destructive mutilating deaths where the bodies have been seen by others, or if survivors have been subjected to close encounters with death in situations of shock and helplessness, then risk of post-traumatic stress disorder may be high. Victims may need early services geared to support, catharsis, and reworking, with an emphasis on gaining control and a sense of mastery. In addition, they may need longer-term interventions to deal with traumatic effects of intrusive memories or inhibitory processes, perhaps along the lines suggested by Horowitz (1976). Disasters that produce dislocation stress may require social and welfare services with counseling to assist family adaptation and network development in new areas.

Consultancy may assist with planning not only for types of mental health skills and services but also for their siting and access. Such services may be optimally developed in the affected communities alongside recovery and rebuilding activities and with use of local expertise and resources (e.g., Valent 1984). There are many difficulties in outreach, as highlighted by Lindy and Green (1981) and Lindy et al. (1983), for many of those in need may be reluctant to make contact or may not perceive their needs as related to mental health services. The presentation of such services may be important, for they are often more acceptable to the public if presented as stress, crisis, disaster, or counseling services, rather than as psychiatric services, which, for many people, still seem to carry some stigma or inference of personal inadequacy.

Apart from such direct mental health services, consultancy during this period aims at increasing the awareness and skills of all those personnel who are likely to be in contact with victims. This is important, as recent reviews (e.g., McFarlane 1984) suggest that some workers lack such awareness in their appraisal of victims' needs and may be unable or unwilling to refer victims to specialized mental health services even when these are clearly required. Furthermore, many workers may see the importance of skills in these areas but feel themselves inadequately trained and thus concentrate on only the material aspects of client care, to the detriment of emotional support.

Educational Consultancy. The educational component is obviously very important in consultancy during this period. The public is on the whole very aware of the mental shock, anguish, and suffering of disaster victims. People see it as appropriate for victims to be distressed and to be helped with distress; but they may be very unsure of the "normal" as opposed to "abnormal" behaviors that might be expected and of what they themselves should say and do. Consultants may provide or develop educational materials for presentation over the radio, on television, or in the print media. These materials may explain common post-traumatic reactions, the processes of grief, family strain in temporary dwellings, the importance of support systems to healing emotional wounds, or many other matters. More specific presentations may be provided to persons who have special contact with victims; for instance, presentations to schools on how to deal with children (Crabbs 1981).

The value of these presentations is great, for they meet needs for information, mastery, and control in the post-disaster period. They not only lessen disaster-related stress or help define ways of dealing with it, but may also provide knowledge that will carry over into ordinary stressful life circumstances. The mental health professionals involved in such programs are usually seen as caring in a time of need, and a more human face is often given to psychiatric services as a consequence.

Following a major transport disaster, media presentations acquainted the public with the needs of bereaved and other victims and with how these could best be handled. Needs for talking through and positive mastery were discussed. Educational presentations were made to welfare, social security, and health professionals in the suburbs where victims lived. These demonstrated in role play and video, as well as in printed handouts, some common reactions and appropriate responses to them. Schools were provided with seminars about needs of children whose parents had died, about likely reactions over time and how these could be dealt with so as to offer most support for the children. Popular magazines produced overviews for the public about recognition of patterns of distress and how to help friends. The *Medical Journal of Australia* was contacted and in rapid time printed an article with guidelines to doctors. Local pharmacies were contacted when newspaper reports suggested that large supplies of tranquilizers were being brought in to deal with victims' distress. Suggestions were made about other more appropriate methods of management.

Following the Ash Wednesday fires, informative leaflets were produced by the Royal Children's Hospital and Prince Henry's Hospital in Melbourne for distribution to victims. These leaflets and outreach educational presentations to the media in several states (television, radio, and newspapers) were seen as supportive and helpful by affected persons and workers, for they explained many of the strange and overwhelming feelings, their likely course, and the best ways to deal with them. Again, programs were provided to schools in which teachers were informed of likely reactions in children and of techniques, such as drawing and storytelling, that might be used in class to help children work through their feelings. A whole booklet or kit of information and teaching was developed by a state health department to these ends. Educational input might be summarized as in figure 10.2.

FIGURE 10.2

Educational Consultancy for Mental Health Aspects of Disaster

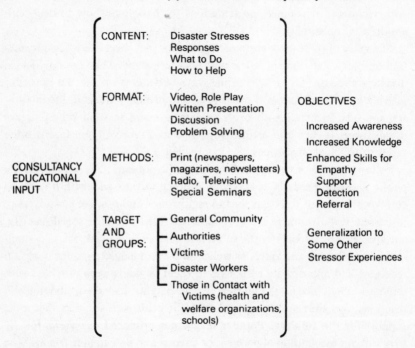

Consultancy Work with Helpers. Consultancy in the aftermath should also be directed toward the "hidden victims," or helpers, and providing for their needs. Specifically designed educational programs may be aimed at increasing the helpers' awareness of the ways in which the various disaster stresses may affect them and of the particular stresses of the helper role (see chapter 9). Helpers may need consultancy to assist them with their role and task definition and boundaries, particularly if they are in diffuse support roles such as counseling. They may also require assistance to help them define lines of authority and responsibility, as well as delegation within the loose-knit post-disaster organization systems of emergent or other groups. This may be very important for helpers whose roles in the disaster are very different from those in their ordinary work situations or who are not linked to emergency-type systems at other times. Consultancy can help the worker recognize the special nature of the victim-helper relationship so that the emotions aroused by it are seen in their proper perspective, as a special caring bond with inherent professional responsibilities.

The opportunity for *psychological debriefing* after the disaster involvement or tour of duty may take place through special discussion groups of workers who have shared a common experience or task. The consultant's role is to facilitate the working through of the experience in this setting. Topics that may usefully be part of such a group's agenda should include the following: disaster stressors personally experienced such as death encounter, survivor conflict, loss, dislocation; roles held; feelings, both positive and negative; the victims and their problems; the stresses of empathy and identification; frustrations and stresses of the task, such as inadequate skills or resources, or uncertain goals and responsibilities; special relationships with friends, colleagues, and others who have been through the experience; the "special" nature of the disaster work; personal and individualistic responses, such as anger, anxiety, and guilt; and the difficulties in transferring both clients and self back to the nondisaster system.

If these aspects are carefully and systematically reviewed in a nonthreatening discussion/education format, the sensitive consultant can facilitate the emotional working through, the psychological debriefing, of the disaster helper's experience. And if helpers conclude with a summarizing review of what has been learned that can be taken to other situations, a carry-over of knowledge and skills is also gained.

This model has proved valuable with workers in a number of major Australian disasters, for example, the Granville disaster. A volunteer rescue team that had worked under the concrete slab crushing the train cars had a psychological debriefing session one week after the disaster. Sitting around in a group and drinking beer, they discussed with the consultant (and in a half-joking fashion) a wide range of topics: the frustrations of their roles and sense of helplessness; the fears several had had about dying themselves in the narrow space; the terror and revulsion at all these deaths, which they could not "accept" despite their frequent experience of death in their other rescue work; the post-traumatic stress reactions of intrusive images, nightmares and fear; the difficulties of sharing the experience with families; and the fact that they could not unload their feelings, because immediately after they had finished their work at the rail disaster, they were called out to several road accident rescues and were still in an alert, aroused state. As the evening progressed, the consultant helped these workers to accept the naturalness of many of their fears and regain their sense of mastery through discussion, release of feelings, and externalization of their experience. The session closed with easier, relieved feelings, less tension, and considerable warmth, evidenced by plans for a get-together of group members and their families. Follow-up indicated that these men perceived themselves as coping well some months later, while their one colleague who had not been able to attend seemed to have major problems.

Consultancy Work with Communities. Following the disaster, the mental health worker might also be involved in organizing or supporting emergent groups or established community systems. Such consultancy has various aims: helping groups to define goals for recovery; assessing and providing for community needs, including those of special and vulnerable groups; facilitating network development; helping reconstitute services or developing new services needed by the community for recovery; ensuring that potential political gains do not interfere with optimal recovery processes for all segments of the community; strengthening adaptive community organizations; preventing scapegoating; and enhancing communication systems.

An understanding of organizations, and of their response and development in crisis, is critical to this component of the consultative process. Assisting current or emergent organizations to assess needs and to define objectives in terms of both these needs and available resources is important, for as Wettenhall (1975) has so ably demonstrated, organizational systems may not function adequately in terms of the disaster requirements.

In terms of organization to facilitate and give legitimacy to mental health services for the disaster, Cohen and Ahearn (1980) suggest that it is valuable to develop as soon as possible a task force to help in planning and implementation. This task force, they suggest, should represent four distinct elements of the community:

Experts: mental health experts
Power group: members of the power structure of the community who can help facilitate decisions for resources and access
Sentiment groups: groups reflecting the broad values of the community who are likely to be concerned for its needs and who may block programs if not involved
Needs group: victims who have experienced the problems directly.

From such a task force the mental health program may evolve following assessment of needs, setting of goals, and definition of suitable procedures for implementation, monitoring, funding, and evaluation. In the United States, special government grants through the Disaster Assistance and

Emergency Mental Health Section of the National Institutes of Mental Health may be used to fund these mental health programs. In other countries, government health departments or institutes may have this role. They may need to be involved in the task force if they are to ensure adequate organizational commitment to mental health component.

Consultancy to "avoid harm." One theme of consultancy advice may be to assist authorities to avoid psychologically harmful practices that might produce further trauma for the victims. Preventive functions served by the consultant's role include: avoiding separation of children from parents; discouraging unnecessary evacuation; lessening the convergence on victims; preventing scapegoating if possible; lessening the passivity that may be forced on victims; advocating for workers and helpers; facilitating role definitions and transitions; and encouraging review and integrative assessment in the post-disaster period. More specific systems of preventive intervention may be developed, as outlined below. One especially valuable function is that of review and integration to assist organizations, leaders, and workers define what has been learned that can carry over positively not only to other disasters but to work and human functioning generally.

PSYCHOLOGICAL FIRST AID AND TRIAGE

As noted previously in the first hours after a disaster, at least 25 percent of the population may be stunned and dazed, apathetic and wandering—suffering from the disaster syndrome—especially if impact has been sudden and totally devastating. The other primary emotional responses during the first hours are distress, sometimes overwhelming, or exaggerated or distorted behaviors. At this point, psychological first aid and triage—the sorting of victims or problems into groups that require similar or emergency services—are necessary (figure 10.3).

Psychological first aid has a number of components:

1. The basic human responses of *comforting* and *consoling* the distressed person are in themselves important. Holding, patting, rocking, and touching the person may convey the emotional meaning of care more than any words, as may quietly sitting beside him or her.
2. At the same time there may be a need to *protect* the victim from ongoing disaster threat or damage of which he is relatively unaware because of his stunned mental state. Staying with the person suffering

FIGURE 10.3
Psychological First Aid and Triage

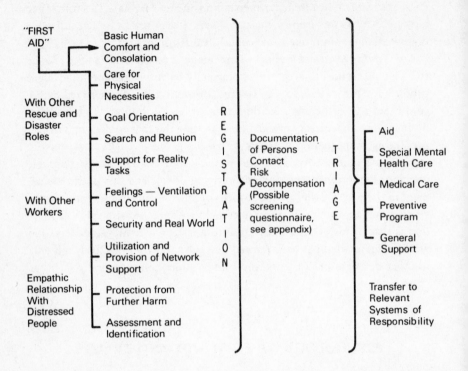

from the disaster syndrome may be sufficient to protect him from harm until emotional reaction and responsiveness to the environment start to return. It is particularly important to identify those who are cognitively affected (disoriented) and to protect and care for them.

3. Primary to these parameters of psychological support must be immediate care for physical necessities, by the treatment of injuries and the provision of warmth, food, clothing, and protection. These elements and psychological first aid are inextricably interwoven. Warm drinks and blankets serve symbolic psychological as well as physiological functions for the shocked victim.

4. Goal orientation has several facets. Individuals who are distressed, wandering, or searching need guidance to a shelter, center, or some other community focus. Aimless activity may need to be channeled by direction to specific tasks. All this involves what Cohen and Ahearn have called "reinforcing the concrete world." Many of these responses of emotional first aid really take into account the degree of regression and need to be cared for that may appear transiently in most victims. As victims' shock lessens, they increasingly become concerned for others and start caring for them in similar ways.

5. Search for and reunion with primary group members, or some contact and reassurance, are critical for most victims, for intense separation anxieties may be experienced if safety and whereabouts of family members have not been established. To emotionally assist, carers need to facilitate this process as far as possible, either helping victims to find those they love or linking them to the appropriate information systems or personnel. This process may also involve assisting in a search for and identification of the dead.

6. Support for reality tasks may be necessary, especially in rescue and recovery tasks and in dealing with the dead. In particular, it may be necessary to provide emotional support while an individual or family identifies the body or bodies of loved ones who have died in the disaster. This is best accomplished by quietly preparing individuals for the state of the body, staying with them for support during the process if they wish or need this support, allowing them the opportunity for touching, time with the deceased and a quiet farewell if at all possible, and then comforting them during any formal procedures required (e.g., statements to police). The worker should ensure that individuals will have ongoing support from family or others, that they are provided with information about care systems and methods of contact, and that outreach follow-up is explained and arranged. Other reality tasks may also be very painful, for instance, making decisions about property, where to go, or the disposal of injured animals. Support may be required for such processes as part of emotional first aid during the emergency.

7. Some ventilation of feelings may occur spontaneously and should be accepted, but always with the idea of helping the victim to reconstitute his defenses and regain control until he is in a more secure emotional situation with support for more in-depth working through of the experience. Nevertheless, many people will want to express to caregivers their initial emotional reactions to the assault of the disaster experience. Anguish, fear, anger, futility, and helplessness are the feelings for which the person is most likely to require understanding and empathic concern. If emotional distress is intense, it is necessary for the carer to stay with the victim until he can be cared for by others or taken into the protective circle of family or friends.

8. Reestablishing some sense of security in the real world is also part of psychosocial first aid. Because the disaster experience is for the most part totally alien from the everyday experience of the victim, one way of lessening stress is to help victims regain some sense of reality by structuring their environment and schedules and by regularizing basic supplies and expectations (for example, meals).

9. Utilization and promotion of networks of support can begin at this stage. Even within the early hours or the first few days, it may be very valuable to link victims together in neighborhood shelters or to link

them with supportive groups of family, friends, or community members. Those who have been through the experience are likely to derive much benefit from sharing their emotions and perceptions of what has happened, from talking through and interpreting events together.

10. Acutely decompensating victims may show states ranging from an acute reactive psychotic episode to intense anxiety and panic reactions, from manic elation to depressive withdrawal. Any victims with such states in the immediate aftermath should be channeled into appropriate systems of psychiatric care if these are available. If victims do not rapidly return to normal, they may require tranquilizers or other psychotropic medication (e.g., benzodiazepine) in the short term, to allow rest and reintegration of defenses.

11. Finally, psychosocial first aid involves linking victims to systems of support that will operate on an ongoing basis. This includes identification of victims as well as documentation and collection of basic data on their future whereabouts (or the address of someone who will know who they are). This is very important because shortly after the disaster victims may become widely dispersed, and it may be difficult to ensure that they have further psychosocial assessment or access to follow-up mental health care. Subsequent assessment and access are crucial because of the latent period before the appearance of some disorders. A screening questionnaire (see appendix) has been evolved for use in this early period to identify those likely to be most at risk psychologically.

As noted in other contexts, documentation and recording often represent a reassuring return to the structures of society and help the person redefine and identify himself. Thus, overall, these techniques are geared to lessening the stress experienced and to comforting and protecting victims until they can master the experience and start to regain control of their lives. It is critical during the first few hours, but also most relevant in early days, at least until the shock passes. While some regression is natural and to be accepted, the independence of the victim should be acknowledged by requesting his opinion or decision on simple issues so that he can increasingly feel his own competence growing with recovery.

Because the roles involved in psychosocial first aid are so linked to many other essential tasks in the immediate aftermath, they should, wherever possible, be carried out in association with these tasks, and with recognition of and collaboration with the other emergency workers. As Cohen and Ahearn (1980) have noted, and as our own experience suggests (Raphael 1979–80), it is easy to become involved in conflict with other groups or in one's own experience of the disaster itself. If this happens, there may be little emotional energy left over to care for those most in need—the victims.

Basic to care in this early phase is the capacity to establish an empathic relationship with the distressed individual. This is accomplished by caring interest, an awareness of common responses to disaster, and especially by experience working with those distressed in other emergency or personal disaster situations. Quiet statements in recognition of suffering and pain, together with gentle probing of the victim's experience, feelings, and current needs and desires, help to this end. As Cohen and Ahearn (1980) note, the worker, in expressing empathy, needs to also be aware of "the healthier parts of the victim's personality, and to mobilize them to enhance the ability to 'hold on' for the time being" (p. 82). The helper must guard against rewarding the victim role and against believing that he can rescue the victims from all distress and suffering. He can comfort them, but he *cannot* take away what has happened.

GENERAL PSYCHOSOCIAL SUPPORT AND COUNSELING

Each worker offering aid, relief, assistance, information, or guidance to the disaster-affected population needs enough knowledge and skills to provide some general psychological and social support alongside whatever other tasks he is engaged in. This applies particularly to those community care-takers to whom affected persons are likely to turn at the time of the crisis —doctors, nurses, ministers, and so forth. Such support is aimed at:

1. Encouraging the *working through* process by reinforcing adaptive coping mechanisms and, wherever possible, discouraging nonadaptive processes.
2. Helping affected persons regain their sense of *mastery and control* so that feelings of helplessness are lessened and the victim feels once more able to deal with his world, even if it is a damaged one.
3. Assessing and identifying *those at risk or in need* of specialized mental health services and either obtaining assistance to deal with them or referring them to appropriate mental health care systems.
4. Facilitating the *reintegration* of affected persons into their own networks and community systems in an adaptive manner.

Most victims, once the state of shock has passed, have a compelling need to talk about what has happened to them and to express the powerful feeling it has evoked. Thus, *empathic listening* is a principal component of what is required to provide the necessary emotional support.

Several key processes are critical in providing such general support and counseling, as diagrammed in figure 10.4.

Exploration of Victims' Experience and Feelings.   Discussion of victims' experience and responses to the experience may be initiated by a gentle, general question such as "Can you tell me all about it—what happened to *you?* And how did you feel?" This usually opens floodgates, and victims will review their experience with much emotional release. Some may stay frozen and nonresponsive, however. If this happens, they may need to be given further time or gently supported through practical tasks. If victims are still not able to speak of their experience, it is useful to recognize their pain, perhaps with comments such as "I can see it's still very hard for you to talk about it. . . . Perhaps, if you would like, we can come back to it again, later." This opening up enables the worker to gain a picture of the specific nature of the victim's experience so that his likely responses may be understood. The more there have been feelings of shock and helplessness with impact,

FIGURE 10.4
General Psychological Support and Counseling

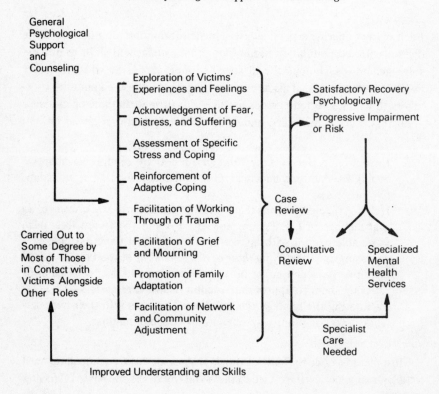

the more the person will need support to gain mastery of these feelings. Other traumatic stresses may also be identified.

Acknowledgment of Fear, Suffering, and Distress.   This may be achieved by empathic comments such as "I can see how awful you must have felt" or "It must have been terrifying . . . " or "I can see that just thinking about it is still very upsetting for you." This is a message to the affected person that his suffering is recognized and his experience made legitimate, especially his own perception of it.

Assessment of Stress and Coping.   Exploration of what has happened, plus evaluation of the person's emotional response to it, both at the time and subsequently, will provide a picture of the degree of psychological traumatization that has occurred and the way the person has attempted to deal with this. The individual who cannot show any feeling may be defending against being overwhelmed by it. The person who repetitively reviews a particular segment of what happened may be attempting, unsuccessfully, to master it emotionally. It is useful to look at the degree to which the victim can recognize and express emotions associated with the experience; the degree to which the victim can master the experience, interpreting it both realistically and in terms of the *past,* as something he can move away from; and the degree to which he can start to orient himself away from his experience to the needs of his family, network, and future realities. All these may be adaptive processes. It is important to ascertain to what extent socially supportive networks, especially family, are available to the victim and can be used by him to facilitate his recovery. Experiences such as encounter with death, shock and helplessness, survivor guilt and conflict, bereavement and other losses, and dislocation should be noted, for each will indicate the need for a degree of preventive support work.

Reinforcement of Adaptive Coping.   This may be achieved in a number of ways. First, actions to facilitate mastery, such as taking part in recovery activities, making presentations about need, and becoming involved in organizational roles may all help and should be encouraged. The process of talking through the experience can also be supported and facilitated, particularly by encouraging the victim to identify his emotional responses and to accept them. Thus, a man who has felt fear and helplessness may perceive such emotions as shameful and cowardly. He may be assisted by comments such as "It seems you handled those *natural* feelings very well." Talking through with others is very adaptive in this context, because it rapidly becomes obvious to the affected person that his fear and helplessness, his guilt and anger, are not unique. Reinforcing the supportive interactions of affected persons with their family and others is also important, especially the sharing of feelings, perceptions, and interpretations of the experience.

Helping people manage their feelings in acceptable "doses" is also important, as has been noted by many workers (e.g., Lindy et al. 1983); after a period of emotional release, it is useful to have a period of activity and mastery or else a rest from the working through of feelings. Throughout assessment of adaptation it is essential to recognize when the person has exhausted his resources and can "hold on" no longer. Then rest is needed, and regression should be temporarily accepted. Rest periods need to be specifically sanctioned and prescribed, because often, the victim's state of arousal, a desire to repair and return things to the pre-disaster state, and survivor guilt may make affected persons reluctant to "indulge" themselves in much-needed respite.

Another important process in reinforcing adaptive coping is the removal of passivity and secondary gain from the "victim" role. Expectations that victims will make their own decisions, control their own destinies, and with assistance, provide for their own needs should be conveyed both implicitly and explicitly, along with supportive empathy for their suffering. The use of different words (e.g., "disaster-affected person") may assist in this process.

Facilitating the Working Through of Death, Shock, and Trauma. In a disaster where a high level of traumatic experience is likely (where there has been extensive death, mutilation, and destruction, helplessness, and shock), some general counseling may help. But if there is indication of a high level of traumatization of particular individuals, then referral for specialized preventive counseling may be necessary. People who show early arousal and anxiety or a return of these feelings, nightmares, or intrusive thoughts should be reassured that these processes are usually of a short-term nature. This may be best understood if comparison is made to the healing of a wound, for the concrete example is more comprehensible than uncertain explorations of mental processes. As Horowitz (1976) has pointed out, for those with excessive intrusive experiences there is a need to reinforce control, cognitive interpretation, and management of feelings. Those who show more inhibitory responses, with an inability to face feelings, may need more support to gradually talk about and express their feelings. Crucial to the working through of trauma seems to be the ability to recognize and come to terms with the helplessness and shock and to set these in the past by gaining understanding and emotional distance from them. However, beyond these general principles it is likely that specialized management will be required, and it is critical that referral is smoothly made where there is indication of ongoing disorder. This is particularly so if (Weisæth 1984) exposure has been intense and, at the end of the first week post-disaster or beyond, anxiety levels are high, irritability is high or rising, or nightmares and other intrusions are increasingly disruptive. Even if such symptoms appear only after a period of delay, referral should be considered, for the risk of chronic, distressing, and disabling post-traumatic disorder is high.

Facilitating the Working Through of Loss and Grief. As some level of loss is inherent in most disaster experiences, grief is a common component of the emotional response. There are many blocks to natural grieving in the disaster, not the least of them the victim's feelings that he should be grateful for all that has been given to him materially (and emotionally in many instances) in endeavors to make restitution. Shock and survival needs may also interfere. Helping the victim to recognize and express grief may be particularly difficult for the worker who has a role of providing aid, for neither he nor the victim may feel comfortable with the emotional currency that can be so easily avoided.

General principles of bereavement counseling may be used in performing other tasks, however (Raphael 1983). The task of documenting disaster losses for necessary administrative purposes can also be used to promote the review process of mourning and the expression of grief. It will be useful to query several main areas. Asking about a loved person who has died can be accomplished by gentle queries along some of the following lines:

> "Can you tell me about *what happened* to J.? . . . what you know? . . . about the time you knew the disaster was coming? . . . through that time and since?"

These questions will provide information about the victim's experience of the death and loss, circumstances of the death that may have evoked particular trauma and guilt, opportunities to see and say good-bye to the dead person, and patterns of emotional responsiveness at the time of the loss and subsequently.

> "Can you tell me *about* J.—your *relationship*—about him as a person, . . . the things you used to do together, . . . your life together, the good times and the bad?"

These questions help promote the psychological processes of mourning and review essential to the gradual coming to terms with the loss. In the early post-disaster period, persisting shock is more likely and the person is often still strongly linked to expectancies that somehow life will return to the way it was before—that the person cannot really be gone forever, even though he is now desperately missed and longed for. Such denial is natural for many people in the face of multiple traumas. It is important to recognize this with the bereaved, while at the same time foreshadowing future working through.

"It must be very *difficult to accept* that J. has really gone . . . when you want him so much . . . and when everything seems so unreal. . . . It's important to let yourself have time to gradually come to terms with it. There will be many opportunities for us to talk about it again, later, and about all it must mean for you. . . . We know it's very hard for people at a time like this—especially if you feel you've got to keep control, just to keep going. . . . But your grief is important too."

Recognition of the intense and complex emotions evoked by bereavement is necessary to the victim and helpful in encouraging release of such feelings. Generalizations about other people's experience may help the victim identify his own feelings as an acceptable part of normal response, while at the same time his particular feelings and their origins can be clarified.

"Most people have very strong feelings at a time like this. . . . It sounds as though you feel really angry, as most grieving people do. Perhaps you can tell me about the things that are making *you* feel this way. You sound as though you've got a lot of guilty feelings. While grieving people often have some feelings of this kind, perhaps it would help if we could see why *you* feel so especially bad about all that's happened. I can see how sad and despairing you are feeling. This is a very terrible time for you with J. gone. Perhaps it will help a little if you can share with me some of the things you feel especially sad about. . . . "

When feeling appears frozen and cannot be released at all, gentle encouragement to review the loss and the relationship may eventually facilitate some working through. But it must be recognized that this may not occur at all for some of the bereaved, or at least not until much later. The longer-term effects of such inhibition of grief post-disaster are not really known, although some people seem to manage to adjust reasonably (Singh and Raphael 1981).

Finally, it is important to help the bereaved use his social network for general assistance as well as support for emotional working through.

"How has the *family* been since J. died? . . . Have you been able to talk about him together? . . . It's important for you to share some of your feelings and memories, but I know this is difficult—family members often feel afraid of upsetting each other—everyone feels he has to keep things to himself for the sake of the others. . . . Yet it's usually an enormous relief afterwards when you do let go. It helps clear the air and helps you all through the painful time, knowing how the others are feeling too. . . . Have you *someone you* can share your feelings with who'll let you cry, or be angry, or talk about J. the way you need to—someone with whom it's alright? We know that this is very important with bereaved feelings. . . . Why don't you try talking with K. about this, too?"

These processes and other skills of bereavement counseling (Raphael 1983) will do a great deal to help the bereaved adjust. Some of the same principles can be transferred to the mourning of the other losses that are so common after disaster, particularly the loss of home and place or of treasured possessions.

"It would be helpful if we could go over what you have lost. I know this is painful for you, but it is natural to grieve for one's home too. I know it's hard to let your feelings go when others seem to have lost so much more—but *your* loss is real and important too and you will *need to grieve* for it. . . . Most people feel angry when the loss really hits them, so it's not surprising that you should feel this way too. . . . I think it will help you in the long run, even though I know it's difficult at present, if we could go over what all this [your home, your . . .] *meant to you.* I know that whatever people give you it's not the same as your own; it's hard to accept for most people, and natural that you should feel sad about it."

Promotion of Family Adaptation. Wherever possible, the impact of the disaster on the family unit should be assessed and the stresses and strains managed. The first step may be to avoid separation of family members from one another for undue periods of time. If separations are inevitable, it is important to help families to communicate and aim at early reunion, and in particular to maintain openness of feelings. Educational input to families about common response patterns and how to deal with them is useful. Families can also be helped to plan joint activities that aim at mastery and recovery but at the same time facilitate the emotional working through of the traumatic experience. Getting families together with other affected families to discuss strains and ways of overcoming them, or arranging times of relaxation and rest from the arduous tasks of the recovery period, may enable the reestablishment of normal relations. In particular, the different response patterns and needs of children should be taken into account and families provided with information about these.

A further useful technique is to arrange a session with the whole family to review its experience and work with members to devise a plan to overcome disaster consequences. Members are given guidelines about the specific tasks and goals of the session. Tasks will generally include reviewing the disaster; assessing damage and losses; defining resources and strengths; planning goals and methods of recovery; and establishing contributions of individual members to these goals; defining specific needs of individual members; developing methods for reviewing progress; and assessing what has been learned from the disaster in both practical and emotional terms. Similar review sessions may be planned for later if necessary, particularly for very needy, damaged, or previously malfunctional families, but in general, the family's skills should be positively mobilized for its own recovery.

"I believe it's important for us to understand the needs of the whole family at this time; it's often a period of great strain for families, especially when . . . your home has gone, you're living under such difficult circumstances. So we would like you all to come—all the children too, and grandma, as she lives with you—next Saturday at 10:00 A.M. We'll be talking about what happened, how it's affected the family as well as each one of you, and, we'll be working out plans to deal with the problems you see as most important."

At the same time practical problems are being identified, communication and emotional release can be facilitated. Models for emotional release can be established and family closeness reinforced, as it is for many who successfully master such stressful experiences and reestablish a sense of personal values related to family life.

Certain families may be especially vulnerable and can be identified in this process:

- Families with preexisting marital or functional problems
- Deprived multiproblem families for whom this disaster may prove to be the "last straw"
- Families who are dislocated into systems that cannot or do not support them
- Families who have suffered overwhelming loss, trauma, and/or separations
- Families severely affected by survivor guilts
- Families who have split, disintegrated, or decompensated following the disaster.

Such families will require supportive referral to special mental health services for preventive or therapeutic work.

Facilitation of Network and Community Adjustment. Relevant information can be obtained through questions about the person's social network, his access to it, and his relationship to and role within his community. It may be helpful to inform the victim of the importance of networks in times of crisis or to link him to groups of other victims. Wherever possible, the emergent groups that frequently arise spontaneously during the disaster aftermath should be encouraged, for they promote mastery and a process of working through of the shared stress. Similarly, there will be groups in the wider community beyond the individual's own network (special interest groups or task-oriented committees) that he or she can usefully join. Thus, it is important for the worker to be aware of such groups and of methods of access to them.

"It would be helpful if you could attend this special meeting. It is going to deal with a lot of problems like yours. . . . I'm sure there'll be quite a few solutions this way."

The isolated, scapegoated, or withdrawn individual in particular may require such support. But it should be remembered that all victims also need times of quiet and privacy to help in the healing of their own wounds.

PREVENTIVE ASSESSMENT AND MANAGEMENT OF THOSE AT RISK

While the overall impression following many disasters is of the resilience and invulnerability of human response, nevertheless there are those at risk of substantial psychiatric morbidity. The preventive component of mental health care involves not only the general supportive and educative models outlined above, but also specific preventive intervention programs. Several workers have commented on the difficulties of implementing these services and on the reluctance of many of those in need to use them. Nevertheless, studies of preventive programs in the United States, Norway, Sweden, and Australia have demonstrated their potential value. A model showing their principal components appears in figure 10.5.

Risk of disorder post-disaster is increased in a number of instances, as has been noted in chapter 8. Sometimes, sociodemographic variables, such as age, socioeconomic status, marital, employment, and education, may indicate groups toward whom preventive programs should be targeted. While past psychiatric disorder may indicate some vulnerability, it often does not, and family history does not seem to contribute greatly. Past disaster experi-

FIGURE 10.5
Preventive Assessment and Management

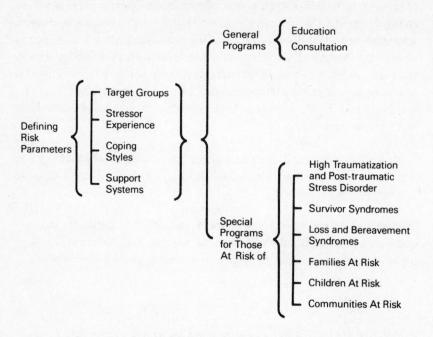

ence may to some extent be a protective factor, although this previous "stress inoculation" is not totally effective for everyone.

A major contributor to post-disaster psychiatric problems is the severity and nature of the stressful experiences related to the disaster, although coping styles and social support may help mitigate this stress to some degree. Therefore, prevention programs should be targeted to those *defined as at risk because of the stresses they have experienced and their perceptions of them as stressful.*

Assessment during emotional first aid or general supportive counseling may indicate individuals and/or groups at risk in the particular disaster. It is possible to then devise and implement preventive programs that are relevant both to disaster stress generally and to the particular disaster and particular individual. That is, there are general and specific components to the intervention program (see figure 10.5). Such preventive approaches have been defined for natural hazard disasters (Raphael 1979b) and for man-made disasters (Raphael 1979–80). Components and objectives may be defined as follows:

1. Educational and general components include a general presentation about disaster stresses to the community at large, to workers, and to groups at risk, so that adaptive approaches may be facilitated in a variety of

ways, as outlined earlier in terms of consultative, emergency, and general counseling aspects.

2. Specific interventions could be planned and provided for those deemed to be at risk of disorder because of levels of stressor exposure, indications of nonadaptive coping, or indications that reactive responses to stress are not settling but are developing into disorder.

Individuals at Risk for Post-traumatic Stress Disorder. Several aspects are of importance in preventing post-traumatic stress disorder. First, if it is at all possible, counterdisaster planning should be used to lessen shock and helplessness, by making people more aware and by providing active planning and objectives to diminish the sense of powerlessness. During impact, any activities that help people maintain some sense of control may help, although such activities are usually difficult to institute unless they are part of some survival-oriented behaviors. In the post-impact period, those likely to be at risk may be identified and provided with intervention aimed at:

- Promoting a sense of mastery of the experience
- Promoting support from significant members of the social group
- Facilitating the working through of the traumatic experience and of emotions of fear, helplessness, anxiety, and depression that have developed as a consequence.

Achievement of these goals may require establishing a relationship with the person on an individual basis or through a supportive group. The cathartic release of feelings that occurs when the experience is talked through and shared with others may be sufficient to prevent the development of disorder, or to allow the reactive processes to settle instead of fulminating into pathology. This *abreaction* has been used naturally by many people who offer informal support.

> "Tell me all about it. . . . You must have felt dreadful. . . . It will do you good to get it out . . . and have a good cry. . . ."

The affected person is thus able to externalize and distance the experience, as well as to gain some emotional release, some retrospective interpretation, and mastery. Getting in touch with and accepting the fear and powerlessness are important, especially when the victim is helped to see these feelings within a cognitive framework:

> "It is very natural and appropriate to feel helpless and frightened with such experiences, . . . most people do. The feelings themselves are often disturbing, too, because they remind us of how we felt when we were

children, and then lots of things made us feel frightened and helpless. Let yourself feel some of those feelings, then think about them now, and let yourself understand them for what they were—natural reactions—and so have some control of them. You'll find that they are not nearly so troublesome and anxiety provoking after a while."

Gentle desensitization to fearful images, memories, or reminders can also be helpful in preventing the development of entrenched disorder. This would be important in the early weeks, if startle, anxiety, and intrusive aspects seem to be increasing, rather than gradually settling, or if phobic components are pronounced. Victims can be encouraged to approach images or places relevant to the experience bit by bit and in the presence of an empathic and supportive person who can offer ego strength while fears are faced. Group process may also serve this function.

Avoidance of withdrawal is important. It may help if the stressed person can be sought out with offers of support and encouraged to gradually talk over what has happened and feelings about it with family members. There is much to suggest that those who show the greatest withdrawal may have most impairment in the long run. Rising irritability may also be a precursor of disorder, and its sources may need to be explored. One of the difficulties with post-traumatic stress reactions may be that the experience is so painfully reawakened by any discussion. People will go to many lengths to avoid this and thus will be inaccessible to outreach preventive programs. Even when such programs are implemented, as by Terr following the Chowchilla school bus kidnapping, there may not be demonstrable preventive effects. Weisæth, who carried out some preventive psychotherapy with his paint factory fire survivors, suggests (Weisæth 1983) that his work may have mitigated disorders to some degree, but here too, the need to avoid the reexperiencing of the pain may have been the limiting factor.

Whether the use of anti-anxiety drugs can help individuals at risk for post-traumatic stress disorder is not known. It seems that medication might have some utility in short-term application where an intrusive component with strong anxiety is established. Its use may really be indicated when disorder is actually developing rather than to prevent it.

Individuals at Risk for Survivor Syndromes. Although it is often difficult to predict those at risk for survivor syndromes, such syndromes are particularly likely where there has been guilt or conflict about living when others have died or where the victim has in some way felt responsible for the deaths of others. Being one of few to survive when many have died may also place the individual at risk. Preventive interventions would here be directed at:

- Reviewing and reinterpreting the experience
- Lessening the guilty conflict
- Facilitating supportive interactions with others.

The individual should be helped to review his decisions and the process of escape and survival, as well as to remember and reexperience his concern for the others he could not save. He should also be helped to reinterpret the experience and to understand the naturalness of the drive for survival. There often must be a process of grief, so that what has happened and what cannot be changed can be sadly and regretfully accepted.

Exploring, expressing, and setting aside guilt can be achieved in some instances when the victim can talk this through with others and see their acceptance. The person with a severe conscience and perfectionist expectations of himself may be unable to do this, however, and may continue his suffering to the level of impairment. It is usually pointless to offer reassurance in a broad way, without review. Formal inquiries may help the victim put what has happened into some perspective.

Enhancing the supportive interactions of the victim's family and social networks is important, for isolation and withdrawal are likely to reinforce the development of disorder.

Individuals at Risk for Bereavement Syndromes. Adaptive responses to loss may be promoted at several levels, from support of the victim to view and say good-bye to the dead person, to general encouragement to grieve the loss, to specific preventive interventions directed toward the bereaved who are at high risk. Such programs aim at:

- Reviewing the death or loss and its circumstances
- Reviewing and mourning the lost relationship, person, or property
- Facilitating the supportive interactions of others.

These aims may be achieved by preventive bereavement counseling, carried out with individuals, families, or in groups.

Reviewing the circumstances of the death or loss helps the bereaved express the feelings evoked by the experience, as well as revealing any indications of further traumatic overload of guilt, shock, and so forth. Feelings expressed may include anger, sadness, anxiety, guilt, and others that are relevant at this stage following the loss. The review is an opportunity to promote the grieving process. The emotions that emerge are generally part of the natural healing process that should follow loss. Where inhibitions or distortions occur, their origins may be explored so that blocks to normal grief can be lessened.

Helping the bereaved to remember and talk about what has been lost—the loved person who has gone, the lost past, and the lost future—will help gradually undo these emotional bonds by promoting the psychological mourning processes. It is important to review, a little at a time, the lost person or relationship, the lost home or place, taking up both positive and negative aspects. Visits to the grave, sorting through remaining possessions, or going through old photographs are concrete rituals that may help the review process. For example, following the Ash Wednesday fires, some families were helped by relatives and friends who collected duplicates of family photos that had been burned in the fires and put these together in new albums of old family memories.

Facilitating support from others and of family members for one another can provide an environment where it is safe to cry, share feelings, and sadly mourn the lost person or valued property. Unless this is done, others who mean well may be so overwhelmed by their own grief or by their fear of the bereaved's feelings that the loss may be avoided.

Specific prescription of grief and mourning may be necessary, for these are often neglected following disaster. Neglect may be due to involvement in the enormous practical tasks of recovery. It may also stem from the fact that disaster bereavements are often complicated by shock, multiple crisis experiences for the bereaved, and much guilt and anger, especially following "man-made" catastrophes.

Families at Risk. Families may be at risk from the consequences of post-traumatic, survivor, and bereavement reactions, and particularly from the ongoing stresses of dislocation in the aftermath period. Preventive interventions aim at:

- Strengthening family coping
- Helping families to share the experience and share feelings
- Linking families to practical and emotional support systems in the community.

Special family sessions may facilitate these goals. At the least, one review session will set the scene for families to incorporate them into their functioning. Such a session can also be used to define special family problems and to help find methods, either within the family itself, or linked to community resources, that will deal with these problems. If necessary, ongoing preventive short-term family counseling can be used to avoid disintegration and disorder.

Children at Risk. To prevent the development of problems among children, it is helpful to follow the general guidelines of avoiding unnecessary separations and supporting parents to recognize and mitigate stressful responses in their children. Outreach and play sessions or group talking through may be used with children in school or other settings, but there is always a need to back this with information and support for parents. Preventive intervention with children aims at:

- Lessening the stressful impact and assisting the child to master what has occurred
- Promoting coping
- Supporting parents to perceive and respond to child's disaster-related experiences and to deal with their own.

Playing through may help the child release feelings and gain a sense of mastery while he externalizes the experience. Support for temporary regression with much physical comforting can help with separation responses, so that these do not become entrenched. Gradual desensitization for separation and fearful responses is also useful. Coping may be further promoted by review of the experience. Children may discuss or write about the experience, or a group of children may even get together to make up a play. Drawing can also be used in this facilitatory way to promote psychological adaptation to the stressful experience so that disorder does not appear.

Bereaved children are likely to need special care, for their losses may be submerged in the general community reaction. They need to review, grieve for, and mourn, together with their parents, whomever and whatever they have lost.

Parents need to be provided with information about children's immediate and delayed behavioral reactions. They should be helped to become attuned to children's fears, comfort them on these specific issues, and involve them supportively in the tasks of family recovery.

Communities at Risk. Preventive interventions at the community level range from providing information about reactions and how to help the vulnerable to facilitating the development of emergent groups and natural leaders who will help the community have a major role in its own recovery. It may be important to assess nonadaptive processes, such as schisms, disintegration, and scapegoating, and to recruit leaders to prevent these processes. Preventive interventions may also take the form of promoting community meetings to review the disaster and what it has meant for the community—what has been suffered and what has been learned. Symbolizing and sanctioning the community's grief is likely to help coping and it is valuable for leaders to identify and support this effort. Leaders should also be encouraged to retain, develop, and facilitate the networks of communality and interaction that will strengthen the social fabric. And, finally, leaders should be helped to reintegrate the community and to concretize its courage and achievements in the disaster and aftermath.

TREATMENT FOR SPECIFIC DISORDERS

When disorder has developed, it is essential that patients be referred to appropriately skilled mental health professionals. Such referral may be direct or may occur during the consultative process, but it must always be sensitive. Mental health professionals are best accepted when they have been part of an integrated outreach to the community. They are also likely to be more sensitive and empathic to the actualities of the disaster experience under these circumstances, but also less "protected" by traditional professional barriers and roles. It should never be implied that the person is in any way inadequate or failing, but rather that he or she is facing a complex problem that is often a natural consequence of such an awful experience, and that the mental health professional is someone with special skills to help in such times of crisis.

> "I think you have been through a great deal—something that would be hard for most people to handle. But I really feel that if we could get some extra help with . . . [symptoms] those nightmares and panic feelings, it would make a big difference. I'd like you to see my colleague Joe Smith; he's been down here looking at the situation and is really helpful. He's had a great deal of experience helping people at times of crisis like this. I really think he could help a lot at this stage. . . . What do you think? . . . We could probably arrange to meet him together in the next few days, if you would be agreeable."

While there should never be any attempt to deceive people about the nature of mental health services, these may be more readily accepted if presented as crisis, stress, counseling, or disaster services, rather than as psychiatric programs. And they are usually more acceptable if, in the initial stages, they are in outreach rather than in psychiatric or mental health centers. Nevertheless, specific psychiatric referral should be made as appropriate.

This approach in no way belittles the skills required to implement preventive or therapeutic approaches. A thorough understanding of patient and family dynamics, plus skills, experience, and knowledge of disaster behavior and the therapeutic approaches, is essential. Special consultative and group skills may also be required, as well as considerable sensitivity to the issues involved in interprofessional and other relationships during the process of assistance. And, finally, a thorough understanding of the meaning of therapeutic relationships in such intense, unstructured crisis contexts is essential, for the therapist faces a danger of being overwhelmed by empathy with the patient's experience.

THERAPY FOR SPECIFIC SYNDROMES

This therapy should be carried out by mental health professionals, either in outreach or informal settings, and should show all the hallmarks of good clinical psychiatric work, with systematic assessment, diagnosis, management planning and implementation, and, finally, evaluation of outcome. Psychotherapeutic approaches are foremost, and may be complemented by behavioral techniques. Medication is usually relevant only for clear-cut indications of severe anxiety or depression. Treatments will be outlined briefly below; for more detail, the reader is referred to specific texts. A model of this aspect of psychosocial care is given in figure 10.6.

TREATMENT OF POST-TRAUMATIC STRESS DISORDER

In addition to the techniques outlined above for preventive management of post-traumatic stress reactions, the guidelines set out by Horowitz (1976) are helpful. He suggests the goal is to help the person to the stage where

FIGURE 10.6
Treatment for Specific Disorders

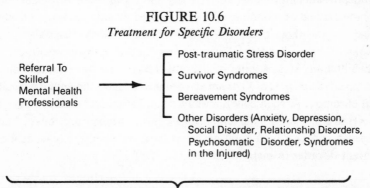

Focal Psychotherapeutic Models, including Behavioral, Abreactive, Individual, Family, and Group Approaches, with Medication if Specifically Indicated

"he is able to freely think about, and freely not think about the event" (p. 265). He explains that the two phases of the disorder, the denial-numbing phase and the intrusive-repetitive phase, require different approaches. For each there are therapeutic techniques aimed at modifying control processes, information processing, and emotional processing.

When the *denial-numbing* aspects predominate there is a need to reduce controls, for example, by suggestions, hypnosis, drug-assisted abreactive techniques, or evocative techniques such as role play. Information processing is developed by encouraging abreaction, associations about the experience, and reconstructions in memory. Feeling release is encouraged through catharsis and emotional relationships.

When the *instrusive-repetitive* aspects predominate, controls need to be developed, for instance, by structuring time, events, and stimulus level, through identification and role models, through the encouragement of group process or leaders, or by behavioral techniques. Information processing is geared to rearranging thinking patterns, with, if necessary, support through tranquilizers, meditation, or alternatives. Support is also given in dealing with emotions; in particular positive emotions are encouraged, and negative emotions suppressed.

This framework is useful but the difficulties in treating entrenched disorder are well-known. The reluctance of many patients to talk about what is so painful, what they wish to deny and shut aside, may mean that they cannot utilize a psychotherapeutic approach, or may drop therapy entirely. Group work in which identification with others sharing similar problems is facilitated may help in relaxing defenses. Systematic relaxation, desensitization, and other procedures may also be of value. For those patients who experience strong panic disorder, medication such as tranylcypramine may assist, and for those where depression predominates trycycline or other antidepressants may be helpful. Anxiety and disturbance of personal functioning may be very chronic and little assisted by anti-anxiety medication, except in the short term. The person who is severely disabled by post-traumatic stress disorder is likely to need extensive expert treatment and rehabilitation. Most studies of therapy, which have concentrated on the treatment of veterans of Vietnam and other wars, have shown the difficulties and chronicity of such conditions. This emphasizes the need to follow the preventive and early intervention procedures outlined previously, but as Weisæth and Terr both point out, even these treatments may be unable to prevent disorder in many people.

Mr. P. had developed severe post-traumatic stress disorder three months after a major plane crash in which many people were killed. He avoided air travel and woke up at night with frightening dreams. He could not talk of the event and tended to isolate himself to avoid others' questions. He had been unable to return to work. His marital relationship was failing because of his sleeping difficulties, exhaustion, irritability, and withdrawal. He showed considerable improvement after ten psychotherapeutic sessions.

At first he was angry that he should have to attend psychotherapy—there was "no point going over that again," he had to "put it out of his mind." When his own experience was gently probed, he initially denied it had any special significance—"others had suffered so much more" than he had. The therapist then clarified issues about his experience on the day of the disaster and his life in general around that time. This led back into a minute-by-minute review of what happened to him during the impact and aftermath. His feelings that he would die, that others would be rescued first, that he would be left trapped, forgotten, and helpless, all flooded back. His terror of death, his feelings of panic, and his shame at calling out for help when others seemed much more severely injured were reviewed over a number of sessions. The shame was seen as related to his perception of himself as a man of extreme independence and control and, ultimately, as related to his childhood. His father, an army officer, had reinforced the idea that boys must be men—brave, never afraid, and always in control of feelings.

As he became able to accept the naturalness of his own response and to express anger at his controlled childhood, he was able to distance himself from the trauma and his fears lessened. He was encouraged to talk through his experience and aspects of his insights with his wife, and this led to a new trust and openness between them. Although he still suffered occasional dreams and said he would always remember the horror of his experience, he claimed he felt himself to be "a new man and a better one—one who wasn't afraid of feelings."

TREATMENT OF SURVIVOR SYNDROMES

A psychotherapeutic approach is indicated, particularly one that concentrates on exploring the sources of guilt, their relationship to the realities of the experience, and their association with earlier unresolved guilts or with aggressive fantasies. The review of the experience and the expression and acceptance of feelings are important. As many survivor patterns show a major impairment of interpersonal relationships, with isolation, withdrawal, lack of trust, and overprotectiveness as some of the themes, the building of a trusting relationship, either in group or one-to-one therapy, may be helpful. The issues of mistrust may then be to some degree worked through. It is especially valuable if group work can be done with other survivors, as there is usually a greater capacity to relate to and trust others who have been through the same experience. Promotion of family and other supportive relationships is also important in this context and may require special sessions. Finally, patients may need permission to relinquish their anguish and isolation and rejoin the world, for there may be a sense that suffering must continue, to atone for not dying and for the deaths of others. The survivor may be difficult to treat, for he may feel he can never be the same again since he has come so close to death and is the "special" one who has seemingly defeated it when so many others did not. He is irrevocably touched by death—this is often a potent theme to be dealt with in therapy.

It is clear that many such syndromes share features with or merge into depression. If feelings of hopelessness, depression, despair, or suicidal preoccupation are prominent, then the victim may need active treatment along appropriate lines, perhaps with anti-depressant medication or, if suicide is likely, even hospitalization. A reworking of issues concerning the disaster experience may be facilitated at the same time as such therapy.

TREATMENT OF BEREAVEMENT SYNDROMES

The therapy of pathological grief in its various forms has been described in detail elsewhere (Raphael 1979a, 1983). However, the general principles of relevance in disaster-related bereavements are as follows:

1. Exploration of the bereaved's perception of the death: this component of psychotherapeutic management aims at defining guilt, shock, and anger that may be linked to the circumstances of the death, and at discovering how these feelings relate to the bereaved's own disaster experience. Blocks or defensive inhibitions of grief may become apparent in the description, and interpretation may be used to facilitate the opening up of emotional expression. In particular need of clarification and interpretation may be any links with earlier deprivations, as well as fears of overwhelming, disintegrating emotions and of facing the future without the dead person. Especially important is how the person died, including issues of mutilation and of suffering. As with the bereavement counseling, this review may include issues relating to aspects of the funeral or legal inquiry, or issues of blame, negligence, or mismanagement. The bereaved's feelings, especially anxiety, anger, and guilt, about all these components may need to be worked through.

2. Exploration of the friendship with the dead person: this helps to promote mourning processes that might be blocked. The bereaved is helped to gradually relinquish idealization of the dead person and face any of the more ambivalent feelings that either already existed or were thrown into focus by the disaster. Unfulfilled dependent needs may lead

to feelings of anger, fear, and helplessness that have to be expressed. Again, photographs or mementos may facilitate this mourning work. So often, anger about untimely deaths, particularly in man-made disasters, provides a block to sadness and relinquishing the relationship, for the bereaved stays locked into the anger rather than expressing it appropriately and moving on.

3. Exploration of responses to the death in the bereaved and significant others: this may give a picture of the ongoing level of grief and of adaptive processes. It may show a need for psychotherapeutic work aimed at promoting emotions and memory processes and at a gradual acceptance of the loss and an emotional reinvestment in the future. Specific sources of denial in terms of personality or coping styles will need to be understood so that they may be interpreted, or supported until the patient is able to do further grief work.

The greatest difficulties are likely to be encountered with patients who face survival issues such as severe life-threatening injury, multiple losses, and ongoing battle for existence. Here the therapist may have to fulfill holding and supporting functions, "staying with" the patient, gradually and even painfully building a relationship of security and trust, so that when the patient is ready, the pain of the loss may begin to be faced. Another major block is that of threatened or reawakened earlier losses, which are unbearable to the patient. Here the therapist may function in a similar, even longer-term, holding mode, serving as a support person through the crisis and beyond and accepting that the patient may not be able to grieve fully or at all for the loss. The goal may be simply protection from future stress and disintegration until coping can be resumed.

Bereavement work may involve practical techniques such as visiting the grave with the patient, systematic desensitization to traumatically stressful memories, or the use of "guided mourning." Family work, including work with children, is very valuable in helping to promote family sharing of memories and feelings about the dead person and in allowing fears about family integrity to be faced. As suggested by Black (1982), family group work may also be helpful to the children. Always, the futility of disaster deaths, the helplessness, anger, and sometimes guilt must be dealt with.

Because there are often many losses, the burden of grief may be very great and may only be shed slowly over time. This needs to be recognized in the therapy. The public nature of the deaths and grief also require support and understanding. The bereaved may need support to grieve in his own way and in his own time, and therapy must be tailored to this, for the syndromes are complex and often resistant to change. Nevertheless, most therapy can significantly improve the bereaved's coping and adaptation (Lundin 1984b; Lindy et al. 1983).

TREATMENT OF OTHER DISORDERS

Whatever other disorders appear, the appropriate assessment and treatment should be carried out. Phobic and anxiety disorders may respond to anxiolytic medication (short-term) and behavior therapies in terms of symptomatic treatment, but almost invariably will need some psychotherapeutic working through as well. Depression and panic disorder are not infrequent. As the incidence of severe mental illnesses apart from the disorder outlined above is not high, these will constitute a small part of the treatment of disaster victims. Any that do arise require therapy per se, plus attempts to manage the stressor components related to the disaster.

The general distress and impairments of social and personal functioning or intimate and family relationships will all require a general therapeutic approach with focus on both disaster stressors and their contribution and long-term (pre-disaster) problems and their origins. Crisis work may focus on the former, with a renegotiation for more in-depth work with the latter if it is clear that old problems are simply surfacing with the disaster and cannot be readily resolved.

One other group of syndromes for treatment may be stress-induced psychosomatic disorders. Here longer-term medical and psychosocial support management needs to be combined with a focused intervention dealing with the disaster stresses. A specific group requiring careful therapeutic work are the injured who may suffer concurrently from any of the above disorders.

Significant therapeutic achievements may be made with such treatment, and for disaster-precipitated illness the prognosis is usually hopeful, especially if the therapist is skilled, has personal knowledge of the disaster, and succeeds in engaging the patient (Lindy et al. 1983).

PSYCHOLOGICAL DEBRIEFING OF WORKERS
AND HELPERS

An essential component of the mantle of psychosocial care after a disaster is the care provided for workers and helpers at all levels. As noted earlier, most people in these roles function in a courageous, dedicated, and highly competent manner. Nevertheless, there is considerable strain from many sources associated with such work: from the personal encounters with death, destruction, and loss and from the empathic concern for other suffering human beings. The aim of the psychological debriefing is to help workers deal with these inevitable stresses so that problems do not arise subsequently. The functions are thus essentially preventive, as was outlined above, although sometimes reactions and disorders may arise requiring specific counseling or referral. Depressed and hopeless feelings are common in the face of the overwhelming nature of the disaster and the little that helpers may be able to do. If these merge into depressive illness, they may require specific treatment, but for the most part, support will be adequate.

The methods of debriefing are best set out in the formal group sessions. The purpose needs to be made explicit to the group of workers so that they do not feel they are being "psychoanalyzed" or there is any inference they have failed to cope.

"There are several aspects of the disaster that it is important to review. This will help us to learn for ourselves and also to make better preparations for any future disasters. It also helps get the disaster in perspective, as an experience. We will go over a number of different aspects, including roles you each filled, frustrations and satisfactions, resources, and how you felt during your work and afterward. This is part of the process we call psychological debriefing, that helps each worker to deal with any strains he or she might have experienced, quite naturally, during such a time. It also helps us to review any positive aspects of the experience. I hope we will be able to conclude with some thoughts or guidelines for others who may be involved in such a situation in the future."

The person who conducts the debriefing should have considerable skills in understanding individual and group dynamics as well as disaster stressors and behavior. Some structuring of the sessions may provide a good framework for dealing with relevant issues, although anxieties, anger, and guilt may also need exploration, expression, and support as they arise. Several themes may be followed (see figure 10.7).

"How did *you* get involved in the disaster? . . . What was your particular role? Was this a role you felt trained for? . . . Did you have warning of the disaster . . . or that you would be involved? . . . How did you feel at this stage? . . . Had you ever been in anything like this before?"

These questions explore initiation into the disaster role and related issues —preparedness or its lack, training, past experience, and degree of shock and other feelings at the early stage. Supportive interpretation or queries may start to facilitate the emotional working through.

Next, there is exploration of the worker's own experience in the disaster and of the role he played in it.

FIGURE 10.7
Psychological Debriefing

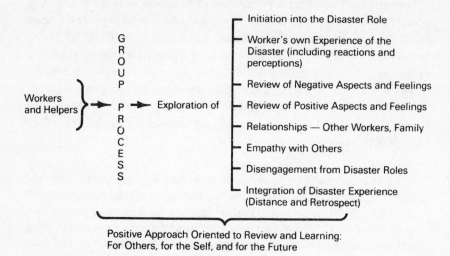

Positive Approach Oriented to Review and Learning:
For Others, for the Self, and for the Future

"Can you go over just what you were called upon to do . . . just what you did at each stage during the impact, rescue, etc.? . . . How did you feel yourself during this time? . . . Was your own life threatened? . . . Did you lose anyone close to you or that you knew well? . . . What sorts of things happened to you personally and what did you feel?"

These areas of inquiry help lead into the psychological perceptions and reactions of the worker. There then needs to be a specific exploration for areas of difficulty.

"What were the most difficult things for you in your role during this time? Were there times when you had difficult decisions to make? Were there things that made you frustrated? Did you feel you knew clearly what to do? Did you have the resources or backup you needed? Did things stop you from doing what you needed to? What were the worst aspects of the experience for you?"

Thus, the frustrations and negative experiences are explored in depth, and the anger, helplessness, and guilt that are so often associated with them are ventilated and lessened. More positive aspects should then be reviewed, to address the balance and help with integration and perspective.

284

"Although there were obviously many terrible, frightening, and frustrating aspects to your experience, it would be helpful if we could also look at the things that went well. Whether you felt good about what you did . . . the satisfying and positive aspects . . . how special it felt to be able to be involved and help at such a time . . . and so forth."

Thus, the more positive and satisfying, even special, aspects of the experience are also reviewed and placed in some perspective so that they do not stay as idealized memories beside which ordinary life pales.

Next, relationships with others should be explored.

"Most people find that their relationships with others during such a time take on special significance. Could we go over how you got on with your colleagues and other workers—the close and positive aspects and some of the conflicts and frustrations?

"It might also be useful to talk about how all this has been for your families. Sometimes families feel out of things . . . mostly they help but don't quite understand . . . and, of course, sometimes it seems to bring you all closer together. Maybe we could talk about how these things have gone with your families."

Thus, the two main areas of interpersonal relationships are explored for stresses and other, more positive responses in terms of the disaster workers' experiences. This allows the ventilation and clarification of feelings and prevents chronic maladaptive patterns from occurring. It is especially useful if some joint session or social event of workers and families can be instituted to allow families to express and share feelings with others who have had similar experiences, thus strengthening intrafamily and interfamily communication and bonds.

Another important aspect for all workers, but especially those in counseling and support roles, has to do with their identification with the experience and feelings of the victims. This experience requires gentle exploration.

"It would be helpful if we could talk about some of the people you were involved with—those you helped. Were there some who had special meaning for *you?* (For example, you knew them; were very distressed by their experience; you saved their lives; you spent a lot of time supporting them; their behavior had a particular impact on you; they reminded you of someone you knew and loved, of your own family, yourself; and so forth.) If so, how did you feel about this?"

This working through of the stresses of empathy is very helpful, for it enables workers to recognize and unload many of the distressing experiences, so that their empathy does not become too painful a burden, blocking them from future close personal caring involvement of this kind.

The worker also needs help in relinquishing his disaster role, integrating it into his overall experience, and making the transition back to everyday life.

"Let us now talk about how it is to finish, to leave this work and go back to ordinary things again. Could we talk about some of the difficulties of transferring back again? The relief that it's finished—but the sadness of not feeling involved in something so needed and special."

This questioning facilitates further the process of disengagement from the disaster experience while integrating it, so that the worker does not become locked into regrets and resentments about his ordinary work functioning. It helps him feel less guilt at relinquishing his task that was adequately but never perfectly accomplished.

Finally, it is helpful to review what has been learned and what can be transferred.

"It would be useful if we could just briefly go over what this work and experience meant. It would be especially helpful if we could define what we have learned that might help: in other future disaster work; for ourselves personally; in the ordinary work we do (stress management, skills, personal disaster aspects). We might also go over any guidance we would offer to others going through this in the future. And, if any of you feel that there are ongoing stresses for you after this experience, then we can talk further about some helpful ways of dealing with these."

This discussion promotes the processes of integration and mastery of the disaster, by actively defining, both concretely and at a feeling level, the experience and its consequences. The experience is given a cognitive structure, and the emotional release of reviewing it helps the worker to a sense of achievement and distancing. He will not forget the experience but neither is he likely to retain an ongoing stressful burden from it.

IMPLEMENTING MENTAL HEALTH CARE PROGRAMS

As has been discussed by workers such as Cohen and Ahearn (1980) and Tierney and Baisden (1979), the overall implementation of mental health care programs to cover aims such as the above will take careful planning and administration. Sanctions and resource support need to be negotiated for the potential provision of care. Then there needs to be assessment of local resources and development of a program that utilizes and links with these resources. Needs may be evaluated at community and individual levels, either in preparation for or immediately following the impact of a disaster, taking into account the variables outlined in this and earlier chapters. All workers who have developed or been involved in such programs emphasize the need to evolve them in liaison with the other rescue and aid systems of the disaster. As Tierney and Baisden (1979, p. 42) point out, "Community mental health center staff must do whatever needs to be done. They must behave as good neighbors would, but it is most important that they *be there;* digging out, saving others and so forth. Especially in sudden disaster, real physical needs are dominant and the situation does not lend itself to playing formal mental health roles."

Similar observations have been made by Valent (1984) with regard to health care provision following the Australian bushfires. Mental health workers spent the early days after the disaster in mud and ashes, working alongside the victims in practical tasks while at the same time offering psychological and social support. In this way, they were also building a relationship of trust for any future in-depth counseling.

It is essential, however, that workers still recognize and specifically deal with the mental health problems in a systematic and skilled way.

Tierney and Baisden (1979) have examined the potentialities for crisis intervention programs for disaster victims in smaller communities, which often have limited mental health resources. They explored the essential service categories, including inpatient, outpatient, emergency, consultation, education, and diagnosis. They felt that twenty-four-hour crisis services and hotlines were especially valuable for use in the disaster context, as a "well-known easily accessible source of information and short-term intervention that can channel effected people towards that part of the systems which best meets their needs" (p. 72). On the whole, the public was more aware of social service agencies than of mental health service agencies. Service provision was often balanced between human services generally and mental health services, and the smaller communities tended to be less well provided for. There seemed also to be a number of groups that might need services in times of disaster but not be provided with them. These groups included the socially and geographically inaccessible, the uninformed, those who feared stigma, and especially, minority groups whose needs might not be recognized. Most people perceived the likelihood of mental health problems, and there was a strong belief that some sort of counseling effort should be directed toward disaster victims.

As this study indicates, there are many different community resources to be assessed and mobilized. Not only are there the local indigenous care organizations, but there are also volunteers and voluntary groups. These provide a large and valuable resource, but it is essential that volunteers be adequately trained and work within their skills and limitations.

While health care will need to be devised to fit the requirements of the particular region and disaster, and while it must have a strong practical and outreach basis, there are general principles, such as those outlined by Cohen and Ahearn, that should be followed:

1. A planning or task force that is representative of mental health professionals, power groups, sentiment groups, and needs groups should be established (see p. 256).
2. Needs must be assessed in terms of community and cultural definitions of health and illness; the extent and nature of existing problems; and available resources.
3. Goals need to be set from analysis of the data on needs and resources, and priorities then allocated.
4. Programs need definition along the following parameters: objectives; methods of implementation; technical requirements for funding, staff, material, space, and other resources; administration of the program; accountability in terms of efficiency, accounting, and monitoring, and evaluation of program effects.
5. Program implementation must be practical and realistic in terms of local resources, needs, and interaction with other community organizations.
6. Staff recruitment and training are important. Potential workers should reflect the ethnic, racial, and class composition of the community, if possible, and should show abilities to relate well to distressed people, as well as personal qualities of maturity, motivation, and stability. Skills should include crisis or disaster counseling, or workers should be provided with training in these spheres.
7. Information, documentation, and data systems need to be developed and maintained for the necessary record keeping and review.
8. Evaluation should be carried on throughout the duration of the program and at its termination. It should, as a minimum, cover groups reached, services provided, outcome, and costs.

Using these guidelines, the potential for mental health programs to aid disaster victims may be developed in pre-disaster planning, to be mobilized should a disaster occur. This development is ideally achieved when disaster services are linked to other crisis counseling and support services, for instance, to those that deal with personal disaster. The program then supplies the "umbrella of care" defined above, melding this with community response and transferring it gradually and appropriately to the regular systems of care. The latter are often enhanced and further developed as a consequence of their disaster work.

The mental health support service mobilized at the city morgue in Sydney to help relatives of those who had died in the Granville rail disaster was so valuable that a full-time social worker was later assigned to the morgue to assist relatives following motor vehicle and other personal disaster deaths. This has generalized to other expertise in emergency mental health care for bereaved relatives (Bray and George 1984).

Many services have been mobilized after disasters, following some of the general guidelines above. Examples discussed in the literature include programs after the Pennsylvania flood of 1972 (McGee and Heffron 1976), the Corning flood of 1972 (Kliman 1976), the ice cream parlor air crash in 1972 (Baren 1976), the Monticello tornado of 1974 (Hartsough et al. 1976), the Managua earthquake (Cohen 1976), the California earthquake of 1971 (Blaufarb and Levine 1972), floods and Hurricane Agnes in 1972 (Okura 1975), a school bus and train collision (Tuckman 1973), a maritime disaster (Carlton 1980), a major rail disaster (Raphael 1977, 1979–80), and bushfires (Valent 1984; Raphael 1984b; McFarlane and Raphael 1984), as well as a program for refugees (Tyhurst 1977). There have been many general descriptions of such programs, but very few have been subjected to any systematic and published evaluation except for those following the Granville rail disaster (Singh and Raphael 1981) and the bushfires (Clayer 1984; McFarlane 1984). General models for such programs have been put forward by many workers, including Berren et al. (1982), Frederick (1977), and Frazer and Spicka (1981). This last study is especially valuable in highlighting the need for a collaborative approach using indigenous resources and promoting skills and knowledge in relevant agencies, such as the Red Cross and mental health organizations. All these papers hold valuable suggestions but remain to be tested. The preventive approach has also been emphasized (e.g., Sank 1979; Raphael 1979b; Gist and Stoltz 1982). Nevertheless, it is clear that the crisis and chaos of disaster have made systematic development of programs and their systematic evaluation extremely difficult. This is an important area of mental health care with a sound theoretical base, and one that will no doubt be more fully developed in the future for the disasters that will inevitably arise.

RELEVANCE TO PERSONAL DISASTERS

Many of the patterns of care, objectives, techniques, and goals discussed are very relevant to the disasters of everyday life. They may be mobilized for accident victims, for the relatives of those who died sudden tragic and untimely deaths, and for those who suffer the assaults of modern society, physical and psychological.

In the case of personal disaster there is also the need to convey a recognition of suffering and strengths, as well as a mantle of care at the time of the emergency that gradually transfers into regular community systems of support. Emotional first aid and triage with the identification of those at risk, general psychological support and counseling, preventive programs for those at risk, and specific therapies, both short and long term, for those who decompensate into disorder are all indicated. Likewise, the consultative and educational models are essential for spreading knowledge and skills to any likely to be in contact with those who experience such crises and to the community as a whole. And, finally, the stressed health workers, at risk of "burnout," may need special support and psychological debriefing to insure their own functioning and psychological health. Such programs have been provided for many, and in some instances, their effectiveness has been tested (Raphael 1977a; Bordow and Porritt 1979; Clarke and Viney 1979). They are increasingly a part of competent health care for those passing through major life crisis.

Thus, there needs to be, in health-care terms, a mantle of general and specific programs that can be linked together. These programs promote caring human involvement. They provide specific skills for all those suffering the powerful personal disasters of life, while recognizing and drawing on their strengths and resilience. At the time of community disaster, they are further mobilized—drawing in extra resources and collaborating with other human service agencies—so that the mantle may be extended to the many different victims of the catastrophe. Again, suffering and strengths are recognized, while care is provided as required. And the altruistic response to those who are hurt by the disaster must surely provide many good legacies that ultimately strengthen the fabric of the community.

CHAPTER 11

Community and
Political Dynamics

"You can't make a career out of disasters."

In earlier chapters much of the consideration of disasters has been at an individual level or, at most, in terms of the family system. But many different systems are relevant in disasters: individual and family, small group, organization, community, and society. Patterns of one system may reverberate through the others or impact may be differential across these systems. The dynamics of disaster and response may be usefully understood from the perspective of these broader systems as well (e.g., Barton 1969; Mileti et al. 1975). And, at every level, the political aspects of power, responsibility, gain, and accountability may impinge on the perception of the disaster event and on the actions that follow.

SYSTEMS PRE-DISASTER

There is evidence from many studies that the nature of the system of community or the societal system may greatly influence how it will be affected by a disaster. Issues of preparation and prevention, the consequences of impact, and the capacity for recovery will all be affected. The most powerful preexisting variable is the degree of deprivation, poverty, underdevelopment, or socioeconomic vulnerability that exists beforehand. Communities may be on the verge of drought, famine, and starvation; may have chronic civil conflict or war; may lack technological or financial resources for anticipating, preparing for, and mitigating the effects of any disaster; may have habitations that cannot withstand the force of natural hazards; and may have poorly developed medical and other response systems. Poor roads, communication, and transport may all add further to the difficulties when disaster occurs. Levels of integration or disintegration of communities may reflect further vulnerabilities, so that social indicators may be used to define communities likely to be in greater need post-disaster, assuming equivalent stresses.

The pre-disaster state may be defined at the individual through family, organizational, and broader social levels, which may include social-class factors (Clausen et al. 1978). Disasters, depending on their severity and nature, will impinge on all these systems to some degree. By definition, most disasters will have impact at least at the community level. Communities will differ in their mix of individuals and family systems, as well as in the nature and values attached to these systems. For example, kinship systems may be small and nuclear or extended, and the value placed on family and other ties will differ widely, as will the importance accorded the individual as opposed to the group.

Communities may or may not have views about or previous experience of disasters in general or particular disasters. They may or may not have disaster subcultures or formal organizational systems whose functions are disaster oriented.

Even when there has been past experience and there are preparatory disaster-specific organizational systems, the structure of the community will be stressed by a disaster of any magnitude. Such stress may be through the deaths of many members of the community, vital in their own right and often for their place in family, community, or society systems. It may be through injuries, their extent, and the resources required to deal with them. It may be through damage to homes, industry, buildings, and physical structures, necessary for the community functioning, or through the alteration of demands upon these structures. And inevitably there is economic impact as well. Common indices of disaster impact on a community are numbers of dead, injured, and of damaged homes and buildings, losses of stock and farm property, damage to forest and ecology, and damage and destruction of industry. Ultimately, of course, these indices represent the estimated costs.

THE RESPONSE OF THE COMMUNITY AS A SYSTEM

Like the individual and the family, the community system goes through a pattern of phasic response to disaster. The community itself may have a sense of invulnerability, reflected in the attitude it takes to the potential for disaster or to actual warning when disaster is imminent. This sense may be concretely indicated by the lack of resources (material or personnel) committed to disaster preparedness or by the lack of organizational systems that have such preparedness as part of their frames of reference. Many characteristics of the community may influence the development of the warning response subsystem described previously (see chapter 2). The trust placed in the authorities, the communicational system, and the costs of preparedness and response may decide the likely outcome in the pre-impact phase.

The response to impact is, like that of the individual, *shock and helplessness.* But, within the community, segments that are not so directly affected rapidly start on the processes of helping the injured, dealing with the dead, and resolving the immediate needs for shelter. How much they can accomplish will be determined by the degree of damage. When damage is nearly total, much of the initial assistance will have to come from surrounding or neighboring systems.

In the immediate post-impact period the community is shattered, fragmented—perhaps dazed and stunned, as the individual with a disaster syndrome. There is a lack of coordinated response, initially, at least.

Communities, of course, function to maintain their systems and achieve their goals through a *wide variety of organizational systems and subsystems,* which form the *infrastructure.* Organizations have been defined by Haas and Drabek (1970) as relatively permanent and complex discernible interaction systems geared to specific tasks of organizational objectives, decision making, enactment of authority and influence, and communication. While organizations show stability over time, they are not static but rather dynamic systems. Gradually or rapidly, these systems will start to respond to the effects of disaster impact proportionately to a number of factors: the relevance of their functions to disasters or emergency; their training or experience in disaster response; the extent to which they have been damaged by the disaster; and the extent to which their authority systems define response for the specific occasion or functions.

In many major community disasters, formal organizational systems may be delayed in response. This may be because, as Mileti's group (Mileti et al. 1975) has pointed out, there are bureaucratic limitations and adaptations. For example, organizations may attempt to adhere to regular roles and activities not appropriate to the disaster, or they may have difficulties in decision making because of inadequate leadership or programs. Increasing stress from the disaster and its consequences may lead to changed patterns of interaction within the organization and between it and other organizations. Stress may also lead to changes in task priorities and decision making. But, when there is rigidity of structure and function, with lack of the fluidity and flexibility necessary for the uncertainty of the disaster situation, then prompt response is difficult. There may be a reluctance to respond if ambiguities in goals and roles lead to fear of taking responsibility for response. Or, the leaders who might normally make such decisions may be unavailable, because of the timing of the disaster, a breakdown of communication, or even because they have been put out of action by the impact.

When formal organizations do start to respond, they do so in terms of roles defined by themselves or some accepted or senior authority system. At the time of crisis and emergency, they may be prepared to give up their autonomy to share tasks and boundaries, or to alter roles for the need of others. Later, however, as will be described further, this may not happen and organizations may retreat into bureaucratic rigidity.

The nature of organizations and their domains of function are vitally important in determining the relative rapidity and appropriateness of their response. As Adam (1970, quoted by Mileti et al. 1975) noted, "the greater the continuity between *disaster* roles and responsibility, the less problematic disaster mobilization is likely to be" (p. 80). Organizations can thus be classified in terms of their day-to-day capacity for emergency functioning and preparedness. Police are a good example of an organization geared to emergency response, decision making, leadership, communication, and control of people and resources. They are likely to respond rapidly in many community emergencies of peacetime and are often given control of other emergency response on the disaster site. Military systems are geared for emergency response, but problems and fears about military control may mean that they often function in association with civilian authority systems. Fire control systems often have capacity and mandate for emergency response and are likely to be mobilized early in many disasters. Rescue and emergency control groups may also be utilized and rapidly mobilized. The other major emergency group with a capacity for response is the medical organization system of hospitals, ambulance and resuscitation workers, doctors, and nurses. Any or all of these emergency groups may spontaneously start to respond to disaster-generated needs in the immediate aftermath.

However, whether or not these formal systems do start to respond, and when, will depend on a number of factors:

- Their knowledge of what has happened and what is needed
- Their access to those who might need their services and help or the access of victims to them
- Whether or not organizational or authority structures operate to fit them into an overall and coordinated response for the stricken community of victims.

When a disaster has been major and to some degree unexpected, there is likely to be, in the shocked, numb phase of the community system response, a period where normal authority systems lapse, and response is spontaneous but not organized. This response is usually massive, as Barton (1969), Dynes (1970), and many other observers have noted. Thus, there are large numbers of individuals, groups, and organizations, each responding as a single entity. This phenomenon is reinforced by that of "mass convergence." Those coming toward the disaster may be seeking to help, seeking those they love, or driven by guilt, curiosity, anxiety, or whatever. They may also have a desperate need to be involved, even showing the intense and heightened activity of what has been called "the counterdisaster syndrome."

These various individuals and groups from within and without the affected community may be difficult to coordinate in their responses because there is likely to be a considerable period of time before the full magnitude of the disaster problem is assessed. Coordination may be particularly difficult if the task is overwhelming, the disaster has occurred during the night and power is lacking, physical disorganization is great, there is a lack of any central coordination mechanism, and communications are impossible or have broken down.

Response of the community system must ultimately address itself to seven basic processes. These processes are, as Mileti's group notes: (1) preservation of life; (2) restoration of essential services, especially power, information, and communication; (3) social control; (4) maintenance of community morale; (5) return of economic activity; (6) emergency welfare and other personal services activity; (7) maintenance of leisure and recreation. At least the first three of these usually form part of the immediate post-impact response.

Thus, out of the initial fragmented and often uncoordinated response must come some way of dealing with these issues, the foremost being preservation of life, through rescue, recovery, and reestablishment of essential services, and prevention of or protection against any ongoing disaster threat. A common, if not universal, phenomenon, occurring before the coordinated mobilization of formal organizations, is the evolution of emergent groups: loosely knit groups of people goal-oriented to specific and immediate practical tasks (Parr 1970; Forrest 1978). Such groups cluster around "natural" or emergent leaders, who seem to facilitate the decision making necessary for coordinated action. These leaders seem to be able to see what needs to be done and to get things organized. They are often people who have had previous disaster experience, have disaster-related skills, and are not torn by family involvements in the disaster. They may be people with prior leadership roles or significant personal prestige. Many, however, are not obvious leaders but simply men and women who rise to the needs of the occasion, achieve much, and then, in many cases, fade back into the community afterward, sometimes without even having been recognized for the contribution they have made.

For example, in the immediate aftermath of a serious community disaster a local truck driver rose to a natural leadership role in his small town. He helped rescue, protect property, and gain support for the community afterward. He was called "the mayor" for this brief period, although the town was too small to have had such formal local government. After the disaster he resumed his ordinary day-to-day life in the community. His leadership had surprised others and himself, yet had been accepted and responded to by all.

Following a severe storm, a young policeman, who had been refused promotion a few weeks earlier because he "lacked leadership potential," proved to be one of the most courageous and effective local emergent leaders.

Wettenhall (1975) described various emergent groups and leaders in the immediate period following the disastrous 1967 Tasmanian bushfires. One such leader was a Methodist clergyman, another a Red Cross state secretary. Afterward, these men essentially settled back into their pre-disaster roles. Emergent groups were both local and more centralized, but in all cases aimed at rescue, relief, and, later, rehabilitation.

This gelling of some group structures for specific tasks, which involve the evolution of decision-making processes and more specified roles, leads to the development of what has been called the *synthetic community*. This temporary synthetic community, as Mileti notes, attempts to coordinate the actions of the various groups and individuals who have started to respond into "a more coordinated weapon to combat the demands generated by the disaster" (p. 90). The temporary coordinating units may develop search and rescue, serve as centers for communication and decision making, and promote interaction between organizations.

Gradually this synthetic community structure is replaced by more coordinated control and formal organizational systems of counterdisaster response through emergency or other services geared to rescue and recovery. Difficulties may still arise here too, however, for organizations may be reluctant to take over coordination unless this is their specific brief. They may not wish to share territory with others or to relinquish responsibility to organizations with which they are traditionally in conflict or competition. Nevertheless, if effective functioning is to take place, complex communication and decision-making processes must occur centrally in a coordinated fashion. Otherwise, duplicative, ineffective, or even harmful actions may result.

The positive charge of altruistic response, the high arousal and involvement, and the intense group processes all contribute to making the community at this time the altruistic (or "therapeutic") community. Close cooperation, solidarity, coordinated action, and the setting aside of conflict and rivalry are all possible in the emergency period. Thus it is that in the early post-impact period those tasks essential for the preservation of the species are facilitated through the strong emotional charge of altruistic responses, which allow and promote the development of coordinated formal and informal organization infrastructures in the damaged fabric of the community.

Special skills required for certain disasters (handling large numbers of dead, dealing with particular types of injuries, resolving certain communication failures) may define the need for specific organizational systems to be involved in or take charge of the coordinating process. Skills with control and coordination from other emergency functioning (e.g., police) may also facilitate the central coordinating function. Access to and capacity to utilize communication systems or headquarters (central ambulance or other radio control) may be critical to the coordinating role. Past disaster training, practice, or experience may further enhance this capacity. Coordination may also be facilitated if the coordinating agency is linked to the other organizations in its day-to-day functions. Formal government or other authority sanctions will also reinforce this effort further.

Thus, the community has been hurt and damaged—has suffered death, destruction, loss, and dislocation—but has survived in whole or in part. Reactions to heal and repair start rapidly and usually develop into an intense and coordinated process. Only when the disaster is total may this process be impossible or very delayed. On the whole, the community will show an increase in solidarity and a decrease in conflict. Priorities are clear and there is a high charge of altruism and hope, a thrust for regeneration.

The broader societal system itself reflects similar responses. Priority is given to the preservation of life, and the political institutions may become less dominant. Here, too, the positive and altruistic themes predominate in this early phase, colored by the culture and texture of the society. The

297

system acknowledges the damage and mobilizes resources, recognizes suffering, and makes special conditions for its affected member. What, then, follows on these themes of promise, reparative altruism, and human concern?

THE REST OF THE WORLD

Depending on the extent of the disaster, it will receive a certain acknowledgment from the surrounding community and "the rest of the world." Once communication with such other systems has been reestablished to a sufficient degree, early reports of the damage and destruction will start to appear. The mass media are the prime mechanism by which a picture of the disaster emerges. With present-day satellite communication systems, the news is likely to be rapid and vivid. Initial reports may under- or overestimate the extent of damage and death. Because greater destruction is likely to be more "newsworthy," overestimation is common and dramatic headlines the rule. Thus, following the 1983 Ash Wednesday fires, television and radio coverage around the world featured sensational reports that thousands had died and the southern half of Australia had been wiped out by fires. Wettenhall (1975) has shown how media presentations of the Tasmanian bushfires, in which sixty-two people were killed, reflected the initial uncertainty.

Headlines following the event included:

"13 Killed in Hobart Fires: Convicts Are Freed to Help Save City" *(Australian)*
"16 Dead in Bushfire Havoc: Flames Raze 450 Homes in Tasmania" *(Sydney Morning Herald).*

These reports serve to highlight the early uncertain and chaotic picture that may appear when disrupted communication and fragmented community response make difficult any accurate estimate of what has happened. Such communication disruption may be due to the physical destruction of systems of communication, the deaths or disablements of those who would communicate through them, or disaster effects that interfere with communication processes.

Scanlon (1978) investigated and described communication patterns within Darwin and to the outside world after the cyclone of 1974. He showed how destruction of means of transportation and damage to local communication systems meant that key agencies, police, fire departments, and medical personnel could not communicate with each other. Mass media were also gone. Scanlon points out that even if communication systems had survived intact, it would have been difficult to inform the public of what was going on, because no one knew. He quotes someone as observing: "Those who had radios that could operate found the absence of news alarming. At one A.M. we lost all radio contact. In the morning we turned on the radio. It was just silence . . . eerie. I tried the telephone. It was dead. There was no way you could communicate. The silence was a sense of loneliness" (p. 9). External communications were also in disarray. Many links were operating but were scattered and ineffective. There was at least one means of communication open to the outside at all times. But such means were often not known to exist by those who might have used them or, because internal communications had failed, were of limited value.

Communication may be further disrupted by convergence phenomena, as anxious relatives, authorities, organizations, and the media try to communicate inward to find out what has happened. Telephones are frequently disabled in this manner. For example, Mileti's group cites estimates that following Hurricane Carla in 1964, telephone calls to the affected Houston area more than doubled.

The extent to which the disaster is newsworthy as well as how it is presented may have much to do with the way the outside world responds. Furthermore, for the sufferers, the media presentations may symbolize public acknowledgment of what they have gone through: something concrete to which they can return.

In a valuable review of the evolving response of the international community to disasters, Kent (1983) notes that a major disaster requiring international assistance occurs about once a week. It is obvious that, with smaller disasters in particular, media presentations will take up only the most major or newsworthy aspects. As the media in a sense may mold and interpret the image of the disaster, what they present and how may have great significance for the pattern of response and aid. The media may also affect the image of organizations of response, which may gain prestige from what is presented, or alternatively, lose it, if media presentations highlight or rumor any inadequacies.

Nimmo (1984) reported on the TV news coverage of the Three Mile Island episode. He suggests that a key emphasis of TV news is in fact story telling and that the major networks produced three different "fables" of this disaster: "CBS narrated a tale of responsible political and technological elites, ABC a nightmare of common folk victimized by elites, and NBC a story of resignation and demystification" (p. 115). These fables must, of course, have significance for victims and the communities they belong to. Nimmo goes on to suggest such fables promote "visions of reassurance, threat and primal assurance." These may be powerfully influential, as well as dramatically artistic.

Political themes also start to appear, often linked to media response. Local leaders, national politicians, and internationally aligned or non-aligned groups are quick to produce statements of concern or sympathy—and are likely to gain prestige by so doing. Prime ministers, presidents, and royalty visit disaster-stricken communities, offer public condolences, and provide funds and reparations. They, too, are consumed by the altruistic benevolence of the post-disaster utopia.

COMMUNITY RECOVERY: CRISES, CONFLICTS, AND COSTS

Just as the individual and family systems are initially euphoric at surviving, or at least numbed, and then gradually give way to despair, fear, sadness, and anger as reality is realized, so, too, do the community and society. The altruistic and therapeutic community of positive feeling in the early days is replaced by a more negative, disillusioned response as organizational systems have to adapt to meeting the longer-term consequences of the disaster.

The demise of the therapeutic community comes for several reasons. First, individual mood and feeling states alter substantially as the reality of the disaster is incorporated—the fact that things will never be exactly the same again and that even return to something like "normal" may take a long, long time. Family stresses begin to emerge, forming a substrate that will further add to the chronic stress level of the community. Dislocation of support networks removes the mitigating effects by which they might have lessened chronic tension.

At an organizational level, as noted by Thompson and Hawkes (1962, quoted in Mileti et al. 1975) "as the bases for normal relationships gradually are restored, the system withdraws resources from the synthetic organization and gradually returns to pluralistic processes" (p. 123). As the various organizations responsible for relief and recovery within the community start to define their territory and boundaries, their roles and limitations, and their jurisdiction, conflicts start to reappear. These conflicts are least between organizations that work cooperatively together in nondisaster periods and have already defined boundaries and mechanisms for dealing with such issues. They may become profound between groups that feel their status is in question or that their territory (as established in the disaster) is being intruded on. Sometimes the public image of an organization may be an important aspect of its role following the disaster, and conflict with other groups may arise because of threat to this public image. Special problems may arise because emergent groups who carried the "dirty work" in the acute phase feel they are being supplanted by outside professionals who were not there and do not really know what the problems are.

Hostility between organizations may also be generated by a sense of guilt or inadequacy, or by frustrations or anger, so that other groups are scapegoated or their expertise and possible contribution denied. This search for blame may be particularly pronounced in man-made disasters where, once the emergency has past, there is a legal impetus need to seek out causation and to investigate effectiveness of response. Groups that are scapegoated may be the different or vulnerable, or those who are negatively viewed for political reasons (e.g., groups that might gain political advantage or leadership). These negative responses come later, of course, and not in the emergency period, when such hostilities are submerged.

Conflicts may arise among relief agencies because of different interpretations of who should provide relief and how. Kent (1983) has commented that it is only in very recent years that international aid has been at all coordinated through agencies such as UNDRO (United Nations Disaster Relief Organization). Poor coordination of relief is also likely at local and community levels until effective coordinating and authority systems are developed for the recovery stage of the disaster.

Competition for victims may even become a political issue between organizations, both in the acute emergency phase and subsequently. Such competition is most likely in developed countries, of course, but reflects the intense need that organizations may have to play a role in the disaster response. In one emergency response to a disaster, for example, two major hospital systems came into conflict, as both were ready to take numerous injured victims of the disaster. Injuries were low in this disaster, although deaths were high. Most of the injured were taken to one or two smaller hospitals, and the major systems, readied to respond, were left with only one or two victims—disappointed and angered that they could not offer more. In the relief period in another disaster several voluntary groups competed to take over the longer-term support needs for victims whose homes were destroyed. Each group differed in what it wanted to provide and few consulted with victims. Until an authoritative superstructure channeled support through a single resource system, victims were bewildered and stressed by the convergence of help upon them.

Differing leadership and organizational expertise is necessary in the longer-term post-disaster period. Special skills, technology, and resources are likely to be required. Once again, organizations whose defined, socially sanctioned role is nearest to what is required are likely to fit best to these tasks. These organizations may nevertheless have deficiencies in the disaster framework, lacking, for instance, rapidity of response, flexibility, or capacity to assess and respond to stress effects that complicate the ways in which victims may present needs and problems. Furthermore, organizations may lack personnel or other resources necessary to carry out disaster tasks alongside or continuing their regular functions. Thus, if they are to fulfill disaster responsibility over a longer period of time, as is essential for relief and recovery, they will need extra resources for that time frame, as well as sanctions. Less disaster-oriented organizations may find it difficult to contribute relevant skills and may not gain a sanctioned place in the disaster relief and recovery response. Sanctions for any agency or organization will usually need to be negotiated at government, local authority, and personal levels, for outsiders may be extruded. Obligations to groups may be feared. Locals usually wish to have ultimate responsibility for the management of relief and recovery in their own communities and for the utilization of resources provided. The two sides of this coin are well exemplified in Kent's comments (1983) about how some groups may see the provision of aid as an entry into a community system, while the system so encumbered may fear the obligation will intrude on autonomy.

For recovery to occur, the community system has to define its tasks and objectives and then develop an organizational superstructure to achieve these objectives. It needs to quantify damage to the various subsystems, to assess needs, to provide and mobilize resources to meet these needs, and, as noted earlier, to restore and maintain the ongoing basic socioeconomic functions of the society. Economic resources may be provided by government, public donation, and aid agencies. They make take the form of goods, services, or money, such as direct grants or loans at special rates. Materials may be provided for rebuilding, subsidies may be given to help meet costs, and insurance funds may be deployed. It is clear that whatever restitution is offered, the community cannot turn back the clock to make things as they were before the disaster. The deployment of resources will have significant structural as well as economic impact. Depending on the situation and on special needs, some parts of the local economy may boom while other parts fall back. For instance, housing and building may boom but farming and livestock be in decline. The fortunes of local businesses may fluctuate greatly, rising or falling. Jobs may no longer be available, leading to second-ary movement of population. Leisure industries may lie fallow, with little time for leisure activities during rebuilding.

Fund raising and disbursement is one special component of the economic recovery that is very likely to be subject to political pressures and usage. It is likely to be a source of conflict and dissatisfaction, even though essential to post-disaster rehabilitation.

Human resources necessary for recovery will include people with special skills, relief agency personnel, appropriate leaders, and often large numbers of volunteers. Determining how best to train and utilize these resources to maximal efficiency and satisfaction may be difficult. This is especially true with the volunteers, who may create further problems in their own reactions to the disaster consequences. Welfare services are important for their role in longer-term recovery, especially in defining goals and dealing with the emotional needs of victims. Sometimes there is conflict among welfare, volunteer, and health services groups as to how the needs for counseling and emotional support may best be fulfilled. Indeed, there may be conflict over who "owns" or "has access to" lists of victims for contact and offer of services. Such lists frequently become the treasured property of one organi-zational system, which does not allow others access to it—at one level preserving the victims from convergence and intrusion on their privacy, at another preserving its own domain of control. In underdeveloped societies such conflicts are less likely to arise: there may not be welfare or health or volunteer systems with any such resources to give, so there is little to fight about. Even here, however, such issues may be relevant for international aid groups, which may fall into similar patterns of competition, as Kent (1983) has suggested.

The ultimate question is, of course, who will bear all the costs—or whether anyone can, for that matter. Insurance will cover some, as will the sources of economic aid noted earlier. And it is likely that, in the post-disaster utopia, political leaders made many promises, which may now seem very costly to keep. Thus, "who will pay" is a source of conflict among organizations in the post-disaster period, as responsibilities are redefined and, in many cases, attempts are made to shift costs to someone else's system. This adds to the victims' difficulties, for it tends to reinforce bureau-cratic administrative procedure—forms and red tape. A cycle of resentment and frustration may arise as a consequence.

The transfer from one coordinating system to another, or from one organization to another, of disaster-relevant roles and responsibilities also causes some difficulty. Transfers often do not proceed smoothly. Rarely are there worked-out mechanisms for transfers to occur. Blame and anger are often an outcome, each system resenting the other when it feels itself to be faced with overwhelming and difficult tasks. Such problems are exemplified in the transfer from emergency counterdisaster such as rescue and resuscitation to intermediate shelter, food, and protection systems to longer-term recovery, rebuilding, and rehabilitation systems. Transfers are times of vulnerability for organizations and victims, during which both services and interorganizational relationships may be threatened.

The coordinating system for longer-term redevelopment may grow from formal organizations and community representatives. It may also be a synthetic community superstructure, or may occur through established departments. In a sense, this system usually consists of some type of emerging group that involves the victims, for their needs and wishes must be fully represented if appropriate action is to occur. Some such groups include, at a local level, citizens action groups and coordinating committees of victims from affected communities, as arose following the Ash Wednesday fires. A Darwin welfare organization and a fire victims welfare organization in Tasmania fulfilled some of these multiple recovery-promoting functions and then disbanded when their tasks were completed.

POLITICS AND POLICY

Disasters have political implications at every level. Government and authority systems may make commitment to preventive, preparatory, or counterdisaster activities, which, in the post-disaster period, will come under critical appraisal for their effectiveness. Priorities of resource allocation may be seen as opportunities for political argument and gain. Government and/ or organizations may have no commitment to disaster-relevant policy, nominal commitment, or true commitment. The uncertainty of disaster occurrence often makes other priorities higher, especially in poorly resourced and underdeveloped countries with unstable political systems.

Severe catastrophe that has shown up the inadequacy of policy and planning, by the extent of effects that might have been prevented, may lead to societal pressures for change and policy development. Many present-day disaster response systems have evolved in this way. As Kent (1983) notes, this type of pressure at an international level resulted in the development of systems of international relief management. These systems, in turn, have led to measures such as food stockpiling, earthquake risk reduction techniques for construction and land use, as well as anti-pollution and conservation measures. Early warning systems such as "Landsat" may technically increase predictive power, with at least the potential for increasing responsiveness.

Recently, Seitz and Davis (1984) have studied the political matrix of natural disasters in Africa and Latin America. They suggest there are three patterns of authoritative allocation in these developing countries: ethnic pluralism, corporatism, and egalitarianism. These political variables, writers believe, operate to influence average numbers killed, amount of change, and victim numbers for disasters such as earthquakes, floods, epidemics, droughts, and storms. Thus, political systems may be significant in impact effects, as well as in molding some aspects of organizational response.

However, several sociopolitical constraints may operate to thwart response. Some constraints, Kent suggests, are structural, that is, "factors deeply ingrained both in the problem itself and the institutions which seek to deal with it." This is exemplified by agencies that cannot or will not address the most relevant problems or allow others access to do so. Another constraint may be the complex interface between underdevelopment and disaster. Countries may have come to accept their level of deprivation (e.g., starvation, poor housing) and be politically sensitive to receiving disaster aid for these, or more in need of aid for development, for, as Kent also suggests, an event may only be a disaster because it has occurred in an underdeveloped area.

Organizational imperatives may also be important: whether an organization can further its real goals by disaster involvement or whether its goals will in fact be threatened. Kent suggests that disasters may not be regarded as "growth areas" for institutional or personal advancement. On the one hand, organizational image may be enhanced by a successful and worthy role in disaster response. On the other, it may be damaged in such a high-profile situation, because of failures that are really outside its control and needs that it cannot hope to meet. The clash of contending interests may lead to symbolic or territorial fights, perhaps in some instances used for political gain. The demands of institutional procedures and systems of the bureaucracy may also constrain effective action and may be intrinsic to the politics of the organization.

Another political difficulty may be in the complications of assistance provided by outside systems. This assistance may show up local inadequacies or deprivations by comparison to some other standard, leading to loss of face or dissatisfaction with the everyday lot in life, perhaps threatening political stability at a local or societal level. It may create obligations to other political systems, as noted earlier. It may also, if aid is at a high level, have significant economic impact with later backlash. Donor governments in the interactional system may also have problems, such as the pressures of media and interest groups, as well as the financial commitment. While these problems have become clear at international levels, they are also relevant in the smaller systems of community and local areas.

Thus, while political aspects fade temporarily in the altruistic phase, they rapidly become significant again during the chronic processes of recovery and rehabilitation, as well as in the attribution of responsibility and in the preparation for future disasters with commitments of policy backed by resources. It is only now, with the development of international systems such as UNDRO, with its policy for preventive action and mobilizing development projects, that some systematic response can be provided that is not *too* vulnerable to the inevitable political constraints and effects. Similar mechanisms and policy are necessary within the different structural levels of the system, from individual to family to neighborhood to community, as well as the broader society. "Regional policy coordination" is necessary at an international level, Kent concludes, with sensitivity to local political and economic problems. This kind of consideration may be necessary at local levels as well, to carefully integrate response systems with local needs and capability, both in planning and in disaster response.

SOCIAL CHANGE AS A LONG-TERM COMMUNITY CONSEQUENCE

Disasters may induce some social change in a variety of ways. They may become reference points for the community systems, just as they may for individuals and families. They may affect, as challenges and stresses, the patterns of organizational functioning and the systems of interaction within the community. This effect may be reflected in their impact on community indices, such as high divorce rates, disruption of families, increased violence, and economic change, all of which have been demonstrated in various studies. Hall and Landreth (1975), for instance, studied longer-term effects of the Rapid City flood of 1972, which killed 237 people and caused 100 million dollars' damage. They found marked social changes such as increases in arrests for public intoxication, divorces, and requests for child care, which were most pronounced in the lower socioeconomic levels. Trailer park groups were particularly at risk. Similar social changes were described by Adams and Adams (1984) after the Mount St. Helen's ashfall. The destruction of community as a result of the Buffalo Creek disaster definitely had long-term negative effects (Erikson 1976). Yet positive changes have been described following some other disasters. Despite severe trauma, the community of Aberfan experienced an increased birthrate and an improved sense of community. And, as noted in earlier chapters, the earthquakes of Managua and Peru led to significant social change in the patterns of labor use and in urban-rural distribution. Migration or resettlement following disaster is likely to produce a very different mix and a different community, quite apart from the structures and buildings.

There is a need to better understand such potentials for change at societal and community levels and, in particular, what factors may mitigate against negative changes and promote positive changes. Anderson (1970), who studied the effects of the Alaska earthquake of 1964, suggested that organizational change might be maximal when changes had been planned or in process when the disaster occurred or when there were great pressures and strains on the organization because of the disaster, and alternative patterns were possible. External support facilitated such adaptive change. Perhaps this is not unlike the crisis effect of the challenge of disaster to individuals and families, who may come through their encounter with greater strengths after they have learned new and more effective ways of coping. Studies of communities show that organizational change may lead also to community change, as may the stressor effects of the disaster in other more general or structural ways. The cohesiveness of the community may be a factor facilitating recovery from a disaster. But community change may be more profound where there is fluidity of the community system in the face of severe disaster stress and where new systems are developed to handle unresolved problems. Whether such change develops the community positively or, on the other hand, leads to its death, will depend on very many factors, perhaps the most significant being the degree to which the disaster has destroyed the fabric of that segment of society. War, refugee status, and physical annihilation of systems must invariably cause such change, but other disasters may do so in more subtle ways. Changes in family composition and customs, patterns of labor, rural-urban distribution, and agricultural or industry patterns all make a substantial social and economic impact. Such changes have been described in a number of situations, but especially following earthquakes, as in Barbina's (1979) description of the Friuli earthquake in Italy.

COUNTRY AND CITY: MEGADISASTERS OF
THE FUTURE

While some of the disasters described in earlier chapters have obviously been "megadisasters" in terms of the numbers of deaths and the amount of destruction, it is clear that society at basic levels may face even greater disasters in the future. As Kent has noted, disasters are rapidly increasing in complexity.

Ecological disasters that result from great devastation of arable and grazing land will affect not only the rural communities directly dependent on them, but also the cities they feed. Cities will be unable to handle vast influxes of rural inhabitants who come seeking work and subsistence. It has been suggested that "15 million acres of arable grazing land became desert every year owing to the destruction of forests and soil erosion" (Kent 1983, p. 710). Such changes have already had a direct impact on the African continent where per capita food consumption is 10 percent less than it was a decade ago and food production is declining by more than 15 percent. Millions of vulnerable people are on the brink of disaster. Rural economies and subsistence in Central America and Southeast Asia may also be at risk. While such figures argue strongly for aid for development and prevention, it is also clear that a point may be reached where little can be done: segments of society, communities, and groups may be at risk of final destruction.

The threat of nuclear war poses megadisaster to the city communities of the world directly and to all ecology. While massive disasters have struck city communities in the past, there have been no real examples of near total disruption of the world's great cities in recent years, since the bombings in World War II, including the atomic bombing of Hiroshima and Nagasaki. Yet, the throbbing and palpable organizations of our giant cities, with their human and technological structures, are at great risk. Should nuclear war occur, there would be little surrounding undamaged social system to respond, support, and heal; nor would there be safe places of refuge.

Integration of Catastrophes
in the Human System

"Perhaps the most hopeful thing is that nuclear war is not unimaginable. Human imagination is our greatest resource—it has given us our greatest creations and advances—it has taken us to the moon and we have viewed the rings of Saturn. It has produced the rich worlds of arts and sciences and the sensitive concern of humanity. It has given us the richness of dreams and fantasy. It allows us human empathy and compassion. Surely the destructive forces of human imagination may yet be mastered"—Beverley Raphael, "Thinking the Unthinkable."

Disasters at both personal and community levels are inevitably part of human life. How does their possibility, their knowledge, and their occurrence become integrated for individuals and societies?

As has been noted in a number of different contexts in this book, the process of review helps the individual master and make meaning of the event, which is outside the natural order of his day-to-day life. This process also takes place at the family level, as the event is integrated into a system of family life. At neighborhood and small group levels, there is also a talking through and sharing of the experience, providing for both emotional release and consoling interaction with others as well as synthesis of perceptions and interpretations. At the organizational level, post-disaster review is frequent and may be formally organized; it serves the same goals. At community and society levels, review processes document and structure in retrospect that which lacked meaning and structure at the time; and the community releases the pain caused by the wound and gains mastery to undo the sense of disintegration and helplessness.

The formal products of review may include reports, documentations, and books. These will undoubtedly carry messages and recommendations regarding ways in which the shock and trauma may be lessened on any future occasion. Thus, this now past experience is both mastered and used for new learning: it may strengthen cognitively and emotionally the fabric of the community and its capacity for future response.

Attempts at mastery in anticipation are also likely: in pre-disaster planning and exercises in a manifest way, but also symbolically in the fascination with disaster films, stories, television shows, books, and with the violence in newscasts. This reworking and mastery may be represented concretely by ceremonies and rituals and by memorials that stem from the disaster, and less directly in the anniversaries of remembering, regrieving, and review. But ultimately, of course, disasters represent on a grand scale the confrontation with death and loss. Thus, for individual and community they symbolize both the cycle of life and the ultimate end.

Survival after disaster symbolizes regeneration and rebirth, a fresh gift of life because death was escaped. Human closeness and warmth are sought as reassurances of life and sexual intimacy, and childbirth may result as individual and society affirm "we will go on and live." The renewal and regeneration of the community convey belief in the future.

Perhaps the most overwhelming theme that epitomizes the integration of disasters past and the adaptation to disasters yet to come is that of hope. Man invests in the future because he hopes for some good experiences, because he can allow himself, for the time at least, to set aside the threat and to forget the pain of the past.

The learning of the disaster experience must surely reinforce this capacity for hope. For the themes of human disaster response are powerful: courage rather than cowardice; compassionate human concern of one for the other; and resilience in the face of overwhelming stress. The altruistic response of individual and community, the intensity of feeling across barriers of class and race must surely symbolize all that is best and strongest in the human species; it is an equation of hope for the future.

Yet there is a dark cloud over this picture, and that is the capacity of humankind to create disaster in the indulgence of its own darkest urges. Nuclear war provides people with the opportunity for the ultimate fulfillment of the sadistic side of their nature, the ultimate climax of aggressive drives. To integrate and deal with disaster these destructive forces, too, must be faced: their reality acknowledged; their sources explored; their mastery achieved; their energy rechanneled (Raphael 1984a).

What human beings have learned from other disasters, from the first nuclear catastrophes, and from the wars of the world must be utilized to lower denial, to resolve conflict nondestructively, and to channel aggressive energies, in socially beneficial ways, into recognition and prevention. Our understanding of disasters at both a personal and community level can evolve into systems of human concern and care for all the day-to-day catastrophes that befall the human species. It can help us develop effective and human counterdisaster systems for our community. To come to terms with catastrophe must reinforce the human values of family and society, of love and hope, and of passionate commitment to life, its value, and its preservation.

Appendix

QUESTIONNAIRE: SCREENING FOR RISK OF POST-DISASTER DISORDERS

BACKGROUND (PAST EXPERIENCE)

NAME:

AGE:

SEX:

MARITAL STATUS:

STATUS IN FAMILY:

RELIGION:

WORK/SCHOOL:

ETHNICITY—FIRST LANGUAGE:

SOURCE: From Beverley Raphael, Tom Lundin, and Lars Weisæth, International Studies in Disaster Psychiatry, Working Paper #1: Draft Guidelines for Research Methodology for Study of Psychological and Psychiatric Aspects of Disaster (Newcastle, Australia, December 1984).

PAST HEALTH:

1. Have you ever had problems/trouble with your nerves?   Yes/No
2. Have you ever had trouble with your general health?   Yes/No

PREPAREDNESS

What was your level of preparedness/training for this disaster?

_____ No preparation
_____ Little preparation
_____ Well prepared
_____ Very well prepared

DISASTER EXPERIENCE—"WHAT HAPPENED TO YOU?"

1. Did you think you were going to die in the disaster?   Yes/No

2. Did anyone close to you die in the disaster, or as a consequence?   Yes/No
   Who?

3. Have you lost your home in the disaster?   Yes/No

   _____ Your farm
   _____ Your job or business
   _____ Possessions very important to you

4. Were you injured in the disaster?   Yes/No

   Severity _____

5. With the actual impact of the disaster do you feel you

   _____ Managed as well as anybody could have
   _____ Did much more than you expected
   _____ Let myself down
   _____ Let others down

Appendix

HOW THE DISASTER HAS AFFECTED YOU

1. How would you describe the thoughts and feelings youhaveaboutwhathappenedinthedisasternow?

    ____ Very unpleasant
    ____ Somewhat unpleasant
    ____ Neither unpleasant nor exciting
    ____ Somewhat exciting

2. These thoughts and feelings affect me in the following ways:

    ____ They come into my mind a great deal, even when I don't want them to.
    ____ I have repeated nightmares about them.
    ____ I have to avoid things or places which remind me of them.
    ____ I am so preoccupied I can't think of anything else.
    ____ They are there occasionally, but don't really worry me.
    ____ I do not have any thoughts and feelings about what happened in the disaster.

3. Are your thoughts in general

    ____ Better
    ____ Same
    ____ Worse
    than they were a week ago?

4. Are you feeling sad or depressed?

    ____ Not at all
    ____ A little
    ____ Quite a bit
    ____ Very much

COPING: HOW ARE YOU MANAGING?

1. Are you still feeling so distressed that you cannot carry on with what you have to do?   Yes/No
2. Do you find that at present being with people:

_____ Helps you feel much better
_____ Is generally all right
_____ Doesn't help me
_____ Is very hard to take

3.   Can you see yourself getting over this with time?   Yes/No

_____ Yes, completely
_____ Yes, mostly
_____ No, probably not
_____ No, never

4.   Is there anything else you would like to tell us
     about the disaster?
     Please write here:

References

Abe, K. 1976. The Behavior of Survivors and Victims in a Japanese Night Club Fire: A Descriptive Research Note. *Mass Emergencies* 1:119–24.

Abrahams, H. A. 1981. *An Analysis of Bushfire Hazard Reduction in the Gumeracha District of the Mt. Lofty Ranges, South Australia.* Master's Thesis, University of Adelaide, Adelaide, South Australia.

Abrahams, M. J.; Price, J.; Whitlock, F. A.; and Williams, G. 1976. The Brisbane Floods, January 1974: Their Impact on Health. *Medical Journal of Australia* 2:936–39.

Adams, D. 1970. The Red Cross: Organizational Sources of Operational Problems. *American Behavioral Scientist* 13:392–403.

Adams, P. R., and Adams, G. R. (1984). Mount St. Helen's Ashfall: Evidence for a Disaster Stress Reaction. *American Psychologist* 39(3):252–60.

Adler, A. 1943. Neuropsychiatric Complications in Victims of Boston's Cocoanut Grove Disaster. *Journal of the American Medical Association* 123:1098–1101.

Ahearn, F. L. 1981. Disaster and Mental Health: Pre- and Post-Earthquake Comparison of Psychiatric Admission Rates. *Urban and Social Change Review* 14:22–28.

Ahearn, F. L., and Cohen, R. E. 1984. *Disasters and Mental Health: An Annotated Bibliography.* Rockville, Maryland: National Institute of Mental Health, Center for Mental Health Studies of Emergencies, U.S. Department of Health.

Anderson, W. A. 1970. Disaster and Organizational Change. In *The Great Alaskan Earthquake of 1964.* Washington, D.C.: National Academy of Science.

Arvidson, R. 1969. On Some Mental Effects of Earthquakes. *American Psychologist* 24(6): 605–6.

Asimov, I. 1979. *A Choice of Catastrophes: The Disasters That Threaten Our World.* London: Hutchinson.

Askevold, F. 1976. War Sailor Syndrome. *Psychotherapy and Psychosomatics* 27:133–38.

Baker, G., and Chapman, D., eds. 1962. *Man and Society in Disaster.* New York: Basic Books.

Barbeau, M. 1980. *Crash Victims: Coping with Disaster.* Personally published document from the University of Southern California.

Barbina, G. 1979. The Friuli Earthquake as an Agent of Social Change in a Rural Area. *Mass Emergencies* 4(2):145–49.

Baren, J. B. 1976. Crisis Intervention: The Ice-cream Parlor Disaster. In *Emergencies in*

Disaster Management: A Mental Health Sourcebook, ed. H. J. Parad; H. L. P. Resnick; and L. P. Parad. Bowie, Maryland: Charles Press.

Barton, A. H. 1969. *Communities in Disaster: A Sociological Analysis of Collective Stress Situations.* Garden City, New York: Doubleday.

Bartrop, R. W.; Lazarus, L.; Luckhurst, E.; Kiloh, L. G.; and Penny, R. 1977. Depressed Lymphocyte Function after Bereavement. *Lancet* (16 April):834–36.

Beach, H. D., and Lucas, R. A., eds. 1960. *Individual and Group Behavior in a Coal Mine Disaster.* Disaster Study No. 13, Publication 834. Washington, D.C.: National Academy of Sciences, National Research Council.

Bell, B. D. 1978. Disaster Impact and Response: Overcoming the Thousand Natural Shocks. *The Gerontologist* 18(6):531–40.

Bell, B. D.; Kara, G.; and Batterson, C. 1978. Service Utilization and Adjustment Patterns of Elderly Tornado Victims in an American Disaster. *Mass Emergencies* 3:71–81.

Bennet, G. 1970. Bristol Floods 1968: Controlled Survey of Effects on Health of Local Community Disaster. *British Medical Journal* 3:454–58.

Berah, E.; Jones, H. J.; and Valent, P. 1984. The Experience of a Mental Health Team Involved in the Early Phase of a Disaster. *Australian and New Zealand Journal of Psychiatry* 18:354–58.

Berren, M. R.; Beigel, A.; and Barker, G. 1982. A Typology for the Classification of Disasters: Implications for Intervention. *Community Mental Health Journal* 18(2):120–34.

Bjorklund, B. 1981. Disaster Studies. Skredet I Tuve. University of Uppsala, Sweden: University of Uppsala Press.

Black, D. 1982. Children and Disaster. *British Medical Journal* 295:989–90.

Blaufarb, H., and Levine, J. 1972. Crisis Intervention in an Earthquake. *Journal of Social Work* 19:16–17.

Bloch, D. A.; Silber, E.; and Perry, S. E. 1956. Some Factors in the Emotional Reaction of Children to Disaster. *American Journal of Psychiatry* 113:416–22.

Boccaccio, G. *The Decameron of Giovanni Boccaccio* (2 vols.), trans. J. M. Riggs. London: Navarre Society Limited.

Bolin, R. C. 1976. Family Recovery from Natural Disaster: A Preliminary Model. *Mass Emergencies* 1:267–77.

———. 1981. *Family Recovery from Disaster: A Discriminant Function Analysis.* Paper presented at meeting of the American Sociological Association, New York.

———. 1982. *Long-term Family Recovery from Disaster.* Monograph No. 36. Bqulder: University of Colorado, Institute of Behavioral Science.

Bolin, R. C., and Bolin, P. A. 1983. Recovery in Nicaragua and the U.S.A. *International Journal of Mass Emergencies and Disasters* 1(1):125–44.

Bolin, R., and Klenow, D. 1982–83. Response of the Elderly to Disaster: An Age-Stratified Analysis. *International Journal of Aging and Human Development* 16(4):283–96.

Boman, B. 1979. Behavioral Observations on the Granville Train Disaster and the Significance of Stress for Psychiatry. *Social Science and Medicine* 13a:463–71.

———. 1982. The Vietnam Veteran Ten Years On. *Australian and New Zealand Journal of Psychiatry* 16:107–28.

———. 1984. *The Vietnam Veteran as a Disaster Victim.* Paper presented at the Conference on Research into Disaster Behaviour, Mt. Macedon, Victoria, April 1984.

Bordow, S., and Porritt, D. 1979. An Experimental Evaluation of Crisis Intervention. *Social Science and Medicine* 13a:251–56.

Bowlby, J. 1952. *Maternal Care and Mental Health.* World Health Organization.

———. 1980. *Loss: Sadness and Depression.* (Attachment and Loss, vol. 3.) London: Hogarth Press.

Bray, C. B., and George, J. 1984. *"Sudden Death" Families and Community Services.* Sydney, Australia: State Health Publication No. (DFM)84–179.

Brett, E. A., and Ostroff, R. 1985. Imagery and Post-traumatic Stress Disorder. *American Journal of Psychiatry* 142:417–24.

References

Bromet, E., and Dunn, L. 1981. Mental Health of Mothers Nine Months after the Three Mile Island Accident. *The Urban and Social Change Review* 14(2):12–15.

Bromet, E. J; Parkinson, D. K; Shulberg, H. C.; Dunn, L. O.; and Gondek, P. C. 1982a. Mental Health of Residents Near the Three Mile Island Reactor: A Comparative Study of Selected Groups. *Journal of Preventive Psychiatry* 1:225–76.

Bromet, E. J.; Shulberg, H. C.; and Dunn, L. O. 1982. Reactions of Psychiatric Patients to the Three Mile Island Nuclear Accident. *Archives of General Psychiatry* 39:725–30.

Brown, R. E. 1969. Mission to Biafra (January 1969): A Study and Survey of a Population under Stress. *Clinical Pediatrics* 8:313–21.

Brownstone, J.; Penick, E. C.; Larcen, S. W.; Powell, B. J.; and Nord, A. 1977. Disaster Relief Training and Mental Health. *Hospital and Community Psychiatry* 28:30–32.

Burke, J. D.; Borus, J. F.; Burns, B. J.; Millstein, K. H.; and Beasley, M. C. 1982. Changes in Children's Behavior after a Natural Disaster. *American Journal of Psychiatry* 139(8): 1010–14.

Burton, I.; Katz, R. W.; and White, G. F. 1978. *The Environment as Hazard.* New York: Oxford University Press.

Butcher, J. N. 1980. The Role of Crisis Intervention in an Airport Disaster Plan. *Aviation, Space and Environmental Medicine* 512:1260–62.

Canter, D., ed. 1980. *Fires and Human Behavior.* Chichester, England: Wiley.

Caplan, G. 1964. *Principles of Preventive Psychiatry.* New York: Basic Books.

Carlton, T. G. 1980. Early Psychiatric Intervention Following a Maritime Disaster. *Military Medicine* 145:114–16.

Chamberlin, B. C. 1980. Mayo Seminars in Psychiatry: The Psychological Aftermath of Disaster. *Journal of Clinical Psychiatry* 41:238–44.

Clarke, A., and Viney, L. 1979. The Primary Prevention of Illness: A Psychological Perspective. *Australian Psychologist* 4: 7–20.

Clason, C. 1983. The Family as a Life Saver in Disaster. *International Journal of Mass Emergencies and Disasters* 1:43–52.

Clausen, L.; Conlon, P.; Jager, W.; and Metreveli, S. 1978. New Aspects of the Sociology of Disasters: A Theoretical Note. *Mass Emergencies* 3(1):61–65.

Clayer, J. 1984. *Evaluation of the Outcome of Disaster.* Health Commission of South Australia: Unpublished paper.

Cobb, S. 1976. Social Support as a Moderator of Life Stress. *Psychosomatic Medicine* 38: 300–14.

Coelho, G. V. 1982. The Foreign Students' Sojourn as a High Risk Situation: The "Culture Shock" Phenomenon Re-examined. In *Uprooting and Surviving,* ed. R. C. Nann. D. Reidel: London.

Cohen, R. E. 1976. Post-disaster Mobilization of a Crisis Intervention Team: The Managua Experience. In *Emergency and Disaster Management: A Mental Health Sourcebook,* ed. H. G. Parad; H. L. P. Resnick; and L. P. Parad. Bowie, Md: Charles Press.

Cohen, R. E., and Ahearn, F. L. 1980. *Handbook for Mental Health Care of Disaster Victims.* Baltimore: Johns Hopkins University Press.

Cook, P.; Wallace, M.; and McFarlane, A. 1984. *The Effects of Bushfire Disasters on Firefighters and Their Families.* Paper presented at Disaster Research Workshop, Mt. Macedon, Victoria.

Crabbs, M. A. 1981. School Mental Health Services Following an Environmental Disaster. *Journal of School Health* 51(3):165–67.

Crawshaw, R. 1963. Reactions to a Disaster. *Archives of General Psychiatry* 9:73–78.

Curran, W. J. 1979. The Guyana Mass Suicides: Medicolegal Reevaluation. *New England Journal of Medicine* 300(23):1321.

Davidson, A. D. 1979. Coping with Stress Reactions in Rescue Workers Following an Air Disaster: A Programme that Worked. *Police Stress* (Spring 1979).

Dekker, T. 1925. *The Plague Pamphlets of Thomas Dekker,* ed. S. P. Wilson. Oxford: Oxford University Press.

Deuchar, N. 1984. AIDS in New York City with Particular Reference to Psycho-Social Aspects. *British Journal of Psychiatry* 145:612–19.

The Diagnostic and Statistical Manual of Mental Disorders, 3rd edition (DSM-III). Robert E. Spitzer, ed. 1980. Washington, D.C.: American Psychiatric Association.

Dimsdale, J. E. 1974. The Coping Behavior of Nazi Concentration Camp Survivors. *American Journal of Psychiatry* 131:792–97.

Dombrowsky, W. 1983. Solidarity during Snow Disasters. In J. Trost and O. Hultaker, eds., *Family in Disasters. International Journal of Mass Emergencies and Disasters* 1 (1):189–206.

Drabek, T. E., and Boggs, K. S. 1968. Families in Disaster: Reactions and Relatives. *Journal of Marriage and the Family* 30:443–51.

Drabek, T. E., and Key, W. H. 1976. The Impact of Disaster on Primary Group Linkages. *Mass Emergencies* 1:89–105.

Drabek, T. E.; Key, W. H.; Erickson, P. E.; and Crowe, J. L. 1975. The Impact of Disaster on Kin Relationships. *Journal of Marriage and the Family* 37:481–96.

Dudasik, S. W. 1980a. Editorial Comment: How to Succeed as a Disaster Victim. *Disasters* 4:127–28.

Dudasik, S. W. 1980b. Victimization in Natural Disaster. *Disasters* 4:329–38.

Duffy, J. C. 1978. Emergency Mental Health Services during and after a Major Aircraft Accident. *Aviation, Space and Environmental Medicine* 49:1004–8.

Dutton, L. M.; Smolensky, M. H.; Leach, C. S.; Lorimor, R.; and Bartholomew, P. H. (1978). Stress Levels of Ambulance Paramedics and Firefighters. *Journal of Occupational Medicine* 20:111–15.

Dynes, R. R. 1970. *Organized Behavior in Disaster.* Lexington, Mass.: D. C. Heath.

Eitinger, L., and Askevold, F. 1968. Psychiatric Aspects. In *Concentration Camp Survivors,* ed. Axel Strom. New York: Humanities Press.

Eitinger, L., and Schwartz, D., eds. 1981. *Strangers in the World.* Vienna: Hans Huger Publishers.

Elizur, E., and Kaffman, M. 1982. Children's Bereavement Reactions Following the Death of a Father, 2. *Journal of the American Academy of Child Psychiatry* 21:474–80.

Engel, G. L., and Schmale, A. H. (1972). Conservation-Withdrawal: A Primary Regulatory Process for Organismic Homeostasis. Physiology, Emotion and Psychomatic Illness. A Ciba Foundation Symposium. New York: Elsevier Associated Scientific Publishers.

Erickson, P.; Drabek, T. E.; Key, W. H.; and Crowe, J. L. 1976. Families in Disaster: Patterns of Recovery. *Mass Emergencies* 1:203–16.

Erikson, K. T. 1976. Loss of Communality at Buffalo Creek. *American Journal of Psychiatry* 133:302–4.

Erikson, K. T. 1979. *In the Wake of the Flood.* London: George Allen and Unwin.

Fairley, M. 1984. Tropical Cyclone Oscar: Psychological Reactions of a Fijian Population. Paper presented at Disaster Research Workshop, Mt. Macedon, Victoria, Australia.

Faschingbauerm, T. R.; Devaul, R. A.; and Zisook, S. 1977. Development of the Texas Inventory of Grief. *American Journal of Psychiatry* 134:6.

Fattah, E. A. 1979. Some Reflections on the Victimology of Terrorism. *Terrorism* 3:1–2.

Feldman, S., and McCarthy, F. E. 1983. Disaster Response in Bangladesh. *International Journal of Mass Emergencies* 1:105–24.

Fenichel, O. 1946. *The Psychoanalytic Theory of Neuroses.* London: Routledge and Kegan Paul.

Forrest, T. R. 1978. Group Emergence in Disasters. In *Disasters: Theory and Research,* ed. E. L. Quarantelli. London: Sage.

Frazer, J. R., and Spicka, D. A. 1981. Handling the Emotional Response to Disaster: The Case for American Red Cross/Community Mental Health Collaboration. *Community Mental Health Journal* 17:255–64.

Frazer, M. 1973. *Children in Conflict.* Greenwood, Victoria, Australia: Penguin.

References

Frederick, C. J. 1977. Current Thinking about Crisis or Psychological Intervention in United States Disasters. *Mass Emergencies* 2:43–50.

Freud, S. 1920. *Beyond the Pleasure Principle.* In *The Standard Edition of the Complete Psychological Works of Sigmund Freud,* 18:1–64. London: Hogarth Press, 1955.

Fried, M. 1963. Grieving for a lost home. In *The Urban Condition: People and Policy in the Metropolis.* New York: Basic Books.

Fried, M. 1982. Residential Attachment: Sources of Residential and Community Satisfaction. *Journal of Social Issues* 38:107–19.

Fritz, C. E., and Marks, E. 1954. The N.O.R.C. Studies of Human Behavior in Disaster. *Journal of Social Issues* 10:33.

Frye, J. S., and Stockton, R. A. 1982. Discriminate Analysis of Post-Traumatic Stress Disorder among a Group of Vietnam Veterans. *American Journal of Psychiatry* 139:52–56.

Furman, E. 1974. *A Child's Parent Dies.* New Haven: Yale University Press.

Garrison, J. L. 1985. Mental Health Implications of Disaster Relocation in the United States: A Review of the Literature. *International Journal of Mass Emergencies and Disasters* 3 (2):49–65.

Gist, R., and Stolz, S. B. 1982. Mental Health Promotion and the Media: Community Response to the Kansas City Hotel Disaster. *American Psychologist* 37:1136–39.

Gleser, G. C.; Green, B. L.; and Winget, C. N. 1978. Quantifying Interview Data on Psychic Impairment of Disaster Survivors. *Journal of Nervous and Mental Disease* 166:209–16.

———. 1981. *Prolonged Psychosocial Effects of Disaster: A Study of Buffalo Creek.* New York: Academic Press.

Goldberg, D. 1978. *Manual of the General Health Questionnaire.* Windsor, England: N. F. E. R. Publishing Company.

Grant, W. B.; McNamara, L.; and Bailey, K. 1975. Psychiatric Disturbance with Acute Onset and Offset in a Darwin Evacuee. *Medical Journal of Australia* 1:652–54.

Green, A. H. 1983. Child Abuse: Dimensions of Psychological Trauma in Abused Children. *Journal of the American Academy of Child Psychiatry* 22(3):231–37.

Green, B. L. 1982. Assessing Levels of Psychological Impairment Following Disaster. *Journal of Nervous and Mental Diseases* 170(9):544–52.

Green, B. L.; Grace, M. C.; and Gleser, G. C. In press. Identifying Survivors at Risk: Long-term Impairment Following the Beverly Hills Supper Club Fire. *Journal of Consulting and Clinical Psychology.*

Green, B. L.; Grace, M. C.; Lindy, J. D.; Tichener, J. L.; and Lindy, J. G. 1983. Levels of Functional Impairment Following a Civilian Disaster: The Beverly Hills Supper Club Fire. *Journal of Consulting and Clinical Psychology* 51:573–80.

Haas, E. J., and Drabek, T. E. 1970. Community Disaster and System Stress: A Sociological Perspective. In Joseph E. McGrath, ed., *Social and Psychological Factors in Stress.* New York: Holt Rinehart & Winston.

Haga, E. 1984. Wet Graves. Unpublished paper.

Hall, P., and Landreth, P. 1975. Assessing Some Long-term Consequences of a Natural Disaster. *Mass Emergencies* 1:55–61.

Hall, W. 1985. Social Class and Survival on the S.S. *Titanic.* Department of Psychiatry, University of New South Wales. Unpublished paper.

Hammerschlag, C. A., and Astrachan, B. M. 1971. The Kennedy Airport Snow-In: An Inquiry into Intergroup Phenomena. *Psychiatry* 34:301–8.

Hannigan, J. A., and Kueneman, R. 1977. Legitimacy and Public Organizations: A Case Study. *Canadian Journal of Sociology* 2 (Winter):125–35.

Harshbarger, D. 1973. An Ecological Perspective of Disaster and Facilitative Disaster Intervention Based on Buffalo Creek Disaster. Paper presented at the National Institute of Mental Health Continuing Education Seminar on Emergency Health Services, Washington, D.C.

Harshbarger, D. 1974. Picking Up the Pieces: Disaster Intervention and Human Ecology. *Omega* 5:55–59.

Hartsough, D. M.; Zarle, T. H.; and Ottinger, D. R. 1976. Rapid Response to Disaster: The Monticello Tornado. In *Emergency and Disaster Mangement: A Mental Health Sourcebook*, ed. H. J. Parad; H. L. P. Resnick; and L. P. Parad. Bowie, Maryland: Charles Press.

Heffron, E. F. 1977. Project Outreach: Crisis Intervention Following a Natural Disaster. *Journal of Community Psychology* 5:103–11.

———. 1979. Decision versus Policy in Crisis Intervention. *American Journal of Community Psychology* 5:543–62.

Henderson, S., and Bostock, T. 1977. Coping Behaviour after Shipwreck. *British Journal of Psychiatry* 131:15–20.

Henderson, S.; Byrne, D. G.; and Duncan-Jones, P. 1981. *Neurosis and the Social Environment.* Sydney: Academic Press.

Hersey, J. 1966. *Hiroshima.* Sydney: Penguin.

Hershiser, M. R., and Quarantelli, E. L. 1976. The Handling of the Dead in a Disaster. *Omega* 7:195–208.

Higgins, M., and Schinckel, H. 1985. Psychiatric Disorder in Primary School Children Following a Natural Disaster: A Follow-up Study. Department of Psychiatry, Flinders University, Adelaide, Australia. Unpublished paper.

Hocking, F. 1965. Human Reactions to Extreme Environmental Stress. *Medical Journal of Australia* 2:477–82.

———. 1981. After the Holocaust: Migrants Who Survive Massive Stress Experience. In *Strangers in the World,* ed. L. Eitinger and D. Schwartz. Vienna: Hans Huber Publications.

Hoiberg, A., and McCaughey, B. G. 1984. The Traumatic After-Effects of Collison at Sea. *American Journal of Psychiatry* 141:70–73.

Holen, A.; Sund, A., and Weisæth, L. 1983a. Survivors of the North Sea Oil Rig Disaster. Paper presented at the Symposium on Disaster Psychiatry, Stavanger, Norway.

———. 1983b. Predictors of Disaster Morbidity. Paper presented at the Symposium on Disaster Psychiatry, Stavanger, Norway.

Horowitz, M. J. 1976. *Stress Response Syndromes.* New York: Jason Aronson.

Horowitz, M. J.; Wilner, N.; Kaltreider, N.; and Alvarez, W. 1980. Signs and Symptoms of Post-Traumatic Stress Disorder. *Archives of General Psychiatry* 37:85–92.

Houts, P. S.; Hu The Wei; Henderson, R. A.; Clearly, P. D.; and Tokuhata, G. 1984. Utilization of Medical Care Following the Three Mile Island Crisis. *American Journal of Public Health* 74:140–42.

Innes, J. M., and Clarke, A. 1984. The Responses of Fire Fighters to Disaster and the Possible Role of Social Support. Paper Presented at the Disaster Research Workshop, Mt. Macedon, Victoria, Australia.

Ironside, W. 1979. *Conservation-Withdrawal and Action-Engagement: On a Theory of Survivor Behavior.* Department of Psychological Medicine, Monash University, Melbourne, Australia. Unpublished paper.

Jaatun, M. G. 1983. Personal communication.

Janerich, D. T.; Stark, A. D.; Greenwald, P.; Burnett, W. S.; Jacobson, H. I.; and McCusker, J. 1981. Increased Leukemia, Lymphoma and Spontaneous Abortion in Western New York Following a Flood Disaster. *Public Health Reports* 96:350–54.

Janis, I. L. 1951. *Air War and Emotional Stress: Psychological Studies of Bombing and Civilian Defense.* Westport, Connecticut: Greenwood Press.

Janis, I. L., and Mann, L. 1977. Emergency Decision-Making: A Theoretical Analysis of Responses to Disaster Warnings. *Journal of Human Stress* 3:35–45.

Janney, J. G.; Masuda, M.; and Holmes, T. H. 1977. Impact of a Natural Catastrophe on Life Events. *Journal of Human Stress* 3(2):22–34.

Jones, Col. D. R. 1985. Secondary Disaster Victims: The Emotional Effects of Recovering and Identifying Human Remains. *American Journal of Psychiatry* 142:303–7.

Kast, S.V.; Chisholm R. F.; and Erkenazi, B. 1981. The Impact of the Accident at Three Mile

References

Island on the Behavior and Well-Being of Nuclear Workers. *American Journal of Public Health* 71 (5):472–95.

Kates, R. W.; Haas, J. E.; Amaral, D. J.; Olson, R. A.; Ramos, R.; and Olsen, R. 1973. Human Impact of Managua Earthquake. *Science* 182:981–90.

Keane, T. M., and Fairbank, J. A. 1983. Survey Analysis of Combat-Related Stress Disorders in Vietnam Veterans. *American Journal of Psychiatry* 140:348–50.

Kent, R. C. 1983. Reflecting upon a Decade of Disasters: The Evolving Response of the International Community. *International Affairs* 59(4):693–711.

Key, P.; Erickson, P. E.; and Crow, E. 1975. The Impact of Disaster on Kin Relationships. *Journal of Marriage and the Family* 37:401–94.

Kinston, W., and Rosser, R. 1974. Disaster: Effects on Mental and Physical State. *Journal of Psychosomatic Research* 18:437–56.

Kliman, A. S. 1976. The Corning Flood Project: Psychological First Aid Following a Natural Disaster. In *Emergency and Disaster Management: A Mental Health Sourcebook,* ed. H. J. Parad; H. L. P. Resnick; and L. P. Parad. Bowie, Maryland: Charles Press.

Koegler, R. R., and Hicks, S. M. 1972. The Destruction of a Medical Center by Earthquake. *California Medicine* 116:63–67.

Krell, G. I. 1978. Managing the Psychosocial Factor in Disaster Programs. *Health and Social Work* 3:140–54.

Krim, A. 1978. Urban Disaster: Victims of Fire. In *Emergency and Disaster Management: A Mental Health Sourcebook,* ed. H. P. Parad; H. L. P. Resnick; and L. P. Parad. Bowie, Maryland: Charles Press.

Krupinski, J. 1984. Studies of Vietnamese Refugees. University of Melbourne. Personal communication.

Krystal, H. 1971. Trauma: Considerations of Its Intensity and Chronicity. *International Psychiatric Clinics* 8:11–28.

Kubler-Ross, E. 1969. *On Death and Dying.* London: Tavistock.

Lacey, G. N. 1972. Observations on Aberfan. *Journal of Psychosomatic Research* 16:257–60.

Lachman, R., and Bonk, W. J. 1960. Behavior and Beliefs during a Recent Volcanic Eruption in Kapoho, Hawaii, *Science* 131:1095–96.

Lachman, R.; Tatsuoka, M.; and Bonk, W. J. 1960. Human Behavior During the Tsunami of May 1960. *Science* 131:1095–96.

Laube, J. 1973. Psychological Reactions of Nurses in Disaster. *Nursing Research* 22:343–47.

Lazarus, L.; Luckhurst, E.; Kiloh, L.G.; and Penny, R. 1977. Depressed Lymphocyte Function after Bereavement. *Lancet* (16 April):834–36.

Lechat, M. F. 1979. Disasters and Public Health. *Journal of the World Health Organization* 57:11–17.

Leivesley, S. 1977. Toowoomba: Victims and Helpers in an Australian Hailstorm Disaster. *Disasters* 1:205–16.

Leopold, R. L., and Dillon, H. 1963. Psychoanatomy of a Disaster: A Long-Term Study of Post-Traumatic Neuroses in Survivors of a Marine Explosion. *American Journal of Psychiatry* 119:913–21.

Lifton, R. J. 1967. *Death in Life: Survivors of Hiroshima.* New York: Random House.

Lin, K.–M.; Masuda, M.; and Tazuma, L. 1982. Problems of Vietnamese Refugees in the United States. In *Uprooting and Surviving,* ed. R. C. Nann. London: O. Reidel.

Lindemann, E. 1944. Symptomatology and Management of Acute Grief. *American Journal of Psychiatry* 101:141–48.

Lindy, J. D., and Greene, B. L. 1981. Survivors: Outreach to a Reluctant Population. *American Journal of Orthopsychiatry* 51:468–78.

Lindy, J. D.; Green, B. L.; Grace, M.; and Titchener, J. 1983. Psychotherapy with Survivors of the Beverly Hills Supper Club Fire. *American Journal of Psychotherapy* 37:593–610.

Livingston, M., and Livingston, H. 1984. Emotional Distress in Nurses at Work. *British Journal of Medical Psychology* 57:291–94.

Logue, J. N.; Hansen, H.; and Struening, E. 1979. Emotional and Physical Distress Following Hurricane Agnes in Wyoming Valley of Pennsylvania. *Public Health Reports* 94:495–502.

Lopez-Ibor, J. J.; Soria, J.; Canas, F.; and Rodrigues-Gamazo, M. 1985. Psychopathological Aspects of the Toxic Oil Syndrome Catastrophe. *British Journal of Psychiatry* 147: 352–65.

Luchterhand, E. G. 1971. Sociological Approaches to Massive Stress in Natural and Man-Made Disasters. In H. Krystal and W. G. Niederland, eds., *Psychiatric Traumatization: After-Effects in Individuals and Communities.* Boston: Little Brown.

Lundin, T. 1984a. Long-term Outcome of Bereavement. *British Journal of Psychiatry* 145: 424–28.

———. 1984b. Disaster Reactions: A Study of Survivors' Reactions Following a Major Fire Disaster. University of Uppsala, Sweden. Unpublished paper.

———. 1984c. Morbidity Following Sudden and Unexpected Bereavement. *British Journal of Psychiatry* 144:84–88.

Lundin, T., and Wistedt, L. A. 1983. Psykiatriska Aspekter daligt Beaktade i Sjukhusens Planer for Medicinska Katastrofer. *Lakartidningen* 80:814–15.

Lyons, H. A. 1972. Depressive Illness and Aggression in Belfast. *British Medical Journal* 1:342–44.

———. 1979. Civil Violence: The Psychological Aspects. *Journal of Psychosomatic Research* 23:373–93.

McFarlane, A. C. 1983. The Ash Wednesday Fires: Effects on Children. Paper presented at the Annual Conference of the Royal Australian and New Zealand College of Psychiatrists, Adelaide.

———. 1984. The Ash Wednesday Bushfires in South Australia: Implications for Planning for Future Post-disaster Services. *Medical Journal of Australia* 141:286–91.

———. 1985a. The Etiology of Post-traumatic Stress Disorders Following a Natural Disaster. Department of Psychiatry, The Flinders University of South Australia. Unpublished paper.

———. 1985b. Post-traumatic Phenomena Due to a Disaster. Department of Psychiatry, The Flinders University of South Australia.

———. 1985c. The Phenomenology of Post-traumatic Stress Disorders Following a Natural Disaster. Department of Psychiatry, The Flinders University of South Australia.

McFarlane, A. C., and Blumbergs, V. 1985. The Relationship between Psychiatric Impairment and Natural Disaster: The Role of Distress. Department of Psychiatry, The Flinders University of South Australia. Unpublished paper.

McFarlane, A. C., and Frost, M. E. 1984. Post-traumatic Stress Disorder in Firefighters: Ash Wednesday. Department of Psychiatry, Flinders University of South Australia. Unpublished paper.

McFarlane, A. C., and Raphael, B. 1984. Ash Wednesday: The Effects of a Fire. *Australian and New Zealand Journal of Psychiatry* 18:341–53.

McFarlane, A. C.; Blumbergs, V.; Policansky, S. K.; and Irwin, C. 1985. A Longitudinal Study of the Psychological Morbidity in Children Due to a Natural Disaster. Department of Psychiatry, The Flinders University of South Australia. Unpublished paper.

McGee, R. K., and Heffron, E. F. 1976. The Role of Crisis Intervention Services in Disaster Recovery. In *Emergency and Disaster Management: A Mental Health Sourcebook,* ed. H. J. Parad; H. L. P. Resnick; and L. P. Parad. Bowie, Maryland: Charles Press.

McIntire, M. S., and Sadeghi, E. 1977. The Pediatrician and Mental Health in a Community-wide Disaster. *Clinical Paediatrics* 16:702–5.

McLeod, W. 1975. Merphos Poisoning or Mass Panic. *Australian and New Zealand Journal of Psychiatry* 9:225–30.

Maddison, D. C., and Walker, W. L. 1967. Factors Affecting the Outcome of Conjugal Bereavement. *British Journal of Psychiatry* 113:1057–67.

Masuda, M.; Lin, K.; and Tazuma, L. 1982. Life Changes among Vietnamese Refugees. In *Uprooting and Surviving,* ed. Richard C. Nann. London: D. Reidel.

Meerven, F. L.; Chapman, J.; Deegan, E.; and Westcott, W. 1979. Decision versus Policy in Crisis Intervention. *American Journal of Community Psychology* 7:543–62.

References

Melick, M. E. 1978. Life Change and Illness: Illness Behavior of Males in the Recovery Period of a Natural Disaster. *Journal of Health and Social Behavior* 19:335–42.

Mileti, D. S. 1983. Societal Comparisons of Organizational Response to Earthquake Predictions: Japan vs. the United States. *International Journal of Mass Emergencies and Disasters* 1(3):399–415.

Mileti, D. S.; Drabek, T. E.; and Haas, J. E. 1975. *Human Systems in Extreme Environments: A Sociological Perspective.* University of Colorado, Institute of Behavioral Science.

Milne, G. 1977. Cyclone Tracy, 2: The Effects on Darwin Children. *Australian Psychologist* 12:55–62.

Moller, D. 1984. Holocaust on Ash Wednesday. *Readers Digest* (February):147–88.

Nadelson, C. N.; Notman, M. T.; Zackson, H.; and Gornick, J. 1982. A Follow-up Study of Rape Victims. *American Journal of Psychiatry* 139:1266–70.

Nann, R. C., ed. 1982. *Uprooting and Surviving.* London: D. Reidel.

Nasr, S.; Racy, J.; and Flaherty, J. A. 1983. Psychiatric Effects of the Civil War in Lebanon. *Psychiatric Journal of the University of Ottawa* 8:208–12.

Newman, C. J. 1976. Children of Disaster: Clinical Observations at Buffalo Creek. *American Journal of Psychiatry* 133:306–16.

Nimmo, D. 1984. T.V. Network News Coverage of Three Mile Island: Reporting Disasters of Technological Fables. *International Journal of Mass Emergencies and Disasters* 2:115–46.

Oates, R. K. 1982. *Child Abuse—A Community Concern.* London and Sydney: Butterworths.

Oates, R. K. 1984. Personality Development after Physical Abuse. *Archives of Diseases in Childhood* 59:147–50.

Oates, R. K.; Peacock, A.; and Forrest, D. 1984. The Development of Abused Children. *Developmental Medicine and Child Neurology* 26:649–56.

O'Brien, D. 1979. Mental Anguish: An Occupational Hazard. *Emergency* 1:61–64.

Ochberg, F. 1978. The Victim of Terrorism: Psychiatric Considerations. *Terrorism* 1:147–67.

———. 1980. Victims of Terrorism. *Journal of Clinical Psychiatry* 41:73–74.

———. 1982. *Victims of Terrorism.* Boulder, Colorado: Westview Press.

Okura, K. P. 1975. Mobilizing in Response to a Major Disaster. *Community Mental Health Journal* 11:136–44.

Oliver-Smith, A. 1977. Disaster Rehabilitation and Social Change in Yungay, Peru. *Human Organization* 36:5–13.

Ollendick, D. G., and Hoffman, S. M. 1982. Assessment of Psychological Reactions in Disaster Victims. *Journal of Community Psychology* 10:157–67.

Palmer, E. L. 1980. Students' Reactions to Disaster. *American Journal of Nursing* (April):680–82.

Parad, H. J.; Resnick, H. P. L.; and Parad, L. P. 1976. *Emergency and Disaster Management: Mental Health Sourcebook.* Bowie, Maryland: Charles Press.

Parker, G. 1977. Cyclone Tracy and Darwin Evacuees: On the Restoration of the Species. *British Journal of Psychiatry* 130:548–55.

Parker, G., and Brown, L. 1982. Coping Behaviors that Mediate between Life Events and Depression. *Archives of General Psychiatry* 39:1386–91.

Parkes, C. M. 1972. *Bereavement: Studies of Grief in Adult Life.* New York: International Universities Press.

Parr, R. 1970. Organizational Response to Community Crises and Group Emergence. *American Behavioral Scientist* 13:423–29.

Patrick, V., and Patrick, W. K. 1981. Cyclone 78 in Sri Lanka: The Mental Health Trail. *British Journal of Psychiatry* 138:210–16.

Perlberg, M. 1979. Trauma at Tenerife: The Psychic Aftershocks of a Jet Disaster. *Human Behaviour* 8(4):49–50.

Perry, J. B.; Hawkins, R.; and Neal, D. M. 1983. Giving and Receiving Aid. *International Journal of Mass Emergencies and Disasters* 1:171–88.

Perry, R. W., and Greene, M. 1982. *Citizen Response to Volcanic Eruptions: The Case of Mt. St. Helen's.* New York: Irvington.

Perry, R. W., and Lindell, M. K. 1978. The Psychological Consequences of Natural Disaster: A Review of Research on American Communities. *Mass Emergencies* 3:105-15.

Petek, W. J., and Atkinson, A. A. 1982. *Natural Hazard Risk Assessment and Public Policy: Anticipating the Unexpected.* New York: Springer Verlag.

Phillips, M. R.; Ward, M. G.; and Reis, R. K. 1983. Factitious Mourning: Painless Patienthood. *American Journal of Psychiatry* 140:420-25.

Pine, V. R., ed. 1974a. *Responding to Disaster.* Milwaukee: Bulfin Printers.

Pine, V. R. 1974b. Grief Work and Dirty Work: The Aftermath of an Aircrash. *Omega* 5:281-86.

Ploeger, A. 1977. A Ten-Year Follow-Up of Miners Trapped for Two Weeks under Threatening Circumstances. In *Stress and Anxiety,* ed. C. D. Spielberger and I. G. Sarason. New York: Wiley.

Popovic, M., and Petrovick, D. 1964. After the Earthquake. *Lancet* (November 28):1169-71.

Poulshock, S. W., and Cohen, E. S. 1975. The Elderly in the Aftermath of a Disaster. *Gerontologist* 15:357-61.

Powell, B. J., and Penick, E. C. 1983. Psychological Distress Following a Natural Disaster: A One-Year Follow-up of 98 Flood Victims. *Journal of Community Psychology* 11:269-76.

Powell, J. W. 1954. An Introduction to the Natural History of Disaster. University of Maryland Psychiatric Institute. Unpublished paper.

Predescu, V., and Niga-Udangiu, S. 1979. Postseismic Reactions, Observations on a Group of Patients Displaying Psychic Disorders Determined by March 4, 1977 Earthquake in Romania. *Romanian Journal of Neurology and Psychiatry* 17:179-188.

Price, J. 1978. Some Age-Related Effects of the 1974 Brisbane Floods. *Australian and New Zealand Journal of Psychiatry* 12:55-58.

Quarantelli, E. L. 1954. The Nature and Conditions of Panic. *American Journal of Sociology* 60:267.

————. 1978. *Disasters: Theory and Research.* London: Sage.

Quarantelli, E. L., and Dynes, R. 1973. When Disaster Strikes. *New Society* 23:5-9.

Rachman, S. J. 1978. *Fear and Courage.* San Francisco: W. H. Freeman.

Raphael, B. 1977a. Preventive Intervention with the Recently Bereaved. *Archives of General Psychiatry* 34:1450-54.

————. 1977b. The Granville Train Disaster: Psychological Needs and Their Management. *Medical Journal of Australia* 1:303-5.

————. 1979a. A Psychiatric Model for Bereavement Counseling. In *Bereavement Counseling: A Multidisciplinary Handbook,* ed. B. M. Schoenberg. Westport, Conn.: Greenwood Press.

————. 1979b. The Preventive Psychiatry of Natural Hazard. In *Natural Hazards in Australia,* ed. J. Heathcote. Canberra: Australian Academy of Science.

————. 1979-80. A Primary Prevention Action Programme: Psychiatric Involvement Following a Major Rail Disaster. *Omega* 10(3):211-25.

————. 1981. Personal Disaster. *Australian and New Zealand Journal of Psychiatry* 14:163-74.

————. 1982. The Young Child and the Death of a Parent. In *The Place of Attachment in Human Behavior,* ed. C. M. Parkes and J. Stevenson-Hinde. New York: Basic Books.

————. 1983. *The Anatomy of Bereavement.* New York: Basic Books.

————. 1984a. Thinking the Unthinkable. In *Preparing for Nuclear War: The Psychological Effects,* ed. G. J. Mann and G. J. Berry. Camperdown, New South Wales: Medical Association for the Prevention of War.

————. 1984b. Psychiatric Consultancy in Major Disasters. Editorial Review, *Australian and New Zealand Journal of Psychiatry* 8:303-6.

Raphael, B.; Field, J.; and Kvelde, H. 1980. Childhood Bereavement: A Prospective Study as a Possible Prelude to Future Preventive Intervention. In Volume 6: *Preventive Psychiatry in an Age of Transition,* ed. E. J. Anthony and C. Chiland. *Yearbook of the International Association for Child and Adolescent Psychiatry and Allied Professions.* New York: Wiley.

References

Raphael, B.; Singh, B.; and Bradbury, L. 1980. Disaster: The Helper's Perspective. *Medical Journal of Australia* 2:445–47.

Raphael, B.; Singh, B.; Bradbury, L.; and Lambert, F. 1983–84. Who Helps the Helpers? The Effects of a Disaster on the Rescue Workers. *Omega* 14(1):9–20.

Raphael, B.; Weisæth, L.; and Lundin, T. 1984. International Study Group for Disaster Psychiatry: Draft Methodology for Psychosocial Study of Disasters. Newcastle, Australia.

Ridington, R. 1982. When Poison Gas Come Down Like a Fog: Native Community's Response to Cultural Disaster. *Human Organization* 41:36–42.

Rogers, R. R. 1982. On National Response to Nuclear Issues and Terrorism. In *Psychosocial Aspects of Nuclear Developments*. Report of the Task Force on Psychosocial Aspects of Nuclear Developments of the American Psychiatric Association. Washington, D.C.: American Psychiatric Association.

Romo, J. M., and Schneider, R. J. 1982. Disaster: Psychiatric Casualties and Implications for Future War. *Journal of the Royal Army Medical Corps* 128:93–99.

Sank, L. I. 1979. Psychology in Action: Community Disasters. Primary Prevention and Treatment in a Health Maintenance Organization. *American Psychologist* 34:334–38.

Scanlon, J. 1978. *Day One in Darwin: Once Again the Vital Communications.* Paper presented at the World Congress on Sociology, Uppsala, Sweden.

Schulberg, H. C. 1974. Disaster Crisis Theory and Intervention Strategies. *Omega* 5:77–87.

Seitz, S. T., and Davis, M. 1984. The Political Matrix of Natural Disasters: Africa and Latin America. *International Journal of Mass Emergencies and Disasters* 2:231–50.

Shanfield, S. B., and Swain, B. J. 1984. The Death of Adult Children in Traffic Accidents. *Journal of Nervous and Mental Diseases* 172:533–38.

Sheets, P. D. 1979. Maya Recovery from Volcanic Disasters: Ilopango and Ceren. *Journal of Archaeology* 32:32–42.

Shore, J.; Tatum, E.; and Vollmer, W. M. 1985. Psychiatric Findings of Mount St. Helen's Disaster. Paper presented at 138th Annual Meeting of the American Psychiatric Association, Dallas, Texas, May 18–24, 1985.

Short, P. 1979. Victims and Helpers. In *Natural Hazards in Australia,* ed. R. L. Heathcote and B. G. Tong. Canberra: Australian Academy of Science.

Silber, E.; Perry, S. E.; and Bloch, D. A. 1957. Patterns of Parent-Child Interaction in a Disaster. *Journal of Psychiatry* 21:159–67.

Simon, J., and Zusman, J. 1983. The Effect of Contextual Factors on Psychiatrists' Perception of Illness: A Case Study. *Journal of Health and Social Behavior* 24:186–98.

Sims, A. C. P.; White, A. C.; and Murphy, T. 1979. Aftermath Neurosis: Psychological Sequelae of the Birmingham Bombings in Victims Not Seriously Injured. *Medical Science and the Law* 19:78–81.

Singh, B. 1984. The Ethics of Research into Disaster. Paper presented at the Conference on Research into Disaster Behavior, Mt. Macedon, Victoria, Australia.

Singh, B., and Raphael, B. 1981. Postdisaster Morbidity of the Bereaved: A Possible Role for Preventive Psychiatry. *Journal of Nervous and Mental Disease* 169(4):203–12.

Singh, B. S.; Lewin, T.; Raphael, B.; Johnston, P.; and Walton, J. 1985. Minor Psychiatric Illness in a Casualty Population. Unpublished paper.

Siporin, M. 1976. Altruism, Disaster, and Crisis Intervention. In *Emergency and Disaster Management: A Mental Health Sourcebook,* ed. H. J. Parad; H. L. P. Resnick; and L. P. Parad. Bowie, Maryland: Charles Press.

Snowdon, J.; Solomons, R.; and Druve, H. 1978. Feigned Bereavement: Twelve Cases. *British Journal of Psychiatry* 133:15–19.

Solomon, S. D. 1984. *Mobilizing Social Support Networks in Times of Disaster.* Center for Mental Health Studies of Emergencies, Division of Prevention and Special Mental Health Programs, National Institute of Mental Health, Washington, D.C. Mimeographed paper.

Sparr, L., and Pankratz, L. D. 1983. Factitious Post-traumatic Stress Disorder. *American Journal of Psychiatry* 140:1016–19.

Stallings, R. A. 1975. Differential Response of Hospital Personnel to a Disaster. *Mass Emergencies* 1:47–54.

Stretton, A. 1976. *The Furious Days: The Relief of Darwin.* Sydney: Collins.

Strumpfer, D. J. W. 1970. Fear and Affiliation during a Disaster. *Journal of Social Psychology* 82:263–68.

Tan, E. S., and Simons, R. C. 1973. Psychiatric Sequelae to a Civil Disturbance. *British Journal of Psychiatry* 122:57–63.

Tatum, E.; Vollmer, W.; and Shore, J. H. 1985. High-risk Groups of the Mount St. Helen's Disaster. Paper presented at 138th Annual Meeting of the American Psychiatric Association, Dallas, Texas, May 18–24, 1985.

Taylor, A. J. W., and Frazer, A. G. 1980. Interim Report of the Stress Effects on the Recovery Teams after the Mt. Erebus Disaster, November 1979. *New Zealand Medical Journal* 91:311–12.

———. 1981. *Psychological Sequelae of Operation Overdue following the DC-10 Aircrash in Antarctica.* Victoria University, Wellington, New Zealand: Victoria University of Wellington Publications in Psychology No. 27.

———. 1982. The Stress of Post-Disaster Body Handling and Victim Identification Work. *Journal of Human Stress* 8 (December):4–12.

Tennant, C. 1984. Vulnerability to Depression. Paper presented at Australian Preventive Psychiatry Workshop on Depression, Newcastle, Australia.

Terr, L. C. 1979. Children of Chowchilla: A Study of Psychic Trauma. *Psychoanalytic Study of the Child* 34:547–623.

———. 1981a. Forbidden Games: Post-traumatic Child's Play. *Journal of the American Academy of Child Psychiatry* 20:741–60.

———. Psychic Trauma in Children: Observations Following the Chowchilla School-Bus Kidnapping. *American Journal of Psychiatry* 138:14–19.

———. 1983a. Chowchilla Revisited: The Effects of Psychic Trauma Four Years after a School-Bus Kidnapping. *American Journal of Psychiatry* 140:1543–50.

———. 1983b. Attitudes, Dreams and Psychic Trauma in a Group of "Normal" Children. *Journal of the American Academy of Child Psychiatry* 22:221–30.

———. 1983c. Time Sense Following Psychic Trauma: A Clinical Study of Ten Adults and Twenty Children. *American Journal of Orthopsychiatry* 53:244–61.

Thomas, H. 1981. *An Unfinished History of the World.* London: Pan Books.

Thompson, J. D., and Hawkes, R. W. 1962. Disaster, Community Organization and Administrative Process. In *Man and Society in Disaster,* ed. George W. Baker and Dwight W. Chapman. New York: Basic Books.

Tierney, K. G., and Baisden, B. 1979. *Crisis Intervention Programs for Disaster Victims: A Source Book and Manual for Smaller Communities.* Rockville, Maryland: National Institute of Mental Health.

Titchener, J. L.; Capp, F. T.; and Winget, C. 1976. The Buffalo Creek Syndrome: Symptoms and Character Change after a Major Disaster. In *Emergency and Disaster Management: A Mental Health Sourcebook,* ed. H. J. Parad; H. L. P. Resnick; and L. P. Parad. Bowie, Maryland: Charles Press.

Titchener, J. L., and Lindy, J. D. 1980. Affect Defense and Insight: Psychoanalytic Observations of Bereaved Families and Clinicians at a Major Disaster. University of Cincinnati (Ohio). Unpublished paper.

Tonge, B. 1984. Psychiatric Involvement in Disaster Teams. Paper presented at the Sectional Meeting of Child Psychiatry, Royal Australian and New Zealand College of Psychiatrists, Warburton, Victoria.

Trichopoulos, D.; Katsouyanni, K.; Zavitsanos, X.; Tzonou, A.; and Dalla-Vorgia, P. 1983. Psychological Stress and Fatal Heart Attack: The Athens (1981) Earthquake Natural Experiment. *Lancet:* 441–44.

Trost, J., and Hultaker, O. 1983. Family in Disaster. *International Journal of Mass Emergencies and Disasters* 1 (special edition).

References

Tsang, L. 1984. Studies of Vietnamese Refugees. Doctoral dissertation, University of Newcastle, Australia.

Tucker, M. B. 1982. Social Support and Coping: Applications for the Study of Female Drug Abuse. *Society for the Psychological Study of Social Issues* 38:117–37.

Tuckman, A. J. 1973. Disaster and Mental Health Intervention. *Community Mental Health Journal* 9:151–57.

Tuckman, A. J., and Kasumi, K. M. A. 1973. Disaster and Mental Health Intervention. *Community Mental Health Journal* 9:151–57.

Tuckman, A. J., and Okura, K. P. 1975. Mobilizing in Response to Emergency Disaster. *Community Mental Health Journal* 11:136–44.

Turner, R. H. 1983. Waiting for Disaster: Changing Reactions to Earthquake Forecasts in Southern California. *Mass Emergencies and Disasters* 1(2):307–34.

Tyhurst, J. S. 1950. Individual Reactions to Community Disaster: The Natural History of Psychiatric Phenomena. *American Journal of Psychiatry* 107:764–69.

Tyhurst, L. 1977. Psychosocial First Aid for Refugees. *Mental Health in Society* 4:319–43.

Tyler, T. R., and McGraw, K. M. 1983. The Threat of Nuclear War: Risk Interpretation and Behavioral Response. *Journal of Social Issues* 39:25–40.

Utson, P. 1978. *War on the Mind.* Sydney: Penguin.

Vachon, M. L. S.; Lyall, W.; and Freeman, S. J. 1978. Measurement and Management of Stress in Health Professionals Working with Advanced Cancer Patients. *Death Education* 1:-365–75.

Valent, P. 1983. A Conceptual Framework for Understanding the Impact of Disasters. *Australian Clinical Psychologist* 15(2):12–25.

————. 1984. The Ash Wednesday Bushfires in Victoria. *Medical Journal of Australia* 141: 291–300.

Van der Westhuizen, M. 1980. Kampuchean Refugees: An Encounter with Grief. *Australian Nurses Journal* 10:53–56.

Volkan, V. 1972. The Linking Objects of Pathological Mourners. *Archives of General Psychiatry.* 27:215–21.

Wallace, A. F. C. 1956. *Tornado in Rochester.* (National Research Council Disaster Study No. 3.) Washington, D.C.: National Academy of Sciences.

Webber, D. L. 1976. Darwin Cyclone: An Exploration of Disaster Behaviour. *Australian Journal of Social Issues* 11:54–63.

Weisæth, L. 1983. The Study of a Factory Fire. Doctoral dissertation, University of Oslo.

————. 1984. Stress Reactions to an Industrial Disaster, Oslo. Unpublished paper.

Weisæth, L., and Sund, A. 1982. Psychiatric Problems in Unifil and the U.N. Soldiers Stress Syndrome. *International Review of the Army, Navy and Air Force Medical Services* 55: 109–16.

Weisman, G. 1974. Psychosocial Model for Limiting Mental Reaction during Stress. *Israel Annals of Psychiatry and Related Disciplines* 12:161–67.

Western, J. S., and Doube, L. 1979. Stress and Cyclone Tracy. In G. Pickup, ed., *Natural Hazards Management in North Australia.* Canberra: Australian National University.

Western, J. S., and Milne, G. 1979. Some Social Effects of a Natural Hazard: Darwin Residents and Cyclone Tracy. In *Natural Hazards in Australia,* ed. R. L. Heathcote and B. G. Thom. Canberra: Australian Academy of Science.

Wettenhall, R. L. 1975. *Bushfire Disaster: An Australian Community in Crisis.* Sydney: Angus and Robertson.

Whelan, J.; Seatone, E.; and Cunningham-Dax, E. 1976. *Aftermath: The Tasman Bridge Collapse: Criminological and Sociological Observations.* Canberra: Australian Institute of Criminology.

Wilkinson, C. B. 1983. Aftermath of a Disaster: The Collapse of the Hyatt Regency Hotel Skywalk. *American Journal of Psychiatry* 140:1134–39.

Williams, H. B., and Rayner, J. F. 1966. Emergency Medical Services in Disaster. *Medical Annals of the District of Columbia* 25:655–62.

Williams, R. M., and Parkes, C. M. 1975. Psychosocial Effects of Disaster: Birth Rate in Aberfan. *British Medical Journal* 2:303–4.

Wolfenstein, M. 1957. *Disaster: A Psychological Essay.* Glencoe: Free Press.

The World's Worst Disasters of the Twentieth Century. 1983. London: Octopus Books.

Yanoov, B. 1976. Short-Term Intervention: A Model for Emergency Services in Times of Crisis. *Mental Health and Society* 3:33–52.

Yates, A. 1983. Stress Management in Childhood. *Clinical Pediatrics* 22:131–35.

Zurcher, W. A. 1968. Socio-psychological Functions of Ephemeral Roles: A Volunteer Work Crew in Disaster. *Human Organization* 27:281–97.

Zusman, J. 1976. Meeting Mental Health Needs in Disaster: A Public Health View. In *Emergency and Disaster Management: A Mental Health Sourcebook,* ed. H. J. Parad; H. P. L. Resnick; and L. P. Parad. Bowie, Maryland: Charles Press.

Zweig, J. P., and Csank, J. Z. 1976. Mortality Fluctuations among Chronically Ill Medical Geriatric Patients as an Indicator of Stress before and after Relocation. *Journal of the American Geriatric Society* 24:264–77.

NAME INDEX

Abe, K., 210
Abraham, H. A., 48
Abrahams, M. J., 187, 188, 192, 198
Adams, D., 294
Adams, G. R., 14, 180, 187, 196, 306
Adams, P. R., 14, 180, 187, 196, 306
Ahearn, F. L., 6, 8, 199, 210, 248, 249, 256, 258, 260, 261, 286, 288
Anderson, W. A., 307
Arvidson, R., 203
Askevold, F., 69, 90, 220
Astrachan, B. M., 212
Atkinson, A. A., 37

Baisden, B., 286, 287
Barbeau, M., 206, 207
Barbina, G., 307
Baren, J. B., 207, 289
Barton, A. H., 291, 295
Bartrop, R. W., 109, 196
Beach, H. D., 209
Bell, B. D., 174
Bennet, G., 180, 187, 188, 192, 197
Berah, E., 224, 239, 240, 245
Berah, J., 10
Berren, M. R., 11, 289
Bjorklund, B., 131
Black, D., 281
Blaufarb, H., 154, 289
Bloch, D. A., 155, 159, 165–67, 169, 201
Blumbergs, V., 83
Boccaccio, G., 12
Boggs, K. S., 170
Bolin, R. C., 113, 116, 126, 129, 130, 136, 140, 142, 170–74, 192, 199
Boman, B., 189, 218, 219
Bordow, S., 199, 290
Bostok, T., 68, 70, 186, 211
Bowk, W. J., 18
Bowlby, J., 106, 163, 165, 167
Bray, C. B., 289
Brett, E. A., 80
Bromet, E. J., 40, 186, 188, 199, 206
Brown, R. E., 21
Burke, J. D., 149, 154, 158, 161, 201
Butcher, J. N., 207

Canter, D., 210
Caplan, G., 248

Carlton, T. A., 289
Chamberlin, B. C., 179
Clarke, A., 234, 290
Clausen, L., 292
Clayer, J., 113, 116, 187, 192, 195–97, 199, 210, 289
Cobb, S., 135
Coelho, G. V., 142
Cohen, E. S., 174
Cohen, R. E., 6, 8, 199, 248, 249, 256, 258, 260, 261, 286, 288, 289
Cook, P., 234
Crabbs, M. A., 253
Crawshaw, R., 203
Csank, J. Z., 143
Curran, W. J., 213

Davidson, A. D., 207
Davis, M., 305
Dekker, T., 12
Deuchar, N. 214
Dillon, H., 189, 211
Dimsdale, J. E., 69, 70
Dombrowsky, W., 212
Doube, L., 142, 147
Drabek, T. E., 136, 170, 293
Dudasik, S. W., 223
Duffy, J. C., 206
Dunn, L., 206
Dynes, R. R., 65, 118, 295

Eitinger, L., 69, 90, 142, 220
Elizur, E., 163, 164, 169, 194
Engel, G. L., 70
Erikson, K. T., 6, 8, 19, 57, 84–86, 96, 116, 117, 131, 134, 142, 170, 173, 307

Fairbank, J. A., 219
Fairley, M., 182, 186–89, 192, 197
Fattah, E. A., 96
Feldman, S., 21
Fenichel, O., 80
Field, 163
Forrest, T. R., 296
Frazer, A. G., 84, 96, 103, 152, 207, 224, 225, 230, 234, 236–38
Frazer, J. R., 289
Frazer, M., 167–69, 217

SUBJECT INDEX